COLLINS GUIDE
TO THE BIRDS
OF NEW ZEALAND

COLLINS GUIDE
TO THE BIRDS
OF NEW ZEALAND
AND OUTLYING ISLANDS

by

R. A. Falla, R. B. Sibson
and E. G. Turbott

illustrated by
Elaine Power

COLLINS
Auckland and London

First published as *A Field Guide to
the Birds of New Zealand* in 1966
Revised in 1970
Reprinted 1972
Reprinted 1975
This edition, revised, extended,
re-illustrated, and re-set in larger
format as *The New Guide to the Birds
of New Zealand* first published 1978
Reprinted with Addenda, 1981
Reprinted 1982
Reprinted 1983
Reprinted 1985
Reprinted 1986
Reprinted 1987

ISBN 0 00 217563 0
© New Zealand Ornithological Society, 1966 and 1978
Set in 8 on 9 pt. Times New Roman by
Monoset Trade Services Limited, Auckland, New Zealand

Printed in Hong Kong by
Dai Nippon Printing Co. (H.K.) Ltd.

CONTENTS

CONTENTS

CONTENTS

New Zealand and its outlying islands

PLATES

PLATES

Although every endeavour has been made to depict all the species described in the text, a few very rare species, which are almost indistinguishable from less rare birds which are illustrated, have not been included in the plates.

PREFACE

Encouraged by the success of the *Checklist of New Zealand Birds*, published in 1953, the Council of the Ornithological Society of New Zealand in 1959 asked the three authors to collaborate in compiling a practical field guide for the birds of the New Zealand region. It was a timely decision for the last half century had been exciting. An increase of critical ornithology in areas formerly rather inaccessible was showing that while a few unique endemic species were becoming ominously rare, others were thriving. New information was being gathered on the status and distribution of birds on the more distant island groups. At the same time many more transequatorial migrants and oceanic wanderers were being added to the already long New Zealand list. Several self-introduced species from Australia appeared to have established themselves in clearly empty ecological niches, and other comparatively recent trans-Tasman newcomers were known to have nested.

The decline in many native birds, so marked in the nineteenth century, seems to have been arrested. Most in fact are holding their own; some have turned the corner and are utilising new habitats, such as hydro-electric dams, reclaimed salt-marshes, man-made forests of exotic pines, swamp-lands now choked with willow and alder. Consequently in 1970 a revised second edition of the *Field Guide* was called for; and in the same year the Ornithological Society issued a new *Annotated Checklist of the Birds of New Zealand* including the Birds of the Ross Dependency. But such is the pace and coverage of current research and such the popular demand for an up-to-date reference book that it was agreed to re-set and re-illustrate the entire work. This has allowed for the inclusion of a great deal of new matter, and improved the book's value to both beginner and experienced ornithologist.

Scope and Aim

For the purposes of this field guide the New Zealand region extends from the Kermadec Islands in Lat. 29°S. to Macquarie Island, Lat. 55°S. (map page 8). Its aim is to enable the serious student, the visitor, the sailor and, perhaps above all, the amateur naturalist, who enjoys watching and identifying birds for the fun of the thing and to satisfy his curiosity, to know what bird he is watching and what birds to expect, anywhere on and around the many islands which make up New Zealand. Here perhaps the first *caveat* should be sounded about the difficulty of identifying with certainty many of the petrels and shearwaters that will be seen at sea.

Extinction and Survival

An ornithologist visiting New Zealand one thousand years ago would have been astounded and delighted at the number and variety of flightless birds which had been able to evolve in the virtual absence of carnivorous predators. But the long peace of this South Pacific avian paradise was rudely broken by the arrival of meat-hungry Polynesian seafarers – Sir Peter Buck's 'Vikings of the Sunrise'. Bone by bone, archaeologist and zoologist are piecing together the sadly fascinating story of the extinction of the Moas and some other flightless birds. Altogether of the twenty-four accepted species or forms of Moa, twenty-one have now been found in association with the middens or hunting-camps of Polynesian man. Some even of the bigger Moas of the genus *Dinornis* survived into the seventeenth century; but when the first European explorers arrived, the giant birds were only a legend, though a few specimens of one of the smallest species may have survived till the nineteenth century. Fortunately all the flightless birds were not equally vulnerable. The Takahe, dramatically rediscovered in 1948, had escaped destruction in its mountain fastnesses – while Wekas and three species of Kiwi survived the impact of Polynesian man unscathed.

In the nineteenth century the land-hunger of European settlers, mainly of British stock, led to the hasty felling of vast areas of bush and to the draining of swamps. Was it not said that a typical pioneer was born with an axe in one hand and a firestick in the other; and that a cow-cocky would sell his soul for an extra blade of cocksfoot? Inevitably the numbers of forest-haunting birds were reduced; but the number of actual extinctions was small, the only loss of a mainland forest species being that of the Huia, which persisted into the first decade of the twentieth century. Some species now extinct on the main islands survive and thrive on off-shore island sanctuaries, e.g. the Stitchbird on Little Barrier; the Saddleback on Hen and, through the dedicated help of the Wildlife Service, on several other small islands; the Shore Plover on South-east Island in the Chathams.

Of course, uncontrolled shooting, based on the philosophy of the inexhaustible, contributed to the general decline. Wekas commonly went into the pot; Kakas were esteemed a delicacy; Kakapo sustained many prospectors; and the *pièce de résistance* of a bushmen's feast might be a pig stuffed with Native Pigeons and Tuis. The endemic ducks and plovers and the so-called Native Quail provided a tasty meal for hungry colonists. In the Auckland Islands shipwrecked mariners probably ate the Merganser to the point of extinction. Rats, black (*rattus*) and brown (*norvegicus*) which came ashore from ships, mustelids deliberately introduced, dogs and domestic cats, abandoned or gone feral, became an additional menace, especially to flightless or ground-nesting birds, which had no experience of eluding mammalian predators. These 'parasites on the Pakeha' still constitute the gravest threat to such colonies of petrels, e.g. the rare Westland Petrel, as survive on the main islands. The effect of introduced deer and opossums on native birds has yet to be assessed. Another danger was disease passed on from domestic poultry or introduced birds. This may partially account for the sudden decline of such different species as Brown Teal, Red-crowned Parakeet and Weka. The range of the Blue Duck seems to have been narrowed by the muddying of formerly clear bush streams, and possibly competition for specialised food by introduced trout.

Much more of the original forest has been permanently reserved – mainly as high country protection forest and National Park – than would have been forecast by an observer in the nineteenth century; and thus the story fortunately is not one of unrelieved gloom. The fast dwindling of some species and the virtual disappearance of others forced the government to act. Protective laws were passed and enforced. The commercial collecting of skins and eggs, trapping of passerines and parrots and their sale or export to aviculturists were strictly prohibited. The season for shooting any ducks was limited to a few weeks in May. The rarer endemic ducks have been absolutely protected for many years and are likely to remain so. In 1894 Little Barrier became the first of many off-shore island sanctuaries. Since 1940 a ban upon the shooting of shore birds has had a most beneficial effect upon the numbers of waders, both endemic and migratory.

Although few species now appear to be in grave danger of extinction, there are regrettable exceptions. Piopio, the so-called Native Thrush but more probably a relative of the Australian bowerbirds, may have gone the way of the Huia. The Kakapo, a large ground-parrot of very ancient lineage, is giving cause for concern, for while the Wildlife Service has been able to track down a handful of males in the mountain fastnesses of Fiordland, so far during the 1970s females have eluded discovery, and it is feared that being more vulnerable at the nest, they may have succumbed to alien hole-exploring vermin. However, the discovery in January 1977 of a population on Stewart Island has strengthened hopes that this remarkable ground-parrot may escape the doom which has befallen so many flightless or near-flightless birds throughout the world.

Some species have clearly benefited from European methods of farming and opening up the country. Among these may be named: Grey Warbler, Kingfisher, Harrier, Paradise Duck, the three gulls, Pukeko, Pied Stilt and probably South Island Pied Oystercatcher, Banded Dotterel, Wrybill and Australian colonists such as Spur-winged Plover, Black-fronted Dotterel, White-faced Heron and Welcome Swallow. Now that the use of pesticides in agriculture is so widespread, the status even of common species needs to be watched continually. The Pipit has almost vanished from some lowland districts, while it remains fairly common at higher altitudes.

Because New Zealand does not possess, and never did possess, the rich variety of passerines and forest-birds such as may be found in Australia or on one of the great continental land masses, casual visitors who see little but the fertile farm-lands of the North and South Islands and may make a brief stay at one of the National Parks, are apt to complain that as far as birds go, the landscape is dominated by aliens. It is indeed true that among the commonest birds in the country must be reckoned most of the dozen or so English passerines which were introduced more than hundred years ago mainly from sentiment, with perhaps some thought of utility. But such a visitor has only to visit the coast, preferably at an estuary with the tide coming in, or one of the well-bushed off-shore islands to realise something of the richness of the birdlife, exemplified in one curious way by the sixteen hundred kilometre overlap of parrots and penguins; for the breeding range of the Little Blue Penguin extends north of Lat. 35°S., and parakeets have successfully colonised many bleak sub-antarctic islands as far as Antipodes and Auckland Islands in Lat. 50°S. Not without reason has it been remarked that the true glory of New Zealand birds is best seen and appreciated in her coastal waters; for there are still many quiet places, far from the madding crowd, where the mind can become, in Darwin's phrase, 'a chaos of delight' at the abundance and variety of birds which pass before the eye or perplex the ear.

Nomenclature
  The common vernacular name is given first, followed by local or Maori names,

if any. For the scientific name the use of binomials instead of trinomials may occasion some surprise among critical readers. The aim has been simplicity. The geography of the New Zealand region, i.e. its length, composition and isolation, has favoured the formation of local races or subspecies. The general rule of the authors has been to use the subspecific name for 'strong' races, e.g. Chatham Island Mollymawk, Brown Teal, Hudsonian Godwit, Black-fronted Tern; and the specific name for 'weak' subspecies, e.g. White Heron, Little Egret, Bellbird, Fantail; and to mention relationships in the text. The order closely follows that used in the *Annotated Checklist* of 1970, beginning with the Kiwis and ending with the passerines.

Treatment

Those species which breed in New Zealand are treated under four headings: (*a*) Description, (*b*) Voice, (*c*) Habitat and Range, (*d*) Breeding. For migrants and stragglers from outside the New Zealand region the section on breeding is omitted.

(*a*) The description begins with a measurement in centimetres of the length of the flying bird from the tip of the bill to the tip of the tail or, in a few instances, of the legs extending beyond the tail. Salient or diagnostic features are printed in italics. Notes on carriage, posture, behaviour, where judged helpful, are included.

(*b*) Syllabification along traditional lines has been attempted. A well-trained ear is invaluable. Many waders and night-flying migrants can be accurately identified by ear without being seen. In thick bush and swamp Kokako and Fernbird, to name but two elusive species, will not be seen easily, although their presence may be revealed by their distinctive calls. In general, the voices and calls of New Zealand birds need much more careful study. This is especially true of petrels and seabirds. Tape recordings already made have been very useful in the search for some secretive species, e.g. Spotless Crake.

(*c*) There are many types of habitat in New Zealand. Perusal of this section will give some idea of their almost infinite variety. In New Zealand many species with a wide distribution in Australia and/or Asia reach the south-east limit of their range. Thus of the ten Ardeidae on the New Zealand list none is endemic, i.e. confined to New Zealand only. Finally, New Zealand is within the regular range of many waders and petrels whose breeding grounds are between 10,000 and 13,000 kilometres distant; the waders coming annually from northern Asia and arctic America; the petrels, as is proved by banding, from as far as the Antarctic coast of the south Atlantic.

(*d*) A summary is here given of what is known of the nesting habits and behaviour of those species which breed in New Zealand. There are still many gaps. It is hoped they will prove a challenge.

Division of Labour

In preparing the text each of the three authors undertook certain families or natural groups. Sir Robert Falla was the obvious choice to describe the penguins, albatrosses, petrels, shags and gulls. Graham Turbott contributed the text on the kiwis, ducks, native pigeon, parrots, native owls, kingfishers and native passerines. I have been responsible for the grebes, tropic-birds, gannets, frigate-birds, herons, ibises, hawks, rails, waders, terns, skuas, cuckoos, introduced pigeons, owls and passerines and stragglers. There has been throughout a free exchange of ideas. As editor, it has been my pleasant task to try to secure a general uniformity of treatment, but differences of emphasis and style remain. Any gross discrepancies should be laid firmly at my door.

R.B.S.
Co-ordinating Editor

1977

Publisher's note on the history of this book

The preparation of the text started about 1960, and the first edition, with illustrations by Chloe Talbot Kelly, was published in 1966. The book had an enthusiastic reception, not only in New Zealand but also abroad.

In 1970 a revised edition was published incorporating fresh data especially on some rarer species which had become better known or more widely distributed in the five years since the original text was completed.

For what is virtually a new book the space now demanded by significant new information has induced us completely to reset the text, thus allowing for improvements in the existing entries and for the inclusion of at least thirty newcomers each in its proper place.

Although the field guide, in its earlier editions, served a most useful purpose for both expert and beginner, and was, in most respects, far fuller in the information it contained than Collins' other Bird Guides, there have been criticisms from the novice that more help was needed in identification. From discussions with the authors it became clear that more colour plates would be the best way to help. As there was no feasible way of splitting up the existing plates painted by Chloe Talbot Kelly, a radical decision was made, with some regret, to abandon these and start afresh on a total of 48 full-colour plates which would illustrate almost every bird described in the text, and would depict some variations due to sex, age or moult. To enlist a New Zealand painter of birds was logical. Such a step would simplify the continual checking required between authors and artist. The choice was not difficult. Elaine Power was on the spot, and she was already experienced both in drawing birds in the field and in painting them for the illustration of books.

Some of Chloe Talbot Kelly's monochrome plates are retained, and some line drawings, as each of these is complete in itself and they serve their purpose as well today as in 1966.

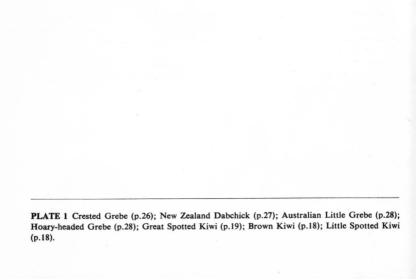

PLATE 1 Crested Grebe (p.26); New Zealand Dabchick (p.27); Australian Little Grebe (p.28); Hoary-headed Grebe (p.28); Great Spotted Kiwi (p.19); Brown Kiwi (p.18); Little Spotted Kiwi (p.18).

PLATE 1

imm.

CRESTED GREBE 50 cm

NEW ZEALAND DABCHICK 28 cm

HOARY-HEADED GREBE 28 cm

AUSTRALIAN LITTLE GREBE 25 cm

GREAT SPOTTED KIWI 50 cm

BROWN KIWI 50 cm

LITTLE SPOTTED KIWI 40 cm

PLATE 2
PENGUINS

GENTOO 76 cm

CHINSTRAP 66 cm

ADELIE 71

YELLOW-EYED 76 cm

LITTLE BLUE 40 cm

EMPEROR 115 cm

KING 92 cm

KIWIS: Apterygidae

Kiwis are flightless birds of robust build standing at most 35 cm high. Their position is evidently that of an early offshoot from the evolutionary line of the ratite birds (moa, emu, ostrich, etc.). They probably branched off at an early stage, and their ancestors are believed to have reached New Zealand at about the same time as those of another group of ratites restricted to New Zealand: the extinct moas. The kiwis are unique amongst the ratites in their small size and adaptations to life on the forest floor, the most noteworthy being the long bill used to obtain worms and other food items in the soft ground.

In the main kiwis are nocturnal. With this is associated weak sight and the development of tactile bristles round the mouth. The long, sensitive bill and the facial bristles are probably the main organs enabling them to move about by night on the forest floor, often in dense undergrowth and fallen debris. The sense of smell of the kiwis is considered to be strongly developed but this should be accepted tentatively pending further investigation. Expiration through the nostrils can be heard as the birds explore the ground for food; the nostrils are situated on the sides at the tip of the bill. To obtain insect larvae, and especially worms, when located underground, kiwis plunge the bill deep into the earth, often right up to the 'hilt'; the bill is also used to pick up fallen forest fruits and ground insects, both of which are important items of diet. The tip of the upper mandible overlaps the lower. The wings of the kiwis consist of remnants hidden beneath the plumage which is loose and hangs in a hair-like fashion. There are no tail feathers and in the resting or walking positions the body with its loose plumage has a distinctive rounded appearance; occasionally the bird may adopt a standing position with bill on the ground so that a tripod is formed by bill and legs together.

There are three species; available information suggests that all three are much alike in mode of life and habits. Early settlement which except in mountain regions brought about a tremendous reduction of forest, caused the extinction of the kiwis in many areas but they have survived in most extensive forests, and even in comparatively small bush remnants. It is especially notable that kiwis now inhabit semi-cleared scrub country and even rough farmland near the forest. They have thus survived in spite of environmental modification, introduction of carnivores and other factors which adversely affected several flightless New Zealand birds.

Although not generally seen, kiwis indicate their presence by their penetrating calls after dark. They are sometimes killed on roads near the bush by traffic at night; dogs or opossum traps (though required by legislation to be set with special precautions to avoid ground birds) account for a few. Various kiwis injured in this way have been kept in captivity and much has been learned of their habits;

PLATE 2 PENGUINS Gentoo (p.21); Chinstrap (p.22); Adelie (p.21); Yellow-eyed (p.20); King (p.20); Emperor (p.20); Little Blue (p.22).

they are now being bred in captivity. They become accustomed to taking food by day. When released in daylight they run with clumsy but powerful strides, and apparently see well enough to enable them to avoid obstacles.

Females are larger and heavier than males. In proportion to the size of the bird, the egg is very big. Incubation is the responsibility of the male.

BROWN KIWI   *Apteryx australis*   *Pl. 1, p. 16*

Maori names: Kiwi; Tokoeka (Stewart Island).

Description: 50 cm (20″). General colour dark grey streaked with reddish-brown and black (feathers grey at the base, terminal portion brown with black tips); the amount of reddish-brown less on the head, which is greyish; bill pale (ivory white to pinkish); legs pale to dark brown.

Females have much longer bills.

Voice: Male a shrill whistle *ki-wi;* female a remarkably hoarse cry, apparently coming from 'deep down in the throat.' (The calls of males of the three subspecies of Brown Kiwis differ in tape-recordings; the two notes are of the same pitch in both North and South Island subspecies, but are more rapidly delivered in the latter, while in the Stewart Island subspecies the second is a descending note).

Habitat and range: Originally common in all forest areas, but the South Island subspecies apparently absent on Banks Peninsula (which was originally forested) and on the Canterbury Plains. Settlement has resulted in a reduction of range as mentioned above: now in many forest areas in the North Island but more restricted in the South Island (no recent records from the south-eastern South Island). Common in Fiordland where it reaches subalpine and alpine zones. In the western and northern South Island now absent or rare (perhaps originally outnumbered or replaced by the two species of Spotted Kiwi in these areas).

Particularly in the North Island, recorded recently in modified conditions; nests have been found in rough farmland under logs and in scrub.

The kiwis of Stewart Island are said to be less strictly nocturnal.

Breeding: Nests in holes, e.g. amongst dense vegetation, in a hollow log, between roots of forest trees, sometimes partly excavated by the birds. Observations in captivity of North Island Brown Kiwis have given the incubation period as 75-80 days; incubation by male. Laying July-February. Eggs (clutch one or two in North Island subspecies, one in remaining subspecies) ivory white or greenish, and highly glazed.

Three subspecies are recognised: the North Island Brown Kiwi (*mantelli*) differs from both South Island Brown Kiwi (*australis*) and Stewart Island Brown Kiwi (*lawryi*) in the stiffened tips of the feathers (harsher to the touch). The North Island and Stewart Island subspecies both have distinctly reddish-brown plumage, especially on the back, the South Island Brown Kiwi being a duller brown; the two southern subspecies are larger on the average than the North Island subspecies. Introduced to Kapiti Island (*mantelli* and *australis*) and Little Barrier Island (*mantelli*).

LITTLE SPOTTED KIWI   *Apteryx oweni*   *Pl. 1, p. 16*

Description: 40 cm (16″). Body is irregularly banded and mottled with brownish black on a faintly buffy pale grey background; head grey; bill pale as in the

Brown Kiwi, and feet pale brown to flesh-white.

Voice: Male and female differ, as in the Brown Kiwi, but the notes have a trilling or tremulous quality.

Habitat and range: Range of the two species of Spotted Kiwi is the western districts of the South Island. In certain areas their range overlaps, or originally overlapped, that of the South Island Brown Kiwi. The present species extends farther both to south (southern Fiordland) and north-east (Marlborough) than the Great Spotted. It has been displaced by settlement from much of Marlborough. In the North Island one record: a specimen from Tararua Range (Mt. Hector) in 1875, but sub-fossil bones indicate a wide distribution in comparatively recent times. Introduced to Kapiti Island where it is well established.

Breeding: No difference from the Brown Kiwi according to early accounts; clutch one. No recent records, except in captivity.

GREAT SPOTTED KIWI   *Apteryx haasti*   *Pl. 1, p. 16*

Maori name: Roa.

Description: 50 cm (20″). Like the Little Spotted, but distinguished by the *strong chestnut tinge* on the back; bill ivory white to pinkish; feet dark to pale brown, claws brown or white.

Voice: Believed to be like those of Brown and Little Spotted, but not enough is known and further study is required.

Habitat and range: According to recent records fairly abundant in forests of western Nelson (especially the Gouland Downs area) and Westland; some doubt as to its occurrence in Westland south of Okarito and in Fiordland. This species has probably suffered comparatively little reduction in range through settlement. It may now be expanding, as there are numerous recent records from the main divide at Arthur's Pass and Lewis Pass; it occurs here at present on both sides of the divide in high altitude beech forest.

Breeding: Only early records, but in the main features evidently similar to the Brown Kiwi. Clutch one, rarely two.

PENGUINS: Spheniscidae

With the addition of the circumpolar species found at Macquarie Island, the New Zealand region has representatives of five of the six genera of penguins, the exception being *Spheniscus*. In 1972 an example of the Magellan Penguin (*S. magellanicus*) came ashore near Napier. Its crossing of the South Pacific is likely to have been ship-assisted.

The breeding range of the smallest (*Eudyptula*) extends from North Cape and Spirits Bay south to Stewart Island.

Within the sub-antarctic belt are several species of *Eudyptes* and the endemic *Megadyptes*. The small birds of the genus *Eudyptula* nest in caves and burrows, the others are surface nesters which, with the exception of the Fiordland Crested Penguin and *Megadyptes*, tend to form large colonies. The Fiordland Crested Penguin has a tendency to seek covered nesting shelter.

EMPEROR PENGUIN *Aptenodytes forsteri*					*Pl. 2, p. 17*
Description: 115 cm (45″). By far the tallest and heaviest of the penguins.
Upper-surface bluish-grey; crown, cheeks, chin and throat black; ear-patches
bright orange, below which a narrowing tongue of black curves upwards from
the 'shoulder'; breast lemon-yellow paling to satin white on belly. Bill long
and down-curved towards tip; bluish-black with a tapering panel of lilac on
the lower mandible. Feet black. There is no yellow in the plumage of first year
birds and the facial pattern is indistinct with a temporary white cheek-patch.
Habitat and range: A circumpolar species seldom straying north of the Antarctic
Circle. At least six breeding colonies are known within the Ross Dependency.
A single bird came ashore in April 1967 at Oreti Beach, Southland.

KING PENGUIN *Aptenodytes patagonicus*					*Pl. 2, p. 17*
Description: 92 cm (36″). The head and the neck are dark glossy black merging
on the nape to a pale blue-grey which is the prevailing tone of the dorsal
plumage. Underparts, as in all penguins, mainly satin white but a pale golden
yellow tinge on the breast deepens on the foreneck to orange-yellow and extends
in two lozenge-shaped patches to the region of the ears. Bill, black; mandibular
plates, orange-rose; feet, black.

Male and female are similar in plumage. Immature birds in first plumage
have the same pattern as the adult with much paler yellow colours. Chicks are
clothed in smoky brown down, uniform over the whole of the body, and this
is retained for some months in the nestling period.
Voice: Resonant squawk; and a somewhat more shrill trumpeting with a
whistling quality during intake of breath.
Habitat and range: In the New Zealand region breeds only at Macquarie
Island. Stragglers sometimes appear at sub-antarctic islands farther north.
In the circumpolar range of the King Penguin no well-defined races have been
recognised.
Breeding: Strongly colonial. Colonies may cover acres. The single pyriform
egg is pale greenish white, chalky outside. Incubation periods, 7½ weeks. The
egg is incubated between the feet in a fold of skin.

YELLOW-EYED PENGUIN *Megadyptes antipodes*					*Pl. 2, p. 17*
Maori name: Hoiho.
Description: 76 cm (30″). The general dorsal colour is slaty grey. The forehead
and crown, pale golden with black shaft stripes. A band of yellow feathers
commences above the eye and encircles the crown posteriorly. Chin and throat
brownish-white which is weakly defined from the satin white of the underparts.
Cheeks pale golden, throat and sides of neck brown. Bill flesh coloured, dull
reddish-brown on the culmen and towards the tip of the mandibles. Feet pale
flesh coloured; iris yellow.

Immature birds in their first year differ from adults in having the yellow band
confined to the sides of the head and not encircling the crown. The chin and
throat also are only faintly marked but are mainly white. Chicks in down are
uniformly dark smoky brown, the texture of the down being fine, rather short
and generally more compact than that of the King Penguin.
Voice: Yellow-eyed Penguins have a considerable range of calls, including a

full trumpet. A contact call note of two syllables, the first one slurred, is closely similar to the cry of the Weka.

Habitat and range: The breeding range is from Cape Wanbrow, Oamaru, south to Campbell Island, but the species has not been recorded from Snares, Antipodes or Bounty Islands. Formerly *Megadyptes* may have bred farther north, and immature birds have a wandering distribution which includes Banks Peninsula where there are recent breeding records, and, rarely, Cook Strait. Otherwise the species is sedentary and there is no indication of true migration.

Breeding: Nesting begins in September and continues until the young are fully fledged about February. Moult takes place later in the same area and the birds are generally present throughout the year. Sites for nests are scattered in the shelter of scrub or low forest at varying distances from the sea and widely scattered within suitable habitat. The full clutch is two eggs and normally two chicks are reared. Incubation period 40-50 days; fledging 110-115 days.

GENTOO PENGUIN *Pygoscelis papua*   *Pl. 2, p. 17*

Description: 76 cm (30″). General dorsal colour dark slate grey, each feather with a bluish-grey tip. Head and neck black with a tendency to ashy grey on the throat. A wide band of white feathers crosses the crown between the eyes and there is usually a scattering of small white plumes as spots about the head and neck. Underparts pure white. Bill black; sides of mandible orange; feet orange; iris brown.

Females are similar in plumage to the males but slightly smaller and the orange coloration of the beak and feet is either paler or tinged with pink.

The immature plumage has the throat mottled with white and the white crescent on the crown is poorly defined, being represented in some examples by irregular white patches only just above the eyes.

The downy young are dark above and white below, the general pattern being similar to that of the adult plumage.

Voice: Trumpeting, braying on two notes by inhaling and exhaling; also hissing.

Habitat and range: With a circumpolar distribution, Gentoo Penguins are found as breeders in the New Zealand region only at Macquarie Island, where they are resident and sedentary. They have occasionally been recorded as stragglers at points farther north – Campbell Island and east Otago coast.

Breeding: Gentoos nest at varying distances from the sea on inland flats or low hillocks of easy gradient. At Macquarie Island they do not form very large colonies; but loosely-knit groups of 20 to 100 nests are scattered around the coastal belt of the island. Two eggs are laid and usually two chicks reared.

ADELIE PENGUIN *Pygoscelis adeliae*   *Pl. 2, p. 17*

Description: 71 cm (28″). Upperparts bluish-black; crown, cheeks and throat black; eye brown; eye-ring conspicuously white. Underparts white. Tail very long. Bill dusky red, short; feet pinkish-white above, black below. First year birds have chin and throat entirely white.

Habitat and range: Circumpolar; breeding in large colonies in Antarctica and nearby islands; occasionally straggling north to Macquarie Island. One record from east coast of South Island may have been ship-assisted.

CHINSTRAP PENGUIN   *Pygoscelis antarctica*   *Pl. 2, p. 17*
Other names: Ringed or Bearded Penguin.
Description: 66 cm (26″). The smallest of the pygoscelid (brush-tailed) penguins. Crown black with a hint of blue. Upperparts dark bluish-grey. Cheeks, throat and underparts white; a thin black line extending from ear to ear, downwards and across throat. Tail rather long. Bill robust, blunt and black; feet white with a buff tinge. The 'chinstrap' is acquired in the first year. Noisy and belligerent.

R. C. Murphy has summed up the reactions of the three pygoscelid species of penguins to intruding man: 'Gentoos turn tail, Adelies stand their ground, but Chinstraps charge.'
Habitat and range: Formerly almost entirely confined to the South American quadrant of Antarctica; but apparently spreading eastwards. Recently found breeding in the Ross Dependency at Balleny Islands. Occasionally wanders to Macquarie Island, and once reported from Campbell Island.

LITTLE BLUE PENGUIN   *Eudyptula minor*   *Pl. 2, p. 17*
Maori name: Korora.
Description: 40 cm (16″). Several distinct subspecies are separable. The southern *minor* is described first.

Dorsal surface deep slate blue, each feather with a flattened black shaft, chin, throat, foreneck and underparts pure white. Bill black; feet pale flesh colour, black on the soles; eyes silver grey. Male and female similar, but the bill of the male is stouter. Immature birds in first plumage have smaller bills and the blue of the dorsal plumage is brighter. Young in down are a dark sooty brown dorsally with an ill-defined patch of whitish down on the underparts. Blue Penguins of the middle region, i.e. about Cook Strait (*septentrionalis*), are uniformly larger; their bills are stouter and longer; and the blue tone of the plumage is lighter even in the darkest examples. In their pale plumage and white flipper marks some are not very different from *albosignata*.

The northern subspecies *iredalei* has a more slender bill, narrower at the base. It closely resembles the common Fairy Penguin of eastern Australia (*novaehollandiae*).
Voice: Blue Penguins have a wide range of calls and are more vocal than any of the larger penguins. Sounds range from mewing notes not unlike those of a cat, to loud screams, trumpetings and deep-toned growls. These are uttered when the bird is ashore at night. The only sounds normally heard at sea are duck-like quacks.
Habitat and range: *Minor* breeds very close to the Sub-Antarctic Convergence from Stewart Island to the Otago Peninsula; and extending up the greater part of the west coast of the South Island. The Chatham Island subspecies *chathamensis* resembles *minor* but has a shorter bill. *Septentrionalis* of the middle region breeds around the coasts of both North and South Islands from the eastern entrance to Cook Strait through to the South Taranaki Bight, Marlborough Sounds and Nelson, south to North Canterbury. *Iredalei* is found mainly north of 40°S. Lat. as far as Spirits Bay and North Cape, but not Three Kings.
Breeding: Nests are to be found from high-water mark to points inland of

several hundred metres distance and sometimes over a hundred metres in altitude. Nests are rarely on the surface and usually in ready-made cavities or burrows which the birds either take over from petrels and enlarge or which they may dig themselves if the soil is soft enough. Two eggs are laid and usually two chicks reared. Incubation period *c.* 39 days; fledging 51-58 days.

WHITE-FLIPPERED PENGUIN *Eudyptula albosignata* Pl. 3, p. 24

Description: 42 cm (16½″). Perhaps best treated as a strong subspecies of *minor*, this is the most robust of the small penguins and is also palest on the back, which is pale slaty grey. The flipper has a broad white edge dorsally, and in males a central white patch which often joins the two white bands.

Habitat and range: Breeds around the shores of Banks Peninsula in Canterbury and in considerable numbers at Motunau Island, North Canterbury, where some of the Cook Strait Blue Penguin may occur.

Voice: As in other forms.

Breeding: Incubation period: *c.* 38 days (O'Brien).

ROCKHOPPER PENGUIN *Eudyptes crestatus* Pl. 3, p. 24

Description: 63 cm (25″). The general dorsal colour is dark slate with a bright bluish tinge on the back and an intensification of the blackish-grey about the head. Chin, throat and cheeks dark blackish slate. The crown in which the feathers are elongated appears even darker contrasting with the narrow golden yellow eyebrow strip, commencing behind the nasal feathers and extending along the sides of the crown to form a long crest. Underparts pure white. Bill, dull orange red. Iris geranium. Feet white; soles black. The female is similar in plumage to the male but has a much smaller bill and apparently an eye of slightly less diameter. Immature birds differ in having the chin ashy white and only a faint suggestion of the superciliary crest. Downy young are dark smoky grey above and white below.

Voice: A loud braying yell.

Habitat and range: In the New Zealand sub-antarctic zone breeds at Macquarie, Auckland, Campbell and Antipodes Islands, with small numbers at Snares and Bounties associated with other species of crested penguin. The Rockhopper is a circumpolar species, represented in the Indo-Pacific sector by the subspecies *filholi*.

Breeding: This species forms nesting colonies on steep and broken coast-line either utilising caves and cavities for nesting places or using terraces and open areas, sometimes to a considerable height above sea-level. Two eggs are laid of which the first is considerably smaller, and the smaller egg does not receive the same amount of care and attention, being sometimes trodden into the debris of the nest. However, in a certain proportion of nests both eggs may hatch and, rather rarely, two chicks can be reared.

FIORDLAND CRESTED PENGUIN *Eudyptes pachyrhynchus* Pl. 3, p. 24

Other name: Victoria Penguin.

Description: 71 cm (28″). Forehead and crown bluish black. The rest of the upperparts dark bluish grey. The chin and throat and cheeks are a dark slaty grey but the feathers have white bases and at the bulge of the cheek below the eye these are exposed in four or five parallel whitish streaks. A rather wide pale line of feathers runs back from the nasal angle above each eye and terminates in a lengthened crest. Bill reddish brown. Eye bright reddish brown. Feet whitish with black soles.

The female is similar in plumage but has a less robust bill than the male. There is no visible bare skin about the gape as in all other New Zealand forms of crested penguin. In immature plumage of the first year the superciliary stripe is poorly developed and indicated only by a few pale cream feathers. The chin and throat are whitish. Plumage otherwise as in adult. The downy young have thick sooty brown down above and dirty white below.

Voice: As in Rockhopper but of a lower tone and more hoarse.

Habitat and range: The range of this species is north of the Sub-Tropical Convergence and extends from the coasts of Otago, western coast of Stewart Island, the Solander Islands and from western Southland through all the fiords north to Okarito and south Westland including Jackson Bay. Unsuccessful attempts at nesting have been recorded from as far north as Cook Strait.

Breeding: Throughout the greater part of the nesting range, these penguins build in caves or in deep cavities beneath the roots of trees in coastal forest. They are seldom seen standing about in the open during daylight hours and conspicuous nesting groups may be met with only on Big Solander Island. Two eggs are laid, the first usually slightly smaller than the second. Under normal nesting conditions both are hatched but two chicks are seldom reared. Eggs may be found in July and chicks in August.

SNARES CRESTED PENGUIN *Eudyptes atratus* Pl. 3, p. 24

Description: 73 cm (29″). Superficially similar to the Fiordland Crested Penguin but darker in colour especially about the chin, throat and cheeks which are almost black, the feathers being dark based and not white based as in the last species. The superciliary yellow crest is brighter, if somewhat narrower, and is more extended and bushy at the free end. Bill light reddish brown. Eye bright reddish brown. Feet flesh colour with black soles.

The female is similar with a slightly smaller bill. Immature birds, which have darker bills are whitish and mottled about the throat and the superciliary crest is represented only by a few yellowish feathers interspersed with black. Nestling down is smoky brown above, white below.

At all ages and especially in the adults, a fleshy exposed line of pale naked skin extends from the gape round the bases of all the bill plates.

Voice:'A staccato bark that sounds in the distance like someone chopping wood; soft musical whistles that may give way to a series of guttural quacks reminiscent of an old drake in a farmyard; harsh screams of anger or alarm, and a number of grunts that sound in the distance like humans talking.' (Stead).

Habitat and range: Known to breed only at the Snares Islands but has been recorded as a straggler from Antipodes and points along the New Zealand

PLATE 3 PENGUINS Erect-crested (p.25); Snares Crested (p.24); Rockhopper (p.23); Fiordland Crested (p.23); Macaroni (p.26); Royal (p.26); White-flippered (p.23).

**PLATE 3
PENGUINS**

SNARES CRESTED 73 cm

ERECT-CRESTED 71 cm

ROCKHOPPER 63 cm

MACARONI 76 cm

ROYAL 76 cm

FIORDLAND CRESTED 71 cm

WHITE-FLIPPERED 42 cm

PLATE 4
ALBATROSSES

ROYAL

ROYAL
(NORTHERN)

ROYAL
75-125 cm

WANDERING (adult)
75-125 cm

WANDERING
imm.

WANDERING
imm.

WANDERING
imm.

coast north to Banks Peninsula. It is possible that the now extinct crested penguin of the Chatham Islands was of this form or closely allied to it.

Breeding: This species forms dense and compact nesting colonies in clearings a short distance from the sea on the Snares Islands. The clearings are usually along the line of small creeks or waterways and form open patches in the heavy coastal scrub which clothes the main Snares Islands. A mile or so away on the Western Reef, where there is no vegetation, the nests on bare rock are very similar in disposition and concentration to that of the Erect-crested Penguin at Bounty Islands. Two eggs are laid and two chicks frequently reared. The laying dates are in September. The young are fully fledged by the end of January.

ERECT-CRESTED PENGUIN *Eudyptes sclateri* *Pl. 3, p. 24*

Description: 71 cm (28″). The dorsal plumage in this species is very dark bluish black, with feathers of the chin, throat, cheeks, head and crown appearing almost jet black. They are however faintly blue-edged on the crown. The crest is comparatively short. The feathers when erected by muscular contraction tend to rise up into a bristle rising at a steep angle from the region of the gape about the eye to the back of the crown. Bill reddish brown. Eye dark reddish brown. Feet fleshy white with black soles.

The female is slightly smaller but otherwise similar in plumage. In immature plumage of the first year the throat is mottled with white and grey feathers and the incipient crest is hardly developed. The downy young are sooty black above and white below.

Voice: Rather a deep-toned squawk or resonant yell. Generally similar to that of the other crested pengins.

Habitat and range: Breeding distribution is at its most dense at the Bounty Islands where practically no other species is nesting: almost as abundant at Antipodes Island where Rockhoppers also occur; and in much smaller numbers associated with Rockhoppers at Campbell and Auckland Islands. As a straggler it has occurred as far south as Macquarie Island and on winter migration has been noted at sea off the coasts of Canterbury and Cook Strait. Immature and moulting birds have been recorded as far north as North Cape. Breeding has also been attempted at Otago Peninsula.

Breeding: Either in dense colonies of their own kind or associated with large numbers of Rockhoppers, Erect-crested Penguins make their nests on the rock surface or ledges a short distance above high-water mark. They seldom ascend to altitudes reached by several of the other related species. They are normally found incubating only one egg (late in October) but it is reliably recorded that two eggs are laid and the first one almost immediately discarded or kicked out of the nest.

PLATE 4 ALBATROSSES Royal (p.29); Wandering (p.29).

ROYAL PENGUIN   *Eudyptes schlegeli*   *Pl. 3, p. 24*
Description: 76 cm (30″). The dorsal plumage is light bluish grey. The under-parts pure white. There is considerable variation in the pattern of facial and head plumage. In most males the forehead, chin, throat and sides of the head and neck are white like the underparts with a faint stain of yellow near the gape. In others a small triangular patch of dark feathers appears as a spot in the middle of the throat. In others this extends to a completely grey area throughout the cheeks and round the eye and in a few examples this is entirely dark slaty grey attaining a condition almost indistinguishable from that of the closely related dark-cheeked Macaroni Penguin (*Pl. 3, p. 24*) (*Eudyptes chrysolophus*) of the South Atlantic and Indian Oceans, whence stragglers some-times reach our sub-antarctic islands. The adult crest consists of golden orange feathers springing from the middle and sides of the crown and bright black extremities. The longest of these are nearly 8 cm long and they either lie back along the crown or droop down on both sides behind the eyes. Eyes bright geranium red. Bill light reddish brown. Feet flesh colour with black soles.

Females resemble the males except that few, if any of them, have the extreme white face and all are somewhat smaller in the dimensions of the bill. Immature birds in their first year show exactly the same range of facial pattern but the crest feathers are incipient and short and are not fully developed until after the third year. Chicks in down are smoky brown above and white below.
Voice: A deep-throated bray.
Habitat and range: Endemic at Macquarie Island. Stragglers are rarely recorded as far north as the New Zealand coast but have been met with fairly regularly at Campbell Island and occasionally in Otago.
Breeding: Around the coast of Macquarie Island, Royal Penguins tend to form very large colonies of up to half a million birds in closely packed groups. Some of these are on flattish coastal terraces and others on rocky face sites similar to those of the Rockhoppers. In one or two valleys the birds trek some distance inland and occupy areas of the valley basins associated with the tributary systems of small streams. Only one egg is incubated and one chick reared but again there are records of a first laid egg being regularly discarded at the time the second egg is laid. Incubation period, *c.* 6 weeks.

GREBES: Podicipedidae

Grebes comprise a small cosmopolitan family of lobe-footed waterbirds with the feet set far back. They are expert divers. Superficially they resemble ducks, but are at once distinguished by their pointed bills and 'tailless' appearance. Two recently recorded as breeding species here raise the total to four.

CRESTED GREBE   *Podiceps australis*   *Pl. 1, p. 16*
Local names: Puteketeke, Topknot Shag.
Description: 50 cm (20″). Upperparts darkish brown; underparts satiny white. Unmistakable in summer plumage when blackish 'horns' and rufous frill (tippets) are developed. In winter cheeks and throat are white. Neck straight

and slender. Bill (6 cm) sharply-pointed. Reluctant to take wing. Flight which is direct and low with head and neck held stiffly forward, rather below level of body, reveals a surprising amount of white in the wing. Sexes alike.

Voice: When agitated near the nest, a series of hoarse, wailing calls.

Habitat and range: Lowland and subalpine lakes of the South Island, most plentiful in South Westland. Appears to be rather sedentary, but sometimes reported in winter on coastal and estuarine waters. Very few recent records from the North Island. Sub-fossil bones have been found at Taupo.

Breeding: Nest usually a floating structure of rushes and waterweeds attached to reeds, sunken branches or a drooping bough; sometimes on land under overhanging cover. Eggs 3–5, pale bluish chalky, quickly becoming stained. Both sexes incubate: period *c.* 23 days. Young grebes in striped downy plumage frequently ride on the backs of their parents. The courtship of the New Zealand race of the Crested Grebe has not been studied. Yet in the words of Julian Huxley, 'The grebes have wonderful mutual ceremonies—their courtship is as strange and fantastic as that of any gaudy tropical creature.'

H. R. McKenzie watched a pair displaying, while accompanied by well-grown young.

NEW ZEALAND DABCHICK *Podiceps rufopectus* Pl. 1, p. 16

Local names: Weweia, Diver.

Description: 28 cm (11″). Top of head and hindneck black glossed with green and faintly streaked; cheeks less dusky with eye showing conspicuously white; upperparts blackish-brown; foreneck and breast rufous; underparts silvery with flanks dusty brown. Dark silky feathers take the place of a tail; but seen from behind the tail-end looks almost white and fluffed up. Bill (2.5 cm) relatively stout. Neck slender when extended. There is no distinct winter plumage.

Voice: A rather shrill sibilant *wee-ee-ee* (hence Maori name). A nest-building pair communicated by a series of low-pitched *tuk-tuk-tuk* notes (Edgar). A low guttural chatter of four notes may accompany the Patter Ceremony when pairs are courting (Storer).

Habitat and range: Widely distributed in the North Island; locally plentiful, especially on the lakes of the Volcanic Plateau up to nearly 900 m, and on the sand-dune pools of the north and south peninsulas of Kaipara. Rather a sedentary species; but there is some evidence of autumn wandering; new dams and reservoirs are being colonised, probably by young birds; gravel pits and even sewage ponds are visited. On the larger lakes of the Volcanic Plateau and of the coastal dunes, loose winter flocks may appear. Dabchicks seem to avoid shallow lowland lakes heavily infested with eels.

Now very scarce in the South Island where it has quite disappeared from many former haunts.

Breeding: Nest 'a flimsy, clumsily-built but bulky structure' of waterlogged material anchored to overhanging branches or rushes but sometimes on a solid ledge or platform; even reported in a boat-shed. Breeding season July-May. Clutch 2–3; eggs white, chalky; quickly yellowish-brown with stain. When a sitting bird slips off the nest, it deftly covers the eggs with weed. Downy nestlings curiously variegated, take to water soon after hatching; often rest by riding on parents' backs.

HOARY-HEADED GREBE *Podiceps poliocephalus* *Pl. 1, p. 16*
  Description: 28 cm (11″). About the same size as the New Zealand Dabchick to which it is closely related. Head and hindneck black, but *white, hairlike feathers on crown and cheeks* give a streaked appearance. Upperparts grey-brown; throat white; upper breast buffy brown; underparts white. A hidden patch of white in the wing becomes prominent when the wing is extended. Bill blackish with paler tip.
  Voice: A low squeaking note is given when young are being attended.
  Habitat and range: An Australian species, sometimes forming large flocks in winter and inclined to visit tidal estuaries and brackish lagoons. First recorded in New Zealand in February 1975 when a single bird appeared in Boat Harbour, Snares Island. In the summers of 1975-76 and 1976-77 a pair bred successfully in Southland, and others sighted in Manawatu, Hawkes Bay and Northland.
  Breeding: In Australia may nest colonially.

AUSTRALIAN LITTLE GREBE *Tachybaptus novaehollandiae* *Pl. 1, p. 16*
  Other name: Black-throated Dabchick.
  Description: 25 cm (10″). Slightly smaller than the New Zealand Dabchick from which the adult is distinguishable at a glance by the *yellowish spot* (teardrop) *between eye and beak*. Head, chin, throat and hindneck black; a rufous band from eyes and down sides of neck. Upperparts brownish-black; underparts whitish to silky white. In flight a clear white band on the inner trailing edge of the wing is revealed. Bill black with white tip.
  A strong flier when the need arises; but perhaps more inclined than *rufopectus* to lurk within the cover of reed-beds.
  Voice: A long chittering, clear and shrill. Also a soft *whit-whit*.
  Habitat and range: An Australian invader first noted in New Zealand near Arrowtown in 1968. Has now been located on several waters between Northland and Otago and from sea-level to 300 m.
  Breeding: After much study, successful breeding was confirmed in 1977 when a pair with three young were seen on a mountain lake. Clutch in Australia 4–6; eggs bluish-white but usually weed-stained.

ALBATROSSES: Diomedeidae

The largest of the petrel family and amongst the largest of flying birds, albatrosses are also noted for their perfection of gliding flight. Except in the Pacific Ocean they are restricted to the southern hemisphere. Identification resolves itself into field characters which can be detected when the bird is on the wing as few people have the opportunity or occasion to see albatrosses when they are settled ashore, nesting places with very few exceptions being on uninhabited and often inaccessible islands. There are two very large species, the Wandering Albatross and the Royal Albatross confined to the southern hemisphere and several more of smaller size frequently called Mollymawks to distinguish them from the larger birds. The breeding places of members of this family in New Zealand seas are all south of latitude 44°.

WANDERING ALBATROSS *Diomedea exulans* *Pl. 4, p. 25*
Other names: Wanderer, Toroa.
Description: 75–125 cm (30″–50″). Beginning their flying life with plumage which is uniformly dark brown except for contrasting white patches on the face and complete underwing, Wandering Albatrosses go through a series of plumage changes which present a bewildering variety of pattern until in old males of the larger of the forms the plumage appears almost entirely white except for the black wing-tips. Beaks in life are pink with a yellowish tip, eyelids pale powder blue, feet a fleshy white with purple veining and eyes dark brown.
Voice: The only sound heard at sea is a hoarse croak, made when they are fighting for scraps. During display, besides beak-clappering, they gobble, neigh and squeal.
Habitat and range: Wandering Albatrosses have a wide oceanic range throughout the southern ocean between latitudes 22°–66° south. Immature birds and non-breeders are at sea throughout the year and many of them probably circumnavigate the globe in high latitudes. Their breeding distribution in the New Zealand region includes Antipodes Island, Campbell Island, Auckland Islands (*exulans*) and at Macquarie Island a breeding population of the large snowy circumpolar form (*chionoptera*), which is found also breeding in the South Indian and South Atlantic Oceans.
Breeding: Starts in late January and for each pair continues throughout twelve months until the single fledgling flies some time in the following January. Adults then miss a year before breeding again. The nest is a well-built mound of tussock and short lengths of vegetation with a plentiful supply of earth for binding. A single elongated white egg is laid; incubation period 66 days and the young bird remains on the nest for about seven months or longer. While still clothed in nestling down it is a very pale grey which becomes much faded by the time it gives place to the chocolate brown immature plumage.

ROYAL ALBATROSS *Diomedea epomophora* *Pl. 4, p. 25*
Maori name: Toroa.
Description: 75–125 cm (30″–50″). As with the Wandering Albatross, there are two races separated by size, the larger race *epomophora* having a more southerly distribution and attaining a much whiter adult plumage. At no stage is the plumage dark as in the Wandering Albatross and young birds are very similar to adults. The whole body except the wings is pure white and the amount of black on the wings varies from total coverage to a pattern heavily flecked with white. Bill horn coloured faintly pink in life; cutting edges of both mandibles black; eyelids black, feet whitish, purple veined.
Voice: As in Wandering Albatross.
Habitat and range: The smaller race (*sanfordi*) nests at Chatham Islands and on Otago Peninsula; the larger at Campbell, where it is very plentiful, and Auckland Islands. Distribution at sea is not generally so widespread as that of the Wandering Albatross but examples of both forms have been observed or collected off the coasts of South America.
Breeding: The cycle follows much the same pattern as that of the Wanderer but the season is about two months earlier, eggs being laid in November, hatching

Key to mandibular plates:
1. Nostrils; 2. Culminicorn; 3. Maxillary unguis;
4. Apical hook; 5. Latericorn; 6. Mandibular unguis;
7. Ramicorn; 8. Mandibular groove or sulcus.

Wandering Albatross

THE TUBENOSES

The Order Procellariiformes (or Tubinares) comprises the family Diomedeidae (Albatrosses and Mollymawks), the family Procellariidae (Fulmars, Petrels and Shearwaters), the family Pelecanoididae (Diving Petrels), and the family Hydrobatidae (Storm Petrels). All four families have distinctive external nostrils, and composite bills which vary remarkably in size, and in the proportions of the parts, even within genera. Modern research seems to show that these nasal tubes are concerned with the rejection of superfluous salt taken into the system with salt water.

Here are some of the variations on a theme.

(Note: The various heads are not reproduced to the same scale.)

Giant Petrel

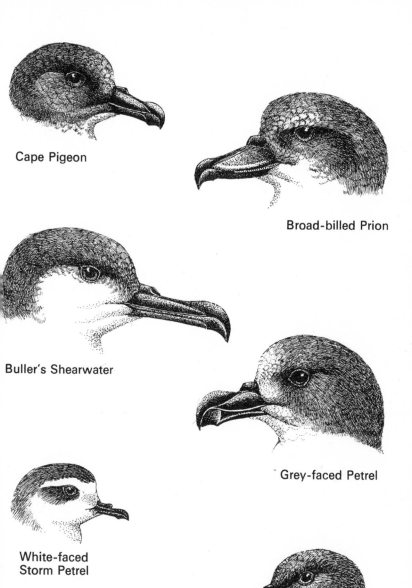

Cape Pigeon

Broad-billed Prion

Buller's Shearwater

Grey-faced Petrel

White-faced
Storm Petrel

Diving Petrel

early in February with the young departing in September. The southern race is about three weeks later. The young at all stages of down are pure white and the first full-fledged condition differs from the adult only in having some dark barring across the 'shoulders'.

BLACK-BROWED MOLLYMAWK *Diomedea melanophris Pls. 5, 6, pp. 32, 33*
  Description: 60 cm (24″). Adult plumage is pure white except for black wings and mantle, dark grey tail and a smudge of smoky grey about the eye. In adult birds the bill is yellow with a pink tip, feet are pale bluish white. Immature birds have a darker bill and there is some blackish feathering under the wings giving the pattern shown in plate 6. The distinctive race of Black-browed Mollymawk (*D.m. impavida*), breeding as far as is known only in the New Zealand area, has a pale honey-coloured eye when adult, whereas the slightly larger circumpolar race (*melanophris*) has a dark eye at all ages.
  Voice: As with most mollymawks a loud plaintive cry, like the bah of a sheep, is characteristic of this species when at the nest.
  Habitat and range: From their sub-antarctic nesting places these mollymawks range north to New Zealand coastal waters and there appears to be an annual movement of young birds along the 'whale route' as far as the Coral Sea. Southwards some frequent the northern limits of the pack ice throughout the year. The New Zealand race breeds at Campbell Island and apparently in smaller numbers at Antipodes Island. The circumpolar race breeds at Macquarie Island.
  Breeding: Egg-laying begins in October and young fly in April. Nests are mounds with a cup-shaped depression ('chimney-pots') and most of the nests are in close proximity in breeding colonies. Frequently the Black-browed Mollymawk occupies sections of areas already used by Grey-headed Mollymawks or alternatively there may be a few Grey-heads associated with larger colonies of Black-brows. The egg is elongated, white with pinkish speckles at the larger end.
  Incubation period *c.* 70 days and the single chick is fed by both parents. Nestling down is pale grey. Fledging *c.* 4½ months.

GREY-HEADED MOLLYMAWK *Diomedea chrysostoma Pls. 5, 6, pp. 32, 33*
  Description: 63 cm (25″). The adult bird has a dark grey head and neck, well defined from the white plumage of the rest of the underparts. There is some white feathering under the wing and in other respects the plumage of the upperparts is similar to that of other mollymawks. The *bill*, however, is distinguished by *dark central stripe edged above and below with rich yellow shading to a bright pink tip*. A dark brown eye set in the midst of the grey plumage of the head is relieved by a half-circle of white feathers at the back of the eyelid. The bill of the immature bird is dusky.
  Voice: As in other mollymawks.

PLATE 5 MOLLYMAWKS

BLACK-BROWED 60 cm

GREY-HEADED 60 cm

YELLOW-NOSED 60 cm

BULLER'S 62 cm

CHATHAM ISLAND 70 cm

**GREY-BACKED
(BOUNTY ISLAND)**
70 cm

SHY (WHITE-CAPPED) 75 cm

**PLATE 6
MOLLYMAWKS**

BLACK-BROWED 60 cm

BLACK-BROWED
imm.

BULLER'S 62 cm

YELLOW-
NOSED
60 cm

SHY
(WHITE-CAPPED)
75 cm

GREY-HEADED
60 cm

imm.

Habitat and range: Another circumpolar species of which no races have been clearly defined. The bird appears to have a more restricted wandering distribution at sea than the Black-browed Mollymawk but the breeding range appears to be almost exactly the same and the one species is seldom found nesting without the presence of the other.

Breeding: Parallels that of the Black-brow except that it starts about two weeks earlier and the young are distinguished by having down of a slightly darker shade of grey. They fledge and leave the nest two weeks or so before the companion species. Incubation *c.* 70 days. Fledging *c.* 4 months.

YELLOW-NOSED MOLLYMAWK *Diomedea chlororhynchus*

Pls.5, 6, pp. 32, 33

Description: 60 cm (24″). The smallest in appearance of the mollymawks resembling the others in plumage pattern except that the *underwing, mainly white, has a dark anterior border slightly wider than the dark posterior one.* The head and neck in adults and young are white like the underparts except that in fresh adult plumage there is a triangular eye-patch or a grey smudge on the cheeks. *Adult bill black with the ridge of the culmen yellow deepening to scarlet near the tip.* The immature bill is entirely black. Eyes brown; feet pale fleshy grey.

Voice: The usual bleat.

Habitat and range: Inhabiting the warmer northerly section of the west wind belt, this mollymawk which breeds only at the Tristan da Cunha group in the Atlantic, and St. Paul and Amsterdam in the Indian Ocean, ranges normally eastward as far as the Tasman Sea; but has been sighted several times near the Three Kings, in the outer waters of the Hauraki Gulf and near Cuvier Island. In January 1975 one landed in a colony of Northern Royal Albatrosses at The Sisters, the northernmost outliers of the Chatham Islands.

BULLER'S MOLLYMAWK *Diomedea bulleri*   *Pls. 5, 6, pp. 32, 33*

Description: 63 cm (25″). This is another small mollymawk of slightly stouter build than the Yellow-nosed. Superficially it resembles the Grey-headed with a central dark band separating the yellow of the upper and lower surfaces of the bill. Cheeks and hind neck are grey but the *forehead is white.* The plumage otherwise is normal as in all mollymawks, the underwing pattern having much the same dark bordering as is found in the Yellow-nosed. Immature birds have a nondescript blackish-grey bill darker towards the tip and somewhat blotchy markings on the neck.

Voice: Not distinguishable from the sheep-like bleat of the other species.

Habitat and range: Breeding only in New Zealand seas in waters along the convergence, a few examples have been found in the Humboldt current region of South America. Feeding range south to 50°.

Breeding: There are anomalies in the breeding season in that at the Chatham Islands (Sisters and Forty-fours) the birds follow the normal cycle of egg-laying

---

PLATE 6 MOLLYMAWKS   Black-browed (p.32); Buller's (p.33); Shy (White-capped) (p.34); Yellow-nosed (p.33); Grey-headed (p.32).

in October-November, with the young fully fledged about April or May. Elsewhere at Solander Island and the Snares the laying period is February, and the young are fledged and flying in August. The two populations are distinguished by slight but constant plumage characters, the dark pigment of the Chatham Islands' birds being blacker.

SHY (WHITE-CAPPED) MOLLYMAWK *Diomedea cauta*

Pls. 5, 6, pp. 32, 33

Description: 75 cm (30″). The largest of the mollymawks approaching in size some of the smaller races of Wandering and Royal Albatross. This and the next two mollymawks differ from the others in that the underwing is practically pure white with a narrow dark border all around. They have the usual pure white body, black wings and mantle and grey tail. The bill is indistinctly coloured, being pale greenish-grey changing to yellow at tip. There is a thin flesh-orange stripe outlining the base of the lower mandible. Apart from the dark eyebrow line, head and neck are pure white in adult males, with a slight dusting of grey on the cheek of females. Bills in immature birds are generally duller and darker.

Voice: During sexual displays breeding birds cackle. Bill clappering to scare intruders.

Habitat and range: Shy Mollymawks have been recorded all round the southern hemisphere, but as breeding birds only to the south of Australia and New Zealand.

Breeding: Australian breeding islands are in Bass Strait and off the southern tip of Tasmania. The New Zealand breeding station is at the Auckland Islands. The breeding season is from October, when eggs are laid, until late March or April, when the young depart. Incubation *c.* 2 months; fledging *c.* 4½ months.

GREY-BACKED (BOUNTY ISLAND) MOLLYMAWK *Diomedea salvini*

Pl. 5, p. 32

Description: 70 cm (28″). Usually regarded as a subspecies of the Shy Mollymawk, the Grey-backed is distinctive enough in appearance to be treated separately. Its bill is noticeably darker along the central area, paler on the culmen and mandible. There is a well-defined patch of grey spreading past the cheeks and down and around the neck. The mantle feathers are paler grey than in any other mollymawk and contrast noticeably with the dark wings.

Habitat and range: This race has also been recorded as a wanderer in all southern seas.

Breeding: Breeds only in New Zealand where it nests at the Bounty Islands and at the Snares (Western Reef). Nesting season, much as for the Shy Mollymawk.

CHATHAM ISLAND MOLLYMAWK *Diomedea eremita* *Pl. 5, p. 32*

Description: 70 cm (28″). No doubt properly regarded as another subspecies of *cauta*, this mollymawk is even more distinctive in appearance. It is slightly smaller than either *cauta* or *salvini* and much darker in overall pigmentation. The crown is pale grey and the cheeks and neck even darker grey, making very little contrast with the mantle. The *bill* is perhaps the most distinctive feature, being *rich chrome yellow* with a dark tip to the lower mandible.

Habitat and range: Restricted as far as is known to the Chatham Islands where it breeds on Pyramid Rock ranging locally; sometimes to Cook Strait, but rarely farther north. This distinctive mollymawk is not known outside New Zealand waters.

LIGHT-MANTLED SOOTY ALBATROSS   *Phoebetria palpebrata*   *Pl. 7, p. 40*
Local name: Pee-oo.
Description: 70 cm (28″). A bird of great distinction. The plumage is dark except for the small half-circle of white feathers on the eyelid. Main body plumage light pearly brown shading to intense chocolate on the head and cheeks, wings and tail dark brown. Tail *wedge-shaped*. Bill black with *pale blue fleshy line* on the mandibular sulcus. Eyes dark hazel; feet pale fleshy white. The immature bird is similar in plumage but the bill usually lacks the pale blue line.
Voice: At nesting places a distinctive call, seldom heard at sea, consists of two clear notes which may be transcribed as 'Pee-oo'. Hence its vernacular name current among sealers and seafarers.
Habitat and range: There are two forms of Sooty Albatross in the southern hemisphere and the Light-mantled is the only one known to occur in New Zealand seas. Breeding at Auckland, Campbell, Antipodes and Macquarie Islands, *palpebrata* ranges widely along a narrow latitudinal belt south to the Antarctic Circle and rarely north of 40°S. Though mainly pelagic, it is sometimes seen in coastal waters and may be blown inland. The true Sooty Albatross, *P. fusca*, belongs to the South Atlantic and Indian Oceans, reaching the Great Australian Bight, but apparently not the Tasman Sea.
Breeding: Nests are situated on cliff ledges and the small terraces of steep slopes. Usually solitary and very rarely in groups of three or four on suitable ledges. Like those of mollymawks they are steep-sided columns of mud and vegetation; the single egg, laid in October, hatches early in January; the young are attended until able to fly in late April or early May. Incubation period *c.* 65 days; fledging *c.* 4½ months.

PETRELS, SHEARWATERS AND FULMARS: Procellariidae

The Order Procellariiformes includes a remarkable variety of families and subfamilies, from the great albatrosses to the small storm petrels and diving petrels. Because all possess distinctive external nostrils, they are sometimes classed as Tubinares (Tubenoses).

Although they are essentially birds of the open seas, many species are abundant in coastal waters, and our long archipelago, with its many outlying islands free of mammalian predators, has been from time immemorial a prolific breeding ground for more than thirty species. Species which breed on the main islands have declined. Some species are highly migratory.

The southern tubenoses grouped as fulmars belong to cold waters and range farther north in winter. They vary in size from the Nelly, large as a mollymawk, to the ethereal Snow Petrel. All have stout bulbous bills.

Nine or ten species of *Pterodroma* breed on islands from the sub-tropical Kermadecs to the sub-antarctic outliers. From their airy drifting flight with sudden drops these petrels are sometimes called 'gadflies'. The smaller white and dusky species have also been separated as 'cookilarias'. (See page 43.)

The four species of *Procellaria* which breed in New Zealand are large petrels, robustly built. Three are essentially pelagic. Only *westlandica* habitually frequents coastal waters.

Most numerous are the shearwaters, *Puffinus*. Seasonally, and in the right weather, large flocks of at least five species or immense flights may be observed from points of vantage along the coasts of the main islands. To watch myriads of Muttonbirds (Sooty Shearwater) passing through Foveaux Strait on a windy day is an exhilarating experience. The true shearwaters have long narrow bills. Flying effortlessly in a fair breeze on scythe-shaped wings, they rise and fall in sweeping arcs.

As is only to be expected, tubenoses from distant oceans stray to New Zealand.

GIANT PETREL   *Macronectes giganteus*   *Pl. 7, p. 40*
Other Names: Nelly, Stinker, Black Molly.

The following composite description covers at least two races, distinguished as the Northern, *M.g. halli*, and the Southern, *M.g. giganteus*. Some authors treat these as two full species. The former has a uniform adult plumage of dull brown with whitish face, and brownish horn bill with darker tip. The latter has more variable plumage, including the white phase, and generally a greenish bill. Brown phase juveniles of both forms are indistinguishable.

Description: 65 cm (26″). Males are noticeably larger than females and have heavier bills. Somewhat variable in colour, adult Giant Petrels in average plumage are dull rusty brown, much paler on the face, throat and neck. As the brown feathers have weak pigmentation they fade rapidly and a mottled variable appearance is not uncommon. Bills vary from horn colour to greenish and feet are from dull brown to almost black. There is also variability in the colour of the eye which may be brown flecked or dull greyish-white. Immature birds in at least their first and second years are a rich glossy brown without the fading variations. The pale beak and dark feet are fairly uniformly so and the eye also is dark. A distinctive feature of the bird's appearance is the heavy bill with the elongated single nasal tube. The white form with scattered black feathers in its plumage is common at Macquarie, but rather rare in the coastal waters of New Zealand proper.

Voice: A hoarse, wheezy croak.

Habitat and range: Mainly scavengers, Giant Petrels are amongst the best documented of ocean wanderers. They have been banded at various breeding places and many recoveries have helped to indicate the extensive wanderings of immature birds in particular. The species is circumpolar in the southern hemisphere and in New Zealand seas is found breeding at Chatham, Stewart, Snares, Auckland, Campbell, Antipodes (*halli*) and Macquarie (both forms) Islands.

Breeding: The laying season extends over a period from August (*halli*) to

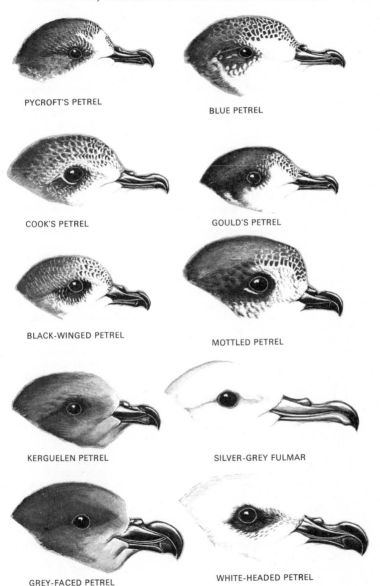

PYCROFT'S PETREL

BLUE PETREL

COOK'S PETREL

GOULD'S PETREL

BLACK-WINGED PETREL

MOTTLED PETREL

KERGUELEN PETREL

SILVER-GREY FULMAR

GREY-FACED PETREL

WHITE-HEADED PETREL

October (*giganteus*). A single white egg is laid on a roughly constructed nest lacking the elaborate build-up of albatrosses and mollymawks. Chicks, when hatched, show the two colour phases found in the adult population and a proportion of them have pure white down, the rest with pattern of grey and white. On leaving the nesting places the young tend to move in a northerly direction and down-wind from the breeding places. A large non-breeding population is thus to be found at sea as far north as Lat. 30°S. Scavenger flocks congregate about whaling stations, coastal meat works, and other sources of offal. These groups are shown by banded birds to include individuals from almost all the known breeding places in the southern hemisphere.

CAPE PIGEON *Daption capensis* Pl. 7, p. 40

Description: 40 cm (16″). This is one of the few members of the petrel family with a strongly contrasting pattern. Head, neck, cheeks, are dark blackish-brown. The back is strongly spotted with black on white, upper tail-coverts white, tip of tail black. There is a broad white bar on the black wings and this often appears as three irregular white lozenge-shaped patches. Underparts white; bill black; feet black; with an occasional splash of bluish-white on the webs. The dark areas of the plumage are more extensive in the subspecies *australis* which breeds in the New Zealand sub-antarctic.

Voice: Often a harsh cackle from flocks at sea. At the nest, among a variety of softer calls, the most notable is a prolonged whirring coo.

Habitat and range: The oceanic range is extremely wide from the antarctic ice to Lat. 25°S. As scavenging flocks, large concentrations of Cape Pigeons are common throughout the year off the coast as far north as Cook Strait, coming boldly into inshore waters where offal from various sources is available. A few in winter enter the Bay of Plenty and Hauraki Gulf.

Breeding: Cape Pigeons breed from the coasts of Antarctica through many high latitude sub-antarctic islands, with a few more northerly outposts at nearly all the New Zealand sub-antarctic islands. The most northerly known is at the Snares. In their sub-antarctic nesting places the birds are almost all inaccessible on high ledges. A single white egg is laid on a rough nest of chips of rock and the chick is reared in the usual way through guard stages by the parents. Egg dates from the New Zealand region are early October, hatching in December; the young flying late March-early April—in plumage not readily distinguishable from adults. Incubation period *c*. 45 days; fledging *c*. 50 days.

SILVER-GREY (ANTARCTIC) FULMAR *Fulmarus glacialoides* Pl. 7, p. 40

Description: 43 cm (17″). This bird is the southern counterpart of the common Fulmar of the northern hemisphere and is similar in appearance being slightly larger and only a little paler in general coloration. Head, neck and underparts are mainly white with a little shading of grey on the hindneck. Back and tail are pearly grey, wings with dark primaries, a pale white patch showing on the upper surface when the bird is in flight. Bill is pinkish horn colour with a bluish tinge on the nasal tube. Feet pale flesh-colour with some darker patches on the outer toes.

Habitat and range: The Silver-grey Fulmar breeds only south of the Antarctic Circle. In New Zealand waters it has been recorded often enough to be regarded as a regular straggler. Between 1935 and 1969 only nine were reported. Subsequently there has been a striking increase of these birds, both dead and alive, along the coasts of the main islands. In 1975 more than 600 were recorded.

ANTARCTIC PETREL *Thalassoica antarctica* Pl. 7, p. 40
Description: 43 cm (17″). Upperparts chocolate brown, contrasting with a white stripe along part of the trailing edge of the wing, broadening to a white patch on the shafts and inner webs of the primaries. Throat and sides of neck brown or mottled. Tail white, broadly tipped with brown. Underparts and underwing white, except for brown leading edge. Bill dark olive brown; legs flesh colour, stained brown on outer toes.
　　Among petrels this contrasting pattern of brown and white is unique.
Habitat and range: Breeds round the edge of Antarctica; moving north with the pack-ice but seldom north of 60°S. Not recorded in New Zealand waters till 1973 when three were found on beaches at Dargaville (September), Oreti (October) and Cape Kidnappers (December), and three more in 1975.

GREY-FACED PETREL *Pterodroma macroptera* Pl. 8, p. 41
Other names: Oi, North Island Muttonbird, Great-winged Petrel.
Description: 41 cm (16″). Entire plumage blackish brown, pale grey on the forehead, face and throat, feet and bill (36 x 14 mm) black. On the wing this bird is a strong and rapid flier wheeling in broad arcs.
Voice: Heard only at nesting grounds, a whistling call with a gutteral undertone rendered roughly by the Maori name.
Habitat and range: Forages widely over the Tasman and South Pacific eastwards nearly to Pitcairn. Other subspecies with less grey on the face occur in the south Atlantic and Indian Oceans in about the same latitudinal belt. Breeds on most off-shore islands and still on a few mainland cliffs within the triangle formed by Three Kings, North Taranaki and East Cape.
Breeding: A winter breeder. Eggs from May onwards, many hatching by the end of August. Young leave, November-January. This is the traditional muttonbird of the North Island Maoris, the taking season being in November.

WHITE-HEADED PETREL *Pterodroma lessoni* Pl. 8, p. 41
Description: 43 cm (17″). Body white, very faintly grey on the crown and hindneck, slightly darker on the back and tail, wings greyish brown and blackish mark through the eye; bill (37 x 15 mm) black, feet parti-coloured, being fleshy pink with brown on the outer toe and terminally on the webs.
Voice: Vocal only at the nesting places, where it has a deep-throated purring call.
Habitat and range: In the New Zealand region breeds at Auckland, Antipodes and Macquarie Islands; and in the south Indian Ocean at Kerguelen. Fairly common at sea to the south of New Zealand, ranging farther north in winter to about Lat. 34°S. where it sometimes associates with *macroptera*. Regularly recorded as a beach casualty, especially on the west coast of the North Island.
Breeding: Nesting season extends from November to April, most eggs hatching in late January or early February.

SUNDAY ISLAND PETREL   *Pterodroma cervicalis*   *Pl. 8, p. 41*
Other name: Black-capped Petrel.
Description: 43 cm (17″). Plumage mainly white with a dark blackish cap and black wings and tail; scapulars and upper wing-coverts frosty grey; bill black (37 x 16 mm); feet flesh-coloured, toes and outer webs black. Strikingly different from other petrels of this region by virtue of its black cap and white collar.
Habitat and range: Known mainly from the vicinity of the Kermadecs where it breeds abundantly on Macauley. Probably closely related to *externa* of the south-east Pacific, which may stray into the New Zealand region.
Breeding: Returns to Kermadecs in October; laying begins in December; young fly in late May and June.

BIRD OF PROVIDENCE   *Pterodroma solandri*   *Pl. 8, p. 41*
Description: 40 cm (16″). A greyish brown petrel, mottled on face and forehead and having a distinctive *whitish patch at the base of primaries* visible when the bird is in flight. This helps to distinguish it from the Grey-faced petrel. Bill (35 x 15 mm) black; feet dark grey.
Habitat and range: Formerly bred in great numbers at Norfolk Island, but now reported extinct there. Breeds in winter at Lord Howe Island. It is curious that a petrel which breeds so close, is known in New Zealand only from a single specimen stranded at Muriwai in 1921.

PHOENIX PETREL   *Pterodroma alba*   *Pl. 8, p. 41*
Description: 38 cm (15″). Dark brown above and white below, the bases of the primaries being only slightly whitish, feet parti-coloured, that is flesh-colour with terminal dark patches on the webs and outer toe. A rather conspicuous field character is the broad *dark band on the chest*, but the variable white throat patch is not easily seen. Bill black (28 x 11 mm).
Habitat and range: Ranges widely in the tropical Pacific mainly south of the equator; westwards to the Kermadecs where four were found on the forest floor of Raoul Island in March 1913. Otherwise not known from New Zealand seas.

TAIKO   *Pterodroma ?magentae*
Description: 38 cm (15″). A large dark-headed, white-breasted 'gadfly' petrel of sub-tropical rather than sub-antarctic affinities. Head, neck and throat deep brownish-black, except for some greyish scalloping on the forehead and a trace of white under the gape. Mantle and upper-surface fairly uniform dark grey; underwing generally silvery grey, but darker along the fore-edge; breast and underparts white; under tail-coverts white edged with dark grey. Bill robust and black (32 x 16 mm); feet particoloured pink, and terminally black.
Voice: No calls were heard from birds flying over what were presumably breeding grounds.

PLATE 7 Light-mantled Sooty Albatross (p.35); Antarctic Petrel (p.39); Cape Pigeon (p.38); Silver-grey (Antarctic) Fulmar (p.38); Giant Petrel (p.36).

PLATE 7

LIGHT-MANTLED
SOOTY ALBATROSS
70 cm

ANTARCTIC
PETREL
43 cm

PE PIGEON
cm

SILVER-GREY
(ANTARCTIC)
FULMAR
43 cm

GIANT PETREL (Southern)
(white phase) 65 cm

GIANT PETREL
(NORTHERN)
65 cm

PLATE 8 PETRELS

GREY-FACED
41 cm

WHITE-HEADED
43 cm

SUNDAY
ISLAND
43 cm

KERMADEC
38 cm

BIRD OF
PROVIDENCE
40 cm

PHOENIX
38 cm

Habitat and range: The Taiko formerly bred on Chatham Island where, to judge by the many bones found in middens, it was for some centuries an important item in the diet of the Moriori. Unknown in our coastal waters or as a beach-wreck, the species evidently ranged north and east of Chatham Island into the vast expanse of the south central Pacific. Believed extinct for more than a century, it was dramatically rediscovered there on 1 January 1978, when two were captured by night, photographed, measured and released.

The Magenta Petrel is known from a single specimen taken in 1867 at 39°38′S., 125°58′ W. by the Italian research vessel *Magenta*.

KERMADEC PETREL   *Pterodroma neglecta*   *Pl. 8, p. 41*
Description: 38 cm (15″). There are three phases of body plumage in this species with some intermediates. They have been described as dark, intermediate and light forms. In the dark form the plumage is brownish grey, the only relief in pattern being the white bases to the primaries which occur uniformly in all phases and at sea show as a pale patch in the extended wing. Wings are otherwise dark brown in all three phases. The intermediate form has a palish body and is often mottled about the face. The pale form is almost white on head and neck and over the rest of the body with the exception of the wings and tail; and except for its wing markings looks at sea something like a small version of the White-headed Petrel. Bill (30 x 13 mm) black in all forms, feet usually parti-coloured, being dark at their extremities, greyish flesh on legs in the intermediate form and pale flesh in the pale form.
Voice: A long-drawn *eeow* often loud, beginning on a high note and descending, commonly followed by three leisurely *yoks*. Brooding birds sometimes make a low, steady purr, lasting more than a minute.

PLATE 8 PETRELS   Grey-faced (p.39); White-headed (p.39); Sunday Island (p.40); Kermadec (p.41); Bird of Providence (p.40); Phoenix (p.40).

Habitat and range: Has a wide breeding range in the sub-tropical Pacific from Lord Howe east to Juan Fernandez. In the New Zealand region breeds at Raoul and Herald Islets, very rarely straying as far south as the North Island. In January 1976 one frequented Cuvier Island and actually landed on a ridge.
Breeding: Nesting takes place all year round on the Herald Islets. Egg laying appears to be at its peak in February. Incubation period 50–52 days.

MOTTLED PETREL *Pterodroma inexpectata*   *Pl. 9, p. 48*
Other names: Korure, Rainbird.
Description: 33 cm (13″). The main tone of the plumage is a dark frosty grey. When the wings are spread there is an obscure blacker tone forming an inverted 'w' pattern. The upper surface of the tail is grey like the back, the face is white with mottled transition to the dark grey of the crown, a dark mark through the eye, underparts white except for a broad grey patch on the lower breast and belly. Bill (27 x 12 mm) black, feet yellowish, toes and outer webs blackish.
Voice: A high-pitched *ti-ti-ti* rapidly and continuously repeated. Another call is a deep resonant bugle-note of two syllables, *Goo-oo* (Stead).
Habitat and range: Compared with its former breeding range, which included both North and South Islands, now much restricted; its main centre of distribution being outlying islands in Foveaux Strait, off Stewart Island and at the Snares. Has a very wide oceanic range, southward to the edge of the pack ice; and northward in the southern winter to the Aleutian Islands.
Breeding: Burrow-cleaning in November; eggs by mid-December; young flying in April. Incubation period *c.* 54 days.

SOFT-PLUMAGED PETREL *Pterodroma mollis*   *Pl. 9, p. 48*
Description: 34 cm (13½″). About the same size as *inexpectata*, and robuster than the typical so-called *cookilaria* petrels. Upperparts slaty grey with a broad blackish stripe across wing-coverts; head brownish, the white-tipped feathers of the forehead giving the scaled appearance that goes with several other 'gadfly' petrels; a black patch before and behind the eye; cheeks, throat and underparts white except for a variable grey collar; underwing mainly sooty grey, but with a paler whitish centre and the leading edge almost black. Bill (35 x 12 mm) black; legs pinkish, webs terminally dark.
Voice: Flight call a shrill *treee-pi-pee*. Over breeding grounds moaning cries accompany aerial flights and chases after dark.
Habitat and range: The typical race breeds on remote islands in the temperate zone of the South Atlantic and Indian Oceans. In February 1969 a few birds, possibly breeding, were found on Antipodes Island; but the existence of a colony was not confirmed. The number of sightings at sea is increasing, viz., one west of Farewell Spit (August 1971); two west of Foveaux Strait (June 1972) and others further north in mid-Tasman in November (J.A.F.J.). Beachcast specimens are very rare; one Hutt Valley (May 1971); one Bay of Plenty (November 1971); one Ruakaka (spring 1974).
Breeding: An extended season in the southern summer. Incubation *c.* 53 days; fledging probably 90–100 days.

KERGUELEN PETREL   *Pterodroma brevirostris*   *Pl. 9, p. 48*
   Description: 33 cm (13"). Almost uniformly dark frosty grey with little variation except for slight mottling on forehead and flanks on some specimens. Compared with the bills of other pterodromas, the black bill of this species is narrow and compressed (26 x 10 mm). Feet purplish flesh colour, darker on the outside.
   Habitat and range: Breeds in the sub-antarctic belt of the Atlantic and Indian Oceans, ranging eastwards in autumn. Mainly known in New Zealand from beach casualties; but may be fairly numerous in the Tasman in some winters, e.g. 1954, when 8 were found wrecked on the Auckland west coast in July and August, and still larger numbers in subsequent years.

PYCROFT'S PETREL   *Pterodroma pycrofti*   *Pl. 9, p. 48*
   Description: 28 cm (11"). Crown, hindneck, back and central tail medium grey. Forehead and all underparts including under wing-coverts and under tail-coverts are white; the outer webs of the outer tail feathers likewise are white. Feet pale fleshy blue, darker on the outer toe. Generally smaller than Cook's Petrel, with shorter bill (24 x 9 mm) and wings, but with a proportionately longer tail. Very hard to distinguish at sea from *cooki* or other members of sub-genus *Cookilaria*, a name sometimes given to the smaller pterodromas.
   Voice: Somewhat similar to that of *cooki*, but thinner and higher pitched; a *tzi-tzi-tzi-tzi* with a buzzing undertone when several birds are overhead calling together. Fleming distinguishes two types of cry, one a soft *ti-ti-ti-ti*; the other somewhat lower and louder *té-té-té-té*. On the ground a bass grunt and a pleasant low crooning note appear to be part of courtship.
   Habitat and range: Oceanic range unknown. Breeds at Hen and Chickens Islands and Poor Knights; and in 1962 discovered in some numbers on Red Mercury. Probably a migrant leaving home waters in April and returning about October.
   Breeding: All the islands on which these petrels are known to breed are well-forested. The burrows may be well inland. The laying season is very short, most eggs appearing in the last week of November.

GOULD'S PETREL   *Pterodroma leucoptera*   *Pl. 9, p. 48*
   Description: 30 cm (12"). Upperparts dark, almost black on crown and nape, much lighter grey on the 'shoulders,' back and central tail. Forehead, underparts, including under wing-coverts, white; feet bluish with dark terminal patches on the webs and the outer toe, bill (24 x 10 mm) black. Distinguishable from several other cookilarias by the darker crown and nape.
   Habitat and range: Not known to breed in the New Zealand region; but among 12 specimens, picked up dead on beaches, of which 10 came ashore at Muriwai in April 1942, representatives of two races are distinguishable. The provenance of the ten which were wrecked together is unknown. A later Muriwai specimen, January 1946, is identical with the breeding birds of Cabbage Tree Island, New South Wales. The most southerly record is of one ashore at Otaki in June 1961.

STEJNEGER'S PETREL   *Pterodroma longirostris*
   Description: 28 cm (11"). Head and nape blackish, back frosty grey, wings black and tail dark grey except for some white mottling on the outer web of

the outer feathers. Forehead and underparts including under wing-coverts and under tail-coverts white, feet bluish, darker on the outer webs. Except for its smaller size, the bird is very similar to Gould's Petrel.

Habitat and range: Known to breed only at Masafuera in the eastern temperate Pacific. Non-breeders in moult occur regularly in the North Pacific and off Japan. In the summer of 1961-2, three were recovered from New Zealand beaches, one at Baring Head, Cook Strait, in December; and two at Ohope, Bay of Plenty, in January.

COOK'S PETREL   *Pterodroma cooki*   *Pl. 9, p. 48*
Maori name: Titi.

Description: 30 cm (12″). Crown, hindneck, back and uppertail pale grey. Forehead white with scalation merging into the grey of the crown. Underparts including under wing-coverts and under tail-coverts, white; feet pale blue, slightly stained with brown on the outer toe; bill (28 x 10 mm) black. Wings are darker grey than the back, but, when extended they show a continuing dark pattern like an inverted 'w'. The strong wheeling flight of Cook's Petrel presents to the eye in turn the characteristic pattern of the back and the pure white undersurface.

Voice: Over their breeding ground at night, Cook's Petrels make a surprising variety of sounds; the commonest being a rapidly repeated *ti-ti-ti* or *whik-kek-kek*. Others described are: a goatlike bleating; a slow deliberate *kek-kek-kek*; a less frequent *hwit-wit*; a cat-like *purrp*; a *borrr* with well-rolled 'r's'. From the burrows comes an undertone of purring and crooning.

    Ti-ti-ti or *kek-kek-kek* calls heard frequently on summer nights over Northland are believed to come from Cook's Petrels based on Little Barrier, as they fly to or from feeding grounds in the Tasman.

Habitat and range: The two known breeding areas, Little and Great Barrier in the north and Codfish Island, are 1,300 kilometres apart; and different average measurements seem to indicate two distinct populations. The range at sea outside the breeding season is extensive. They are known as migrants during the southern winter along the coast of South America, Mexico and California.

Breeding: On Little Barrier, the burrows are mostly on the high forested slopes above 300 metres. Burrow-cleaning in October; eggs from early November; young fly in March and April, sometimes crashing in the suburbs of Auckland, perhaps dazed by the city lights. At Codfish Island, where the colony is now very small, the breeding season seems to be some weeks later.

CHATHAM ISLAND PETREL   *Pterodroma axillaris*   *Pl. 9, p. 48*
Maori name: Ranguru.

Description: 30 cm (12″). Superficially, similar to Cook's Petrel, but differing in being rather darker and having feet of a different colour. Crown, hindneck, back and uppertail are medium grey and the wings blackish. Forehead and underparts pure white, but the *axillaries are black*, a distinctive mark when the bird is on the wing. Bill (24 x 11 mm) short, stout, black; feet fleshy colour with terminal dark patches on the webs and outer toe.

Habitat and range: Known to breed only at South-east Island, and not definitely recorded away from the Chathams, even as a straggler.

BLACK-WINGED PETREL *Pterodroma nigripennis*   *Pl. 9, p. 48*
Description: 30 cm (12"). Crown, hindneck, back and the uppertail, medium grey, wings blackish, forehead and underparts, including under wing-coverts, white. Bill (24 x 11 mm) short, stout, black; feet fleshy colour with terminal dark patches on the webs and outer toe. On the wing, can be distinguished from the Chatham Island Petrel by the white axillaries, the *underwing showing white with a firm black edging.* Both *axillaris* and *nigripennis* are sometimes treated as races of the North Pacific *hypoleuca.*

In the north Tasman in February pairs (? of young adults) have been noted indulging in spirited chases, perhaps courtship flights; often soaring considerably higher than 30 metres.
Voice: A shrill high-pitched *tee-tee-tee*, audible even by day both at sea and over its breeding grounds.
Habitat and range: Its main breeding stations are at the Kermadecs and Norfolk Island—where it flies about the cliffs in broad daylight—whence it ranges west to Lord Howe and eastwards into the Pacific across the Wellington-Panama shipping route. Discovered breeding at Three Kings Islands in 1945; now known to breed on all major islands in that group, and more recently has been found breeding at South-east Island in the Chathams. Reported as flying on board ships in mid-ocean probably more frequently than any other petrel of its size. Seldom found storm-wrecked in New Zealand proper; but the great gale of mid-April 1968 cast more than forty ashore in the region of Hawkes Bay and Cook Strait.
Breeding: Returning birds are first heard at Kermadecs in October; burrow-cleaning in November; eggs laid from mid-December to mid-January; young leave towards the end of April.

BLUE PETREL *Halobaena caerulea*   *Pl. 10, p. 49*
Description: 30 cm (12"). This petrel conforms closely in appearance with the prions described later. In flight the upper surface appears bluish-grey with a dark marking extending from the blackish primaries to the carpal flexure at an angle across the lower secondaries and connected by a dark patch on the rump to the similar pattern of the upperwing. This forms an inverted 'w'. Upper tail-coverts and tail are the same blue-grey as the back, but *the tip of the tail is pure white.* On the crown the feathers darken to a cap which is almost black. There is a mottled forehead, mainly white, underparts including under-wing, pure white; bill (26 x 10 mm) black; feet pale blue with pinkish webs.
Habitat and range: Blue Petrels are probably circumpolar in the southern hemisphere and the origin of the birds frequently found throughout winter on New Zealand coasts may be any of the breeding places known from the South Atlantic and South Indian Oceans. They are not known to breed for certain in the New Zealand area although nesting at Macquarie Island is strongly suspected as they are found there throughout the breeding season and remains are plentiful in older deposits on the shore. There is a normal summer breeding season with eggs in October and young flying late February—early March. Beachcombing has shown that Blue Petrels may be present in the Tasman Sea from May to October. In 1954 between these months, eighteen were picked up on the Auckland west coast.

PRIONS The group of petrels which make up this genus is peculiar to the southern hemisphere. It has given much trouble to systematists who are unable to agree on the best classification to express relationships. On superficial view, all prions, or whale-birds as they are sometimes known in sealers' usage, look very much alike, only the extremes of the large Broadbilled Prion and the smaller Fairy Prions being distinguishable on sight at sea. A study of birds from breeding places shows that there is an almost bewildering variety of distinguishable forms, if minute details of bill sizes and plumage characters are taken into account. It is considered that the subdivision given here will enable most observers to place a specimen in the right species.

BROAD-BILLED PRION *Pachyptila vittata* Pl. 10, p. 49
Other names: Parara, Blue Billy (Chathams).
Description: 28 cm (11″). Upperparts mainly grey-blue, slightly darker on the crown with blackish patches behind and below the eye, and dark areas of the wing forming the pattern already described for the Blue Petrel. The upper tail-coverts are the same shade as the back. Tail feathers likewise, but broadly tipped with black terminally. Bill (34 x 20 mm), which is unusually broad, is usually steel grey above and bluish along the side of the mandible. A few individuals have bluish bill plates above also as all the smaller prions have. The generally darker bill and large head, are features which permit the Broad-billed Prion to be identified sometimes at close quarters. Eyes brown, feet blue with pale webs.
Voice: A dove-like coo with some guttural undertones.
Habitat and range: Broad-billed Prions have a restricted breeding range along the convergence region of all the southern oceans. The New Zealand populations are found nesting from the mainland coasts of Foveaux Strait and the south-western fiords through the Stewart Island region, including the Snares, and at Chatham Islands. This species does not wander very far except for ranging in winter into northern New Zealand waters.
Breeding: Egg dates early September, hatching October-November, and young flying in December and January. Incubation period *c.* 56 days; fledging *c.* 7 weeks.

LESSER BROAD-BILLED PRION *Pachyptila salvini*
Description: 28 cm (11″). As for Broad-billed Prion but with narrower bill (30 x 15 mm), the upper plates of which in life are always bluish and not steel grey.
Habitat and range: Recorded in New Zealand only as a winter visitor, the Lesser Broad-billed Prion and several forms very similar to it may be found at sea or blown ashore in very large numbers along the west coasts of New Zealand. There is no evidence that any forms of this prion breed in the New Zealand area and their origin must be the South Indian Ocean. Most New Zealand specimens are immature, many in fresh first-year plumage.

ANTARCTIC PRION *Pachyptila desolata*
Description: 27 cm (10½″). In plumage as for Broad-billed Prion. The specific distinctions are in the form of the bill (28 x 13 mm) which is moderately wide,

that is, width about half the length; the sides of the bill seen from above are fairly straight without convexity; the *lamellae* or fringe of thin plates, well developed in Broad-billed and Lesser Broad-billed Prions, are *small* and *not usually visible* at the gape when the bill is closed.

Habitat and range: Although races of the Antarctic Prion are known to nest at Auckland Islands and Macquarie Island, the flocks found in New Zealand seas throughout the winter are composed for the most part of the distinguishable races breeding much farther west in the sub-antarctic zone.

NARROW-BILLED PRION *Pachyptila belcheri*

Description: 25 cm (10″). Plumage distinguishable from the prions already described mainly by more extensive white areas about the face. The *very narrow bill* (24 x 10 mm) with width less than half the length, is the significant character.

Habitat and range: The known breeding range is Kerguelen and Falkland Islands but Narrow-billed Prions are regular winter visitors to New Zealand seas. It has been ascertained that large mixed flocks of prions ranging as far north as the Kermadec Islands include many of this species.

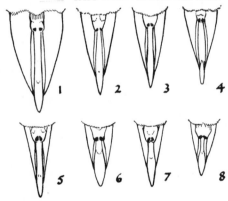

A Beachcomber's Guide to Prion Bills

1. Broad-billed Prion, *Pachyptila vittata;* 2. Lesser Broad-billed Prion, *P. salvini;* 3. Crozet Island Prion, *P. salvini crozeti;* 4. Auckland Island Prion, *P. desolata alter;* 5. Narrow-billed Prion, *P. belcheri;* 6. Fulmar Prion, *P. crassirostris;* 7. Fairy Prion, *P. turtur;* 8. Lesser (Southern) Fairy Prion, *P. turtur fallai.*

FAIRY PRION *Pachyptila turtur*   Pl. 10, p. 49

Maori name: Titiwainui (Stewart Is.).

Description: 23 cm (9″). In general, this species is like the others but is smaller, more stockily built, with a relatively smaller head and generally lacking in any darker tone on the crown. The most useful distinguishing mark, however, is the *greater extent of black at the end of the tail*. When the bird is on the wing this band appears to be fully half the exposed tail and, in fact, it may be ascertained from a specimen in the hand that the tips of the upper tail-coverts are also blackish in this species of prion only. Bill (22 x 10 mm) blue, feet bluish with pale webs.

Habitat and range: This is the common resident breeding prion of New Zealand and South Australian seas. Found on islands off the coast from Poor Knights to the Snares, and at the Chatham Islands. A small sub-antarctic race occurs at Antipodes Islands and probably elsewhere in the same water zone. Flocks are at sea throughout the year and there appears to be no extensive migratory movement either north or south of the main breeding range. A vagrant in the South Atlantic. One banded in Cook Strait was taken by a Peregrine Falcon off the Australian coast.

Breeding: Eggs are laid from late September through October; and young, hatching early in December, are fledged at the end of January when the main exodus flights occur. Incubation period *c.* 55 days; fledging *c.* 7 weeks.

FULMAR PRION *Pachyptila crassirostris*

Description: 24 cm (9½″). Very similar to Fairy Prion in plumage pattern, but more sturdily built, usually a shade paler overall and distinguished by a *robust swelling of the bill plates*. Actual measurements are not very helpful in distinguishing this form from the others, but the shape of the bill (23 x 11 mm) is diagnostic.

Habitat and range: Fulmar Prions range farther south than Fairy Prions. They nest at Chatham Islands on two steep rocky islets and at Auckland Islands in the New Zealand area. Another race occurs on Bounty Island where they nest in fairly exposed crevices, and at the Snares (Western Reef).

GREY PETREL *Procellaria cinerea*   Pl. 10, p. 49

Other name: Pediunker.

Description: 48 cm (19″). The general colour of the upper-surface is ashy grey, darker on the crown, wings and tail. Underparts are white merging into the darker upper-surface without any strongly defined line. Under wing-coverts are grey and this is a good field character when the bird is seen on the wing. The bill (47 x 17 mm) is parti-coloured having horn-coloured nail and tip, side plate and bottom of the lower mandible. The nostril, the ridge just in front of it and the dark sulcus on the lower mandible are blackish. Feet dull flesh colour, darker on the outer side, webs distinctly yellowish.

Habitat and range: This is a bird of the southern oceans and a circumpolar breeder. In the New Zealand area breeds plentifully at Antipodes Island and in smaller numbers at Campbell Island. They occur at Macquarie Island and probably breed there but have not yet been recorded at the Auckland Islands. At sea they keep to the regions of cooler water and so are found only occasion-

PLATE 9 PETRELS Pycroft's (p.43); Chatham Island (p.44); Cook's (p.44); Gould's (p.43); Black-winged (p.45); Soft-plumaged (p.42); Kerguelen (p.43); Mottled (p.42).

PLATE 9 PETRELS

CHATHAM ISLAND 30 cm

PYCROFT'S 28 cm

COOK'S 30 cm

GOULD'S 30 cm

BLACK-WINGED 30 cm

KERGUELEN 33 cm

SOFT-PLUMAGED 34 cm

MOTTLED 33 cm

PLATE 10
PRIONS AND PETRELS

BROAD-BILLED PRION
28 cm

FAIRY PRION
23 cm

BLUE
PETREL
30 cm

GREY PETREL
48 cm

BLACK PETREL 43 cm

WESTLAND BLACK
PETREL 51 cm

WHITE-CHINNED
PETREL 51 cm

ally off the main coastline, where they may be cast ashore as far north as Muriwai and the Bay of Plenty.

Breeding: A winter breeder. Eggs in May, the young leaving the nesting grounds early in November.

BLACK PETREL   *Procellaria parkinsoni*   *Pl. 10, p. 49*
   Description: 43 cm (17″). Entire plumage is dark blackish brown, feet black and the bill (41 x 15 mm) is parti-coloured. It is bluish horn on the nostril, side plates and mandible with a dark line along the ridge of the culmen and dark tip.
   Voice: Incoming birds around the summit of Little Barrier seemed to be silent; but a staccato rapidly-reiterated angry-sounding *clack-clack-clack-clack* was traced to birds sitting at burrows. A soft deep-toned hissing call has also been recorded.
   Habitat and range: Black Petrels are known to breed on the tops of Little Barrier and Great Barrier and on a few bush-clad mountain-tops some distance inland in Taranaki, Nelson, Westland, Fiordland and Stewart Island. Evidently migratory. Occurs as a non-breeder in the region of the Galapagos Islands.
   Breeding: A late breeder. Eggs laid in December and the young flying in May and June.

WESTLAND BLACK PETREL   *Procellaria westlandica*   *Pl. 10, p. 49*
   Description: 51 cm (20″). The entirely dark plumage is exactly similar to that of the Black Petrel, as are the bill (49 x 20 mm) and feet. There is, if anything, less tendency to bluish horn on the lighter parts of the bill and most specimens are yellowish horn.
   Voice: At dusk the birds fly into the colonies rather quietly. Then subterranean sounds increase and within an hour there is a crescendo of shrieking. This lasts less than half an hour. During the night there are intermittent calls. Towards daybreak a sustained chorus begins and lasts for about two hours, as the birds leave.
   Distribution and habitat: Known to breed on coastal ranges a few kilometres inland along a section of the west coast of the South Island between Barrytown and Punakaiki. At sea they have been observed off the west coast and in Cook Strait; and they range across the Tasman to eastern Australia. The most northerly records are of two found ashore in New South Wales and of two wrecked at Muriwai on the Auckland west coast.
   Breeding: A winter breeder. Eggs in May, the young flying in November.

WHITE-CHINNED PETREL   *Procellaria aequinoctialis*   *Pl. 10, p. 49*
   Other names: Cape Hen, Shoemaker.
   Description: 51 cm (20″). Entire plumage dark blackish brown, feet black, bill (52 x 21 mm) yellowish horn with black nostril, black along the ridge of the culmen and along the immediate sulcus of the lower mandible. A variable

---

PLATE 10 PRIONS AND PETRELS   Fairy Prion (p.47); Broad-billed Prion (p. 46); Blue Petrel (p.45); Grey Petrel (p.48); Black Petrel (p.49); White-chinned Petrel (p.49); Westland Black Petrel (p.49).

amount of white chin, sometimes reduced to one or two feathers between the mandibles at the base and sometimes more extensive on one side than the other, distinguishes the New Zealand race from those of the South Indian and South Atlantic Oceans, which usually have more white on the chin.

Voice: A clacking sound is made from within the burrow and is said to be uttered also by birds sitting at the mouth of the burrow. Hence the old sealers' name, 'Shoemaker'.

Habitat and range: A circumpolar, mainly sub-antarctic species, breeding in the New Zealand region at Macquarie, Campbell, Antipodes and Auckland Islands. Favours the cold water zone and not common off the coast of the main islands. Occasionally stranded as far north as Muriwai.

Breeding: Breeds in the southern summer. Burrows are conspicuously large. Many of them are in wet situations with water seeping out of the tunnels; but the nest is usually built up beyond the water-level. Eggs in December; the young leaving April-May.

NORTH ATLANTIC SHEARWATER *Calonectris borealis* *Pl. 11, p. 56*
Other Name; Cory's Shearwater.

Description: 46 cm (18″). This large shearwater, dull brown above, white below, has been recorded only once in New Zealand as a straggler, a dead bird being found on Foxton Beach in January 1934. It is described briefly here in case additional strays should turn up, as there is a general trend for Atlantic petrels to drift occasionally south of the Cape of Good Hope and reach Australia or New Zealand. It is somewhat similar to the Grey Petrel but could be distinguished at sea by the decidedly darker brown colour of the head and back, the mottled upper tail-coverts, black tail and pure white undersurface of the wings. The *bill* (55 x 21 mm) *is dull yellow*, darker at the tip and the feet flesh colour stained brown on the outer toe and outer surface of the tarsus.

FLESH-FOOTED SHEARWATER *Puffinus carneipes* *Pl. 11, p. 56*
Description: 46 cm (18″). An all brown shearwater distinguishable on sight by its *pale bill* (42 x 13 mm), darker only at the tip, and the pale *flesh-coloured feet*. In plumage, these birds are not noticeably different from any other dark shearwaters but they are more compactly built than any others in the New Zealand area and are likely to be confused only with the still blacker *Procellaria parkinsoni*.

Voice: As with most petrels, vocal activity is mainly on shore at the nesting place. A variety of calls includes a cat-like mew.

Habitat and range: This is a migrant shearwater breeding only in the southern hemisphere and normally visiting in the northern hemisphere during the non-breeding season. Breeding places in the New Zealand area range from the Hen and Chickens Islands to the region of Cook Strait. At sea the range is southward to the latitude of the Chatham Islands and off the New Zealand coast in the same belt.

Breeding: Laying dates are from late November to early December, hatching starting in mid-January and fledglings taking their departure in April. Nestling down is uniformly dark grey and the first plumage of young birds is similar to that of adults.

WEDGE-TAILED SHEARWATER *Puffinus pacificus* *Pl. 11, p. 56*
Other name: Black Burrower (Raoul).
Description: 46 cm (18″). An all brown shearwater with a long wedge-shaped tail, pale feet, and a dull compressed bill (38 x 13 mm) more slender in outline than that of the Flesh-footed Shearwater with which it might otherwise be confused. The breeding birds of the Kermadecs all seem to be of the dark phase.
Voice: Strange and weird, resembling the growls and snarls of fighting cats.
Habitat and range: Widely distributed over the tropical Pacific and Indian Oceans. Known to breed in the New Zealand region only at the Kermadecs; and rarely recorded farther south. A specimen of a white-breasted form, picked up at Makara on 26/1/61, is thought to be from a breeding area in the north Pacific.
Breeding: Adults return and start cleaning out burrows in October. Eggs mostly in early December; young hatched generally by the end of January; a few birds may linger at breeding grounds till early June.

BULLER'S SHEARWATER *Puffinus bulleri* *Pl. 11, p. 56*
Description: 46 cm (18″). A large wedge-tailed shearwater with distinctive plumage pattern. Crown, hindneck, and mantle are dark, shading to grey on the back and on the upper wing-coverts. The pattern of primaries and the outer part of secondaries forms an inverted 'w' pattern separated from the dark wedge-shaped tail by grey upper tail-coverts. Underparts, including underwing, pure white, bill (41 x 12 mm) bluish-grey dark on the ridge, feet flesh colour, dark on the outer sides.
Voice: Heard only at the nesting places, a mewing call is the main feature with some low cackling notes.
Habitat and range: From the only known breeding place at the Poor Knights Islands these shearwaters disperse widely throughout New Zealand seas from early September to mid-May as far south as Otago Peninsula and Westland. Migrates to the north Pacific in the off-season. In summer conspicuously abundant in the Hauraki Gulf and Bay of Plenty.
Breeding: Late November—early December is the laying period; hatching in January and fledglings ready to leave at the beginning of April.

SOOTY SHEARWATER *Puffinus griseus* *Pl. 12, p. 57*
Other names: Muttonbird, Titi.
Description: 43 cm (17″). Another shearwater all brown except for the greyish tinge of the underparts and the sprinkling of white and mottled feathers in the under wing-coverts. As the bill (42 x 13 mm) is dark grey and the feet dark lilac with brown markings on the outer side, the general impression is of a dark bird, except for the conspicuous *silvery flash of the under wing-coverts*.
Voice: The predominant sounds are 'oo' and 'ah' in various combinations in which the tempo increases and the series frequently ends with a yell.
Habitat and range: With a wide breeding range in the south temperate zones and extensive migrations to the northern hemisphere, this is one of the best known of shearwaters. Apart from the little known nesting regions of South America, the largest breeding concentration is in New Zealand seas mainly

south of 44°S. and extending to Macquarie Island, 55°S. Smaller breeding colonies are scattered as far north as the Three Kings Islands. In the Stewart Island area, there is extreme density of population and a restricted commercial industry known as mutton-birding.

Breeding: Adults come ashore in October and start cleaning out burrows. Eggs laid mid-November to early December, hatching mostly in late January; young leave late April or early May. Incubation period *c.* 8 weeks; fledging 86-106 days. Both parents incubate.

SHORT-TAILED SHEARWATER   *Puffinus tenuirostris*   Pl. 12, p. 57
Other name: Tasmanian Muttonbird.

Description: 38 cm (15"). Similar to the Sooty Shearwater in colour of plumage, but usually lacking the pale areas under the wings. Tail short and rounded. Bill and feet similar to *griseus* in colour, but the bill (32 x 11 mm) is proportionately shorter in this species, and the general smaller size is also a useful field character. **Habitat and range:** Cool temperate waters of the Australian coast with concentration of breeding at islands in Bass Strait where there is a regular industry similar to that conducted in New Zealand with other muttonbirds. Egg dates, general life history and departure dates are similar, and there is a mass migration to the northern hemisphere. This has been well documented by banding studies in Australia and significant recoveries. In some years many are 'wrecked' on the long west coast as they set out on their northward migration. Judged by the frequency of strandings, Tasmanian Muttonbirds regularly occur also in summer in the outer waters of the Hauraki Gulf and Bay of Plenty. Three were watched closely at the Poor Knights on 20/12/58 as they fed among Red-billed Gulls. The northward migration in some years takes thousands close past Cape Reinga in mid-April.

CHRISTMAS SHEARWATER   *Puffinus nativitatis*   Pl. 11, p. 56
Description: 35 cm (14"). Smaller than a Sooty Shearwater and about the same size as a Short-tailed Shearwater, but with a greyish chin and a *wedge-shaped tail*. Upperparts generally chocolate brown; underparts lighter. Bill (40 x 10 mm) and feet black.

Voice: Crooning at daylight and dusk, May-June, on Canton Island (Buddle). **Habitat and range.** Breeds widely in the tropical Pacific; but rarely reaches New Zealand. One found ashore near Dargaville (1976).

FLUTTERING SHEARWATER   *Puffinus gavia*   Pl. 12, p. 57
Maori name: Pakaha.

Description: 33 cm (13"). One of the smaller shearwaters, brown above and white below. The brown is seldom of dark tone except in fresh moulted birds and becomes somewhat faded and rusty for most of the year. In the region of the neck there is a faintly mottled darkish collar and breast patch; under wing-coverts are conspicuously white and the under tail-coverts likewise. Legs and feet dark on the outer side and pale fleshy in the inner surfaces; bill (33 x 9 mm) darkish olive appearing blackish at a distance. Fluttering Shearwaters spend much time resting on the surface of the sea and in flight they skim the water with a rapid wing-action. In high winds or a rough sea, they assume the rising and falling gliding flight characteristic of most shearwaters. When feeding they also dive frequently and can swim well under water.

Voice: Exceptionally strong for a bird of such small size. A cackling call is sometimes heard even when the birds are feeding or resting at sea. On their approach to nesting grounds after dark, they are very noisy with a rapid staccato repetition of a call which can roughly be rendered by one of the Maori names for the bird, 'Pakaha' with the emphasis on the last syllable. 'The normal full call sounded like *kahów kahów kahów kahów, kehék kehék kehék kehék— errr*; the *Kehek* is sharper, faster and slightly higher pitched than the *kahow*; and the final *errr* tails off as a rather drawn-out note at a lower pitch. There are many variants.' (Edgar).

Habitat and range: Cool temperate waters of the New Zealand coast. Known to breed at many islands from Three Kings to Cook Strait. Their normal feeding range is not far off shore and they regularly penetrate the deeper inlets and harbours. Also recorded from the eastern seaboard of Australia, but not as a breeder.

Breeding: The first adults return to the breeding islands in August. Eggs, September-October. Young birds leave December-January.

HUTTON'S SHEARWATER *Puffinus huttoni* Pl. 12, p. 57

Description: 36 cm (14″). Very similar to the Fluttering Shearwater in appearance and habits. Its area of distribution is rather more southerly, although formerly it was not distinguished from it. The plumage pattern is the same except for a few scattered dusky under wing-coverts and these, together with the fact that the plumage is of a uniformly darker brown, give Hutton's Shearwater the general appearance of a darker bird altogether. *Brown flecks on lateral under tail-coverts.* The bill (37 x 9 mm) is slightly longer and appears more slender than in the average Fluttering Shearwater, but in other respects *huttoni* is almost indistinguishable.

Voice: Apparently similar to that of the Fluttering Shearwater but has only been recorded from stray birds held in the hand. From these it appears to have a slightly harsher and deeper tone, although the sequence of notes is the same.

Habitat and range: Abundant in Cook Strait and ranges down the east coast of the South Island. There are unconfirmed records from Snares Island but these are based on a series of commercially collected skins, of which the origin seems to be doubtful. The only known breeding place, discovered by G. Harrow in 1965, is at more than 1000 m in the Seaward Kaikouras. The breeding season is fully two months later than that of the Fluttering Shearwater. Young birds fresh from the nests on their first flight are regularly taken on board ships in Cook Strait or found along the adjacent shoreline in the latter half of March each year. Only rarely wrecked as far north as the Auckland west coast. Outside New Zealand occurs regularly on the coast of South Australia, with casual records as far as Western Australia.

LITTLE SHEARWATER *Puffinus assimilis* Pl. 12, p. 57

Other name: Allied Shearwater.

There are several well-marked subspecies from different breeding localities from the sub-antarctic to the sub-tropics. Three actually breed in the New Zealand region.

The following description relates to the North Island race *haurakiensis*.

Description: 30 cm (12″). The smallest of the New Zealand shearwaters; dark bluish-black above and pure white below. The pattern is well defined except for a slight mottling about the cheek and ear patch. Feet pale bluish with fleshy webs; bill (25 x 8 mm) dull lead blue and black along the ridge and tip.

Voice: The normal call is a rapid *kakakakakakak-urrr* repeated; the *urrr* sounding as if uttered while drawing breath. (Edgar)

Habitat and range: *Haurakiensis* is the breeding bird on islands off the north-east coast of the Auckland Province and in the Bay of Plenty. This subspecies does not seem to range much beyond its breeding area and is replaced both north and south by birds of lighter build and smaller size in the sub-tropics and by a heavier and more stoutly built race in the sub-antarctic (*elegans*). There are small differences of measurement and plumage characters by which they can be distinguished in the hand or as museum specimens; but for field identification, it is not possible to define subspecies.

Breeding: Colonies consist of rather scattered groupings of burrows in terrain that is often fairly heavily wooded. The season extends through the winter, the birds occupying the nesting burrows from about April, with eggs in May and June and most of the young on the wing by the end of October. On Meyer I. young of *kermadecensis* with little down remaining may still be in the burrows in mid-November.

STORM PETRELS: Hydrobatidae

LEACH'S FORK-TAILED STORM PETREL   *Oceanodroma leucorhoa*
Pl. 13, p. 64

Description: 19 cm (7½″). Plumage blackish brown, the secondaries paler at the tips and forming a dull rusty band on the upper wing. Upper tail-coverts white, forming a band on the rump. Bill, legs and feet black; iris brown. The feature that distinguishes Leach's Petrel on the wing is that a V-shaped wedge of dark plumage invades the white tail band in front. This is variable in extent, sometimes almost dividing the white patch into two, but the irregularity of marking is always clearly visible.

Habitat and range: Leach's Petrel has a wide breeding range in the northern hemisphere in both Atlantic and Pacific Oceans. The one New Zealand specimen, washed ashore at Muriwai in winter 1922, is not distinguishable from typical specimens of the Atlantic form.

WILSON'S STORM PETREL *Oceanites oceanicus*   *Pl. 13, p. 64*
Description: 19 cm (7½″). Plumage black except for the pale brownish patch on the greater wing-coverts and secondaries and a *white rump patch* formed by the upper tail-coverts extending to the lower flanks on either side. Iris brown; bill black; feet black, *with middle portion of the webs yellow*. Tail square; legs very long.

Habitat and range: The circumpolar race of Wilson's Petrel which breeds in Antarctica seems to be the largest of several. In the southern winter it migrates through Atlantic, Pacific and Indian Ocean tropics to the northern hemisphere. Birds taken in New Zealand, where the species is known only as a straggler, have invariably been of the large Antarctic form (*exasperatus*) and not of the smaller races that are known to breed in Chile, Patagonia and Kerguelen.

GREY-BACKED STORM PETREL *Garrodia nereis* Pl. 13, p. 64

Description: 18 cm (7″). A diminutive species without white on the rump. Head, neck, throat and upper breast dark greyish black. The back is ashy grey with pale white edges, giving a scalloped appearance, and this colour continues to include the upper tail-coverts and the upper part of the tail which is also grey. The tail terminates in a dark band and the wings, with the exception of the secondary coverts which are pale grey, are dark brownish black. Breast and underparts, including under tail-coverts and the central wing-coverts, white.
Voice: A high-pitched twittering is made by birds on the wing over the nesting-grounds.
Habitat and range: A circumpolar species breeding at many sub-antarctic islands, including Chathams, Antipodes, Auckland Islands and probably Campbell. Ranging north in winter to about Lat. 36°S.; but rarely reported.
Breeding: The season extends from October to February or March. Burrows, like 'rat-holes', have been found in a belt of *Anisotome* among sitting molly-mawks on Disappointment Island, and succulent vegetation of *Cotula* on Pyramid Rock. Elsewhere, the burrow may be in the heart of clumps of tussock.

BLACK-BELLIED STORM PETREL *Fregetta tropica* Pl. 13, p. 64

Description: 20 cm (8″). General colour sooty black, brownish grey on the secondary wing-coverts. There is a slight contrast between the ashy tone of the head and the browner tone of the mantle. The upper tail-coverts are white and some of the feathers of the rump are white based and white tipped. *Flanks on both sides are also white*, as are most of the axillaries and a mottled area of the central wing-coverts. There are white bases to the feathers of the throat and in worn plumage this results in a whitish throat patch. Bill black; iris brown; legs and feet black. At sea, this petrel has an erratic flight and tends to zigzag, more so than Wilson's Petrel which it much resembles. In swinging from side to side, it exposes the under-surface of the body so that *the extensive white flank patches* are clearly seen, giving the appearance of a white bellied pattern, unless the thin, dark central line of the belly feathers can be detected.
Voice: A piercingly shrill piping note repeated singly at intervals of four or six seconds. 'This call might be imitated on a piccolo fife in the key of G or F.' (Eaton on this species at Kerguelen Island.)
Habitat and range: A circumpolar species breeding at many sub-antarctic islands, including Auckland, Bounty and Antipodes Islands, off which it is commonly seen at sea. Stragglers reach Lat. 36°S.; but are seldom reported.
Breeding: Seems to be a late nester at the Auckland Islands where Stead found eggs only slightly incubated on 1st February. At Kerguelen Island, the season seems to be some weeks earlier.

WHITE-BELLIED STORM PETREL *Fregetta grallaria* *Pl. 13, p. 64*
Description: 19 cm (7½"). Head, neck and throat sooty black, underparts white, the contrast together with the shape of the head being reminiscent of a Pied Tit; back and mantle greyer; rump white; tail black and virtually square cut; wing black above, but undersides white except for dark edges. Bill and feet black.

This robust storm petrel should perhaps be regarded as the sub-tropical counterpart of the sub-antarctic Black-bellied species, which has been named so misleadingly, *tropica*.

Habitat and range: A circum-subtropical species known to breed in the New Zealand region only on the vermin-free outliers of the Kermadecs. Seldom sighted in coastal waters. Two west of Farewell Spit in November 1969 may have originated from Lord Howe Island.

WHITE-FACED STORM PETREL *Pelagodroma marina* *Pl. 13, p. 64*
Other names: Takahikare-moana, Skipjack, Jesus Christ Bird (shortened to 'J. C. Bird'), Dancing Dolly.
Description: 20 cm (8"). Crown, nape and patch below the eye smoky greyish-brown, mantle and back and upper wing-coverts brownish. Rump and upper tail-coverts grey; tail and wings blackish brown. The lores and a line above the eye, chin, throat and underparts including under wing-coverts, and the inner webs of primaries, white. Iris brown; bill black; feet black; webs yellowish or dull ochre with pink veins. The only storm petrel commonly seen in coastal waters; easily distinguished by its wholly white underparts. Occasionally during a flat calm may be seen sitting on the sea, riding high, with wings and tail held at quite a sharp angle. Rump and upper tail-coverts in the well-marked Kermadec race (*albiclunis*) are white.
Voice: At a nesting colony after dark an animated twittering.
Habitat and range: The common subspecies (*maoriana*) of the New Zealand region breeds on many islands and islets from the Three Kings to the Chatham and Auckland Islands. Apparently absent from late-April to early August; destination unknown, but has occurred near Galapagos Is.
Breeding: On some islands the colonies are dense; and after dark the returning birds drop in like a snowstorm, bouncing daintily on a mat of ice-plant or low-growing taupata as if they were at sea. The egg is white with faint pinkish-brown specks at the larger end. Eggs, in the north mostly in second half of October; young leave mostly in February; but some may still be in the burrow in March. On Whero, the peak of egg-laying was about 6 November (Richdale). Incubation period 55-56 days; fledging 52-67 days. Near nesting colonies Harriers, Black-backed Gulls and Southern Skuas take their toll.

PLATE 11 SHEARWATERS Christmas (p.52); Buller's (p.51); Flesh-footed (p.50); Wedge-tailed (p.51); North Atlantic (p.50).

PLATE 11 SHEARWATERS

CHRISTMAS 35 cm

BULLER'S 46 cm

FLESH-FOOTED 46 cm

WEDGE-TAILED 46 cm

NORTH ATLANTIC 46 cm

WEDGE-TAILED (light phase)

PLATE 12   SHEARWATERS

SOOTY
43 cm

SHORT-TAILED 38 cm

HUTTON'S 36 cm

HUTTON'S

FLUTTERING
34 cm

LITTLE
30 cm

DIVING PETRELS 20 cm

DIVING PETRELS: Pelecanoididae

This specialised group of the petrels, or tube-nosed swimmers, is confined to the southern hemisphere. They are small stocky birds, all much alike, with short powerful wings which they use under water for swimming and in the air for rapid whirring flight near the surface of the sea, into which they frequently dive. They are apparently flightless during a short period of moult. Dark above and white below, they resemble superficially the Little Auks of the northern hemisphere, but are true petrels both in structure and habits.

DIVING PETREL *Pelecanoides urinatrix*   *Pls. 12, 13, pp. 57, 64*
Local names: Dipchick, Kuaka (Stewart Island only).
Description: 20 cm (8″). Crown, neck, back, tail and upper surface of wings black, except for white edges on new secondaries. Cheeks grey. Underparts pure white, smoky under the wings. Bill black; legs blue.

The northern subspecies *urinatrix* is slightly larger than the southern *chathamensis*. In the sub-antarctic subspecies, *exsul*, the bill is proportionately wider at the base so that the sides looked at from above are less parallel. Usually, but not always, the grey speckling on the breast and foreneck is more pronounced.
Voice: Silent at sea; but wailing, chattering, cooing and mewing in the air over nesting places at night, with a considerable range of powerful calls.
Habitat and range: Typical *urinatrix* is found in coastal waters from Three Kings to Cook Strait, breeding in burrows on many offshore islets; *chathamensis* ranges from Cook Strait to about Lat. 47°S., breeding on offshore islets at Chatham, Stewart, Solander and Snares Islands; *exsul* occurs in sub-antarctic seas south of Lat. 48°S., breeding at Antipodes and Auckland Islands, probably at Campbell Island and straggling to Macquarie Island.
Breeding: In the north the season is from August to December. Incubation period, five weeks. The first down of the chicks is pale; the second darker grey. In full first plumage, the young resemble the adults. With *chathamensis* the season comes about a month later; and in the sub-antarctic islands it lasts from October to February.

SOUTH GEORGIAN DIVING PETREL *Pelecanoides georgicus*
Description: 17 cm (7″). Crown, neck, back, tail and upper surface of wings black, except for patches of white scapulars, white edges to secondaries and white inner webs to the outer wing feathers seen when the wings are spread. Bill black above, bluish along the edges of the mandibles; feet pale blue.
Voice: Not recorded for the New Zealand race.
Habitat and range: This is an antarctic diving petrel of circumpolar range, occurring in New Zealand seas, as far as is known, only at the Auckland Islands, where it is now exceedingly rare. Nothing is known of its distribution

---

PLATE 12 SHEARWATERS Sooty (p.51); Short-tailed (p.52); Hutton's (p.53); Fluttering (p.52); Little (p.53); Diving Petrels (p.57).

at sea nor the extent of its feeding range, except that it has not been detected amongst large flocks of diving petrels in coastal waters and possibly is more pelagic.

Breeding: The season is from October to February and the sequence appears to be similar to that of other diving petrels, except that at the Auckland Islands burrows have been found to be shallower and in more sandy soil than those of *exsul*. They were first collected in 1840 on Enderby Island, where the sandy coastal areas have since been much consolidated by trampling of cattle and reburrowed by rabbits. The only colony known was on a small islet, and the burrows were round a fringe of consolidated sand. It was occupied when discovered in 1943 but could not be found in 1972.

TROPIC BIRDS: Phaethontidae

A small family (3 species) of beautiful white seabirds, superficially pigeon-like, well-named because they are confined almost exclusively to the tropics. In adult birds the two central tail feathers are very much elongated. Hence they are also known as Bo'sun Birds after the 'marlinspike' in the tail. Tropic Birds range far from their nesting grounds and may appear suddenly, approaching with a steady flapping flight, and briefly escorting a ship when it is far from land.

Of the two species which occur in the south-west Pacific, one, the Red-tailed, breeds at the Kermadecs and Norfolk Island and may range to S. Lat. 38°; the White-tailed is widespread in Polynesia, but seldom reaches New Zealand.

RED-TAILED TROPIC BIRD   *Phaethon rubricauda*   *Pl. 14, p. 65*
    Other names: Amokura, Strawtail.

    Description: 46 cm (18″) plus up to 41 cm (16″) for the *two scarlet central tail-feathers*. Plumage mainly white with a pinkish hue; but there is a conspicuous black crescent before and over eye; the tail-feathers and longer wing-feathers have black shafts; and some feathers on flanks and undertail have black centres. Bill yellow or coral red with black streak through nostrils; feet black. Young have upperparts broadly barred with black; bill black; legs yellowish or bluish-white; central tail-feathers undeveloped.

    Voice: A harsh grating sound, repeated two or three times, is frequently heard in fine weather at the breeding grounds. A shrill, rasping call has been heard from birds circling a ship.

    Habitat and range: The breeding range of the sub-species of the western Pacific (*roseotincta*) extends from northern Queensland to Lord Howe, Norfolk and the Kermadec Islands. Recent sightings suggest that in summer some regularly reach the outer waters of the Hauraki Gulf and Bay of Plenty and may penetrate the Tasman as far as Lat. 38°S.

    Breeding: At the Kermadecs most eggs are laid between mid-December and mid-January. Clutch one; egg commonly pinkish, closely blotched reddish-brown; nest a mere hollow on a ledge of a cliff. Incubation period *c.* 35 days. Most birds leave the breeding grounds in April and May; a few linger over the winter months; most return in October.

WHITE-TAILED TROPIC BIRD *Phaethon lepturus*   *Pl. 14, p. 65*
  Description: 38 cm (15″) plus up to 40 cm (16″) for the four white central tail-feathers. Plumage mainly white, sometimes with a flush of pink. Black line before and over eye. *A broad black bar across the base of the wing* shows conspicuously. There is also a black line along the fore-edge of the wing. Bill yellowish with grey base; legs yellowish; feet black. Young have shorter tail and crescentic black bars on upperparts and flanks.
  Habitat and range: This is the species which not infrequently crashes on board ships in tropical waters. In the Fiji-Samoa-Tonga triangle of ocean it greatly outnumbers *rubricauda*. A very rare straggler to New Zealand waters, presumably swept south by tropical cyclones.
  One beached specimen, Whakatane (January 1973).

GANNETS AND BOOBIES: Sulidae

The members of this family are large strong-flying seabirds (wing-span nearly 2 metres) related to the shags and pelicans; but somewhat gooselike when resting on the sea or standing near their nests. Physically they are especially characterised by their stout, pointed conical bills, an area of bare skin on face and throat and their wedge-shaped tails. The family is mainly tropical and its tropical species are commonly known as Boobies, while those which frequent cooler waters are the true Gannets.

They nest in colonies, most of which are on small islands. Their food, mainly fish, is obtained by diving and their almost vertical plunges from a considerable height can be truly spectacular.

The Australian Gannet is the commonest of the really big seabirds around the coast of the North Island, but south of Cook Strait it becomes rather scarce. Two tropical boobies at the southern limit of their range reach the northern waters of New Zealand.

Included in the same order (*Pelecaniformes*) are the true pelicans.

AUSTRALIAN GANNET *Sula serrator*   *Pl. 14, p. 65*
  Local name: Takapu.
  Description: 91 cm (36″). 'The finest and most majestic of the birds of coastal waters.' (Buddle.) Mainly white; crown and nape pastel yellow; primaries, secondaries and at least four, occasionally as many as ten, central tail-feathers black. Bill and bare skin of face, bluish grey; feet dark brown, with vivid light green lines running down to the toes.
  The nestling at first black and naked becomes fluffy white in just over a month. By three months it is mainly brown on the upper surface of neck, body, wings and tail, but a white dot at the end of each feather gives a generally speckled appearance. Under surfaces are mainly white.
  Flight strong and direct; also glides, soars and planes. Catches its prey both by steep plunges from up to 30 m and also by shallow low-angled torpedo-like dives.
  Voice: Even in the hatching egg the chick yaps like a small puppy. Later the

voice deepens but it is still like a short, sharp bark and is used mainly to greet a parent returning with food. Adults at sea are generally silent, but a gruff *aak-aak* and a softer throaty *kook-kook-kook* have been heard. On nearing their nesting sites adults may utter a pleasantly rhythmic throaty call, produced by a very rapid movement back and forward of the tongue as in *ooh-lah-ooh-lah-ooh-lah*. A not unmusical quavering *kee-er-up*, *kee-eree* or *skee-ree* is also described.

Habitat and range: According to a census taken in 1946-7, *c.* 21,000 pairs were then breeding in New Zealand, but in ten of the colonies which have since been checked the count is now higher, so that the estimated breeding population in 1961 was 27,000 pairs which together with roosting non-breeders would make the total number of adults about 60,000. A reassessment in 1973 gave 32,000 pairs.

The colonies, with one notable exception at Cape Kidnappers, are on small islands, mostly north of Lat. 38°S.; but two very small colonies, Nuggets and Little Solander, are in much colder water at Lat. 46½°S. Strays reach Campbell Island.

Adults are common in coastal waters, sometimes penetrating muddy creeks, around the North Island throughout the year. In the vicinity of the colonies Gannets may often be seen flying in lines, especially when returning to roost at night. The formations, which are often roughly V-shaped, with one arm longer than the other, vary in size from a few birds to over eighty.

Few mottled immatures are seen after May; for on leaving the nest most of them set off across the Tasman to spend two or three years around the Australian coast south from Queensland and west to the Indian Ocean, before returning to New Zealand to breed.

The Australian breeding colonies are confined to the region of Bass Strait and Tasmania. Closely allied forms are found in the North Atlantic (*S. bassana*) and around South Africa (*S. capensis*).

Breeding: Banding has shown that a few Gannets return to their home colony at the end of their third year, and some have been found breeding at the end of their fourth. Most breed in their fifth year or later; a few are eight years old when found breeding for the first time. The nest is a mound of seaweed, soft plants, earth and guano. In the north eggs are laid from late August to early December; in the south over a month later. Only one egg is laid, but if it is lost in the early stages of incubation, a second may be laid about five weeks later. Parents take turns in incubating for 43 days. Fledging, 15½ weeks. Within six months of departing the young lose some of their mottled plumage, and within a year they resemble adults but are not as white on the body or as yellow on the head, and the dark feathers of the wings and tail do not present the same contrast as in the adults.

BROWN BOOBY *Sula leucogaster* Pl. 14, p. 65

Description: 74 cm (29″). Adults with dark chocolate brown plumage and white belly are unmistakable, *the sharp line of demarcation being on the lower breast.* In flight the white axillaries and median under wing-coverts become visible. Naked face of skin and throat greenish yellow or bluish; bill yellowish or bluish; feet pale yellow. In immatures the bill can be shining bluish horn-colour and the feet bright orange-yellow; the underparts are smudged brown, but a sharp line usually separates the darker breast from the lighter belly and the contrasting pattern of the underwing is helpful in distinguishing them from the mottled immatures of *S. serrator*.

Habitat and range: Though the subspecies *plotus* is the commonest of the tropical boobies in the south-west Pacific, it has seldom been recorded from New Zealand; but increased sightings since the 1950s may indicate that Brown Boobies, probably immature non-breeders, visit our northern waters every summer. One is known to have frequented the Hauraki Gulf for three consecutive seasons and to have roosted with the Gannets on Horuhoru. Brown Boobies occasionally reach Cook Strait, and one visited Wellington Harbour, typically resting on buoys, in late summer 1975. The most southerly record is of one just south of Timaru in March 1969.

BLUE-FACED BOOBY *Sula dactylatra*   *Pl. 14, p. 65*
Other name: Masked Gannet.
Description: 86 cm (34″). Largely white and at first glance rather like *S. serrator*; but the tail and flight feathers are dark brown, appearing in flight as a *broad black band on the rear edge of the wing*. Head white; beak stout and yellow; naked skin on face and throat blue-black; feet greenish blue. Immatures are mainly white, but head, throat, mantle, upperwing surface and tail are brown.
Habitat and range: The subspecies *personata* is widespread in the western and central Pacific, the nearest colonies being at Norfolk Is. and the Kermadecs. Seldom sighted much further south; but one west of North Cape, February 1964 and one (?2) Firth of Thames October 1977.
Breeding: Nest a slight hollow in the ground. Eggs August-November. Clutch commonly two, but only one young is reared.

AUSTRALIAN PELICAN *Pelecanus conspicillatus*
Description: 170 cm (66″). Wing-span up to 2.4 m. Mainly white. 'Mane' greyish; rump, tail and sides of back black, also flight feathers so that *a large black V appears in the flying bird on the upper surface*: huge bill (45 cm) with pinkish pouch; bare skin round eyes yellow; legs dark blue-grey.

After laboured take-off, pelicans fly strongly, gliding and soaring majestically. Flocks in the air tend to fly in formation and on the water to 'hunt in packs'.
Voice: A grunt.
Habitat and range: Widely distributed in Australia, ranging to New Guinea but rarely straying to New Zealand. Three records: one on the Wanganui River 1890; one on the Northern

Wairoa August 1976; one died of starvation (?) in Southland November 1977. Sub-fossil remains prove that formerly New Zealand had its own large distinctive pelican.

SHAGS OR CORMORANTS: Phalacrocoracidae

Birds of this group are well represented in New Zealand. The number of species recognised depends on the form of classification adopted, and on an extreme view, sixteen forms can be recognised. A useful sub-division can be made by the colour of the feet. The four black-footed species are all associated, to some extent with freshwater habitat, although they also occur coastally. On the other hand there are six or seven races of sub-antarctic shags with pink feet and one with yellow feet which are exclusively marine, some of them inhabiting outlying oceanic islands. In the latter group, a field identification key must concern itself mainly with the facial markings and colours. Like the Penguins, the pink-footed shags seem to have their main recognition characters in the head, the body plumage otherwise being remarkably uniform and similar throughout. The eggs of all shags are whitish or very pale bluish or greenish with a chalky encrustation.

Closely related to the Shags are the Darters (*Anhingidae*), distinguished by their sharp-pointed bills and long snaky necks. In 1874 the skin of a freshly dead Australian Darter (*Anhinga novaehollandiae*) (Pl. 17, p. 80) was found nailed up inside an old shed at Hokitika. This waterbird, which is common in Queensland, is rare in New South Wales and unrecorded in Tasmania.

BLACK SHAG   *Phalacrocorax carbo*   *Pl. 15, p. 72*
Other names: Kawau, Common Cormorant.
Description: 88 cm (35″). The adult in breeding plumage has generally black plumage glossed with green. There is a well-developed crest of black feathers extending on to the nape. The upper back plumage is dull bronze brown, each feather widely bordered with dark green. The naked gular pouch is narrowly bordered with white feathers and there are narrow white filo-plumes on the head and neck in breeding plumage, also a large patch of white feathers on each flank. The skin about the eye and the gular sac yellowish. Bill greyish brown. Iris green. Legs and feet blackish. The white filo-plumes on the neck and the thigh patches are transitory and seasonal, being found usually in May and October.

The plumage of the female, which is smaller, is similar. In immature birds in their first year, the underparts are dirty white and the facial colours not strongly developed. The young, hatched naked, are later covered with a blackish down.

Voice: A hoarse croak and a wheezy whistling note.
Habitat and range: The Australian race (*novaehollandiae*) of this cosmopolitan cormorant ranges throughout the main islands, inland to mountain lakes and streams, and eastwards to the Chathams; stragglers penetrating south to Campbell and Macquarie Islands. Most feeding appears to be inland; but in autumn and early winter flocks, numbering hundreds of birds, may fish

sheltered tidal waters such as the Firth of Thames.

Breeding: Nesting colonies are commonly in clumps of tall trees or on the ledges of inland cliffs and river-gorges; some colonies are on coastal cliffs or off-shore rockstacks. Nests with eggs or young may be found at almost any season. Clutch 3–4. Precise information on incubation and fledging periods is lacking. The young, hatched naked, are later covered with a blackish down. A high proportion of the fish brought to the young consists of freshwater eels.

PIED SHAG *Phalacrocorax varius* *Pl. 15, p. 72*
Maori name: Karuhiruhi.

Description: 81 cm (32″). Upperparts, including top of the head and hindneck are black glossed with dark green. Dorsal wing feathers are bronze grey with a greenish gloss, each feather bordered with black. Sides of the head, chin, throat and underparts pure white. Iris sea-green, a bright yellow spot of bare skin in front of the eye, naked blue skin around the eye, and gular sac yellow. Bill, dark horn colour, with some variable marking. Legs and feet black.

In the first year, immature plumage upperparts are somewhat browner and the pale underparts are mottled with occasional brown feathers.

Voice: Varies from a deep croak to a light and monotonous wheezy call.

Habitat and range: Restricted to the warmer parts of New Zealand, being most plentiful in the north; but the range is discontinuous, viz: Northland, Hauraki Gulf and Bay of Plenty where many off-shore islands possess breeding colonies; virtually absent from Hawkes Bay and the Wellington coast; occurring again in the Marlborough Sounds and around Nelson with a small group nesting on the coast of North Canterbury; not found again until Stewart Island. In New Zealand Pied Shags rarely venture far inland and their food consists mostly of estuarine fishes, but in eastern Australia it is often an inland species.

Breeding: The typical colony is in trees, especially pohutukawas in the north, on an exposed sea-cliff; but a few colonies are in trees beside freshwater lakes which are near the coast, e.g. Pupuke, Takapuna; Lake Paritu, one of the crater lakes on Mayor Island, and Lake Rotorua, about 3 km inland from the Kaikoura coast. Around Auckland, nesting goes on throughout the year, with two peak seasons of egg laying. August-September and March-April; and apparently as many pairs breed in autumn as in spring. Clutch 2–4. After the naked stage, chicks have white down on the underparts.

LITTLE BLACK SHAG *Phalacrocorax sulcirostris* *Pl. 15, p. 72*
Description: 61 cm (24″). Generally smaller but otherwise similar to the big Black Shag. The entire plumage is black with a dull green gloss and the usual dark bordered ashy feathers on the 'shoulders' and wing-coverts. There are seasonal white plumules on the side of the head and about the eye in the breeding season, but they are not clearly visible at a distance, and no white thigh patches are developed. The rather long bill (4.5 cm) is dull lead colour, appearing black at a distance. The iris is deep emerald green. Occasionally, there is a bluish-purple tinge about the skin of the face; otherwise this is the most sombrely plumaged of all the New Zealand shags. Females are similar to males, and immature birds differ only in being slightly duller.

Habitat and range: An Australian species, which has tended to escape notice in New Zealand; but actually not uncommon and probably increasing in the northern part of the North Island; regularly reported from Wellington and Hawkes Bay and more rarely from the South Island. In early winter, there appears to be a northward movement into coastal waters of the Bay of Plenty, Hauraki Gulf, Manukau and Northland. One characteristic of this species is to hunt in packs, presumably rounding up fish. A flock, containing anything from a dozen to 150 birds, will swim round a lake or about an estuary diving. As birds surface and find that they are at the rear of the flock they fly over the main body and dive again to be in the forefront of the chase.

Breeding: So far has been found breeding in few localities, e.g. lakes of lower Waikato, and Pupuke, a few pairs, the nests being in trees; but almost certainly breeds regularly in the Bay of Plenty and Rangaunu Bay and probably elsewhere, even on rocky islets offshore. Competition with other shags may force it to breed rather late, i.e. about midsummer or in early autumn. Clutch 2–5, commonly 3. Chicks clothed in a dark blackish-brown down are not easily distinguished from the young of Black and Little Shags. At Lake Waikare, they were fed largely on carp and eels.

LITTLE SHAG   *Phalacrocorax melanoleucos*   *Pl. 15, p. 72*

Other names: Kawaupaka. The name White-throated Shag is also in general use for the most abundant phase of a rather variable species which, at its other extreme, is identical with the Little Pied Shag of Australia. However, as intermediates occur, and the Little Pied form is relatively uncommon, it seems more convenient to treat the New Zealand population as a variable one under a distinctive name.

Description: 56 cm (22″). In the dark phase the entire plumage is glossy black with the face, cheeks and chin white, a patch which commonly extends to the throat and foreneck. The feathers of the crown are elongated and form a ruff-like crest. The naked skin of the face and the gular pouch are yellow. Bill (3 cm) black above yellowish below. Feet black. In the other extreme of plumage the entire underparts are pure white.

Most immature birds are dull brownish black over the entire plumage, including the throat, with conspicuously yellow bill and face, although it should be noted that immature birds of the extreme pied phase are often dull smoky white below. Chicks are covered with blackish-brown down dotted with tufts of white in birds that are ultimately of the pied phase. As a field character, all these Little Shags can be readily distinguished from the Little Black Shag by the fact that the *bill is short and stout and the tail relatively long*.

Voice: Wheezy and guttural. During courtship, low urgent cooings; a muffled sound something between a low bark and a coo.

Habitat and range: The most widespread of the freshwater shags, being found far inland up into the mountains and along the whole coastline south to Stewart

PLATE 13 STORM PETRELS

WHITE-FACED
0 cm

LEACH'S
FORK-TAILED
19 cm

WILSON'S
19 cm

GREY-BACKED
18 cm

BLACK-BELLIED
20 cm

DIVING PETRELS 20 cm

WHITE-BELLIED
19 cm

PLATE 14

RED-TAILED
TROPIC BIRD
46 + 41 cm

WHITE-TAILED
TROPIC BIRD
38 + 40 cm

GREATER FRIGATE BIRD
102 cm

LESSER FRIGATE BIRD
78 cm

BROWN
BOOBIES
74 cm

imm.

BLUE-FACED
BOOBY 86 cm

AUSTRALIAN GANNETS

imm

Island; recorded as a visitor to most northern off-shore islands but only rarely straggling to sub-antarctic islands. The Little Pied form is most plentiful in Northland where the proportion of Little Pied to White-throated is about 1 to 3 or 4, but, rather anomalously, Little Pied Shags started to breed at Campbell Island *c*. 1967. The food in inland waters includes eels, koura, native freshwater fish, and an assortment of larvae of aquatic insects.

Breeding: Nests are in trees or shrubs commonly with other species of black-footed shags in swamps, on lakes, in river gorges or on sea-cliffs. These shags have an extended breeding season; but near Auckland, they appear to have a fairly rigid annual breeding cycle with egg laying at a peak in September or early October. Clutch 3 or 4.

NEW ZEALAND KING SHAG *Phalacrocorax carunculatus* *Pl. 16, p. 73*

Description: 76 cm (30″). Head, cheeks, neck, sides, back and outer thigh feathers dull metallic bluish green. Inner scapular regions, scapulars, and wing-coverts glossed with green. Quills and tail blackish brown. A wide white alar bar is formed by the inner median wing-coverts. Another white patch appears among the outer scapulars in most specimens, and there is usually a central dorsal patch of white variable in size. No crest. The bill is horny brown. Facial skin and gular pouch, dark reddish brown. Ring round the eye bright blue. Patches of chrome yellow caruncles above the bill at the base. Iris dark hazel. Feet pink. The caruncles are generally larger in males than females. Immature birds in their first plumage have the upperparts mainly dull brown with very little of the greenish gloss in the first plumage. The alar bar and scapular patch, when present, are indicated by paler buffy feathers but the dorsal patch is rarely indicated except by a slight weakness of pigmentation in the middle of the back. Facial colours about the bill have not developed and they remain purplish brown. Nestlings after hatching naked are clothed in dark smoky down.

Voice: The usual croak of which the pitch and tone has not been precisely distinguished from that of other cormorants.

Habitat and range: The habitat is entirely oceanic. The only known nesting places are on rocky islets adjacent to oceanic water which in Cook Strait contains many elements of the Sub-Tropical Convergence. The food consists of bottom-haunting and weed-inhabiting fishes or seasonal crustacean supplies. A radius of about 50 km encompasses all the known breeding stations from the White Rocks in the east to Trios in the west.

Breeding: Large built-up nests of marine growth and coastal plants are placed on rock platforms and ledges in close proximity. The full clutch of eggs is three and the laying season appears to vary. In a normal year most of the colonies are winter breeders having eggs in June and a considerable batch of fledglings in late August. In some seasons the various separate colonies are out of step by several months and the situation suggests breeding by some groups of birds all the year round although this has not been precisely demonstrated.

PLATE 14 Red-tailed Tropic Bird (p.58); White-tailed Tropic Bird (p.59); Greater Frigate Bird (p.70); Lesser Frigate Bird (p.70); Brown Booby (p.60); Blue-faced Booby (p.61); Australian Gannet (p.59).

The numerical strength of the King Shag is only a few hundred birds but its present status is quite healthy and protection is more effective than in the past.

STEWART ISLAND SHAG   *Phalacrocorax chalconotus*   Pl. 16, p. 73
  Description: 68 cm (27″). The description given above for the King Shag applies in most details to this species, at least in its pied phase. The southern bird is, however, *dimorphic* and approximately half the populations are entirely and uniformly bronze green with the colours of soft parts the same in both phases. The soft part colours are also similar to those of *carunculatus* except that a few yellow to orange papillae take the place of the robust caruncles of the northern bird. Also the white scapular patch found in the latter, is lacking in *chalconotus*.
  Habitat and range: The birds are restricted to coastal waters from Otago Peninsula to Foveaux Strait and Stewart Island. There is a marked cline in the size of birds in this range, those of Otago Peninsula being much larger and heavier and having more pronounced development of papillae above the beak.
  Breeding: Rock-stacks and flat-topped rocks are favoured for the close grouping of nests which are built up into raised cups on a fairly solid base of organic debris and guano. Mated pairs may be of either phase or mixed and although this appears to be indiscriminate, the young develop into the two distinct phases without many intermediate plumages being produced. The only variant that has been noted in a small percentage of examples is an occasional 'bronze' bird with irregular scatterings of white feathers, usually on the belly.

CHATHAM ISLAND SHAG   *Phalacrocorax onslowi*   Pl. 16, p. 73
  Description: 63 cm (25″). The description given for the King Shag applies also to this species except that the plumage is in all respects more sleek and glossy, with heightened colour and strong metallic reflections. It has well developed orange caruncles and an alar bar of white as well as some white in the scapulars and the dorsal patch. Facial colours are much brighter than *carunculatus*, being reddish on the cheeks and gular pouch; bright blue ring round the eye; iris brown. The same brown stages of immaturity and nestling down apply equally to this form.
  Habitat and range: Found only at the Chatham Islands, this shag has not been known to occur elsewhere and has probably a restricted home range. Nesting sites chosen are similar in all respects to the larger colonies of the other races already described and are to be found around the coasts of the main Chatham Islands and their outliers. They have not been recorded as nesting on the more exposed outlying stacks.

BOUNTY ISLAND SHAG   *Phalacrocorax ranfurlyi*   Pl. 16, p. 73
  Description: 71 cm (28″). In general plumage and in size similar to the largest examples of the Stewart Island Shag, the bird exclusively inhabiting Bounty Islands differs mainly in having almost entirely bright red facial skin although lacking either caruncles or papillae. It has both alar bar and dorsal patch although the latter is poorly developed and often broken in the specimens available for study. Its general group relationship, however, seems to be clearly with the *carunculatus*, *onslowi*, *chalconotus* group.
  Habitat and range: Restricted to the rocky Bounty Islands and appears to be

restricted there to roosting and nesting on a few narrow ledges not already occupied by penguins and mollymawks, or on small islets not used by them. As there must be abundant feed in the area, the controlling factor responsible for the comparatively small numbers must be lack of nesting space.

Breeding: Nests are similar to those of the other forms and the full clutch of eggs appears to be three.

Immature plumages are probably indistinguishable from those of the other forms, and nestlings have not been described.

AUCKLAND ISLAND SHAG *Phalacrocorax colensoi* *Pl. 16, p. 73*

Description: 63 cm (25″). This bird and the Campbell Island Shag form a group separable from the other Blue-eyed Shags. In the main, they are smaller and more delicately built. There is no trace of papillae or carunculation. The general plumage pattern and colour is hardly distinguishable from that of *carunculatus* group. However, the dark feathering on the back and sides of the neck almost meets on the foreneck and in a few examples is joined by a complete dark band. This is variable in the Auckland Island Shag but fixed and regular in the Campbell Island Shag. The gular pouch is red. Facial skin reddish-brown. Ring round the eye mauve or pinkish-violet. The feet are pink as in all the other sub-antarctic cormorants. Iris brown.

Immature birds have the plumage pattern much the same, but instead of the metallic colours have dull lustreless brown and the foreneck is almost always mottled or brown plumaged in immature birds.

In comparison with *carunculatus* the alar bar is much reduced and the white dorsal patch normally missing, although it does occur in a few examples.

Habitat and range: Around the many harbours and inlets of the Auckland Islands and along their eastern coastlines, this shag is plentiful, and occupies a large number of nesting sites which may be changed from year to year. Either coastal rock terraces or a series of narrow ledges may be occupied and the nests are the usual built-up piles of debris and guano. Clutch 3.

There is an abundant food supply of post-larval fishes and kelp-haunting fish as well as a considerable range of surface crustaceans.

CAMPBELL ISLAND SHAG *Phalacrocorax campbelli* *Pl. 16, p. 73*

Description: 63 cm (25″). Just separable from the Auckland Island Shag, being of exactly the same size but having less variable plumage pattern and generally darker pigmentation, especially in the colours of soft parts. The remarkable uniformity of plumage is indeed in contrast to the variability of the Auckland Island Shag: although chin and throat are white, there is a black throat band about 8 cm in depth. The white alar bar is not present nor has the white dorsal patch been recorded. Facial skin and gular pouch are deep red and the eye is dark purple mauve, as distinct from the more pinkish tinge of the Auckland Island Shag.

Habitat and range: Restricted to Campbell Island and its outliers and much less abundant than the Auckland Island form. After the breeding season 'rafts' gather in sheltered inlets such as Perseverance Harbour. On 11/8/60 it was estimated that more than 2000 were fishing Tucker Cove.

Breeding: The nesting season for both Auckland and Campbell Island Shags is the same, the earliest eggs appearing in November.

MACQUARIE ISLAND SHAG   *Phalacrocorax purpurascens*   *Pl. 16, p. 73*
Description: 71 cm (28″). This sub-antarctic cormorant resembles the others in having pink feet; but it clearly belongs to a circumpolar chain of races grouped about *P. albiventer* of the Falkland Islands. The metallic colours are much closer to royal blue than to bluish green. The abundant caruncles are yellow and the ring about the eye bright electric blue set in an area of facial skin and gular pouch of dark brown. There is an alar bar but no record of dorsal white or white scapulars in this form. It differs also from the others in having the dark feathers of the cheek commencing about the gape and not at the base of the lower mandible. This means that the facial pattern is much whiter and the ear opening is to be found along the line of demarcation of the dark and white feathers and not in the dark area as in all the others. Immature birds are brown above and white below, with dull facial colours; nestlings in down are smoky: irises at all ages, brown.
Habitat and range: In the New Zealand region found at Macquarie Island only and does not wander.
Breeding: Forms fairly compact nesting colonies, sometimes on low-lying rocks and occasionally on coastal ledges. There are numerous colonies scattered along the shores of Macquarie Island and other birds are breeding on the more distant outliers north and south. There appears to be a stable population of Macquarie Island Shags and the limiting factor on increase of numbers is probably food supply. None of the sub-antarctic cormorants is migratory and their sedentary range is quite small.

SPOTTED SHAG   *Stictocarbo punctatus*   *Pl. 15, p. 72*
Local name: Flip-flap (Canterbury).
Description: 73 cm (29″). A very handsome bird in full plumage, but for the greater part of the year it appears in non-breeding dress and there are several stages of plumage in the progress to maturity. In a fully adult bird at the beginning of the breeding season the crown of the head and the longish double crest rising at the forehead and again at the nape are greyish black with a faint metallic gloss. The back of the neck is glossy greenish blue and this dark metallic colour occurs again on the lower back and rump. The scapulars and wing-coverts are pale grey, each feather with a round black spot at the extremity. The underparts are silvery grey from the chin to the under tail-coverts which like the thighs are glossy greenish-black. Two white lateral strips of plumage start at the base of the bill, pass above the eye and are continued down the sides of the neck to the shoulder. There may also be scattered white feathers sprouting from the darker portions of the plumage. Bill long and slender (70 mm), light horn colour. Iris hazel. Naked skin around the eye opalescent blue and green. The gular pouch bright blue and the feet bright orange-yellow. In non-breeding plumage, the clear white areas are invaded by mottled feathers and the conspicuous pattern is effectively broken down.

Immature birds which are dark grey above and very pale grey almost white below, have no conspicuous pattern until they begin to assume the first adult plumage. Their feet also are seldom bright yellow and may be dull brownish-pink.

Voice: Adults croak; nestlings make a thin, reedy whistle and almost musical warble.

Habitat and range: Entirely marine and rather sedentary, occupying throughout the year cliff stations adjacent to fairly deep water from which large quantities of post-larval and small fish may be obtained. Locally common in the North Island, where there are three groups of breeding colonies (*a*) in Hauraki Gulf, Noises to Waiheke, Tarakihi and Ponui Islands, and east to the islets off Coromandel Peninsula; (*b*) on the Auckland west coast, Oaia, Ihumoana and Girdwood Point; (*c*) Somes and Ward Islands in Wellington Harbour, where formerly it was a winter visitor, as it still is to Waikanae and Palliser Bay.

Abundant in the South Island from Marlborough Sounds down the east coast, especially Goose Bay, Banks Peninsula and Otago Peninsula, where long lines of these shags flying between cliffs and feeding grounds make an impressive sight.

Breeding: Nests in colonies on ledges, in fissures on steep cliffs or in sea-caves. A fairly substantial nest is made of old sticks, cliff-plants and seaweed. Clutch commonly 3, rarely 4. Incubation period *c.* 4½ weeks. An extended breeding season seems to vary according to locality. The elegant nuptial plumes and colours are lost during incubation.

BLUE SHAG   *Stictocarbo steadi*

Local name: Bravo Duck (Stewart Is.).

Description: Probably best treated as a subspecies of the Spotted Shag, the Blue Shag is nevertheless distinguishable by being slightly darker in tone of plumage, having a narrower white line on the sides of the neck in breeding dress and occupying a restricted zone of coastline around Stewart Island, at some islands in Foveaux Strait, at Open Bay Islands and on the coast of Westland north to Perpendicular Point. Some of the plumage characters are clearly trends in the direction of the pattern found in the more distinct Pitt Island Shag of the Chatham group. Little has been recorded about the breeding behaviour, which appears to be erratic and similar to that of the Spotted Shag.

PITT ISLAND SHAG   *Stictocarbo featherstoni*   *Pl. 16, p. 73*

Local name: Double-crested Shag.

Description: 63 cm (25"). This is clearly the Chatham Island representative of the Spotted Shag/Blue Shag group. Very similar to the two already described, but entirely lacking the white neck stripes and much darker altogether. Head, both crests, chin, throat, foreneck and the entire back rump and upper tail-coverts as well as the under tail-coverts and thighs, black glossed with dark greenish-blue. The grey plumage of the wing-coverts and scapulars is of a deep tone with a green gloss, each feather having the triangular black spot on the extremity. The rest of the underparts is dark silvery grey and the only white plumes are the scattered filo-plumes on head and neck in breeding condition. The naked skin about the eye is purple. Iris dark hazel. Legs and feet orange.

In the immature plumage there is a strong suffusion of brown tone and no clearly marked pattern except on the scapulars and wing-coverts, which resemble the adult condition.

Habitat and range: Restricted to the Chatham Islands, with its greatest numbers south of Pitt Strait.

Breeding: Favourite nesting sites are in eroded pockets or ledges in vertical cliff faces. Eggs are said to be laid in August. Most nests are deserted by the end of December.

FRIGATE BIRDS: Fregatidae

With their long forked tails and narrow angular wings Frigate Birds are very easily recognised. They are the most aerial of oceanic birds and they are said never to settle on the water. In the tropics they hang poised in the sky, dark sinister shapes, ready to swoop upon other seabirds and to harry them till they force them to disgorge whatever they have caught. Because of their marauding habits they are also called Man-o'-War Birds. Their long slender bills are sharply hooked at the tip.

Five species are recognised, all breeding in colonies on tropical islands. Two species, rather different in size, occur in the south-west Pacific; but as they seldom travel far from land, it is not surprising that they reach New Zealand waters only when driven south by tropical cyclones.

In identifying the two species which may occur in New Zealand it is important to note carefully the position and extent of the whitish areas of the underparts.

GREATER FRIGATE BIRD   *Fregata minor*[1]   Pl. 14, p. 65
Description: 102 cm (40″) wing-span *c.* 2 m. Adult male entirely dark, with no white, and with a red distensible gular pouch; female has a greyish-white throat and foreneck and the lower neck, breast and sides of the body are white. Both sexes have a brownish bar across the upper side of wing. In immature birds the head and neck are white and the underparts tinged reddish.

Habitat and range: A very rare straggler from distant tropical breeding grounds south to Cook Strait; *c.* 12 records.

LESSER FRIGATE BIRD   *Fregata ariel*   Pl. 14, p. 65
Other name: Least Man-o'-War.
Description: 78 cm (31″); wing-span nearly 2 m. Plumage generally black with a metallic sheen. *Male has a white patch on either flank under the wing* and a bright red distensible gular pouch; female has throat black, breast buffy white and a grey-brown patch on the upper side of the wing. Immature birds have head, neck and breast white mottled with rusty brown.

Habitat and range: Commoner in the south-west Pacific than *F. minor*;

[1]The curious may wonder why somewhat anomalously the specific name of the Greater Frigate-bird is *minor*. The adjective survives from the eighteenth century when this bird was called the Lesser Pelican (*Pelecanus minor*).

breeding from Queensland to Fiji, but rarely wandering to New Zealand; c. 10 records up to 1964 mostly from the north during or after tropical blows, but has reached Cook Strait and the Chatham Islands. One in Kaipara Harbour was seen to harry gannets, gulls and terns. In January 1971 hurricane Rosie swept several towards the coast of Northland and the number of sightings was doubled.

HERONS, EGRETS AND BITTERNS: Ardeidae

As a general rule herons and egrets are birds of the open; bitterns and night-herons are shy skulkers in reed-beds or thick cover. Nine of the ten species which occur in New Zealand are widely distributed in Australia and/or south-east Asia. In New Zealand they reach the south-east limit of their range.

Three species, Reef Heron, White-faced Heron and Bittern, breed widely in the main islands, the most numerous now being the White-faced Heron, a highly successful recent immigrant. There is a single small breeding colony of White Herons. Since 1950 there have been so many records of Little Egrets that it is not implausible to suggest that a small breeding colony may by now be established. The status of the Little Bittern is quite unknown. Although the Nankeen Night-heron is very rare, there is reason to believe that breeding occurs occasionally. Cattle Egrets are now being found frequently and sometimes in substantial flocks. This species has spread so fast in Australia that its arrival here was not altogether surprising. The colours of bill, facial skin and legs may become brighter or change considerably as adult birds come into breeding condition.

With their broad wings and slow, heavy flight, herons are especially susceptible to wind drift. A remarkable example, if the record is true, of drifting by an over-carried migrant is that of the Grey Heron (*Ardea cinerea*) of Eastern Asia, said to have come aboard a schooner off the east coast about 1898.

WHITE-FACED HERON   *Ardea novaehollandiae*   Pl. 17, p. 80
  Other name: Blue Crane.
  Description: 66 cm (26"). Bluish grey with *white on forehead, chin and around eye*; long pale grey plumes on back; undersurface light grey with chestnut or bronze feathers on breast; wing quills blackish, *the contrasting tones in the wing showing clearly in flight*. Bill black; legs greenish yellow, *sometimes reddish*.

  Flight leisurely and strong. Can gain height quickly. When not foraging often to be seen perched on a post in a vulturine attitude with neck tucked in between hunched shoulders.
  Voice: Flight call a guttural *graaw*; 'a similar call is used when alighting at the nest but on these occasions it ends with a repeated *gow-gow-gow* which becomes quieter as each syllable is repeated.' (Moon.) A higher pitched *wrank* used near the nest seems to be an alarm call.
  Habitat and range: This common Australian species, only rarely reported in New Zealand before 1940 when breeding was suspected at Okarito and con-firmed in Otago, has become in quarter of a century, the most plentiful heron

in the country. Widespread in coastal districts of North and South Islands, but scarce inland above 500 m. Its rapid spread has been aided by the construction of farm-dams which are quickly colonised by the introduced Australian Green Frog (*Litoria aurea*). When nesting is over, flocks of 20 or more are now quite usual at roosts or in sodden paddocks; and as numbers increase, even larger gatherings are being reported in areas where the incoming tide drives them off their feeding grounds. There may be some northward movement in autumn, viz. in May 1962 more than 400 were counted on Farewell Spit, where few breed.

Now established on some off-shore islands, e.g. Waiheke, Kawau, Ponui, Great Mercury. Southwards, has straggled to Campbell Island. The northward thrust has taken this species to Mokohinau, Kermadecs and Fiji, and it is breeding freely on Norfolk Island.

Breeding: First proved in the South Island at Shag River, 1941 and in the North Island at Porirua, 1951. In Northland some pairs are nesting by midwinter. Pairs commonly nest singly; but with increasing numbers a few pairs may form a loose colony. The untidy nest frequently flimsy and surprisingly small, is usually high up in a tree. Exotic pines, especially *Pinus radiata*, are preferred; but gums, cypress (*macrocarpa*), kahikatea, tanekaha, totara, kauri and the tall crowns of manuka are used. In 1962 a pair nested successfully in an old passenger ferry beached on Ponui Island. Eggs, June to December, 3–5, pale blue-green, unglossed. Incubation 25 days; fledging *c.* 6 weeks. Both sexes incubate.

WHITE-NECKED (PACIFIC) HERON   *Ardea pacifica*

Description: 76 cm (30″). Larger and more conspicuous than the White-faced Heron with which it is likely to associate. *Head, neck and breast white*, lightly shaded with grey; body mainly dark blue-grey with some reddish feathers on back and upper breast; *a white patch on the leading edge of the wing at the bend*, conspicuous in flight. Bill and legs black or dark grey-green.

Wing beat slow and strong.

Habitat and range: A typical heron of inland swamps and waters in Australia; but of irregular occurrence in the south-east coastal region and Tasmania, where periodical irruptions may occur. So far only once recorded in New Zealand, autumn and winter 1952, at Methven.

WHITE HERON   *Egretta alba*   *Pl. 17, p. 80*

Maori name: Kotuku.

Description: 91 cm (36″). Uniformly white, with elegant dorsal plumes (ospreys or aigrettes) in nuptial dress. Bill yellow, except for a brief period during the nesting season when it is purple-black; skin between eye and bill yellowish green; upper leg (tibia) yellowish; tarsus black, with yellow tinge on the inner side; and with a distinct purplish bloom in nesting season. The double kink in

PLATE 15 SHAGS

SPOTTED 73 cm

imm.

Spotted imm.

PIED 81 cm

BLACK 88 cm
breeding plumage

BLACK 88 cm

LITTLE (White-throated form)

LITTLE BLACK 61 cm

LITTLE imm.

LITTLE (White-throated form) 56 cm

LITTLE (Pied form) 56 cm

PLATE 16 SHAGS

PITT ISLAND 63 cm

AUCKLAND ISLAND 63 cm

MACQUAR ISLAND 71 cm

CHATHAM ISLAND 63 cm

STEWART ISLAND (Bronze) 68 cm

STEW ISLAN 68 c

CAMPBELL ISLAND 63 cm

NEW ZEALAND K 76 cm

BOUNTY ISLAND 71 cm

the long thin neck is characteristic.

Voice: In flight a frog-like croak is sometimes uttered.

Habitat and range: An almost cosmopolitan species, common in Australia (subspecies *modesta*) the outlying breeding colony of 12–20 pairs in South Westland being of this race. After the nesting season, these herons disperse all over the country, especially northwards so that there are few lowland lakes, estuaries, coastal lagoons or mangrove creeks which they do not visit at one time or another. Numbers in New Zealand seem to vary between *c.* 50 and *c.* 200. Strong winds at the time of dispersal may reduce the population. Stragglers which reach the sub-antarctic islands may be considered lost beyond reprieve. Local numbers may be substantially augmented by wind-drifted strays from Australia. Thus during and after the winter of 1957 numbers were exceptional. Immature non-breeders commonly summer away from Okarito. In the far north they are particularly partial to Rangaunu Bay, where more than forty have been reported in winter; and 15 have been present even in January (R. B. S.).

Breeding: New Zealand-bred White Herons are evidently strongly conservative. The one known breeding place is near Okarito in a kahikatea swamp through which the sluggish Waitangiroto crawls. Some of the herons' nests are in the crowns of tree-ferns; others in kowhai or kamahi which they share with Little Shags, while Royal Spoonbills prefer the taller kahikateas. It is curious that no colony has been established in any of the big northern harbours, where many White Herons pass the winter and there are areas of swamp-bush which appear quite suitable for nesting.

Eggs, September-October, 3–5, pale bluish-green. Incubation *c.* 25 days; fledging *c.* 6 weeks.

PLUMED EGRET *Egretta intermedia*

Description: 62 cm (24″). White; rather larger than *garzetta* but distinctly smaller than *alba*; bill robuster but hardly longer than that of *garzetta*. Stragglers to New Zealand are likely to be young birds with yellow bill and blackish legs.

Breeding adults have filamentous plumes *only on back and breast* and at full length the dorsal plumes extend well beyond the tail; facial skin bright blue-green; bill orange; upper legs reddish contrasting with black of lower legs and feet.

Habitat and range: The subspecies *plumifera* of this primarily tropical egret is common in northern Australia, but uncommon in the south-east. Not known from Tasmania and a very rare vagrant to New Zealand. This species seems to prefer swampy grasslands and the margins of freshwater lakes to tidal areas and brackish lagoons.

LITTLE EGRET *Egretta garzetta*   *Pl. 17, p. 80*

Description: 56 cm (22″). Pure white. In nuptial plumage two long narrow-

---

pointed plumes fall from the nape and there are ornamental filamentous plumes on back and breast. Bill, black with base of lower mandible yellow; bare skin of face yellow; legs black; soles of feet greenish yellow.

In flight gains height quickly with comparatively fast wing-beats; and in the distance, flying away looks not unlike a very white Caspian Tern.

Voice: Nothing recorded in New Zealand.

Habitat and range: A cosmopolitan species with a number of weakly defined subspecies, of which *nigripes* extends into our region. First recorded in New Zealand in 1951; since when, reported from many coastal lagoons and estuaries between Parengarenga and Bluff; rarely inland. Often solitary; greatest number seen together in New Zealand five. Associates freely along the shore with other herons and the larger waders; but likely to be harassed by gulls.

The reappearance of Little Egrets, winter after winter in certain localities, favoured also by Great White Heron, almost suggests a regular dispersal or migration from a breeding place within New Zealand. But banding of nestlings in Australia has proved that some cross the Tasman to spend at least their first winter in this country.

BLUE REEF HERON   *Egretta sacra*   *Pl. 17, p. 80*

Other names: Blue Crane, Matuku moana.

Description: 66 cm (26″). Generally slaty grey, darker above, paler below with a tinge of brown on the abdomen; a narrow streak of white on chin and throat. During courtship and nesting long plumes are visible on back and lower neck. Bill brown or yellowish; skin between bill and eye greenish-yellow or grey, depending on age and season; legs yellowish-green.

A bird of coastal rocks and the tideline. Its crouching gait, rather heavy bill and shorter legs give it quite a different silhouette from that of the more graceful White-faced Heron, which is now invading its habitat. In flight which is nearly always low over the water, the uniformity of its colouring is plain to see.

Usually solitary or in pairs; but in northern harbours flocks of about a dozen may gather at high-tide or night-roosts.

Voice: During the breeding season a guttural croaking is made, often accompanied by bill snapping. Alarm note a guttural *crraw* (Moon).

Habitat and range: Sparingly distributed around the rocky coasts of the main islands, but absent from long sandy stretches; commonest north of the Bay of Plenty and Raglan and present on many coastal islands. Very seldom inland, two at L. Taupo in 1961 being quite exceptional. A rare straggler to some sub-antarctic islands, e.g. Chatham.

The wide range of this species includes the coasts of south-east Asia, Australia and Polynesia. The Reef Heron is dimorphic but New Zealand is outside the range of the white phase.

Breeding: Preferably the nest is in a cave on a rocky islet—sometimes several pairs together; it may also be in a crevice or among vegetation on a cliff, on a rotting hulk or a tumbledown jetty.

Eggs, September-February, 2–3, typically 3; pale greenish-blue. Incubation period 25–28 days; fledging *c.* 5½ weeks. Both sexes incubate.

CATTLE EGRET   *Bubulcus ibis*   *Pl. 17, p. 80*
Other names: Buff-backed Heron, Tickbird.
Description: 51 cm (20″). A small stocky heron with a rather short bill (6 cm) and neck. At first glance appears wholly white; especially in flight, when easily confused with Little Egret (q.v.). Unmistakable in breeding dress when plumes on crown, nape, back and breast become orange-buff; and legs and bill redden. Juveniles and adults in eclipse are mainly white with *yellow bill* and yellowish or grey-green legs.

Habitually consorts with grazing animals, eating the insects which they disturb and often perching on their backs.
Habitat and range: A vigorous coloniser now widespread in warmer regions of both Old and New Worlds; and still extending its range. The eastern race (*coromanda*) appears to be spreading fast in Australia.

First recorded in New Zealand in 1963, when a single bird spent the cold winter, May-September, near Christchurch, alternating between two herds of Friesian-Holsteins 'on town supply'. It may have left the Australian coast in company with Little Egrets. In the spring it developed nuptial plumes. At the same time a second example was discovered at Lake Ellesmere. A vagrant reached Stewart Island in 1967. Now reported widely, especially in winter when flocks containing 20–40 birds may settle into a district for some months, only to disappear in the spring, by which time many may be showing nuptial plumes.

Evidently at present a rather secretive breeder.

AUSTRALIAN BROWN BITTERN   *Botaurus poiciloptilus*   *Pl. 18, p. 81*
Other names: Brown Bittern, Black-backed Bittern, Matuku, Matuku-hurepo.
Description: 71 cm (28″). A large brown heron-like bird, normally not easily seen because of its skulking habits; but one surprised in the open may 'freeze' in surroundings where it is absurdly obvious. Upperparts dark-brown mottled with golden buff; underparts light buff with dark brown streaks and flecks. Superciliary stripe and throat pale cream. The neck is thickly feathered with a smoky brown expandable ruff. Bill, dark brown above, lighter beneath; skin between eye and bill pale green; legs and feet pale green.

Wings broad and rounded. Rises with long dangling legs. Flies with neck tucked in. Sometimes climbs reeds to survey surroundings. Several bitterns may soar and spiral over their nesting swamp. One has been seen to assume a loon-like attitude and to swim across a deep channel.
Voice: Flight call a hoarse *cr-a-ak*. The resonant boom of the male *woomph* following an audible intake of breath, may be heard especially in the evening from July to February. A bubbling call, accompanied by a distinct soft flutelike note, is sometimes made by the female as she approaches the nest (Moon).
Habitat and range: Less plentiful than formerly, but still widely distributed in the main islands in marshy places and reed beds up to more than 300 m a.s.l. at e.g. Taupo and Wakatipu. Young wander in autumn and are quite often flushed on salt-marshes. An occasional visitor to off-shore islands, e.g. Kapiti, Great Mercury. Believed to breed at crater-lake on Mayor Island.

B. poiciloptilus, whose range includes Australia and New Caledonia, is closely related to *B. stellaris* of the Old World.
Breeding: The female builds the nest which is a firm platform of sedge or rush,

usually surrounded by water, in a thick reed bed, preferably raupo. Eggs, September to January, 3–5 (typically five in the north) smooth, greenish cream. Incubation period *c*. 25 days. Only the female incubates. Chicks are thinly clad in a long greyish down with silky tips.

NANKEEN (RUFOUS) NIGHT HERON *Nycticorax caledonicus*

Pl. 18, p. 81

Description: 56 cm (22″). A short-necked heron with beautiful rich chestnut plumage; unmistakable if well seen, but not easily located. Crown and nape, blue-black; back and wings chestnut red; underparts whitish; superciliary streak white; throat and neck rich buff. Bill sharp, stout, black; skin between eyes and bill greenish yellow; legs yellowish to reddish orange. In breeding plumage one, two or three white plumes with brown shafts drop over the nape. Young are dark brown, heavily spotted and streaked with buffy white.

Voice: Said to call harshly at night.

Habitat and range: Widely distributed in Australia and the south-west Pacific; straggling to New Zealand. Some were liberated unsuccessfully near Wellington in 1852. There are very few records for the present century. Young may have been reared near Blenheim, 1957-9. One was present near Kaitaia in 1961, regularly roosting in a pine.

Mainly nocturnal. Spends the day in leafy cover, emerging to feed towards dusk. Night Herons watched at Blenheim were perching well up in the leafy canopy of elm and walnut.

LITTLE BITTERN *Ixobrychus novaezelandiae* *Pl. 18, p. 81*

Maori name: Kaoriki.

Description: 30 cm (12″). Small, secretive and hard to flush. Crown and nape greenish black; hind neck deep chestnut red; back and mantle dark brown; tail black above, slaty below; neck and chest buff with an irregular streak of reddish brown running from the chin and down the foreneck; underparts buff with darker streaks; wings chestnut buff and dark brown, the contrasting pattern very evident in flight. Bill yellowish green with black tip; legs long, green.

Voice: Alarm notes 'a peculiar snapping cry' and also 'a cry not unlike that of the Kingfisher, though not so loud' (Buller).

Habitat and range: Has commonly been treated as a subspecies of *minutus*, which is widespread in the Old World and Australia; but the few skins in museums are so markedly distinct that it is not easy to dismiss New Zealand Little Bitterns simply as wind-blown strays of *minutus* from Australia. However recent finds in Australia of birds very like the New Zealand Little Bittern, and unlike *minutus* leave the question open.

Twenty recorded in the South Island mostly from Westland, where it probably bred in the extensive swamps and may do so still, though none has been recorded there in the twentieth century. Neither of the two North Island records, Tauranga 1836 and Meremere 1963 is wholly satisfactory.

IBISES AND SPOONBILLS: Threskiornithidae

The members of this cosmopolitan family of large water-birds bear a superficial resemblance to herons, but are readily distinguishable by the shape of their bills and their manner of flight. The family is strongly represented in Australia whence vagrant Royal Spoonbills have recently established a small breeding colony in South Westland. Two species of ibis occur as irregular stragglers, most often, so it would seem, during periods of prolonged drought in inland Australia, where some mixed breeding colonies contain many thousands of pairs. It is curious that the commonest of the three Australian ibises, the Straw-necked (*Threskiornis spinicollis*) has not yet been reported from New Zealand, though one was seen on Norfolk Island in 1962.

GLOSSY IBIS   *Plegadis falcinellus*   *Pl. 18, p. 81*
   Description: 56 cm (22″). At a distance appears black; actually deep purplish-bronze, darker on wings and tail, with greenish gloss. Bill (13 cm) strong and arched. In winter head and neck show whitish streaking. Not to be confused with Far Eastern Curlew which is about same size but is mottled brown and has a markedly longer bill. Flies with neck and legs extended and with faster wing-beat than herons and egrets. Can gain height quickly. A flock when descending swiftly makes a noise like Shoveler Ducks. Often glides. Seen in a flock, these ibises may show considerable variation in size.
   Voice: A harsh grating *gra-a-k* described as a 'decidedly corvine prolonged guttural croak'. Flocks make subdued grunting sounds.
   Habitat and range: The Glossy Ibis is a notorious wanderer, especially when the colonies disperse after the breeding season. To New Zealand, it is a casual visitor widely reported, sometimes appearing in flocks, from the big river swamps of Australia where the race *peregrinus* breeds. They are most likely to visit New Zealand when forced by prolonged drought to seek new feeding grounds. There was a notable irruption in 1953-54, when the biggest flock seen contained 24 birds; and another in the summer of 1968-69, when up to 10 visited Stewart Island, Southland lagoons and Taieri Lake. In the autumn of 1975, 16 descended upon open spaces in the Hutt Valley, but soon dispersed.
      Not primarily a bird of the coast but of freshwater swamps and lakesides, likely to remain for some weeks where food is plentiful, e.g. tadpoles. Described as feeding busily like Starlings on marshy ground.

AUSTRALIAN WHITE IBIS   *Threskiornis molucca*   *Pl. 18, p. 81*
   Description: 73 cm (29″). Uniformly dull-white with wings tipped black; head and upper neck of adults bare and black, with nape banded rose-pink; neck of immature birds feathered; bill long (18 cm) down-curved; legs black. On the ground the black tips of the folded wings make it appear that this ibis has a black tail; actually the tail is white. Distinguished at once from all white egrets by shape of bill and silhouette in flight.
   Voice: A short goose-like cry or corvine croak.

Habitat and range: The Australian White Ibis which occasionally reaches New Zealand – scattered irruptions in 1925, 1957-58 and 1975-76 – is sometimes considered a race of the Sacred Ibis (*T. aethiopicus*) of ancient Egypt, the range of the species including Africa, India and Australasia. In New Zealand these ibises have freely associated in swampy places with domestic geese, ducks and fowls, feeding by stabbing their strong bills full length into the soft ground. They fly strongly and roost at night in trees.

ROYAL SPOONBILL   *Platalea regia*   *Pl. 18, p. 81*
Maori name: Kotuku ngutu-papa.
Description: 78 cm (31″). A large white heron-like bird, distinguishable at once by its *curious black spatulate bill* (18 cm) slightly decurved. Breeding birds have a drooping crest on the nape and show sandy-buff on the foreneck. Forehead and ocular region bare and black. Legs black. Young birds show some brown in the primaries. Flight strong and direct, with *neck held forward*, not as in herons. Also glides and soars on extended wings. Usually near water in marshes or tidal creeks; but will perch in a tree or on a post. Feeds by sweeping bill from side to side in shallow water as it moves forward. Roosts without friction among waders especially Pied Stilts, at high tide.
Habitat and range: Widespread in Australia whence vagrants have become established in New Zealand. Apparently in the 1940s one or two pairs began to breed in the White Heron sanctuary near Okarito and by 1960 10–12 pairs were known to be nesting. Birds disperse in autumn and have been met with from Parengarenga to Paterson Inlet but rarely inland. Flocks of a dozen or more visit estuaries near Nelson and Farewell Spit; usually at least a score winter in the Manawatu estuary. Smaller flocks have been noted in Hawkes Bay and most of the northern harbours, where non-breeding sub-adults may also remain throughout the summer. New blood for the established breeding stock may be coming with further stragglers from Australia.
Breeding: Nests observed in New Zealand have been high, 15 to 20 m in the forks of big swamp trees, e.g. kahikatea. Eggs 3–4, dull white lightly smeared with brown, November-December.

YELLOW-BILLED SPOONBILL   *Platalea flavipes*
Description: 89 cm (35″). Slightly larger than a Royal Spoonbill. White, but with *bill dull yellow*, sometimes tinged pink and *legs yellowish*. Facial skin lilac-blue narrowly edged with black. Pendant hackle feathers on lower neck.
    Flies like *regia*, with strong slow wing-beats, alternating with long glides.
Habitat and range: An Australian species, frequenting shallow water both fresh and salt. Apparently more sedentary than *regia*. Seven on Lord Howe Island in March 1957 were the first reported away from the Australian continent. Not recorded in Tasmania. In August 1976 one was seen and photographed in Rangaunu Bay. It may have crossed the Tasman Sea in company with other large white Australian nomads. Still present a year later.

GEESE, SWANS AND DUCKS: Anatidae

A cosmopolitan family comprising three subfamilies: the Anseranatinae (a single species, the unique Australian Magpie Goose); Anserinae (whistling ducks or tree-ducks, swans and geese); the Anatinae (shelducks, river or dabbling ducks, etc.). Some Australian members of the last-named family are popularly known as geese – including the Cape Barren Goose and Maned Goose (Australian Wood Duck) – but their similarity to the true geese is only superficial.

Two Australian species, Pink-eared Duck (*Malacorhynchus membranaceus*) and Musk Duck (*Biziura lobata*), are known in New Zealand only from sub-fossil bones. Our extinct so-called goose *Cnemiornis*, which together with a large extinct swan and a small extinct duck survived in New Zealand till the arrival of man, was related not too distantly to Australia's Cape Barren Goose.

GRASS WHISTLING DUCK *Dendrocygna eytoni* *Pl. 20, p. 89*
Other name: Plumed Tree Duck.
Description: 43 cm (17″). Long neck and upright carriage is characteristic. Brown, with buff face, and pink bill and legs. Stiff, yellow flank plumes are held outside the wings. Tail black with a broad buff band at base; abdomen white. Sexes are almost indistinguishable. Head feathers can be erected to a crest when disturbed.
Voice: A loud piping.
Habitat and range: Inland waters; feeds on grass and other vegetation. A straggler in New Zealand, the four records being: Thames (1871), Kaitangata (1871), Ashburton (1894–6), Little Wanganui (1975).

MUTE SWAN *Cygnus olor* *Pl. 21, p. 96*
Other name: White Swan.
Description: 150 cm (60″). Pure white plumage, size and generally loosely folded wings on the water ensure identification at any distance. Orange bill, with black base and black knob on forehead (knob of male is enlarged in spring). Downy young, pale grey. First plumage brownish-white above, almost white below.
Voice: Has a penetrating trumpeting note, rarely heard; also snort and hiss of annoyance.
Habitat and range: Introduced from Great Britain as an ornamental bird and still exists mainly in a semi-domestic state except for the well-established breeding population (50–70) on Lake Ellesmere, Canterbury, and smaller populations (12–20) on L. Poukawa, Wanstead Lagoon and other lakes in central and southern Hawkes Bay.
Breeding: Nest massive, in raupo, etc., at water's edge, or on stream or lake shore in secluded location; eggs 5–7, September-January. Incubation, mainly by female, *c.* 38 days; fledging 4 months or more.

BLACK SWAN *Cygnus atratus*   *Pl. 21, p. 96*
Description: 100 cm (40″). Black; primaries and secondaries white, producing *flashing white wing-tips prominent in flight*. Bill crimson, with white band crossing the upper mandible near tip, and extreme tip also white. On the water white flight feathers occasionally show as a patch on the folded wings. Downy cygnet a little darker (brownish-white) than Mute Swan; immature plumage ashy brown, becoming darker after later moults.
Voice: Musical and far-reaching crooning note; also a whistle especially when disturbed on breeding grounds.
Habitat and range: Introduced as an ornamental waterfowl from Australia, and now widespread throughout New Zealand, especially on the larger lakes and estuarine harbours: main concentrations on Lake Ellesmere, Lake Waihola, Vernon Lagoon (Marlborough), Lake Wairarapa, Whangape and other lower Waikato lakes, and at Farewell Spit; also at the Chatham Islands (the central lagoon on the main island).
Breeding: A substantial mound nest on river or lake shore, forming colonies on the latter; may be surrounded by tall lakeside vegetation, or in open. The numbers of Black Swans are controlled on Lake Ellesmere by disturbance of undesired colonies and commercial egg-collecting. Clutch 4–7, June-December, in some districts also autumn; greenish-white; incubation by both sexes *c*. 37 days; fledging *c*. 6 months.

CANADA GOOSE *Branta canadensis*   *Pl. 21, p. 96*
Description: 100 cm (40″). Body brown above and pale brown to white below; lower back black; band above base of tail and whole of tail-coverts white; tail black; *black* head and neck with a conspicuous *white mark on the cheek*. In flight black tail contrasts with white undertail and rump. When seen on the water with Black Swans the two species may be confused but Canada Goose has shorter and less curved neck; in favourable light the white undertail is visible for some distance. Downy young, olive-yellow, marked with brown above. Immature plumage tinged grey.
Voice: Musical double honk delivered on the water and in flight. High-pitched call when disturbed on breeding grounds.
Habitat and range: Introduced from North America as game (possibly more than one race, but predominantly *B.c.maxima*). Abundant in Canterbury and North Otago, breeding mainly in grassy mountain valleys and by high country lakes. In Otago remains mostly in vicinity of the breeding grounds for the winter; Canterbury breeders migrate to lowland lakes (mostly to Lake Ellesmere) in February-May, returning to the high country in early September; a few (10–15 pairs) breed on Lake Ellesmere, 150–200 pairs on nearby Lake Forsyth. (Non-breeding Canterbury birds leave the high country in December to moult at Lake Ellesmere.) Breeds more sparingly in other parts of the South Island. Very few breed in the North Island but stragglers appear in all districts.

PLATE 17 Blue Reef Heron (p.74); White-faced Heron (p.71); Cattle Egret (p.75); Australian Darter (p.62); Little Egret (p.73); White Heron (p.72).

PLATE 17

BLUE REEF HERON 66 cm

HITE-FACED HERON
cm

AUSTRALIAN DARTER 92 cm

CATTLE EGRET
51 cm

TTLE
GRET
6 cm

CATTLE EGRET, breeding plumage

WHITE HERON 91 cm

PLATE 18

LITTLE
BITTERN
30 cm

NANKEEN
(RUFOUS)
NIGHT HERON
56 cm

AUSTRALIAN
BROWN
BITTERN
71 cm

AUSTRALIAN WHITE IBIS
73 cm

GLOSSY IBIS 56 cm

ROYAL SPOONBIL
78 cm

CAPE BARREN GOOSE
85 cm

Recently liberated in Wairoa district.

Breeding: A mound nest is built where the incubating bird can obtain a wide view; eggs 2–11 (usually 4 or 5), September-December, creamy white, incubated by female. When nest is approached, the female lowers her neck to ground level, remaining quite motionless, and nest is detected with the greatest difficulty. Incubation period *c.* 28 days; fledging 8–9 weeks.

CAPE BARREN GOOSE *Cereopsis novaehollandiae* *Pl. 18, p. 81*

Description: 85 cm (34″). An upstanding, goose-like species (related to Paradise Duck, not to geese); colour *grey*, faintly spotted dark on wing-coverts; tail and end of quills *black*; yellowish-green soft skin (cere) covers base of black bill; feet pink. Sexes alike.

Voice: Grunt-like (thus local name in Australia 'Pig Goose').

Habitat and range: Introduced from Australia in 1915; now rare in Australia, being found only on islands off the south and south-western coast. Liberated on Lake Hawea, and subsequently reported (in 1936) from Lake Hawea and Lake Thomson. Has also been recorded in Fiordland (1947) although this may be the result of immigration from Australia. Inhabits grasslands and swampy areas in Australia, feeding on vegetation.

Breeding: In Australia a grass nest, lined with down, on the ground in the open; eggs 4–6, June-September, white.

PARADISE SHELDUCK *Tadorna variegata* *Pl. 19, p. 88*

Other names: Putangitangi, Paradise Duck, Pari, Rangitata Goose, Painted Duck.

Description: 63 cm (25″). Of intermediate size between the ducks and the larger species (Canada Goose and swans). The female's *conspicuous white head* is generally the first field characteristic recognised (commonly observed in pairs or family groups); body of adult female mainly bright chestnut. Male predominantly dark; black barred with fine white lines, reddish-brown abdomen, head black with a metallic sheen. Bill and feet black. At a distance on the water recognised by stout build and relatively short neck. In flight, the *white coverts form a prominent wing patch* on both upper and under wing. Speculum green. (As in other ducks these wing markings may or may not be visible when the wings are folded.) Runs strongly, legs relatively long. Immature plumage of both sexes similar to that of adult male, females assuming white head within 1–2 months of fledging. Downy chick has striking pattern of white and brown.

Voice: Loud alarm note different in male and female: male a deep *zonk-zonk* . . . and female a shrill, penetrating *zeek-zeek* . . . In the breeding season the pairs rise and call on sighting an intruder, and the calls are given as a duet in the air or from some high point on the ground. Call carries for some distance – especially the high-pitched call of the female – in mountain valleys, and is thus well known as a cause of disturbance to deer-stalkers.

PLATE 18 Little Bittern (p.76); Nankeen (Rufous) Night Heron (p.76); Australian Brown Bittern (p.75); Australian White Ibis (p.77); Glossy Ibis (p.77); Royal Spoonbill (p.78); Cape Barren Goose (p.81).

Habitat and range: Widely distributed along eastern foothills of the Southern Alps and in lowland Southland; scattered elsewhere in South Island. In the North Island there are concentrations in the Gisborne-East Cape area, National Park and Northland; scattered elsewhere although uncommon in Waikato and southern Wellington. Readily adapts to hill country pastoral land, using stock ponds for rearing young. Moults in large flocks in traditional localities on rivers, lakes or ponds, December-February. A game bird, but protected in some districts.

Breeding: Nest a depression lined with down, completely hidden on the ground or up to a height of 6 m in hollow trees (hollow logs, holes in ground and haystacks are common sites). Eggs 8–12, August-January, white; female incubates.

MALLARD *Anas platyrhynchos* *Pl. 19, p. 88*

Description: 58 cm (23″). Although the female may be confused with the Grey Duck, there is no possible confusion between the males, the *male* being unmistakable, viz. glossy dark green head, white collar, purplish-brown breast, grey body varied with brown, and iridescent black rump; the middle tail feathers are black and the side feathers white, the four centre black feathers curled; *white vertical stripe on flank*; bill greenish-yellow. *Female* mottled brown, *without the pale chin or striking facial pattern* present in the Grey Duck (there is a comparatively faint dark line through the eye and indistinct pale eyebrow stripe); the pale tip of each feather much more extensive than in Grey Duck, and tips strongly buff in colour; bill yellowish-green with black nib in male, orange mottled with black in female. In both sexes underwing white; *speculum blue* with black border in front and behind, and a *double wing bar*. *Feet orange in both sexes.*

Swifter and more irregular flight in comparison with the Grey Duck, and take-off is generally more sudden.

The bright plumage of the male is replaced in summer or autumn, for a period of about a month, by an 'eclipse' plumage: this resembles plumage of female, but not evenly mottled, and distinguished further by darker brown (almost black) crown, brownish-black rump and greyish upper surface; curled tail feathers absent. Moult back to the breeding plumage during February-May.

Mallard and Grey Duck may hybridise, but observation has shown that this is rare in the wild in New Zealand; however, there are well-established hybrid populations in certain parks, etc., the best-known being on the River Avon, in Christchurch city (hybrid plumage varies: a common type has general plumage, especially strong facial pattern, derived from Grey Duck, in combination with the Mallard's conspicuous double wing bar and either orange or orange-tinged feet).

Voice: Female has a loud, deep *quark* and softer 'conversational' notes; male softer, higher-pitched *quek*.

Habitat and range: Introduced as early as 1867, the stock originating from the British Isles, but did not become established until intensive breeding and liberation was carried out *c.* 1930: at about the same time introductions were made from the United States. The stock is thus of mixed origin, and it is not known whether both migratory and sedentary races were included. Research on migration of this species and the Grey Duck in New Zealand shows that while the Grey Duck performs widespread movements (possibly migratory), the Mallard is rather more sedentary; however, movements of up to 1300 km have been recorded and one bird banded at Lake Tuakitoto, in South Otago, was shot near Adelaide in 1962.

In general habits the Mallard bears a strong resemblance to the Grey Duck; the two species probably compete for food.

The Mallard now outnumbers the Grey Duck in most closely settled districts and in all highly developed farmlands. Present on the Chatham Islands but in small numbers.

Breeding: Nests under cover, rarely far from the water, and like the Grey Duck often chooses a hollow tree or fork; nests may be simply in tall grass. Constructed of grass (sometimes nest material is practically absent), down being added as incubation progresses. Eggs 10–15 (average 13), August-January, greenish- to bluish-white, or creamy. Incubation 28 days, sometimes less.

GREY DUCK   *Anas superciliosa*   *Pl. 19, p. 88*
Other names: Parera, Black Duck (Australia).
Description: 55 cm (22″). 'Grey' plumage (dull brown with a pale greyish or buff crescentic tip on each feather), paler over-all on the lower surface, the distinctive markings are the *pale chin and throat* and *conspicuous horizontally striped pattern of the face* (latter consists of dark brown stripe through the eye and above it a pale buff eyebrow-stripe which divides the eye-stripe from the dark crown); a second dark stripe from the gape across the cheek, but less distinct. *Speculum green*, black borders and *narrow white posterior band*; in front of the speculum a narrow pale buff band, but often indistinct. No difference between the sexes (cf. Mallard). Underwing white; bill dark bluish-grey; feet olive or yellowish-brown.

May be confused with the female Mallard, but in addition to the above plumage characters, the Grey Duck is of somewhat slighter build, the head being larger in proportion.
Voice: The female's loud quacking is typically duck-like, but the male has a higher-pitched call like that of the Mallard.
Habitat and range: Universally distributed, and on Kermadec, Chatham, Snares, Auckland, Campbell and Macquarie Islands. Although the modification of swamps and inland waters as the result of settlement, together with other factors, have caused a general decrease in numbers, it remains a common duck in many parts of New Zealand; it is also adaptable, although appearing to need more cover than the introduced Mallard and thus avoiding the more developed farmlands. Habitat includes mountainous areas, estuaries and sheltered inlets, as well as all inland waters. Food is both plant and animal, obtained by typical 'up-ending', or dabbling in shallower water, or on land; marine organisms commonly taken on mud in estuaries.

Banding records of movements to date include regular recoveries between the Waikato district and Southland – the longest (1100 km) recorded within New Zealand; and several from Chatham Islands and from Australia.
Breeding: Generally away from water (cf. Mallard) concealed in herbage; frequently in a tree fork or hollow tree; a favourite site is in masses of perching *Astelia*; dry grass and other vegetation is used, with much down as a lining.

Average clutch 10 (5–6 if re-nesting when first clutch lost through flooding, predation, etc.), August-December (peak October-November), greenish-white, or pale cream tinged with green. In this and related ducks incubation is performed by the female; incubation period 27 days.

GREY TEAL   *Anas gibberifrons*   *Pl. 19, p. 88*
Maori name: Tete.

Description: 43 cm (17″). Like the Grey Duck has pale throat, but noticeably smaller and differs in having no conspicuous eyebrow- and eye-stripes on the face; from the female Mallard is distinguished by greyer plumage; from the female Shoveler by more rounded outline, neat head and small bill. The Grey Teal is distinguished in flight from all these three species by the *prominent white triangle* on the upperwing in front of speculum, and by having less white on the underwing. Speculum green, with narrow white bar behind. Bill bluegrey upper and yellow lower mandible; feet greyish-brown. Sexes alike. Wing beats are faster than in other New Zealand ducks, and flocks often wheel rapidly in flight.

Voice: A rapid *cuck-cuck-cuck*, and a muted *eep* given by adult to young.

Habitat and range: A common species in Australia, but in New Zealand established in several districts and apparently spreading to new localities every year. It is probably self-introduced fairly regularly from Australia (an influx is believed to have occurred in the autumn of 1957, when a banded bird from Victoria was shot in the Waikato district); there have been established breeding populations for at least 50 years in the Rotorua and Wairarapa districts, and more recently it has been observed regularly on lakes and ponds from Kaipara to Oreti gravel pits, breeding (1961) as high as L. Tekapo at 700 m a.s.l. Sometimes visits salt water.

Breeding: On ground under vegetation near water; nest of grasses, normally lined with down but down sometimes absent: sites recorded in New Zealand include top of 'niggerheads' (*Carex*) (Wairarapa district) and tree forks (Waikato). Eggs 5–9, September-January, dark cream.

BROWN TEAL   *Anas chlorotis*   *Pl. 19, p. 88*
Other names: Pateke, Brown Duck.

Description: 48 cm (19″). General colour is warm brown. *Male* dark brown head with green reflections on nape and along a line to eye; white collar (on front portion of neck only) between this and the vivid reddish-brown breast; some indistinct fine barring on back; a black line passes back from each shoulder; on flanks is an area of fine wavy lines of alternate pale and dark, and behind this is a *white flank patch*; undertail-coverts black; speculum green broadly edged behind with black, and behind this a *white posterior bar;* another narrow bar of buff in front of speculum. *Female* uniformly brown, head closely freckled with dark brown; wing markings as in male: no white flank. In both sexes, the underwing-coverts partly white; bill bluish-black; feet slate grey.

Some males breed in a dull plumage almost identical with that of the adult female (Peter Scott); it is not known whether these birds ultimately assume the brighter plumage. The immature male is similar to adult female.

Voice: Low *quark* and a high-pitched piping (G. R. Williams).

Habitat and range: Once very widely distributed, especially on swampy streams and ponds and tidal creeks shaded by trees, coming out at night to feed on open ground. Widely taken for food in the early period of European settlement. Various factors probably caused its sharp decline especially swamp draining. It is now rare, but there are considerable numbers on Great Barrier Island, and localities where it has persisted in small groups are North Auckland (Waipu, Kara, Helena Bay, Kerikeri, Takou Bay, Kaeo), Little Barrier Island, Fiordland and Stewart Island. Recently introduced to Kapiti Island and Manawatu district. In Fiordland and about Stewart Island its habitat includes sheltered portions of the coast and it may rest and feed in beds of bull-kelp. Dives well, and has strong flight, although it takes to the wing infrequently.
Breeding: Grass, lined with down, in a well-concealed situation near the water; eggs 5–7, July-December, cream.

AUCKLAND ISLAND TEAL   *Anas aucklandica*   Pl. 19, p. 88
Other name: Auckland Island Flightless Duck.
Description: 43 cm (17″). Resembles Brown Teal in both sexes, but there is no white collar or dark line on the back in the male; male has only a faint patch (brownish-white) on the flanks; speculum and wing-bars almost absent, reduced to greenish gloss and faintly indicated brownish-white bar at rear edge; abdomen of female whitish. Underwing white mottled with brown in both sexes.
Voice: A piping or whistling note resembling that of the Brown Teal; no other call recorded.
Habitat and range: This form is essentially flightless, with much reduced wings which are of use only to aid the bird when scrambling up to coastal rocks. It feeds regularly amongst kelp on the coast, which is much indented and provides many sheltered locations. Also on the streams and lakes, which are never far from the coast in this group. Like the Brown Teal, habits are nocturnal: feeds on land at night.

A slightly smaller and browner form (*nesiotis*) on Campbell Island (now breeding only on adjacent Dent Island and straggling to the main island).
Breeding: Nests on the smaller members of the group, but cats probably now prevent it from breeding on the main island. Nest lined with grass, *Dracophyllum* leaves and down, concealed under vegetation; eggs 3–5, October-December, cream.

NEW ZEALAND SHOVELER   *Anas rhynchotis*   Pl. 20, p. 89
Other names: Kuruwhengi, Spoonbill, Spoonie.
Description: 48 cm (19″). *Male* is the most colourful New Zealand duck, striking features being: bluish-grey head combined with black round base of bill and *vertical white line in front of eye*; *bright chestnut undersurface* and breast freckled dark-brown and white; *prominent white patch on flanks*; *pale cobalt blue upperwing-coverts* (and outer webs of scapulars), *green speculum*, and coverts and speculum divided by a *white bar*; bright orange-yellow feet; rump and tail-coverts (upper and under) are black with a green gloss. Adult males show much variation in extent of white on breast. The plumage of the *female* is mottled brown, but *wing markings similar to those of male*; feet

yellowish-brown. Bill comparatively long, strikingly spatulate at the tip. In both sexes underwing white.

On the water where the full pattern may not be seen, this species has a distinctive squat outline – in proportion a *shorter neck and bigger bill* than the Grey Duck or Mallard. The bright chestnut sides are conspicuous in good light (chestnut distinctly brighter than the purplish-brown breast coloration in the Mallard drake and more conspicuous at a distance); white more extensive on flanks than in the Mallard drake. *Female* distinguished from Grey Duck by absence of facial pattern, and from both Grey Duck and Mallard by smaller size and different outline.

Males in dowdy eclipse plumage somewhat resemble females. Flight is swift and impulsive, with a tendency to turn suddenly.

Voice: Female *cuck-cuck-cuck* very similar to that of Grey Teal, with which easily confused; male a muted *clonk* given only in evenings or when disturbed.

Habitat and range: Spread throughout, and considered to be increasing in numbers; at the Chatham Islands until *c.* 1925; straggler to the Auckland Islands. Visits most lakes up to about 700 m a.s.l. (e.g. Rotoaira); readily colonises new ponds and dams; seldom in small streams in forested regions such as those favoured by the Grey Duck. Feeds predominantly on small aquatic animals and seeds; unlike Grey Duck and Mallard does not graze on pasture.

A slightly different (duller breast) subspecies in Australia (*rhynchotis*). The subspecific name of the New Zealand Shoveler is *variegata*.

Breeding: Recent records mainly in very open grassy sites a short distance (*c.* 100 m) from water, often in the ranker patches found on pasture land; an early record under tussock at some distance from water (Potts); also recorded under a small lupin on a shingle-ridge in a riverbed. Occasionally in trees in Australia, but no records of this in New Zealand. Nest of grass and other vegetation, lined plentifully with down; eggs 9–13 (average clutch 11), October–January, pale bluish-white; incubation period 25 days.

NORTHERN SHOVELER   *Anas clypeata*   *Pl. 20, p. 89*
Description: 50 cm (20″). About the same size as the New Zealand Shoveler; but drakes in full plumage are conspicuously different. Head, not blue, but a *dark glossy green and lacking the white crescent on the cheeks*; breast a clear white; this means that in flight *clypeata* is much more variegated than the

whitest of *variegata*. The females cannot surely be distinguished in the field, and the eclipse plumage of the two species is very similar.

Habitat and range: A holarctic breeder which in its southward migration outdistances most of the other dabbling ducks, frequently reaching the tropics and sometimes passing through them. First recorded in New Zealand in 1968 in the Lower Waikato. Since recorded on or near Lake Horowhenua.

BLUE DUCK *Hymenolaimus malacorhynchos*   *Pl, 19. p. 88*
Maori name: Whio.

Description: 53 cm (21″). Dove-grey with strong bluish sheen; brownish-grey on crown; heavily *spotted red-brown* on the breast; on the inner secondaries each feather has a black margin, and inner secondaries have narrow white tips; underwing pale grey; *pinkish-white bill* is a prominent feature, and has a *black tip* (including flexible lobe on each side); feet dark brown. Female has reduced red-brown spotting on breast; spots are completely absent in the first immature plumage.

If it remains motionless seen with difficulty against stones in stream bed.
Voice: Male has a shrill, somewhat hoarse whistle (denoted by Maori name); female has a characteristic cry *cr-ack* that has been appropriately described as a 'rattle'; also recorded is a *ra-ra-ruk*.

Habitat and range: North (south of Coromandel Peninsula) and South Islands; originally to sea-level in areas with turbulent streams, i.e. fiords and hilly areas; restricted at present mainly to more mountainous regions where modification of the habitat is at a minimum. Adapted to feeding upon aquatic insects and obtains much of its food from stones and boulders amongst rapids, where insect life is abundant. Caddis-fly larvae most important food item. It can dive freely, even in swifter currents. Emerging adult insects, etc., are also taken on the surface of streams and lakes. Flight is strong and direct; but when disturbed, will escape more often by diving and swimming out of sight. In pairs or family groups throughout the year. Activity increases towards dusk.

Remarkably tame, and has thus sometimes been severely depleted in unfrequented areas, but now that total protection is more generally observed is believed to be increasing.

Breeding: Under thick vegetation near a stream, often on a steep bank above water; eggs 4–9, August-November, creamy-white. Downy young in olive-brown and pale creamy-white down, with narrow stripe through the eye, are strong divers and swimmers, and accompany their parents along the stream-beds.

WHITE-EYED DUCK *Aythya australis*   *Pl. 20,p. 89*
Other names: Karakahia, Hardhead, Australian Pochard, Australian White-eyed Duck.

Description: 48 cm (19″). Like the following species (New Zealand Scaup) this is a 'diving duck', a group in which the legs are set well back on the body and the body outline is distinctly rounded; diving ducks tend to swim in the deeper portions of lakes and lagoons, and there dive for their food. The White-eyed Duck and Scaup are alike in the mainly dark plumage of the male, but in the present species *white rump and undertail* are distinctive. In both sexes *wide* *white wing-stripe across whole wing*; underwing white. Female brown. The male has a *white* iris (female *brown*).

Habitat and range: While a number of Australian species have reached New Zealand during the last 50 years, some settling permanently, this duck had disappeared by the 1930s after an early period (1867-95) of some abundance in certain districts; it was present in numbers in the lower Waikato, and recorded from Lakes Rotomahana and Tarawera, Manawatu district, Hawkes Bay, Lake Wairarapa, Lake Ellesmere and finally an isolated sight record in 1934 at Hamurana, on Lake Rotorua. In 1973 one of a flight of eight was shot in Hawkes Bay.

Common in Australia, where it is recorded as taking a wide variety of plant and animal foods.

Breeding: In Australia the nest, a deep cup, is placed in dense vegetation or shrubs above swamps. Eggs 9–12, creamy-white.

NEW ZEALAND SCAUP   *Aythya novaeseelandiae*   *Pl. 20, p. 89*
Other names: Papango, Black Teal.
Description: 40 cm (16″). Male black above with purple sheen (greenish on head), and blackish-brown below; the abdomen with white mottling. *Female* blackish-brown, darker above; in breeding plumage has a white band (sometimes incomplete) on forehead; abdomen mottled with more white than in male. In both sexes, a *broad white wing-bar on secondaries*; underwing greyish-white with brown mottling; bill bluish-black; feet dark brown. Iris *yellow* in male, *brown* in female.

Readily distinguished by dark plumage and rounded outline; sits high in the water as compared with other ducks, and patters along the surface to take off. Dives for food.

Voice: Male a soft whistle, female a muted quack.

Habitat and range: Lagoons and lakes, including mountain lakes up to *c.* 1000 m a.s.l. and numerous small coastal ponds and sand-dune lakes in both islands. It is still found throughout, but numbers greatly reduced following settlement probably both through modification of the habitat and extensive shooting; now completely protected. It has increased greatly on North Island hydro lakes, colonising some within a few months after flooding. Established on artificial ponds in some areas.

Flocks of non-breeders persisting throughout the nesting season may indicate that this species does not breed till two or more years old.

Breeding: Nests close to water in dense cover, occasionally under an overhanging bank; material mainly grasses, lined plentifully with down; eggs 5–8, October-March, creamy-white; large for the size of the bird. Commonly nests in close groups. The chicks can dive shortly after hatching, and go down to a considerable depth.

PLATE 19 Grey Teal (p.84); Brown Teal (p.84); Grey Duck (p.83); Mallard (p.82); Blue Duck (p.87); Paradise Shelduck (p.81); Auckland Island Teal (p.85).

PLATE 19

GREY TEAL 42 cm
♂
♀

BROWN TEAL
48 cm
♂
♀

AUCKLAND
ISLAND
TEAL 43 cm

GREY DUCK
55 cm
♂
♀

MALLARD
58 cm
♀
♂

BLUE DUCK 53 cm

PARADISE SHELDUCK
63 cm
♂
♀

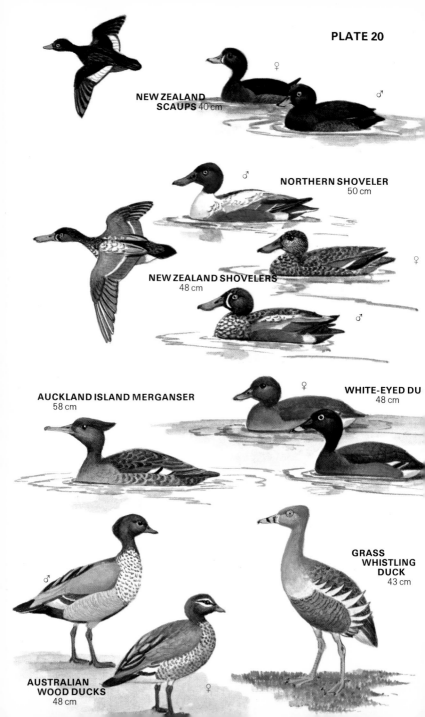

PLATE 20

NEW ZEALAND SCAUPS 40 cm
♀ ♂

NORTHERN SHOVELER 50 cm
♂

NEW ZEALAND SHOVELERS 48 cm
♀
♂

AUCKLAND ISLAND MERGANSER 58 cm

WHITE-EYED DU 48 cm
♀

GRASS WHISTLING DUCK 43 cm

AUSTRALIAN WOOD DUCKS 48 cm
♂
♀

AUSTRALIAN WOOD DUCK *Chenonetta jubata* *Pl. 20, p. 89*
Other name: Maned Goose.
Description: 48 cm (19″). Recognised by goose-like head in association with small size. *Male* has *chocolate head*; mane-like black feathers on the back of the neck; mottled brown and white breast; back, undertail-coverts and tail black; and *blue-grey wing-coverts and flanks. Female* mainly mottled and barred brown and white; pale buff face and dark line through the eye; undertail-coverts white. Speculum *green*, with *white bar above and below*, in both sexes; underwing white; dark brown bill and black feet.
Habitat and range: Four records, apparently of stragglers, from Wanaka (1910), and Orawia, Linwood and Wairaki (Southland) (all 1944). In Australia a widespread species, obtaining much of its food on land, including grassland and sometimes crops. Nests in tree hollows.

AUCKLAND ISLAND MERGANSER *Mergus australis* *Pl. 20, p. 89*
Description: 58 cm (23″). Belongs to the Sea Ducks (Mergini), which include the eider ducks and their relations as well as the mergansers – the latter are distinguished by their slender bills, serrated along the cutting edge on both mandibles. Apart from a species on the eastern coast of South America, the Auckland Island Merganser is the only Sea Duck found in the southern hemisphere. Except that both sexes resemble the female of northern mergansers it is not markedly distinct, and thus probably arose as an offshoot of the northern hemisphere stock comparatively recently. Has been found sub-fossil in the South Island. Plumage *mainly dark greyish-brown*, with *dark red-brown head*; the feathers on the back of the head hair-like forming a crest; *white wing-patch*; underwing white mottled grey; *abdomen with plentiful white mottling*; bill orange-yellow, brown above; feet orange. Note slim shape and narrow bill. Female similar to male, but plumage slightly duller (*note* – both sexes are very like the female of northern species, especially the Red-breasted Merganser, *Mergus serrator*; in all northern mergansers the male has a green head).
Habitat and range: Almost certainly extinct as it has not been recorded since 1905; further, a thorough search in 1942–5 by the coast-watching parties stationed on the Auckland Islands, and by subsequent expeditions, in nearly all localities on Auckland, Adams, Disappointment and other members of the group had no result. Lived mainly on the fiord-like inlets of the east and south coasts, and on the extensive coast of Carnley Harbour, but also on the lower reaches of streams. Only food recorded is fish (a species of *Galaxias*).
Breeding: Nest and eggs not known; downy chick olive-brown above, yellowish-white below with reddish throat and foreneck.

PLATE 20 New Zealand Scaup (p.88); Northern Shoveler (p.86); New Zealand Shoveler (p.85); White-eyed Duck (p.87); Auckland Island Merganser (p.89); Grass Whistling Duck (p.79); Australian Wood Duck (p.89).

HARRIER-HAWKS AND EAGLES: Accipitridae

This large cosmopolitan family which in Australia alone numbers nearly twenty species, has only one representative in New Zealand. The common Australian Sea Eagle (*Haliaeetus leucogaster*) might be expected to wander to these islands, but the evidence that it has done so on a number of occasions is inconclusive. Sub-fossil bones of a large long-legged, short-winged eagle *Harpagornis moorei* are known from both North and South Islands; and those of a sea eagle with Asiatic affinities, *Icthyophaga australis*, have been found in the Chatham Islands.

HARRIER   *Circus approximans*   *Pl. 21, p. 96*
  Other names: Hawk, Swamp Harrier, Gould's Harrier, Kahu.
  Description: 60 cm (23″), females being slightly larger than males. Plumage rather variable. Head and upperparts commonly dark brown, upper tail-coverts white; usually some white feathers on nape; tail lighter brown with dark bars; underparts reddish-brown with dark streaks; legs and feet yellow. Young birds are dark and lack the pale rump; plumage becomes lighter with age and some old birds, especially males, are almost grey.

  A bird of open country, quartering the ground with slow, leisurely flight, sometimes soars in wide effortless circles; often a roadside scavenger, feeding upon car-killed rabbits, hares, opossums, etc. Will wade into shallow water after frogs and tadpoles. Persistently badgered by Australian Magpies where they are present; and often mobbed by flocks of Starlings.
  Voice: Mewing accompanies playful courtship flights. A high-pitched squeal *Kee kee kee* is used during display; also by the male to call the female from the nest.
  Habitat and range: Fairly common throughout, except in heavily forested districts (up to 2000 m); straggling south to Auckland and Campbell Islands. By opening up great tracts of country and increasing its food supply, European farming has benefited this hawk which despite persecution survives in settled districts. Young birds wander in autumn and there is some evidence that they tend to drift northwards. Communal ground-roosts in winter may contain scores of birds. The species is found throughout Australia and the south-west Pacific.
  Breeding: Courtship flights observable in September. Nest, preferably in a swamp among raupo or niggerheads, often in scrub and fern, sometimes on saltings. Eggs 2–7, commonly 4, white, chalky, October-December; incubation period 31–34 days; fledging about six weeks. The passing of food in mid-air when the female rises from the nest and turns on her back to receive it from the male is sometimes observed.

FALCONS: Falconidae

Falcons with powerful strokes of their long pointed wings are among the fastest of fliers and are noted for the boldness with which they attack and strike down their prey. Of the two species on the New Zealand list, one is endemic, the other is a rare straggler from Australia. It is remarkable that the almost ubiquitous Peregrine Falcon (*F. peregrinus*) has never been known to occur in New Zealand.

NEW ZEALAND FALCON *Falco novaeseelandiae* Pl. 21, p. 96
  Other names: Bush Hawk, Sparrow Hawk, Quail Hawk, Karearea.
  Description: 45 cm (18″). Like many falcons, a variable bird; females generally bigger and more richly coloured than males, but the largest males are hardly smaller than the smallest females. Upperparts brownish-black, darkest on the crown, barred with brown in older birds, chin and throat whitish with dark brown streaks; dark line through eye beneath pale superciliary stripe; dark streak at sides of chin like drooping moustache. Underparts pale buff to white, striped with dark brown on chest and belly, barred on flanks (adult); dark rufous brown with obscure round spots and splashes of pale buff (imm). Thighs and undertail-coverts rufous brown ('red trousers') with darker streaks. Legs, feet and cere yellow, claws black. The first flying plumage is uniformly dark above and lacks the rufous tones below; feet and cere bluish-grey.
    A fierce and fearless predator, preying mostly upon birds, especially now apparently on the common introduced species, and occasionally on sea birds and small mammals. Intolerant of intruders, particularly of the Harrier, on its breeding territory.
  Voice: A loud piercing whistle or shrill scream on the wing. Alarm calls near the nest are a repetitive *kek-kek-kek*. Also during play or exercise a series of single *heks* with pauses between.
  Habitat and range: Apparently now only a winter vagrant north of Rotorua; commoner to the south, mainly in the back country, but young birds wandering in autumn visit settled country and even urban gardens. Thrives conspicuously at the Auckland Islands, sometimes visiting Campbell Island, at the southern limit of its range.
  Breeding: Nest usually on the ground on the ledge of a cliff or on a bare slip in steep bush, sometimes in a tree. Eggs 2–4, rich reddish brown with chocolate blotches, typical of falcon, October-December; incubation period 30 days.

NANKEEN KESTREL *Falco cenchroides* Pl. 21, p. 96
  Other names: Australian Windhover, Hoverer.
  Description: 33 cm (13″). Above a beautiful cinnamon brown, feathers with black centres; wing quills dark brown; underparts white or light yellowish buff, the breast feathers having narrow brown shaft lines. Rump and tail grey in male, rufous in female with black sub-terminal band and white tip. Legs orange-yellow.
    A typical Kestrel distinguished at once by its size, colouring and *habit of hovering*, poised in mid-air with head facing into wind and tail more or less

91

depressed according to the strength of the breeze. Drops by stages. Hunts over open country especially short grass, in search of lizards, large insects, small birds and mammals.

Habitat and range: Widespread in Australia but scarce in Tasmania. Rare straggler to New Zealand, reported about 15 times between 1889 and 1965. After a minor irruption in 1969, there were scattered sightings and it was hoped some pairs might stay and breed, as happened on Norfolk Island. Worth watching for after strong autumn westerlies on the West Coast.

GAME BIRDS: Galliformes

The only indigenous member of this order, *Coturnix novaezealandiae*, became extinct about 1875. It was a close relative of the Stubble Quail which is still common in Australia.

NEW ZEALAND QUAIL *Coturnix novaezealandiae* *Pl. 22, p. 97*

Other name: Koreke.

Description: 15 cm (6"). Above and on flanks warm dark reddish-brown, mottled dark brown and black and each feather centrally streaked with buffy white; paler, mottled dark brown below. *Male* has face (from a line above the eye) and throat *reddish-chestnut*, female face and throat whitish with dark brown spots.

Note that male is readily distinguishable from that of Australian Brown Quail, as the latter has no chestnut on face and throat; the pale stripes are bolder in the New Zealand Quail; underparts in Australian Brown Quail are barred rather than mottled. The *axillary feathers* (under wings) are *white* in the New Zealand Quail cf. grey in Australian Brown Quail (this can only be seen when specimens are examined).

Voice: Low purring and call *twit, twit, twit, twee-twit* (Potts) (cf. the characteristic double call *ker-wee*, accented on the second syllable, of the Australian Brown Quail).

Habitat and range: Presumed extinct, the last acceptable recorded date being 1875 (Buller). Formerly North, South and Great Barrier Islands, being 'excessively abundant in all the open country, and especially on the grass-covered downs of the South Island' (Buller). In the early days of settlement it was widely taken for food (and for sport); other factors contributing to its reduction were widespread burning of native grasslands, and mammalian predators; however, the ultimate cause of its extinction remains difficult to trace.

Food: seeds and grass (Buller).

The New Zealand form is subspecifically related to the Australian Stubble Quail, *Coturnix novaezealandiae pectoralis*, and, in view of the persistence—even under modern agricultural conditions—of the latter, the possibility should not be overlooked that an invasion may still occur from Australia (in *pectoralis* general colour is paler, but chestnut throat in male more extensive).

Breeding: Nest a depression lined with grass. Eggs 10–12, yellowish-brown to buff, with heavy spots and blotches of dark brown (cf. Australian Brown Quail, eggs of which are evenly freckled with small dark brown spots).

BROWN QUAIL   *Synoicus ypsilophorus*   *Pl. 22, p. 97*
Local name: Rat Quail, Swamp Quail.
Description: 18 cm (7$\frac{1}{4}$″). Two forms of this Australian quail, *ypsilophorus* and *australis*, were introduced in the mid-nineteenth century; but the possibility of there having been natural colonisations should not be ruled out. Sexes alike. Upperparts generally brown, mottled black and chestnut; feathers of back centrally streaked with white; throat buffy white; underparts greyish buff with black zig-zag bars. Females are slightly bigger than males. Crouches, runs and flies briefly on short rounded wings.
Voice: A plaintive long drawn rising whistle—*Ker-wee*, *ffweep*, or *mooreete* (this being its Australian Aboriginal name).
Habitat and range: Widespread in lowlands of North Island; scarce in the southern half. Locally faithful to swamps or the edges of salt-marshes (? descendants of Tasmanian Swamp Quail). Often seen in Northland along the dusty edges of scrub-fringed roads. Also, rather enigmatically on several offshore islands from Mayor and Aldermen to Three Kings.
Breeding: Nest a slight depression lined with grass and leaves. Eggs October-January, dull white evenly freckled with brown. Fledging *c*. 10 days.

BOBWHITE QUAIL   *Colinus virginianus*   *Pl. 22, p. 97*
Description: 23 cm (9″). A plump reddish-brown quail with a grey tail; smaller than *californicus*, larger than *australis*. Head vividly patterned black, white and chestnut; throat and eyebrow-streak of males white, of females buffish; chest rufous; underparts greyish, lightly and irregularly barred with black.
Outside the breeding season these quails move in coveys, roosting at nightfall in a circle on open but weedy ground, each bird facing outwards to facilitate, if disturbed, a swift and direct escape.
Voice: A whistled *ah-bob-white* or simply *bob-white*.
Habitat and range: Near the end of the nineteenth century more than 1,000 were introduced from North America and liberated between Auckland and Southland. They did not thrive; but isolated pockets became tenuously established in at least two districts. Only in northern Hawkes Bay are they known to have survived till the 1950s.
Breeding: Little known in New Zealand. Nest a hollow hidden in thick herbage. Eggs white; clutch 7–28. Incubation period *c*. 23 days.

CALIFORNIA QUAIL   *Lophortyx californicus*   *Pl. 22. p. 97*
Description: 25 cm (10″). A plump stocky gamebird with a jaunty crest. Male, forehead pale grey; crown dark brown; top-knot plume black and curving forward; back mostly brown; tail grey; throat black encircled by a narrow white band; breast bluish-grey; upper belly buff, feathers edged with black; rich chestnut patch in middle of belly; lower belly buff; flanks brownish-grey streaked conspicuously with white. Female smaller; chiefly brown; belly scaled and flanks streaked as in male; top-knot shorter.
Runs fast, rises with a whirr and glides on short wings stiffly held. Will perch

in a tree or watch alertly from an eminence, e.g. fencepost, wall, rock.

Voice: A sharp clucking *tek-tek*; an anxious *whit-whit* when a flock is scattered. Most characteristic is a clear, triple call, variously interpreted as *tobacco, chicago, where are you*; frequently mimicked by Starlings.

Habitat and range: Widely spread in both North and South Islands; and on some settled offshore islands, frequenting both farmlands and scrub. Not common in areas of high rainfall.

Breeding: Flocks split up in late winter. Nest commonly in long grass near thick cover of brambles, gorse or fern. Eggs October-December. Clutch 9–16 pyriform, creamy white, spotted dark and yellowish-brown. Incubation 22–23 days.

GREY PARTRIDGE *Perdix perdix*   *Pl. 22, p. 97*

Description: 30 cm (12″). Larger than California Quail; plump and squat with short rounded wings and a short rufous tail. Has a crouching gait but can run fast. Forms coveys outside the breeding season. Rises suddenly and flies fast and low on whirring wings with spells of gliding.

Face and upper throat rich reddish brown; upperparts brown streaked with buff; neck and underparts grey with fine wavy markings; flanks barred with chestnut. Males usually distinguishable from females by a conspicuous dark chestnut horseshoe-shaped mark on the lower breast.

Voice: A sharp tuneless *karwit* or *kirric* with far carrying power.

Habitat and range: Introduced from Europe in 1962 and widely liberated, but with little success. Possibly persisting in Southland. Requires the rough cover provided by hedges and weedy ground. Not well adapted to a system of farming in which the emphasis is on pasture, topdressing, herbicides and pesticides.

Breeding: Nest a hollow scrape commonly in thick growth on waste ground; sometimes in fields of corn, hay or clover. Eggs, rather pyriform, evenly olive-brown; clutch size very variable. Incubation period *c*. 24 days; fledging *c*. 16 days.

CHUKOR *Alectoris chukar*   *Pl. 22, p. 97*

Description: 33 cm (13″). Two of the numerous races of this Asiatic rock partridge were introduced into the South Island and have prospered. For a time *chukar* was considered a race of *A. graeca*, but recent authorities treat them as distinct species.

Upperparts ashy tinged on crown and shoulders with vinous red; a black band across forehead, continuing through eyes and down sides of neck to join above breast; cheeks, chin and throat buffy white; breast ashy tinged with brown; abdomen buff; flanks barred with chestnut and black. Bill and legs bright red. Sexes similar.

Voice: Cackles or clucks rather like a barnyard fowl.

Habitat and range: High country mainly east of the Southern Alps from Nelson to Otago, up to 1800 m, preferring dry rocky faces.

Breeding: Nest usually in a rocky place under shelter, e.g. snowgrass or tussock. Eggs September-February. Clutch 10–18, greyish-freckled with brown spots. Average size of coveys 8–10. In autumn larger flocks are formed.

PHEASANT *Phasianus colchicus* *Pl. 22, p. 97*
  Description: Males 80 cm (32″), females 60 cm (24″). At least two forms of this popular and colourful game-bird have been introduced, the so-called English Pheasant *colchicus* and the Chinese Ring-necked Pheasant *torquatus*.

  Plumage of males is rather variable; but the glossy dark green head and neck, red wattles around eyes and short ear tufts are unmistakable; and most have complete or partial white neck rings. Females are soberly mottled in light brown, chestnut and black; tail shorter than in male, distinctively pointed.
  Voice: Male has a loud, abrupt crowing *kok-kok*.
  Habitat and range: Widely and frequently released. Appears to thrive best in the coastal scrubland of the north.
  Breeding: Polygamous. Nest a hollow scratched by female, scantily lined and usually in thick cover. Eggs 7–15, uniform olive brown, September-January. Incubation *c.* 23 days. Young accompany mother and can fly at *c.* 14 days, though far from full grown.

TUFTED GUINEA FOWL *Numida meleagris* *Pl. 22, p. 97*
  Description: 63 cm (25″). About the size of a barn-door fowl; plumage grey peppered with white spots; head and throat unfeathered; cheeks whitish; wattles red; skin of the neck blue-grey. The head has a casque and a line of coarse hairy feathers extends from nape down the hindneck. Gregarious, alert and nimble. At dusk Guinea Fowl fly up into trees to roost.
  Voice: A noisy raucous cackle.
  Habitat and range: First introduced in 1864, the familiar Guinea Fowl of the farmyard, long domesticated in Europe, has gone bush in a few districts, favouring rough country with scrub or wooded gullies. In one isolated coastal region, distinctive black and white feathers lining a Welcome Swallow's nest proved the unsuspected presence of Guinea Fowl.
  Breeding: In the wild virtually unknown in New Zealand. Clutch probably 8–12; eggs, glossy, evenly pinkish-buff with strong pitted shells.

RAILS, CRAKES, WEKAS, GALLINULES AND COOTS: Rallidae

With few exceptions, among which are the Weka, the Pukeko and the Takahe, the rails are a diversified family of secretive, sombre birds of swamp and reed-fringed waterway. The bill varies in dimensions, being long in typical rails (*Rallus*), shorter and thicker in crakes (*Crex* and *Porzana*), reaching its greatest size in the gallinules (*Porphyrio*, *Notornis*), where it is sub-conical. In some species a bony shield covers the forehead. Rails are characterised by short wings, heavy bodies and long legs. Most species fly only under duress, and some have lost the power of flight. Yet rather surprisingly, despite their short wings, rails have successfully spread to many remote islands, and from ancestral types some very distinct forms have been evolved. All over the world the rails tend to disappear before settlement and the advance of urbanisation.

In New Zealand only one species, the Pukeko, is conspicuously common. The Weka is locally numerous. Three species, Banded Rail, Spotless Crake and Marsh Crake, are widely distributed, but like the Scarlet Pimpernel 'demned elusive'. The Australian Coot, though still rare, is expanding its range yearly. The remarkable Takahe, a highly specialised gallinule, survives only in a few remote valleys of Fiordland.

Two distinctive rails of the Chatham Islands, *Rallus dieffenbachi* and *Cabalus modestus*, became extinct in the nineteenth century. The Auckland Island Rail, which was rediscovered in 1966, is doubtfully distinct from a small Australian rail, which is common in Tasmania, *Rallus pectoralis*, the Lewin or Slate-breasted Rail.

An extreme example of ralline wandering is provided by the Corncrake (*Crex crex*) said to have been killed near Nelson about 1865.[1] Among the lost rails of New Zealand known only from sub-fossil bones are: a small weka, a small gallinule, a flightless coot and the giant rails, *Diaphorapteryx* and *Aptornis*.

Included in the same order Gruiformes are the Cranes, of which two species, *Brolga* and *Sarus*, breed in northern Australia. It appears that vagrants, specific identity uncertain, have reached New Zealand at least twice.

WEKA *Gallirallus australis* Pl. 23, p. 104

Other names: Woodhen, Woodrail.

Description: 53 cm (21"). Wekas are large flightless rails with strong bills and feet and reduced wings. The plumage is mainly brown and black, but the tone of the brown and the amount of black vary. On these colour differences, and also on slight differences in size, several forms have been defined.

The Weka of the North Island (*greyi*) has more grey on the underparts and brown rather than reddish legs, the colour becoming brighter in the breeding season.

The Buff Weka (*hectori*) was found in low rainfull districts east of the main range in the South Island. It became extinct in its old haunts, but throve at Chatham Island, whence 16 were re-introduced in February 1962 to Arthur's Pass National Park.

The Weka of the western region of the South Island from Nelson to Fiordland (*australis*) has a streaked red-brown and black breast. In South Westland and Fiordland it is dimorphic, the dark form showing much more black in the plumage. 'Black' Wekas are not uncommon along the Milford Track and range to the top of the Mackinnon Pass (1000 m).

The Stewart Island Weka (*scotti*) is slightly smaller. It also is dimorphic, but the dark phase is less black.

The Weka walks deliberately with tail flicking, but can run very fast and

[1]The Corncrake, a western palaearctic breeding species, normally migrates to South Africa. The New Zealand occurrence, though suspect, is not impossible. The bird has twice been recorded in Australia; the first from a few miles south of Sydney in June 1893; the second from Jurien Bay, Western Australia, in December 1944.

PLATE 21 New Zealand Falcon (p.91); Nankeen Kestrel (p.91); Harrier (p.90); Canada Goose (p.80); Black Swan (p.80); Mute Swan (p.79).

PLATE 21

NEW ZEALAND FALCONS
45 cm
imm.

♀

♂

NANKEEN KESTRELS
33 cm

HARRIER
imm.

HARRIER
60 cm

CANADA GOOSE
100 cm

BLACK SWAN
100 cm

MUTE SWAN 150 cm

PLATE 22 GAME BIRDS

NEW ZEALAND QUAIL
15 cm

BROWN QUAILS
18 cm

BOBWHITE QU
23 cm

GREY
PARTRIDG
30 cm

CALIFORNIA QUAILS
25 cm

CHUKOR
33 cm

TUFTED
GUINEA FOWL
63 cm

PHEASANTS
60 cm
80 cm

swims without hesitation. Inquisitive, omnivorous, a ready snapper-up of unconsidered—or unguarded—trifles, especially if they are bright and shiny. In association with man can become a shameless raider of rubbish-bins and fowl runs. Near the sea frequently feeds on beaches among kelp and tidewrack. A capable rat-killer. Becomes more active at dusk.

Voice: A shrill, far-carrying whistle, *coo-eet*, many times repeated. When one Weka starts calling, others in the vicinity are likely to join in. Also described as a 'thin, fairly high-pitched *wee-ee-eek*, *wee-ee-ee-eek*, which seemed to sound all round the hills' (Gee).

Habitat and range: Not primarily a swamp bird, preferring drier scrub country or the edge of the forests.

In the North Island the Weka became confined to the Gisborne district, where it continues to thrive in a variety of habitats, both urban and rural. Its sudden disappearance from districts where it was plentiful is probably to be attributed to disease. In Taranaki its disappearance is dated to 1918. In parts of Northland Wekas were plentiful in 1936 and very hard to find by 1940. In an attempt to re-establish Wekas in some of their old haunts, hundreds have been caught near Gisborne and released elsewhere in the North Island, where conditions for their survival appear favourable. Some colonisations seem to have succeeded.

In the South Island Wekas are to be found mainly west of the main range. Plentiful in north-west Nelson, especially on Farewell Spit, they are said to be increasing in Westland and becoming plentiful again in parts of Fiordland. The decline of the Buff Weka in Canterbury became apparent about 1917; and the last record known to Stead was in 1924. Luckily, in 1905 this form had been introduced to Chatham Island, where it prospered exceedingly. The Weka of the Stewart and adjacent islands is in no danger. This form was introduced to Macquarie Island, where it is now numerous. The nearest allies of this endemic species are the flightless woodrails (*Tricholimnas*) of Lord Howe Island and New Caledonia.

Breeding: Matures early. A pair of North Island Wekas, aged about nine months, nested and reared a chick. Nesting season very extended, eggs commonly September to April, 3–6, creamy-white or pinkish with scattered brown and light purplish blotches. Incubation 20–27 days. Chicks are clad in brownish-black down. Broods commonly reduced to one or two, but a pair may nest repeatedly in a season.

BANDED RAIL *Rallus philippensis*   *Pl. 23, p. 104*

Other names: Landrail, Striped Rail, Mohopereru, Mioweka. (The old sealers' name for the Macquarie Island race was Wigeon!)

Description: 30 cm (12″). A secretive bird, more often heard than seen and most often glimpsed as a disappearing shape, close to the ground. The rich colouring

---

PLATE 22 GAME BIRDS New Zealand Quail (p.92); Brown Quail (p.93); Bobwhite Quail (p.93); California Quail (p.93); Chukor (p.94); Grey Partridge (p.94); Tufted Guinea Fowl (p.95); Pheasant (p.95).

and the subtle pattern of its markings are not easily seen. Upperparts olive brown spotted with black and white; superciliary streak whitish; broad chestnut band through eye to hindneck; another chestnut band across the breast; chin whitish; throat and foreneck grey; underparts black with narrow irregular white bars. Bill reddish-brown; feet brown.

Voice: A creaky *swit-swit* or high-pitched *quee-quee* often heard at dusk. Near the nest a low *kik-kik-kik*. An intruder near the nest is greeted by a growl or throaty croak.

Habitat and range: This species is represented by many races in south-east Asia, Australia and the islands of the south-west Pacific. Apparently once widespread in New Zealand, but now seldom reported except coastally north of Raglan and the Bay of Plenty and in north-west Nelson. Not uncommon along mangrove creeks and the adjacent salting and sedgy swamps, surviving even in urban surroundings despite rats, cats and tin cans. Still occurs inland in some districts. A scarce resident on some off-shore islands, from Three Kings to Weka-free islets off Stewart Island.

Sometimes in secluded creeks may be observed foraging in the open, especially in rainy weather or when there are downy chicks to feed. May fly a short distance with dangling legs, if suddenly flushed.

Breeding: The nest is well hidden in thick grass or rushes near water. It has also been found supported on the trailing stems of ribbonwood in a tangle of saltmarsh herbage. Eggs September to February, 4–7, buff or pale pinkish marked with dark reddish-brown and purplish-grey spots and blotches. Incubation 19–25 days. The chicks are covered with black down. Both sexes incubate. Probably double-brooded.

Note: Dieffenbach's Rail (*Rallus dieffenbachi*), once abundant in the Chatham Islands, was similar to the Banded Rail in so many respects that it may be regarded as a strong subspecies of *philippensis*. The last specimen was obtained in 1840.

AUCKLAND ISLAND RAIL   *Rallus muelleri*   *Pl. 23. p. 104*

Description: 21 cm (8½″). Crown chestnut streaked with black; upperparts chestnut obscurely streaked with blackish-brown; superciliary stripe, cheeks, side of neck and nape rich rufous; chin whitish; throat and breast slate-grey, lower tinged with olive; wings, belly and flanks black barred with white. Bill reddish-brown; legs pinky-grey or light grey-brown.

Voice: A metallic *clink* or *cree-eek* repeated loudly; also a typical ralline grunt. A double note, *kek-kek*, may indicate mild alarm.

Habitat and range: Possibly exterminated by feral cats on the main Auckland Island, surviving on Ewing Island and (?) Adams Island. Clearly a small representative of the species *pectoralis* of which several forms occur between Australia and the Philippines.

Breeding: Nest not known in New Zealand. In Australia the nest is a saucer of rushes and grasses, in a swamp. Eggs 4–6, pale stone, spotted with red and lavender.

SPOTLESS CRAKE   *Porzana tabuensis*   *Pl. 24, p. 105*
Other names: Sooty Rail, Putoto, Puweto.
Description: 20 cm (8″). Upper surface dark slate merging with chocolate brown; chin greyish; underparts leaden grey; undertail-coverts black barred with white. Bill black; legs reddish. Eye red.

An elegant little rail which 'seldom takes wing, and then only for a very short distance; but it runs with rapidity, swims very gracefully and often dives to escape its enemies' (Buller).

Voice: Three distinct calls were noted by Buddle at the Poor Knights:

(*a*) a high-pitched squeak repeated steadily at short intervals by both birds of a pair;

(*b*) a very low crooning—the purring note of other authors—audible only at close range, used by the female when in nesting cover, evidently a call to the young;

(*c*) a harsh scolding *crack-crack-crack* repeated rapidly which seemed to be the male driving the female back to the nest.

Hadden in the lower Waikato also distinguished a slightly nasal *mook*, which was sometimes rapidly repeated to become a bubbling noise like water running out of a narrow-necked bottle; a harsh very nasal *harr*-ing, not often used; soft, high-pitched murmurings made by both adults at once and 'all run in together'; a rarely heard *mint mint*.

Habitat and range: This small dusky rail is generally a skulking denizen of swamps, fresh and saline. Much of our knowledge of its distribution in New Zealand depended on specimens brought in by cats. On Aorangi in the Poor Knights, where there is no true swamp, and also on the Southwest King, it forages on the open forest floor. At the Kermadecs it scavenges around petrel burrows and climbs trees. On Tiritiri from which cattle and sheep have been removed, it thrives in the lush growth of long grass and bracken.

Its quick response to the playing of its tape-recorded calls has proved that it is present in many small raupo-choked swamps.

The range of the species includes Australia and most of the south-west Pacific, *plumbea* being the name of the southern race which is found in Tasmania, southern Australia and New Zealand south to Stewart and Chatham Islands.

Breeding: The nest is not easily found, and our knowledge of nesting habits long leaned heavily on the findings of Buddle at the Poor Knights. In 1967 Hadden learnt how to find nests near Waingaro and shed much light in dark places.

Nest a bulky, clumsy structure loosely woven of grass or sedge, preferably, it seems, in cutty-grass where available, and up to a metre above water level. Apparently several spare nests may be built. Eggs August to December, 2–3, typically 3; pinkish-cream, occasionally pale bluish, flecked all over with light brown spots varying considerably in size. Incubation period *c.* 23 days. Chicks are clothed in a woolly black down, the hair-like tips on back and head having a greenish sheen.

MARSH CRAKE   *Porzana pusilla*   *Pl. 24, p. 105*
Other name: Koitareke.
Description: 18 cm (7"). The smallest of our rails. Very secretive. Distinguished from Spotless Crake by white markings and brownish colouring. Upperparts brown spotted with white and streaked with black; breast pale blue-grey; flanks and abdomen barred with black and white. Bill, legs and feet brownish-green. Sexes similar. One flushed by a dog at Lake Wainono flew with rapid wingbeats for about 100 m, not rising more than a metre.
Voice: Call notes a harsh *krek-krek* or *creak-creak*. A quick jarring trill has also been described.
Habitat and range: A bird of swamps and the thick reedy margins of lakes up to over 350 m (Taupo), it has been widely reported from the main islands and recorded at Stewart and Chatham Islands, but is nowhere common. It falls an easy victim to introduced vermin.

The Marsh Crake ranges very widely over the Eastern Hemisphere. It has been divided into five subspecies, *P. p. affinis* being the name given to New Zealand birds.
Breeding: This small elusive rail obviously breeds in many swamps throughout the country; but although broods have been seen, a nest with eggs is seldom found. An egg from Awanui in the Buddle collection, now deposited in the Auckland War Memorial Museum, is dark olive brown. This tallies with eggs, clutch 7, in a nest studied in Southland. According to Sharland, the clutch in Tasmania is 4–8 and the eggs are brown, spotted olive. Eggs: October–December. Incubation period *c.* 20 days.

DUSKY MOORHEN   *Gallinula tenebrosa*   *Pl. 24. p. 105*
Description: 37 cm (14½"). Looks slightly smaller than a Coot. Generally slaty-black with olive brown tone on back and scapulars, which in a good light can assume a greenish sheen; underparts paler becoming almost white at vent; *undertail with dark centre but white at sides*. Frontal plate orange-red; bill red with yellow tip; legs greenish. These vivid colours are dulled in moulting adults. In subadults the colour of bill and shield varies from greenish-yellow to dark horn with a reddish tinge.

Moorhens feed in weedy shallows or on the edge of reed beds, sometimes diving but generally avoiding open water. They may also forage on land and to rest they may perch on low branches overhanging water. Both on land and water, the white sides of the tail are very conspicuous.
Voice: A sharp, explosive, high-pitched *koot* or *kurk*.
Habitat and range: Common in eastern Australia, excluding Tasmania; preferring fresh to salt water and readily adopting suburban habitats where there are parks with ponds. First recorded in New Zealand in August 1968 when a subadult, which later acquired adult plumage, was found on Lake Hayes.
Breeding: Not known to have bred in New Zealand. Could easily become established.

AUSTRALIAN COOT *Fulica atra* *Pl. 24, p. 105*
Description: 38 cm (15″). Plumage appears wholly black; actually upperparts are sooty black and underparts dark grey; *no white under tail. Bill* and *frontal shield* pale bluish-grey, *appearing creamy-white* at a distance; legs and feet steel grey with fleshy lobes.

Juveniles lack the frontal shield and have a dusky bill.

Flight laboured at take-off, as feet patter along the surface. Bobs its head while swimming. Dives frequently to bring up weed.
Voice: A variety of calls includes a harsh *crark-crark* and a noise very similar to the sound of someone's chopping with an axe, *kratack, krat, krat.*
Habitat and range: A cosmopolitan species, represented in Australia and Tasmania by the race *australis*. Rare but increasing in New Zealand, especially in the last two decades. The most aquatic of the rails, frequenting reed-fringed lakes both subalpine and lowland.

In the South Island Coots now occur sparingly from Southland to Marlborough. Breeding has been proved at Lake Hayes (1958), St. Anne's Lagoon, Cheviot (1961), Lakes Alexandrina and Macgregor (1962).

In the North Island Coots were found in 1954 at Tutira, where they have since bred successfully. They have now been reported from other lakes in Hawkes Bay; from Lake Wairarapa (1957); Lake Pupuke (1957-9), Lake Okareka (1962), Virginia Water, Wanganui (1962). The colonisation of other lakes on the Volcanic Plateau is now well on the way.

Gregarious in winter, the biggest flocks noted numbering *c.* 80 birds.
Breeding: Nests at Lake Hayes were placed on a solid foundation in a tangle of willow, made of willow rootlets and lined with raupo. Eggs October to November, 5-7, creamy-white evenly and sparsely marked with small and medium-sized black spots. Incubation *c.* 22 days. The dusky down of nestlings is strikingly tipped orange to orange-rufous; bill crimson with a white line. May be double or treble-brooded like the typical Eurasian race.

As the population on some lakes increased, clutch size decreased and few young were being reared.

PUKEKO *Porphyrio melanotus* *Pl. 24, p. 105*
Other names: Swamp-hen, Pukaki, Pook, Old Swampie.
Description: 51 cm (20″). The most conspicuous of our rails. Head black; upperparts black with green gloss; throat, neck, breast and flanks purplish-blue; abdomen and thighs black; *undertail coverts white. Massive bill and frontal plate scarlet*; legs and feet pale red or orange. Females are slightly smaller than males. Juveniles lack the iridescence and the bright colours.

Walks jauntily and delicately, flirting its tail. Can run fast and, if pressed, swims freely. Flight at first laboured with legs dangling, then strong. Habitually climbs about swamp vegetation. Has a parrot-like habit of sometimes holding its food firmly in one foot.

The species is prone to albinism, complete or partial. A colony containing several buff-coloured birds has been described from the Wairarapa.
Voice: An ear-piercing screech *kwee-ow* seems to be both an alarm note and also a contact note used, e.g. when Pukekos are flying high at night. A variety

of sounds emerges from a raupo-swamp which holds a colony of Pukekos; a drawn-out, almost booming *poo-koo-koo-koo*, a sighing *kwee-uk*; a bleating *kwairk*; an anxious *pee-ewk* and agitated *a-yik* or *k-yik* quickly repeated.

Habitat and range: Closely related to the Purple Gallinule which has a very wide range in the Old World. Apparently only locally common in New Zealand before 1850; but increased greatly in second half of nineteenth century and now plentiful in the main islands in swampy places up to 600 m from which it may emerge to raid crops or feed in open grassland, e.g. Rotoaira.

Often flies by night. Has recently colonised swamps on some inshore islands, e.g. Waiheke, Great Mercury; and has straggled to Three Kings, Fanal, Little Barrier, Mayor, Campbell Island. Resident on Raoul and Norfolk Islands.

Breeding: Frequently polygamous. The nest, a bulky structure, is normally in marshy surroundings but is sometimes ill-concealed. Eggs 4–7, buff or reddish-stone with dark brown, grey and reddish blotches all over; commonly August to March; but midwinter nesting has been recorded. Incubation period *c.* 25 days; apparently mostly done by male at least during the day-time. Chicks are clad in a silver-tipped black down.

TAKAHE   *Notornis mantelli*   *Pl. 24, p. 105*

Other name: Moho.

Description: 63 cm (25″). A ponderous, flightless, brilliantly coloured gallinule with massive bill and legs. Head, neck, breast and flanks iridescent indigo blue; shoulders peacock blue; mantle, back and rump suffused with shades of green; wings blue (greater coverts) and green (lesser coverts); thighs and abdomen bluish-black; undertail-coverts white. Frontal shield and base of bill scarlet; rest of bill pink; feet red. The plumage of the immature bird contains more brown and is without the brilliant gloss. Sexes similar.

Voice: Alarm call *oomf* repeated slowly. Possibly a contact call is a weka-like duet, *coo-eet* many times repeated by a pair as a two-part canon (Fleming). The cry of the chick is a slow *wee-a* or a repeated wheedle, the parent meanwhile keeping contact by the *cowp-cowp* call.

Habitat and range: Known from the North Island only by sub-fossil bones, though it may have persisted till the nineteenth century. Formerly ranged over much of the South Island, but only four specimens were obtained (1849, 1851, 1879, 1898), all in the south-west. Dramatically rediscovered in 1948 by Dr. Orbell, the Takahe has since been the subject of much expert study. It is now known to survive only west of Lake Te Anau in the Murchison and Kepler Ranges, where its main habitat is the tussock grassland of the valleys at 600–1000 m a.s.l. More especially in winter it enters the adjacent beech forests.

Breeding: The nest is a kind of bower between tussocks of *Danthonia*. Eggs October to March, 1–2, dull cream with brown and mauve blotches. Chicks are covered with a black down and have a white patch on the fore-edge of the wing.

BLACK-TAILED NATIVE HEN   *Tribonyx ventralis*   *Pl. 24, p. 105*

Description: 35 cm (14″). Generally dusky, considerably smaller than a Pukeko and not unlike a handsome little bantam. Upperparts dark bronze brown;

throat and breast bluish-grey; abdomen black; *conspicuous white spotting on the flanks*; frontal shield and upper mandible dark pea-green; lower mandible orange-red, green towards tip; *legs brick red*.

Runs but seldom flies. Tail carried erect and continuously flicked.

Habitat and range: An Australian species ranging widely in swampy districts, but apparently rather scarce near the south-east coast and replaced in Tasmania by a much larger water-hen, the non-flying *Tribonyx mortieri*.

This Australian Water-hen is known as a nomad, prone to mass movements. Numbers will suddenly arrive in a district after rains and may disappear just as suddenly. The overflow of such irruptions may occasionally reach New Zealand, but the only satisfactory records are of a bird shot at Colac Bay, Southland, in June 1923; and of one which frequented the Tukituki river-bed, near Patangata, Hawkes Bay, in 1957 and 1958. Other specimens lack authenticating data.

WADERS

After the Petrels, the Waders are the largest order of birds on the New Zealand list. They are primarily birds of the coast, though some, e.g. Pied Stilt, Black Stilt, Banded Dotterel, Wrybill, South Island Pied Oystercatcher, move inland to breed, even high into the mountains, and two, the Spur-winged Plover and the Black-fronted Dotterel, are hardly shore-birds at all.

There can be few estuaries on the long New Zealand coastline which are not frequented or visited by a variety of waders in the course of the year; and the study of wader-migration is perhaps one of the most fascinating aspects of ornithology. For the benefit of the beginner, some of the more important areas where waders may be successfully studied are now briefly mentioned.

In the far north, Parengarenga, Rangaunu and Kaipara have begun to reveal their secrets and have richly repaid regular watching. Manukau and the Firth of Thames are the largest areas which have been studied systematically. Much has been published both on the commoner and the rarer waders for which they provide ideal feeding grounds. Where Bar-tailed Godwits occur in large flocks, other waders will be found. Ohiwa and Tauranga are known as good 'godwit harbours' in the Bay of Plenty, and so are Raglan, Aotea and Kawhia west of the Waikato. The sandy beaches and river mouths of the south-west and south-east coasts of the North Island are visited by many passing migrants, and have their quota of breeding Stilts, Dotterels and Oystercatchers. In the South Island, the vast flats inside Farewell Spit have proved an area of major importance. Nelson is a well-known 'godwit harbour'. Westland has received little attention, but a harbour such as Okarito must have great possibilities. On the east coast of the South Island, the many river mouths are admirable, but little-studied wader habitats. The Heathcote-Avon estuary is dominated by impressive numbers of Godwits and Oystercatchers. Lake Ellesmere was a wonderfully rich area in the first half of this century, when Edgar Stead was collecting information on the birds of Canterbury, and probably still is. Otago Harbour and nearby inlets attract many waders both resident and migrant. In the far south the lagoons and estuaries along Foveaux Strait support a large and varied population, the study of which has proved most rewarding and has sprung several surprises on its devotees.

For the correct identification of waders it is essential to note not only size, shape, general colour and behaviour; but also the length and shape of the bill; markings on back, tail or wings; and, if possible, voice. An added complication is that the plumage of many species varies according to age and season. An obvious example is the Banded Dotterel. Adults in breeding dress may be quite unmistakable; but adults in the post-nuptial moult, when the bands have disappeared, and juveniles look very different. Much the same is true of other species of

---

PLATE 23 Banded Rail (p.97); Auckland Island Rail (p.98); Weka (p.96).

PLATE 23

AUCKLAND ISLAND RAIL 21 cm

BANDED RAIL 30 cm

SOUTH ISLAND WEKA (Black) 53 cm

SOUTH ISLAND WEKA (Buff)

STEWART ISLAND WEKA

NORTH ISLAND WEKA

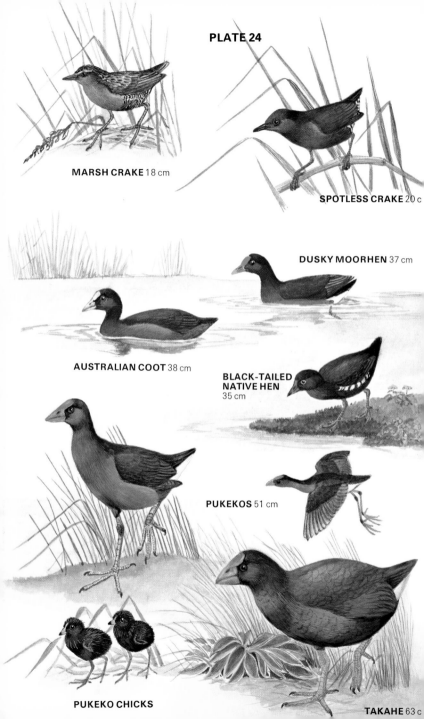

PLATE 24

MARSH CRAKE 18 cm

SPOTLESS CRAKE 20 c

DUSKY MOORHEN 37 cm

AUSTRALIAN COOT 38 cm

BLACK-TAILED
NATIVE HEN
35 cm

PUKEKOS 51 cm

PUKEKO CHICKS

TAKAHE 63 c

dotterels which sometimes stray to New Zealand from Australia or Asia and may attach themselves in summer or autumn to flocks of Banded Dotterels which contain moulting adults and bandless juveniles. Only after a very close and critical scrutiny will these rare visitors be acceptably identified. Even the most experienced observers have to check and re-check such occurrences.

Several species also of the migratory arctic waders show striking differences between the comparatively drab colouring of adults in eclipse or first-year birds and the vivid reds, deep blacks and rich variegated spangling of breeding dress. Between January and April the plumages of adult male Godwits, Knots, Curlew Sandpipers, Red-necked Stints, Golden and Grey Plovers, undergo a spectacular change. The plumage of the females too becomes more colourful. Other more subtle changes are less easily detected, e.g. the development of crescentic spots on the flanks of Sharp-tailed Sandpipers or an increase of barring on the underparts of Tattlers. Traces of nuptial colouring are still visible in the plumage of some adults when they return to New Zealand in September or October.

Geographically, the waders of New Zealand fall into three groups:

(a) Those which breed in New Zealand.

(b) Those which breed in Australia and have strayed across the Tasman Sea, perhaps to become established in New Zealand, e.g. Spurwinged Plover, Black-fronted Dotterel.

(c) The trans-equatorial migrants which breed in northern Asia, Siberia and north-west America and, by flying south, avoid winter in the northern hemisphere and enjoy the temperate summer of New Zealand.

(a) Of those which breed in New Zealand, the commonest are Banded Dotterel, Pied Stilt and South Island Pied Oystercatcher. All are migratory within New Zealand so that, if the birdwatcher lives on the coast or is able to visit an estuary, he should soon be able to recognise these three distinctive birds even if they do not breed in his district. It should perhaps be mentioned that even in the North Island, the commonest oystercatcher is the one which breeds on the riverbeds of the South Island and flocks of uniformly marked black and white oystercatchers, occurring in northern New Zealand even in summer, are likely to be migrants from the south.

Some of the waders which breed only in New Zealand must be considered among the rarer birds of the world. The population of Wrybills, estimated from counts of wintering flocks in the northern harbours may be 5000. Much scarcer are the Red-breasted Dotterel with perhaps 1500 individuals, the Variable (Northern) Oystercatcher, the Black Stilt, the Shore Plover now confined to Rangatira Island in the Chathams and the primitive snipe with its four or five subspecies on remote sub-antarctic islands.

Regular watching of an estuary where migratory waders pause to rest and feed is the kind of field-work which can prove most rewarding. Outside Canterbury there are curiously few records of the Wrybill in the South Island. On its migrations, it occurs on both west and east coasts of the North Island. The Red-

---

PLATE 24 Marsh Crake (p.100); Spotless Crake (p.99); Dusky Moorhen (p.100); Australian Coot (p.101); Black-tailed Native Hen (p.102); Pukeko (p.101); Takahe (p.102).

breasted Dotterel is a puzzling bird with a curious distribution. The two areas where it is known to breed are 1200 km apart and there are few recent reports of this fine dotterel between Foveaux Strait in the south and the Waikato estuary in the north.

The oystercatchers of New Zealand are a notoriously difficult family. Something has already been said of the South Island Pied Oystercatcher, a successful bird with distinctive habits and the representative in New Zealand of the common oystercatcher of the northern hemisphere. Larger and rather scarce is the Variable Oystercatcher, a bird of unstable plumage characters, some being black, some fully pied, while there are all sorts of intermediate phases with smudgy markings. The ranges of this and the Black Oystercatcher overlap. It is taxonomically convenient and probably biologically correct to unite the Variable and Black Oystercatchers and regard them as a polymorphic species, with the black form dominant in the south and the mixed form most numerous in the north, though nowhere abundant enough to form big flocks. Quite distinct also is the oystercatcher which inhabits the Chatham Islands.

The Black Stilt which some ornithological workers consider to have been the original stilt of New Zealand before the invasion of the Pied Stilt from Australia, is known to breed in only a few loose colonies which may total 30—40 pairs.

The Spur-winged Plover and Black-fronted Dotterel are examples of vigorous colonisers. Both are steadily extending their ranges.

(b) The field-naturalist should find it worthwhile to familiarise himself with the appearance of the commoner plovers which breed in south-east Australia just in case he is lucky enough to encounter one or more of them as stragglers. In recent years a Red-capped Dotterel has been found sitting on eggs in Canterbury and others have been reported from widely scattered localities. Climate and terrain being suitable, these small plovers could become established as breeding species. Indeed they may already have taken the first steps towards becoming naturalised New Zealanders, as other species have done. The beautiful Australian Avocet evidently bred in the South Island in the middle of the nineteenth century. Probably collectors, rather than a lack of suitable habitats, are to be blamed for frustrating its efforts to become established. Hopes were raised when one spent two years, 1968-70, near Westport.

(c) The third group of waders comprises about forty species, and they form a very important part of the bird life of our tidal flats which, without them, would be comparatively barren for long periods of the year. These far-travelling visitors come from northern Asia, Siberia and north-west America, arriving from about mid-September and departing in March and April, though flocks of immature non-breeding birds remain throughout our mild winter, growing up and conserving their strength for the time when they, too, will have to face a flight of 9000–13000 km to reach their breeding grounds.

At least twelve species of waders may be considered regular annual migrants from arctic or sub-arctic regions. Of these, the most numerous is the Eastern Bar-tailed Godwit. Absolute protection came in time to save it; for the experience of other lands has shown that the larger shore-birds which form dense flocks are very vulnerable to shooting.[1]

[1] In America the Eskimo Curlew was shot virtually out of existence and the Hudsonian Godwit whose numbers sank dangerously low is still rare.

Godwits are sometimes referred to as 'snipe' or 'curlew'. Both these names are quite incorrect. A constant companion of the Godwit is the Knot. Mixed flocks in favoured localities often contain many thousands of these two 'fellow-travellers'. Third in order of abundance are Turnstones and after them Eastern Golden Plovers. In a few chosen coastal districts, these two very different birds regularly form sizeable flocks and feed together.

An examination of the classified summarised notes which are published yearly in *Notornis* shows that Sharp-tailed Sandpipers, Red-necked Stints, Curlew Sandpipers, Far Eastern Curlews, Whimbrels, Pectoral and Terek Sandpipers and Siberian Tattlers are regular migrants in small numbers; and few years now pass without reports of Large Sand Dotterel, Greenshank, Asiatic Black-tailed and Hudsonian Godwits. Especially in the north, the patient watcher has a fair chance of finding some of the more unusual visitors which, drifted by the wind or caught up with a flock of strong-flying regular migrants, have missed Australia or overshot the normal southern limits of their kind.

The name of Edgar Stead, the great Canterbury naturalist and collector, is closely linked with the discovery that the migration of several species of arctic waders could take them to New Zealand and indeed did so regularly. His impressive list of 'firsts' includes Little Whimbrel (1900), Hudsonian Godwit (1902), Curlew Sandpiper (1902), Red-necked Stint (1902), Pectoral Sandpiper (1903), Sanderling (1917), Red-necked Phalarope (1929). It is unfortunate that, since the golden age of Edgar Stead, Lake Ellesmere where most of these birds were collected has not been the scene of much critical ornithology. Fortunately the study of the migratory shore-birds has been maintained with increasing keenness elsewhere, and, while much has been learnt about the numbers and movements of the commoner species, several arctic waders new to New Zealand have been found and the evidence is that some of them reach New Zealand much more frequently than was formerly supposed. As the result of painstaking field work, Auckland ornithologists now have several 'firsts' based on sight records to their credit, viz. Large Sand Dotterel (1943), Grey Plover (1946), Siberian Tattler (1950), Terek Sandpiper (1951), Asiatic Black-tailed Godwit (1952), Oriental Dotterel (1954), Marsh Sandpiper (1959), Broad-Billed Sandpiper (1960). The first Least Sandpiper to be reported in New Zealand was found by R. H. D. Stidolph in Hawkes Bay in 1952. Farewell Spit produced a Mongolian Dotterel in 1961; Porirua a Yellowlegs in 1962; Taranaki a Common Sandpiper in 1964; Manawatu Great Knots and Manukau an Upland Plover in 1967; Miranda a Ringed Plover in 1970. Several species of small sandpipers breed across the sub-arctic wastes which border the Bering Sea. Besides the regular Red-necked Stint, at least six of these may reach New Zealand as vagrants. Correct identification in the field is very difficult and a challenge to the most acute observer. Nor is the list of possibilities exhausted, e.g. Wood Sandpiper is still missing from the New Zealand list. Careful scrutiny of flocks of Wrybills in northern harbours has often led to the discovery of stray sandpipers and plovers which seem to seek the sanctuary afforded by the Wrybills as they trustingly rest in compact groups.

One unusual experience which sometimes happens to the observer of shore-birds in New Zealand is that he is able at the same time to watch closely related species or subspecies, the southern limits of whose ranges overlap in New Zealand. Siberian and American Pectoral Sandpipers have been encountered together again and again at Lake Ellesmere, Manukau Harbour and the Firth of Thames and perhaps elsewhere. Two forms of the Black-tailed Godwit, Hudsonian and Asiatic, have been noted within a few yards of each other in Manukau. Dark-backed American Whimbrels have been found consorting with the pale-rumped Asiatics.

WADERS CLASSIFIED ACCORDING TO
SIZE AND BREEDING CENTRE

Size	*New Zealand (a)* *Australia (b)*	*Northern Asia, Siberia, North-west America*
Very big		Far Eastern Curlew Bristle-thighed Curlew
Big	S.I. Pied Oystercatcher (*a*) Variable Oystercatcher (*a*) Black Oystercatcher (*a*) Chatham Island Oystercatcher (*a*) Spur-winged Plover (*a, b*) Pied Stilt (*a, b*) Black Stilt (*a*) Red-necked Avocet (*b*) (*formerly a*)	Asiatic Whimbrel American Whimbrel Bar-tailed Godwit Hudsonian Godwit Asiatic Black-tailed Godwit Greenshank
Medium	Red-breasted Dotterel (*a*)	Grey Plover Eastern Golden Plover Oriental Dotterel Little Whimbrel Lesser Yellowlegs Marsh Sandpiper Wandering Tattler Grey-tailed Tattler Upland Sandpiper Ruff Turnstone Japanese Snipe Knot Great Knot Oriental Pratincole

Classified List of Waders (continued)

Size	New Zealand (*a*) Australia (*b*)	Northern Asia, Siberia North-west America
Small	Banded Dotterel (*a*) Red-capped Dotterel (*b*, ?*a*) Black-fronted Dotterel (*a*, *b*) Shore Plover (*a*) Wrybill (*a*) Sub-antarctic Snipe (4 insular races) (*a*) Chatham Island Snipe (*a*)	Large Sand Dotterel Mongolian Dotterel Ringed Plover Terek Sandpiper Common Sandpiper Sharp-tailed Sandpiper Pectoral Sandpiper Curlew Sandpiper Dunlin Baird's Sandpiper White-rumped Sandpiper Sanderling Broad-billed Sandpiper Grey Phalarope Red-necked Phalarope
Very small		Red-necked Stint Least Sandpiper Long-toed Stint Western Sandpiper Semi-palmated Sandpiper

OYSTERCATCHERS: Haematopodidae

Oystercatchers are sturdily built waders, black or pied, with red or pinkish legs and strong orange-red bills (7.5 cm). Hence in some districts they are commonly called Redbills.

SOUTH ISLAND PIED OYSTERCATCHER *Haematopus finschi*

Pl. 25, p. 112

Other names: Torea, Redbill, Pied Piper.

Description: 46 cm (18″). The plumage of the South Island Pied Oystercatcher presents a strikingly clear-cut pattern of black and white, especially in flight. Head, neck, chest, upper back, wings and tail black; underparts, wing-bar and lower back vividly white. Females are slightly larger and have longer bills. Immature birds have bills with dusky tips and their legs are paler.

By far the most plentiful of the oystercatchers of New Zealand even in the North Island.

Voice: A shrill far-carrying *hu-eep* or *kleep*. Song, a long musical piping with considerable variation, commonly heard on breeding grounds and sometimes in northern winter-quarters; similar to the piping ceremony described by

Huxley for the closely related European Oystercatcher (*ostralegus*), but needs studying in New Zealand.

Habitat and range: Breeds inland in the South Island only (not Stewart Island) —not common west of the Alps. When inland may feed on arable land. After nesting forms large flocks at estuaries and on tidal flats. While the bulk of the population stays on the east and north coasts of the South Island in winter, some even going to Paterson Inlet in Stewart Island, many thousands move north to Auckland and Northland, a few annually reaching Parengarenga. The northward movement begins in December, reaches a peak January-February and continues till April. The southward movement starts in July. Flocks of immature non-breeders summer in the northern harbours.

A thriving race which appears still to be increasing. The size of wintering flocks near Auckland has shown a spectacular increase since 1940.

Breeding: A fairly early nester on river-beds and lake shores up to 1000 m. A rising population now breeds above the tree-line on sub-alpine tundra up to 1800 m. Eggs September to November; clutch 2–3; incubation period 24–28 days; fledging *c*. 5 weeks.

VARIABLE OYSTERCATCHER   *Haematopus unicolor*   *Pl. 25, p. 112*

Local names: Torea, Northern Oystercatcher, Mudpigeon, Black Oystercatcher, Musselpicker.

Description: 48 cm (19″). The plumage of the oystercatchers (formerly called *reischeki*) which breed on northern beaches is very variable. Pied examples can usually be distinguished from *finschi* by their larger size – very marked in some individuals – less angular and more 'humped up' carriage and by the smudgy blurring of their markings. A few are almost as pied as *finschi*; but the contrasting pattern is not as clear-cut; and even in the most pied specimens the white recess on the 'shoulder' which *finschi* shows so clearly when standing, is seldom present; nor are the wing-bar and lower back so conspicuously white. Some show only a trace of white on the belly; some are entirely black. It has been stated that the black form of the Variable Oystercatcher is a browny black and lacks the purple gloss of true *unicolor*, but this needs verification. The plumage of black oystercatchers breeding on the northern coast of the North Island can be distinctly glossy; and black oystercatchers seen in flocks on Stewart Island are not noticeably glossy. Females are usually larger and have longer and more pointed bills. Dull colouring of legs and bill distinguishes young birds in their first winter.

Voice: Very similar to that of *finschi*; call note *kee-eep* perhaps a little huskier and less piercing. Piping ceremony accompanies pair formations and courtship.

Habitat and range: A bird of the coast frequenting both sandy beaches and rocks. Occurs most commonly near sandy estuaries among the extensive dunes of Northland. Some pairs appear to occupy their territory throughout the year; but there is some local wandering; small flocks may be formed and odd *unicolor* may be sometimes found among the big flocks of visiting *finschi*. On Coromandel and in the Bay of Plenty the pied form of the Variable Oystercatcher is much outnumbered by the black. In the South Island smudgily pied oystercatchers occur as far south as Kaikoura and Fiordland but the dominant form is black. The oystercatchers which breed on the coast of Otago, Southland and

Stewart Island are mostly typical *unicolor*.

Breeding: Rather a late nester even in the north. Eggs commonly December-January, stone-buff spotted with dark brown; normal clutch 3. Both sexes incubate. Where variable oystercatchers occur, it is not unusual for one of a breeding pair to be black and the other pied.

On Stewart Island some pairs of *unicolor* are almost troglodytic. They hold narrow territories in small rocky bays overhung with trees and when danger threatens may secrete their brood in caves.

CHATHAM ISLAND OYSTERCATCHER *Haematopus chathamensis*
                                                                            Pl. 25, p. 112

Description: 48 cm (19″). A pied oystercatcher without any tendency to melanism although the distinctions—and these are constant—between this form and *finschi* are all additional dark elements—viz., the line of colour demarcation on the chest is less distinct; the area of white on rump and lower back is smaller; there is less white in the pattern of the wing. Important characteristics are its stouter short bill and larger feet correlated with the rock-dwelling habit.

In plumage and behaviour this form seems to be more closely related to *unicolor* than to *finschi*. It has also been linked with *longirostris* of Australia.

Habitat and range: Confined to the Chatham Islands where it is widely distributed around the coast. Sedentary, non-migratory and strongly territorial; apparently not forming flocks.

Breeding: Does not appear to have been studied.

PLOVERS AND DOTTERELS: Charadriidae

SPUR-WINGED PLOVER *Lobibyx novaehollandiae*   *Pl. 26, p. 113*

Description: 38 cm (15″). A true 'lapwing' strikingly patterned, quite unlike any other plover in New Zealand. Suggestive of a small heron, as it rises or flies low with slow, deliberate beats of its rounded wings. Brown above, white below; crown and shoulders black; bill and face-wattles yellow; legs reddish. In flight the wings are seen to be whitish beneath with a dark band along the rear edge; rump white; tail white with black tip. Bony spur (1 cm) on wing at carpal flexure. Has a sedate walk and also a nimble, tiptoe run.

Voice: A noisy grating rattle variously interpreted as *kitter-kitter-kitter*, *rikka-rikka*, or *kerrick-kurrick*, also described as a long crackling call in a descending scale. This call is commonly used when a passing Harrier is being mobbed.

Habitat and range: A common breeding species of south-east Australia and Tasmania, which *c.* 1940 became firmly established in Southland whence it has now spread north so that it breeds over much of the South Island, occasionally up to 1000 m a.s.l. By the mid-1970s the invasion of the North Island was well under way; and a few pairs were breeding annually in districts bordering Cook Strait, and possibly up the east coast as far as Waiapu. Southwards two reached Campbell Island in 1945. Others have been reported at Stewart Island since 1967.

Flocking takes place after nesting season, but no large-scale movements so far noted in New Zealand.

In the South Island these plovers may congregate in fields of root crops while Black-billed Gulls and Black-fronted Terns are hawking insects overhead. They also visit the seashore and have been seen feeding in a runnel among gulls of three species, and resting among Godwits at a high tide roost.

Breeding: An early nester in open country, sometimes on dry stony ground, usually near a swamp. Normal clutch 4. Young sometimes hatched by August, but some pairs still have eggs in December. Incubation period *c.* 28 days. Both sexes incubate.

EASTERN GOLDEN PLOVER *Pluvialis fulva*   *Pl. 28, p. 121*

Other names: Least Golden Plover, Pacific (Asiatic) Golden Plover.

Description: 25 cm (10″). A medium-sized plover without any salient characteristics in juvenile or winter plumage; mottled brown and buff above with the golden suffusion showing more clearly as breeding dress is assumed; throat and breast grey and yellowish-buff; eyebrow pale buff; underparts buffy white; tail and rump like back showing no white; underwing and axillaries uniform grey. Summer and winter plumages are very different. In February some adults start to show black on the underparts and the moult into nuptial plumage is complete by April when they leave; forehead broadly white and line over eye extending down side of neck to white patch on breast white; lores, spot in front of eye, cheeks, middle of breast and abdomen black. Bill black; legs slaty grey; rump and tail appear dark in flight and there is no wing-bar. Adults may retain traces of nuptial black when they return to New Zealand. The flight is rapid with strong, regular wing-beats. An alert and shy species.

Voice: Described as a shrill but melodious double whistle, *tuill tuill*, a clear sounding *kleee-yee*, or a harsh whistled *queedle*.

Habitat and range: A summer visitor from Northern Asia and perhaps Alaska, arriving from September onwards and frequenting certain favoured stretches of coast every year from Parengarenga to Bluff; and on Kermadec and Norfolk Islands. Small parties have reached the Auckland Islands. Flocks sometimes fly a short way inland to marshes, ploughland and pastures, where herbage is thin and short. In some districts frequently accompanied by Turnstones. Occurs usually in small parties, but flocks of more than 200 birds occur. Flocks resting at full-tide do not form compact groups but are usually in a straggling line, apart from other shore-birds.

There are few reports of these plovers in New Zealand between May and August, but subadults in partial breeding dress normally overwinter on islands in the tropical Pacific.

Fulva is usually treated as a race of the American Golden Plover (*P. dominica*), but because of marked differences in plumage and behaviour it has strong claims to full specific status.

PLATE 25 South Island Pied Oystercatcher (p.109); Variable Oystercatcher (p.110); Black Oystercatcher (p.110); Chatham Island Oystercatcher (p.111); Pied Stilt (p.139); Black Stilt (p.139); Red-necked Avocet (p.140).

PLATE 25

SOUTH ISLAND
PIED OYSTERCATCHER
46 cm

VARIABLE OYSTERCATCHERS
48 cm

BLACK
OYSTERCATCHER
48 cm

CHATHAM ISLAND
OYSTERCATCHER 48 cm

BLACK STILT
38 cm

imm.

PIED STILTS
38 cm

RED-NECKED
AVOCETS 45 cm

PLATE 26

WRYBILLS 20 cm

winter

sum

BLACK-FRONTED DOTTEREL
18 cm

SHORE PLOVER 20 cm

imm.

winter

RED-CAPPED DOTTERELS 15 cm

BANDED DOTTERELS
18 cm

summer

NEW ZEALAND DOTTERELS 27 cm

winter

summer

SPUR-WINGED PLOVER 38 cm

GREY PLOVER   *Pluvialis squatarola*   *Pl. 28, p. 121*
Description: 28 cm (11″). Distinctly larger and lighter-coloured than an Eastern
Golden Plover and with a robuster bill; but not always easily distinguishable
on the ground. Upperparts brown dappled with white; tail barred white and
brown with a *broad white band* across the upper tail; underparts white except
the *black axillaries* which, in flight, are diagnostic; but if the bird is flying away
from the observer, they are not easily seen; the white upper tail also is an
important aid in identification; whitish wing-bar visible in flight; bill black;
legs ash-grey. Grey Plovers seen in New Zealand are likely to be in the winter
plumage described above. In very handsome summer plumage adults have
back spangled silver and black, and underparts black. A bird of the tideline,
unlikely to be found far from the seashore.
Voice: A rather melancholy trisyllabic *hee-oo-ee* or *hee-er-ee*.
Habitat and range: Perhaps the most cosmopolitan of the true plovers. A
circumpolar breeder, migrating south; some birds reaching the southern tips
of the great continents. Rare in Tasmania.
    Since the first confirmed sighting in the Firth of Thames (1948) single birds
have been reported from most northern harbours. There is also a wide scatter of
records from Grassmere, Southland lagoons, and even Chatham and
Macquarie Islands. The most popular venue seems to be Farewell Spit, where
several have been found since 1961 and three were watched together in January
1977.

BANDED DOTTEREL   *Charadrius bicinctus*   *Pl. 26, p. 113*
Other names: Double-banded Dotterel, Mountain Plover, Tuturiwhatu,
Pohowera.
Description: 18 cm (7″). A handsome small plover easily recognised in breeding
dress, i.e. from May to January when both male and female have *two bands*—
one black and narrow on the lower neck, the other chestnut and wider on the
breast. Males are a little bigger and more showy than females, but the intensity
of the colour and distinctness of the bands vary considerably. Forehead white,
edged above with black; a black band from bill towards eye; some white above
and below eye but facial markings show some variation. Upperparts brown;
underparts white; bill black; legs dull greenish yellow or yellowish grey. In
eclipse plumage, February to May, the bands disappear or are much reduced.
Juveniles in their first autumn have upperparts sandy and speckled, are not so
white underneath and lack the pectoral bands.
    Occurs in flocks of some size from January to July scattered over tidal flats
or short-cropped pastures near the sea.
Voice: An incisive *chip chip* or staccato high-pitched *pit pit* is commonly used
by pairs on territory and by birds in flocks. Courting and breeding males trill
excitedly—hence Maori name 'tuturiwhatu'. A rippling liquid *qreep* and a

---

PLATE 26 Black-fronted Dotterel (p.114); Wrybill (p.119); Shore Plover (p.119); Red-capped
Dotterel (p.115); Banded Dotterel (p.113); New Zealand Dotterel (p.115); Spur-winged Plover
(p.111).

high-pitched whistling *twirp* have been described (Moon).

Habitat and range: The most numerous and widespread of the smaller plovers which breed in New Zealand. But comparatively few breed in northern districts, viz. doubtful if fifty pairs nest within 100 km of Auckland city, though large flocks appear in autumn. Common also at the Chatham Islands. A few pairs breed on off-shore islands, e.g. Great Mercury, Kapiti. A larger race, apparently non-migratory, inhabits the Auckland Islands.

After nesting, these dotterels move down to the coast, form flocks and begin to move northwards but some winter in the South Island. In early January, flocks numbering hundreds appear in districts where few or none have bred. Many cross the Tasman to Australia where between February and August they occur on the south coast from Queensland to Swan River. The trans-Tasman migrations of the Banded Dotterel make it unique among waders. Nesting in Australia has never been proved, though some non-breeders remain throughout the normal nesting season. Occurs on passage at Norfolk and Lord Howe Islands. Regular migrant in small numbers to Fiji.

Breeding: Some nest on ocean beaches but most nest inland on riverbeds, beside lakes, sometimes on ploughed land, sometimes in arid or stony fields or on mountain slopes up to 1800 m. Eggs August to January, pyriform, greyish or greenish, closely marked with dark brown and black spots or blotches. Normal clutch 3. Incubation period 25–30 days. Both sexes incubate.

BLACK-FRONTED DOTTEREL   *Charadrius melanops*   *Pl. 26, p. 113*

Description: 18 cm (7″). A small distinctive plover whose plumage presents a sharp contrast of black, white, tawny and red. Upperparts brown; forehead, eye-line and *V-shaped breast-band* black; eye with bright red orbital ring: a white line passes above the eye and round the back of the head; throat white; *shoulders deep chestnut red*; wing-tips black; broad white wing-bar visible in flight; *bill bright red, tipped black*; *legs thin, red*. Does not assume an obvious eclipse plumage. On wing most undotterel-like. Flight jerky and dipping, recalling that of a short-tailed passerine. Runs very fast. Seems to feed mostly at water's edge.

Voice: A high-pitched metallic whistle or soft *tink tink* of a considerably higher pitch than that of a Banded Dotterel. Also a fast clicking *tik-tik-tik-tik*.

Habitat and range: Widely distributed and plentiful in Australia, where it is a bird of the inland rarely seen on estuaries or sea beaches. River shingle and the dried caked mud at the edges of lagoons are favoured resorts. Often forms small flocks in winter. Uncommon in Tasmania.

First recorded in New Zealand in 1954, near Napier, the Black-fronted Dotterel is now strongly established in Hawkes Bay, where breeding was suspected in 1958 and proved in 1961 (several pairs). By the mid-1970s these dotterels had colonised several shingle rivers in the southern half of the North Island, and the lower reaches of some South Island rivers. Flocks are now formed in autumn. Stragglers have been seen in the north of the country.

Breeding: Nests seen in Hawkes Bay have been on river-shingle usually a few metres from the water's edge. The nest may be well formed of small pebbles carefully collected. Eggs September to January, pyriform, heavily marked; but rather variable, occasionally yellowish. Typical clutch 3.

RED-CAPPED DOTTEREL *Charadrius ruficapillus* *Pl. 26, p. 113*

Description: 15 cm (6″). An obvious dotterel, distinctly smaller than the common Banded Dotterel. Upperparts light greyish-brown; outer tail-coverts white, centre dark-brown; *crown of head and nape rusty red*; forehead broadly white, bordered above by a narrow black line; lores black; underparts white; a black and rufous patch at the sides of the neck; bill and legs black. Females lack the reddish head and are generally duller.

Voice: Call note a faint *wit-wit-wit* or *twink-twink*.

Habitat and range: The commonest of the small Australian dotterels, usually treated as a race of the very widely distributed Kentish Plover (*C. alexandrinus*). A very rare wanderer to New Zealand. A few recent sightings in Manukau Harbour when Banded Dotterels are on the move.

Breeding: On the Ashley river-bed (1947-9) it appears that a female mated with a male Banded Dotterel and young were reared showing characters clearly derived from both parents.

NEW ZEALAND DOTTEREL *Charadrius obscurus* *Pl. 26, p. 113*

Other name: Red-breasted Dotterel.

Description: 27 cm (10½″). A squat, broad-winged dotterel with a robust bill. Sexes in winter similar. Upperparts brown, feathers with paler edges; forehead and superciliary streak white; dark line through eye, thinning or fading towards bill; underparts whitish or unevenly rufous. Males in breeding dress, June to December, have red breasts and bellies, the red varying in extent and in intensity from dark chestnut to a pale cinnamon. (Latham's name, 'Dusky Plover', is evidently based on a darkly red-breasted male.) Females, too, may show some red, but some breeding pairs show very little colour on the underparts at all. Bill black; legs grey.

Voice: The common call is a cricket-like *krik* or *kriki*. Breeding birds in flight make a variety of sharp calls, *weet, huit, rit, turr* or *torrt* with the *rr* emphasised. When they have young, an excited screaming may accompany the 'rodent run' during distraction display.

Habitat and range: A bird of very curious distribution, apparently with two breeding populations separated by about 1200 km and living under very different climatic conditions, one in the north from the Aotea harbour and Bay of Plenty to Spirits Bay, with a few pairs on offshore islands, e.g. Waiheke, Great Mercury, Great Barrier, Cavallis; the other on Stewart Island and the coast of Southland, with no known breeding pairs in between these populations, although a few are normally present on Farewell Spit; and strays visit the coasts of Manawatu and Wairarapa. Frequents both ocean beaches and also sandy flats in harbours and estuaries, often in autumn and winter visiting grassy paddocks near the sea. Formerly said to have occurred high in the mountains and still does on bare tops over 500 m on Stewart Island.

Rather a sedentary species, but first-year birds are known to wander locally. No evidence that southern birds move north. Forms small flocks in late summer; but one recorded gathering of 218+ in late May at Old Neck, Stewart Island, may represent the normal winter flocking of the southern population.

Breeding: In the north, breeds among coastal dunes preferably not far from running water or on sandy spits at estuaries, sometimes on pebbly beaches or

NEW ZEALAND DOTTEREL, winter

MONGOLIAN DOTTEREL, winter

ORIENTAL DOTTEREL, winter

BLACK-FRONTED DOTTEREL, summer

LARGE SAND DOTTEREL, winter

RED-CAPPED DOTTEREL, summer

BANDED DOTTEREL, winter

BANDED DOTTEREL, summer

EASTERN GOLDEN PLOVER, winter

EASTERN GOLDEN PLOVER, summer

GREY PLOVER, winter

GREY PLOVER. summer

shell-banks. Eggs August to February, buff or olive, heavily blotched with black and dark brown. Normal clutch 3. Incubation period 28–31 days. Both sexes incubate.

ORIENTAL DOTTEREL   *Charadrius veredus*   *Pl. 28, p. 121*
Description: 25 cm (10″). About the same size as a New Zealand Dotterel or Eastern Golden Plover, but the *upright carriage* and *longer legs* are distinctive. Upperparts smooth greyish-brown; underparts off-white or very pale buff; forehead and eyebrow line dull white or pale brown; crown and sides of face dark brown; throat whitish; breast sandy buff or washed grey; abdomen whitish; no white on tail. A dark line shows along the edge of the primaries; legs dull yellow and rather long; bill brown and slender. In nuptial dress, the breast-band is chestnut and black and the legs become a clear yellow.

The head is held high and bobbed when the bird is alarmed. Runs and feeds actively.
Voice: A piping *klink* heard as a flock rises.
Habitat and range: Seldom seen on sea-beaches, preferring dried mud and sandy wastes near lagoons. A very rare summer migrant to New Zealand from northern Asia, reported Raoul Island 1908 (1), Firth of Thames 1954-5 (flock of 10), and *c.* 5 subsequent sightings of single birds south to Manukau Harbour. Should be looked for loosely attached to flocks of other species of dotterels or plovers.

LARGE SAND DOTTEREL   *Charadrius leschenaulti*   *Pl. 28, p. 121*
Other names: Greater Sand Plover, Large-billed Dotterel.
Description: 22 cm (8½″). Rather larger and leggier than a Banded Dotterel with a conspicuously white forehead and a *stout black bill* (2.5 cm), a *blackish patch in front of and around eye*; lores grey; pale superciliary stripe; upperparts brownish grey, markedly greyer than those of Banded Dotterel; underparts white with a *grey wash at sides of foreneck*. In breeding dress this becomes a collar of a rich tawny or rufous colour, traces of which may remain till November—a useful aid to identification. Legs grey-green or greyish-brown. In flight, it is a distinctly larger bird than a Banded Dotterel with broader wings and a slow, buoyant wing-beat over short distances.
Voice: Rather a silent bird. A quiet *treep* or *tir-rip* slowly repeated three or four times, quite distinct from any note of Banded or Red-breasted Dotterel. Also described are a musical *peeph* and a melodious trill.
Habitat and range: First recorded in 1943, this dotterel, a migrant from northern Asia, is now known to visit one or other of our northern inlets most summers, and sometimes it overwinters. Further south, this far-ranging species has occurred in Taranaki and Hawkes Bay. There is an inland report from Taupo. In the South Island an increasing number of reports come from Farewell Spit and even from the Southland lagoons. Its winter quarters extend from South Africa to the islands of the south-west Pacific.

In New Zealand Large Sand Dotterels have usually been associating with Wrybills or Banded Dotterels near their high-tide roosts; once with Eastern Golden Plovers on ploughed marshland. Also noted in winter feeding near Turnstones and Red-breasted Dotterels on a shelly beach and among Banded

Dotterels on close-cropped pasture.

MONGOLIAN DOTTEREL   *Charadrius mongolus*   Pl. 28, p. 121

Other name: Lesser Sand Plover.

Description: 19 cm (7½″). About the size of a male *bicinctus* (Banded Dotterel), but with a longer and deeper bill (2 cm) with a strong dertrum—not however as heavy as the bill of *leschenaulti* (Large Sand Dotterel). In juvenile or eclipse plumage, in which this 'difficult' species is most likely to be seen in New Zealand, closely resembles *bicinctus* and *only separable with very great care.* Conspicuously white-faced; upperparts *greyer* lacking rufous tone; *dark patch below and behind eye* tapering forwards towards bill; underparts white with narrow grey band faintly visible at sides of lower breast; legs slate grey; rather upright stance and proportions reminiscent of an undersized *obscurus*. In nuptial dress, which might be seen in April or early May, crown and breast are brilliantly brick-red.

In eclipse plumage this is a rather nondescript and featureless dotterel. Among flocks of moulting or juvenile *bicinctus* it could easily escape notice. **Voice:** One at Farewell Spit uttered a clear *trik* and a soft *tikit*, less incisive than the typical note of *bicinctus* and lacking its carrying quality. Also described are a clear penetrating *drrriiit* or sharp plaintive whistle, a chittering tern-like note uttered in flight, and a soft melodious trill.

Habitat and range: Breeds in eastern Asia, migrating south and annually reaching south-east Australia in some numbers. A rare visitor. One at Farewell Spit in January 1961 fed near Banded Dotterels, but tended to keep apart and returned again and again to the same green oasis of closely grazed saltmarsh among the sand-dunes. One at Karaka in Manukau Harbour, January to March 1963, was loosely attached to Banded Dotterels and Wrybills, both for feeding and for roosting. Three on Farewell Spit, January 1967, and others since. Sightings are now reported almost yearly, especially from the northern harbours. Additional South Island records come from Southland lagoons and Kaitorete Spit, Lake Ellesmere.

RINGED PLOVER   *Charadrius hiaticula*   Pl. 28, p. 121

Description: 19 cm (7½″). Black, white and brown pattern of the head, white chin and *complete white collar* narrowest on the back, black chest band also narrowing to form a collar, stubby *orange bill with dusky tip* and *orange-yellow legs* at once distinguish *hiaticula* from other small plovers in New Zealand. Upperparts generally light brown; tail brown in the centre, white at the sides and with a black band across the end. Underparts except for chest band, clear white. Flight reveals a clear white wing-bar.

Voice: The typical call of birds in flocks or on migration is a liquid piping *queep*.

Habitat and range: Breeds across northern Eurasia, the far eastern population migrating almost exclusively towards Arabia and Africa; and very rarely to Australia. One spent much of the summer of 1970-71 at Miranda in the Firth of Thames, preferring the company of Wrybills and small arctic sandpipers to that of Banded Dotterels, its much closer relatives.

On migration and in its winter quarters this is a bird of the seashore and coastal marshes where the turf is short.

SHORE PLOVER *Thinornis novaeseelandiae* *Pl. 26, p. 113*
Maori name: Tuturuatu.
Description: 20 cm (8"). In flight recalls a Turnstone, 'the wing pattern, glistening white breast, dark collar, orange legs and general manner of flight being remarkably similar' (Fleming).

Forehead, cheeks, throat, forepart of neck and narrow nuchal collar black in males, brownish in females; crown and hind part of head greyish brown, separated from the dark area by a band of white which passes from the top of the forehead above the eye to the nape; rest of upper surface greyish brown; wing-coverts tipped with white; primaries dark brown with central white streak; underparts white. Bill orange-red with dark tip; in females the dark tip is more extensive; legs pinkish orange. Sexes are readily distinguishable by their plumage and soft parts. Though the measurements of males average slightly larger, in life females appear heavier.
Voice: A high-pitched *peep*. Agitated adults with downy young pipe in chorus.
Habitat and range: Former distribution and movements ill-documented and rather puzzling. Now apparently confined to South-east Island (Rangatira) in the Chathams, where in 1937 the population was estimated at about 70 pairs, most densely distributed over the salt meadow in the bays, but with a few pairs on the top of the island. Feeds mainly in salt and brackish rock pools. Windblown stragglers may sometimes reach other islands.
Breeding: Mated pairs indulge in 'pursuit flights' following a zigzag course together with perfect co-ordination. The nest, quite a bulky structure, is generally in a sort of horizontal tunnel, rarely open to the sky. Nest sites are commonly a hole or crevice among boulders, but may be a muttonbird burrow, a hollow log, a tunnel in thick bidi-bidi, under buttress roots of a shrub. Eggs, November to February, 2–3, vary considerably in shape, colour and markings. Both sexes incubate.
Note: *Thinornis rossi* described from a unique specimen said to have been collected by the *Erebus* and *Terror* Expedition (1841) at the Auckland Islands, may be a vagrant *T. novaeseelandiae* in sub-adult plumage.

WRYBILL *Anarhynchus frontalis* *Pl. 26, p. 113*
Other names: Wry-billed Plover, Crook-bill Plover, Ngutu-parore.
Description: 20 cm (8"). A small grey and white plover about the size of a Banded Dotterel, but with a longer bill (3 cm) which is unique because the *tip turns to the right*. Adults in breeding dress (June to January) have a clear cut pectoral band; forehead white edged above with a thin blackish line more pronounced in male; whitish superciliary streak. Except in breeding season, a bird of the open seashore, sometimes sheltering among low vegetation such as glasswort, to avoid wind. Runs fast with head tucked closely in to the body. Often rests on one leg and hops without untucking the other leg. In its winterquarters usually confiding and approachable.
Voice: 'A high-pitched staccato whistle' (Stead). A shrill reedy *weet or peep*. A flock may keep up a thin soft chattering *wik-a-wik* or *chitter-chitter*. *Skürr, skürr* may denote anger: *zwee, zwee zweep* almost a trill, may be the start of a courtship song: *wee-te-ti* also recorded. A subdued bubbling trill *quit-wurr* repeated denotes sexual excitement.

Habitat and range: Known to breed only on some of the larger river-beds of Canterbury and North Otago up to the mountains. After breeding small flocks have been noted on the Canterbury coast, but elsewhere in the South Island it is rarely reported, though a few may regularly pass along Farewell Spit. A few are now being recorded annually on the Southland coast, and in April 1974 five were found at Sandspit, Stewart Island. Apparently from late December onwards the main population quickly moves northwards in small flocks; some pausing on the south-west and south-east coasts of the North Island, to winter-quarters mainly in the Firth of Thames, Manukau and Kaipara. Small numbers annually reach Parengarenga. The only inland localities from which passing migrants have been reported are Lake Rotorua and Lake Hatuma. In 1960 the total population, based on counts of wintering flocks, was conservatively estimated at about 5000.

Small flocks of immature non-breeders summer in the north where they are joined by the first of the returning migrants about Christmas-time. The south-ward movement begins in July, reaches a peak in August and may continue till October. Infected by pre-migration excitement towards the end of winter, large flocks in the Firth of Thames perform lengthy and complicated aerial evolutions, a superb display of controlled flying *en masse*.

Breeding: Breeding pairs reappear on Canterbury river-beds in August. Nests are near water in wide areas of clean shingle where the stones are rather large and clear of all growths and drift. Eggs, September-November; normal clutch 2, rarely 3, pyriform, pale grey faintly tinged with blue or green, closely and evenly peppered with minute dark and pale blotches, spots and lines. Incubation period *c.* 30 days; fledging *c.* 30 days.

CURLEWS, WHIMBRELS, GODWITS, SNIPES AND SANDPIPERS: Scolopacidae

FAR EASTERN CURLEW   *Numenius madagascariensis*   *Pl. 27, p. 120*
   Other names: Long-billed Curlew, Australian Curlew.
   Description: 61 cm (24″). The largest of the arctic waders which visit New Zealand, easily recognised by its size, *long down-curved bill* (19 cm) and distinctive call. Streaked brown and buff, both above and below, the underparts being lighter; pale eyebrow line; back and rump much the same shade of brown as wings and tail. Legs bluish-grey.
   Voice: A tuneful *croo-lee*, a husky *kérr-eep* or *keep* and a harsher *ker-woik*. Also a rather husky *ker-kerup*. Often curiously silent; but when calling, audible a long way off.
   Habitat and range: Breeds in north-eastern Siberia, migrating south and widely

---

PLATE 27 Asiatic Whimbrel (p.121); American Whimbrel (p.121); Little Whimbrel (p.122); Eastern Bar-tailed Godwit (p.122); Asiatic Black-tailed Godwit (p.124); Far Eastern Curlew (p.120); Hudsonian Godwit (p.123); Bristle-thighed Curlew (p.122).

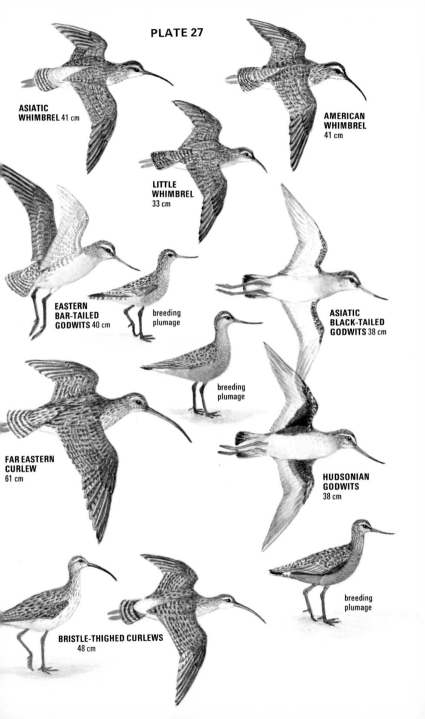

PLATE 27

ASIATIC
WHIMBREL 41 cm

AMERICAN
WHIMBREL
41 cm

LITTLE
WHIMBREL
33 cm

EASTERN
BAR-TAILED
GODWITS 40 cm

breeding
plumage

ASIATIC
BLACK-TAILED
GODWITS 38 cm

breeding
plumage

FAR EASTERN
CURLEW
61 cm

HUDSONIAN
GODWITS
38 cm

BRISTLE-THIGHED CURLEWS
48 cm

breeding
plumage

PLATE 28

RINGED PLOVER
19 cm

MONGOLIAN DOTTERELS

winter

summer

LARGE SAND DOTTEREL 22 cm

breeding plumage

ORIENTAL DOTTERELS
25 cm

GREY PLOVERS
28 cm

breeding plumage

EASTERN GOLDEN PLOVERS 25 cm

winter plumage

breeding plumage

distributed on the coast of Australia. A few regularly reach New Zealand. Tired migrants may drop in on almost any stretch of coast, more often the west; but soon move to estuaries and harbours much frequented by other waders. A bird of the tide-line, associating with godwits and oystercatchers at high-tide roosts; but an uneasy mixer tending to keep apart and so easily noticed. May rest and feed among and sometimes actually under low-growing mangroves. Godwits tend to resent stray curlews and have been seen to mob and chase them. As in Australia immature non-breeders may stay over the southern winter.

Observations since 1940 in Manukau and the Firth of Thames seem to show that these large curlews are occurring more frequently in New Zealand. Many reports are of single birds; but small flocks also appear in a few inlets south to Awarua Bay. The Firth of Thames and Farewell Spit are the most favoured termini for summering flocks.

ASIATIC WHIMBREL   *Numenius variegatus*   *Pl. 27, p. 120*
Description: 41 cm (16″). About the same size as a Bar-tailed Godwit but generally looks darker and robuster with a distinctly *decurved bill* (9 cm). Smaller size and boldly streaked crown *with pale median stripe* and *voice* (q.v.) distinguish the whimbrels from the true curlews. A *whitish rump*—white feathers boldly barred with brown—distinguishes the Asiatic from the American Whimbrel in which the rump is of a warm brown uniform with mantle and tail. When a whimbrel is seen in flight, the '*pale blaze pointed up the lower back*' should be looked for, as it is the only means of separating in the field the two forms which occur in New Zealand. Females are rather larger than males and in a flock obvious differences in size, especially in the bill, may be noted. Legs bluish. At high tide among other resting waders, a whimbrel often remains alert and holds its head aloft.
Voice: An even rippling whistle of about seven notes. Hence its Scottish names 'Titterel' and 'Seven Whistler'. The tittering call *ti-ti-ti-ti-ti-ti-ti* can be the first indication that there is a Whimbrel with a passing flock of godwits. The ordinary calls of Asiatic and American Whimbrels are indistinguishable. Sometimes whimbrels call repeatedly; sometimes they are curiously silent.
Habitat and range: Asiatic Whimbrels reach New Zealand annually from September onwards; and immature non-breeders may remain over the following winter. Single birds or small flocks make their landfall almost anywhere along the coast, but soon move to tidal estuaries and harbours, where flocks of up to *c.* 30 birds are now being reported.

AMERICAN WHIMBREL   *Numenius hudsonicus*   *Pl. 27, p. 120*
Other name: Hudsonian Curlew.
Description: 41 cm (16″). On the ground indistinguishable from Asiatic Whimbrel, but in low flight upper surface including lower back and rump are

PLATE 28 Ringed Plover (p.118); Mongolian Dotterel (p.118); Large Sand Dotterel (p.117); Oriental Dotterel (p.117); Grey Plover (p.113); Eastern Golden Plover (p.112).

seen to be uniformly brownish.

Habitat and range: Although the first whimbrel to be obtained in New Zealand was of the dark-backed American form, it remained unrecognised in the Dominion Museum for more than half a century. The next was found and identified in Ohiwa Harbour, Bay of Plenty in June 1949, a bird overwintering with godwits. Now in the mid-1970s, *hudsonicus* is being reported almost annually, especially from the northern harbours; but some reach Farewell Spit and the Southland lagoons. They may associate temporarily with flocks of Asiatic Whimbrels.

LITTLE WHIMBREL   *Numenius minutus*   *Pl. 27, p. 120*

Description: 33 cm (13"). Looks rather like a Golden Plover in size, shape and colour, except that in flight the wings appear longer and the *primaries blackish*, but easily recognised as a miniature curlew or small whimbrel by its strongly decurved bill (4.5 cm). Crown dark brown with *median streak of buff*; eyebrow conspicuously light buff; upperparts variegated dark and light brown; upper tail-coverts brown with light grey crossbars not showing noticeably pale in flight; tail grey-brown with dark bars; throat and abdomen dull white, breast streaked with brown. Legs dull bluish-grey.

Voice: A flock feeding busily may keep up a soft not unmusical chatter *te-te-te*. Alarm notes are a rather harsh *tchew-tchew-tchew*.

Habitat and range: Breeds in north-east Siberia and winters mainly in north-east Australia. A rare visitor which has been reported from Lake Ellesmere at scattered intervals since 1900 and at Farewell Spit in 1961, and several times from the North Island, including both east and west coasts as well as the major northern harbours. In Queensland, where large flocks occur in autumn, said to prefer grasslands to the seashore; but freely associates with Sharptailed Sandpipers. In New Zealand Little Whimbrels should be looked for in grassy paddocks which are visited by dotterels and plovers as high tides force them off the flats.

Note: Some taxonomists make the Little Whimbrel conspecific with the very similar Eskimo Curlew, now probably extinct. If this view is correct, the Little Whimbrel must be treated as the Asiatic race of *Numenius borealis*.

BRISTLE-THIGHED CURLEW   *Numenius tahitiensis*   *Pl. 27, p. 120*

Description: 48 cm (19"). Slightly larger than a whimbrel, lighter underneath and *generally tawnier*, with back and wing-coverts more obviously speckled. Upper tail-coverts sandy or buffy white forming a band across lower rump; *tail rusty buff with dark bars*. Legs greyish-blue.

Voice: Recorded as a 'whistled long-drawn-out *pee-u-wit* or *krreeep*', slightly rising and quite unlike the usual tremulous trill of a whimbrel.

Habitat and range: Breeds in north-western Alaska, migrating south to Pacific islands and atolls; and, at the south-west limit of its range, sometimes reaching Norfolk and Kermadec Islands.

EASTERN BAR-TAILED GODWIT   *Limosa lapponica*   *Pl. 27, p. 120*

Local names: Godwit, Kuaka. (Also, quite incorrectly, 'Snipe' and 'Curlew'.)

Description: 40 cm (16"). Colour, proportions, long legs and long slightly upturned bill (9 cm), readily distinguish godwits from other shore birds, e.g.

stilts and oystercatchers, with which they commonly associate. Upperparts mottled brown and grey; lower back, rump and tail barred white and brown; underparts dull white, clouded with grey. The assumption of breeding dress starts in January and by the end of February many males have bright brick-red underparts; females show a buffy tinge on breast and some fine barring on the flanks. Traces of nuptial red are still visible in the plumage of some adults when they return to New Zealand in September. Females are distinctly larger than males, the difference in size being especially noticeable in the bills. Flight fast and direct; no wing-bar. Flocks commonly fly in long lines or chevrons.

Voice: A clear excited double note *kew-kew* is commonly used. A soft *kit-kit-kit-kit* is heard from passing flocks. Roosting flocks, if uneasy, may keep up a steady conversational chatter.

Habitat and range: Breeds in north-eastern Siberia and north-western America (possibly two subspecies), migrating south to Australia and New Zealand, the bulk of the population apparently coming to New Zealand, where it is by far the commonest of the migratory arctic waders. Plentiful, October-March, in all suitable harbours and estuaries from Parengarenga to Paterson Inlet, Stewart Island; flocks in a few favoured localities containing thousands of birds. A regular visitor to Kermadec and Norfolk Islands. A regular migrant to Chatham Island and a straggler to Campbell, Auckland and Macquarie Islands.

Feeds mostly on tidal flats; also visits marshes and pastures near the sea at spring tides or during very wet weather. Seldom reported inland. Some thousands of non-breeding juveniles overwinter, especially in the big harbours of northern New Zealand.

HUDSONIAN GODWIT *Limosa haemastica*   *Pl. 27, p. 120*
Other name: American Black-tailed Godwit.
Description: 38 cm (15″). About the same size as a male Bar-tailed Godwit, but upperparts greyer and less speckled; breast distinctly washed grey. Can be satisfactorily identified on the ground only if it raises its wings; or in flight when the *clear white upper tail-coverts strongly contrast with the sooty black tail* with its narrow white tip. A narrow white wing-bar is not always very noticeable; nor at certain angles are the *sooty axillaries and underwing linings* by which alone in the field the American can be distinguished from the Asiatic Black-tailed Godwit (q.v.). Most Hudsonian Godwits seen in New Zealand are in the grey and white plumage of juveniles or adults in winter; but some adults have been seen in late April with underparts reddish, finely barred with black and the white superciliary stripe much more definite than in winter. Bill flesh-coloured or yellowish, darkening towards the tip. Legs greyish-blue. Females are rather larger than males. Some males look curiously small and dusky, especially in flight.
Voice: Flight call a low double *ta-it* or a sharp, but not far-carrying *kit-keet*.
Habitat and range: A rare but possibly regular migrant from arctic America, where in autumn strays may be caught up in the southbound stream of Bar-tailed Godwits. So far all records in New Zealand are of single birds, usually attached to flocks of Bar-tailed Godwits and seldom inclined to leave them to join other waders in shallow waters away from the tideline. But tired migrants, just arrived, have been found among flocks of non-breeding Pied Stilts. Most

frequently recorded from the northern harbours; casually also from estuarie, on both east and west coasts south to Oreti.

ASIATIC BLACK-TAILED GODWIT *Limosa melanuroides* Pl. 27, p. 120
Description: 38 cm (15"). About the same size as a male Bar-tailed Godwit, from which it cannot with certainty be distinguished on the ground unless it raises its wings, though generally it looks slimmer and more elegant; and with birds in winter plumage the uniform smooth grey of the breast is a useful pointer. In flight its salient characteristics are *pure white upper tail-coverts* contrasting with *broad black terminal band of tail, conspicuous white wing-bar* and *gleaming white underwing* narrowly edged with black. Bill long, pinkish, darkening towards the tip, straight or very slightly upward-curved. Legs greenish-grey. Breeding dress, with deep orange rufous underparts partly barred with black and with the brown-grey of the upperparts darkening, is assumed in March and April. Traces of this may still be seen on adults in September-October. Adult males in full breeding dress are richly coloured, females are slightly larger than males and less showy.
Voice: Rather a silent bird in its southern winter quarters. Feeding birds sometimes utter a single *kuk* or *kik*. The flight call has been described as a loud clear *wicka-wicka-wicka* or *gritto-gritto*.
Habitat and range: A rare migrant from northern Asia recorded only from the Firth of Thames and Manukau Harbour till January 1963, when one was seen at Enderby Island, nearly 1600 km farther south (B. D. Bell). May be looked for wherever Bar-tailed Godwits occur; although, unlike the Hudsonian Godwit, it may often desert the tidal flats to join Pied Stilts on flooded grassland and freshwater pools. First recorded in New Zealand in 1952; but may be coming more frequently, even occurring in small flocks which may stay for some months in localities which obviously suit them, viz. 4 at Puketutu and 6 at Miranda. These godwits have now been reported from several estuaries south to Bluff; and in 1976 one again reached the Auckland Islands. Immature non-breeders have overwintered.
Note: The only feature by which the Asiatic Black-tailed Godwit can be separated with certainty in the field from the Hudsonian Godwit is by its *white underwing* as against the *sooty underwing* of its American counterpart.

UPLAND SANDPIPER *Bartramia longicauda* Pl. 31, p. 136
Other names: Bartram's Sandpiper, Prairie Whistler, Quailie.
Description: 30 cm (12"). An upstanding, ploverlike, buffy sandpiper, with a slender neck, small head, conspicuous eye, comparatively short bill (3 cm) and longish tail. Chin and belly white. Throat and breast lightly streaked, the streaks darkening into crescentic bars lower down and on the upper flanks. In flight, long tail with dark centre and creamy margins, black lower back and white sides of rump, and dark primaries are exposed. On alighting the wings are often held upright long enough to reveal the pied barring of the underwing. Legs yellow.
Habitat and range: This unique species differs from other sandpipers in its preference for dryish grasslands where it has a habit of perching on posts and poles.

Breeds in north America, migrating mainly through the interior to South America, east of the Andes. Apt to wander, especially eastwards across the Atlantic; but very rare in the Pacific. One record for Australia, Sydney (1848). One sighting in New Zealand, Manukau Harbour (February 1967). This bird alternately ran and paused on the fringe of a mixed flock of arctic and indigenous waders gathered on a semi-marine flat.

GREENSHANK   *Tringa nebularia*   *Pl. 29, p. 128*
Description: 33 cm (13″). About the same size as a male Bar-tailed Godwit. Upperparts grey, lightly flecked with white, with *white lower back and rump*; tail feathers so lightly barred as to appear almost white; wings blackish; underparts white. *Legs grey-green*; bill (5 cm) bluish-grey, slightly upcurved.

In flight the Greenshank looks to be an almost black and white bird, the blackish wings contrasting with the *inverted V of white up the back*. Often calls as it rises.
Voice: A musical ringing *tchew*, *tlooi* or *chewey*, sometimes single, more often repeated. Three which flew high over Manukau Harbour calling were audible at more than a mile on a calm day in May 1954.
Habitat and range: Though a regular summer visitor from the northern hemisphere to southern Australia and Tasmania, where some also spend the winter, few seem to straggle to New Zealand; yet most coastal haunts of waders have been visited, and strays have reached even the Snares, and Macquarie Island.

Greenshanks show a marked liking for the company of Pied Stilts, avoiding the big packs of Godwits and Knots. A wader of muddy creeks and lagoons rather than of the open shore. Most untypical of New Zealand were three Greenshanks and a Little Egret sharing the top of a small mudbank in Manukau on 14/10/53.

LESSER YELLOWLEGS   *Tringa flavipes*   *Pl. 29. p. 128*
Description: 27 cm (10½″). About the size of a Knot in body and wing-span, but with *long, slender bright yellow legs* which in flight extend beyond the tail. Upperparts greyish-brown, the pale tips of the feathers giving a spotted appearance, especially in summer plumage; less so in winter; flight feathers darker. Rump white, tail light grey with dark bars but showing almost white in

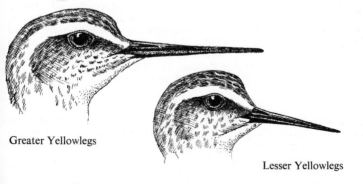

Greater Yellowlegs

Lesser Yellowlegs

flight. A dark line runs through the eye and there is a white superciliary stripe. Underparts generally white, but neck and breast streaked with brown, more heavily in breeding season. Bill (3.5 cm) fine and straight.

Walks with a jerky strut when feeding, but can run very fast.

Voice: The typical call is a dissyllabic *ti-tu* or *kit-to*, softer and flatter than the ringing notes of Greater Yellowlegs.

Habitat and range: Breeds in Alaska and northern Canada, migrating mainly in a south-easterly direction to West Indies and South America. Said to occur regularly in Hawaii during the fall and spring migrations; but elsewhere in the central or western Pacific a rare vagrant. Reliably reported in New Zealand from Napier, November 1963 and April 1973; Lake Ellesmere, January 1964; Washdyke, February 1971; Lake Wainono, February 1972; Manukau, October-December 1973; Lake Pukepuke, March-April 1974; Farewell Spit, March 1974 and January 1977.

Note: The first Yellowlegs sighting recorded in New Zealand was on a shallow brackish pool at Porirua in November 1962. After much careful deliberation it was identified as a Greater (*T. melanoleuca*) and this identification was widely accepted. However a dissentient view soon emerged and now prevails.

MARSH SANDPIPER *Tringa stagnatilis* Pl. 29, p. 128

Other name: Little Greenshank.

Description: 25 cm (10"). An elegant wader resembling a small Greenshank (except that its *legs are disproportionately long*) or, in flight, a miniature stilt with legs projecting well beyond the tail. Upperparts dark grey, underparts white; forehead and face white; lower back and rump white, showing clearly as bird flies away from observer; tail so lightly barred that it appears almost white; thin grey flecking on throat and breast is a mark of breeding dress; legs greenish; bill (4 cm) fine and straight.

Voice: A single *tew*, *teeoo* or *kewip*, not very loud; reminiscent of Greenshank's *tchew*.

Habitat and range: A palaearctic species wintering from Africa through southern Asia to Australia, only recently discovered in New Zealand. One in Manukau Harbour (1959) associated closely with Pied Stilts from March to May, wading up to its belly and feeding off the surface of the water. Essentially a wader of fresh and brackish pools, not of the tideline. One in Firth of Thames on 28/4/63 rested inland with Pied Stilts at full tide and later flew with them to feed on the exposed mudflats. Presumably the same bird after wintering appeared at Miranda, where it was frequently seen between September and December. Another which visited a farm-pond near Hawera, Taranaki, on 1/11/63 was identified from colour photographs. Other sightings include one near Gisborne in 1964; four at Kaituna, Bay of Plenty, in January 1970; one near Napier, February 1972. One near Westport, May 1968, is the first South Island record.

TEREK SANDPIPER *Tringa cinerea* Pl. 29, p. 128

Description: 23 cm (9"). Long, thin, *distinctly upcurved bill* (4.5 cm) (hence an old but apt name, Avocet Sandpiper) and *orange* or *bright yellow legs* distinguish this from other small sandpipers, none of which at all resemble it. Crown and upperparts brownish-grey; underparts white; faint streaks on neck and breast varying according to the season. In flight the white-tipped secondaries forming a *white rear-edge to the rather dark wings* show up clearly. Runs actively and bobs tail.

Voice: A pleasant musical trill *weeta-weeta-weet*; also interpreted as a fluty *du-du-du-du* or a melodious *tiririr*. Often calls when it rises; sometimes on the ground, as it runs.

Habitat and range: A northern palaearctic breeder wintering in Africa, Asia and Australia. Now recorded annually either in the Firth of Thames, where it was first discovered in New Zealand in 1951, or elsewhere, south to Bluff, and seen often enough to suggest that some are reaching New Zealand every year. A bird of the wide tidal flats, often in company with Wrybills. In the hot summer days when these are drowsing at their high-tide roosts, a Terek Sandpiper will remain alert; and one has been seen to run from one end of a dozing flock to another, the one moving bird in a gathering of hundreds. In mid-winter two Terek Sandpipers edged away from a big close flock of Wrybills soon after the tide began to fall and fed eagerly while the Wrybills continued to rest. In flight with Wrybills, often takes the lead. The overwintering of immature non-breeders first proved in 1952 is now known to be normal.

SIBERIAN TATTLER *Tringa brevipes* *Pl. 29, p. 128*
Other names: Grey-rumped Sandpiper, Grey-tailed Tattler.
Description: 25 cm (10″). A slim, graceful wader. Upperparts almost uniformly slate-grey, the evenness of the grey especially noticeable in flight, but some fine white barring on the rump may be visible at close range; underparts white except for some finely pencilled barring on breast. Dark line through eye, clear white superciliary stripe. Bill straight and long (4 cm); *legs yellowish* becoming yellower about April. *Nasal groove* extending *half length of bill.* In breeding plumage barring on underparts develops, but *undertail-coverts remain white.* A typical *Tringa* when alerted, bobbing its head, tipping its tail and perhaps running to and fro. Inclined to be solitary; and, when disturbed, to fly low across water, sometimes without calling.

Voice: Usual call a sharp, high-pitched, double whistle *twhéet* or *too-wéet* resembling the call of an Eastern Golden Plover but less melodious. Also described as *whew-rit* or *whewew-réet*, the final syllable being emphasised and higher in pitch. Also a soft trill of three or four notes, *ter-wee*, repeated in fluty tones. Apparently less vocal than Wandering Tattler.

Habitat and range: Breeds in alpine zone of eastern Siberia, migrating south, reaching south-eastern Australia and Tasmania. Rare but regular migrant to New Zealand, especially Parengarenga and Farewell Spit. Since 1950 recorded from most coastal habitats frequented by waders, south to Stewart Island (1976) and even Snares (1968).

Tattlers may stay some months or even years in some estuary or on a stretch of shore which clearly satisfies their requirements, frequently resorting to a favourite perch on a post, a piece of driftwood or an isolated rock. What was evidently the same individual used the same distinctive resting places for more than four years on the Karaka coast of Manukau.

Several instances of overwintering seem to indicate that most of the tattlers which reach New Zealand are first-year birds.

WANDERING TATTLER *Tringa incana* *Pl. 29, p. 128*
Other name: Alaskan Tattler.
Description: 28 cm (11″). In winter plumage only separable with extreme care from *T. brevipes* (with which some authors consider it conspecific); but slightly larger, of a darker grey and looks robuster. In breeding plumage the underparts *including undertail-coverts* are heavily barred. Relatively *longer nasal groove*, *extending two-thirds* of bill, is visible in a good light with a strong telescope. One at Kawakawa Bay assumed breeding plumage in February and March (1949) but remained throughout the following winter.
Voice: A clear sweet whistle or rippling trill of 6–10 notes with the accent on the second note, the following notes diminishing a little in volume and given more rapidly than the first two or three.
The quite distinct calls of the two forms of tattler are perhaps the safest guide to correct identification, especially when tattlers are in winter plumage as they usually are in New Zealand.
Habitat and range: Breeds along mountain streams in Alaska. Winter range includes the islands of the central Pacific and Polynesia south to Fiji and Tonga, occasionally straggling to south-eastern Australia and New Zealand. Recorded from Raoul Island in Kermadecs, Portland Island and Kawakawa Bay, where for more than a year one frequented the vicinity of a ridged shingle reef, Cape Kidnappers, Ashley rivermouth, South-east Island (Chathams), and Farewell Spit. Unspecified tattlers perhaps belonging to this form have been reported on the east coast from Napier, Gisborne, Kuaotunu, Port Jackson.

COMMON SANDPIPER *Tringa hypoleucos* *Pl. 29, p. 128*
Description: 20 cm (7¾″). A typical well proportioned straight-billed sandpiper, inclined to be solitary and avoiding exposed sea-shores; preferring either quiet lakesides or fast-flowing estuarine waters where there are rocks or stumps on which it may perch. Upperparts olive-brown except white wing-bar, sides of rump and tail which are revealed in flight. Eyebrow stripe white. Underparts white except for shadowy spotting on sides of breast. Bill brown; legs greenish-grey.
The jerky flickering flight low over the water – a few short sharp wing-beats followed by a brief gliding with wings held stiffly down-curved – is distinctive. Bobbing the head and dipping the tail are part of its natural gait.
Voice: A shrill *twee-dee-dee* or *kitty-dee*, often given when flushed or in low flight.
Habitat and range: Breeds across northern Eurasia; migrating south. Uncommon in south-east Australia and only six sightings in New Zealand (all between October and April): five on west coast of North Island – Taranaki

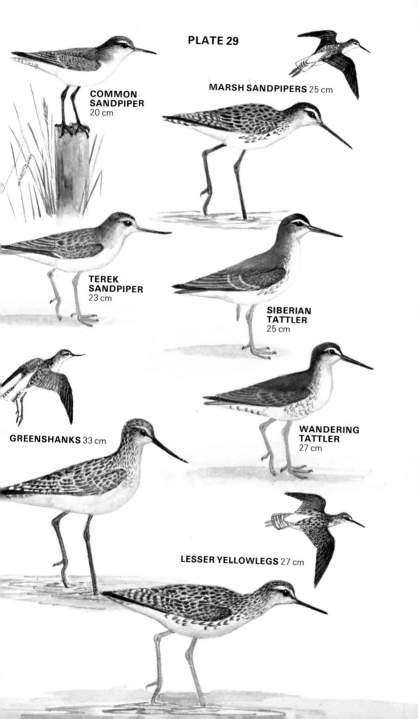

PLATE 29

COMMON SANDPIPER 20 cm

MARSH SANDPIPERS 25 cm

TEREK SANDPIPER 23 cm

SIBERIAN TATTLER 25 cm

GREENSHANKS 33 cm

WANDERING TATTLER 27 cm

LESSER YELLOWLEGS 27 cm

PLATE 30

winter

RED-NECKED STINTS 15 cm

breeding plumage ♂

PECTORAL SANDPIPER 22 cm

SHARP-TAILED SANDPIPER 22 cm

SANDERLING 20 cm

♂ breeding

winter

CURLEW SANDPIPERS 22 cm

GREAT KNOT 29 cm

♂ breeding plumage

winter

LESSER KNOTS 25 cm

(1964 and 1972), Waikanae (1972), Port Albert (1964), Manukau (1977) – and one from Kerikeri Inlet (1969).

TURNSTONE   *Arenaria interpres*   *Pl. 31, p. 136*
Description: 23 cm (9″). Distinguished at all seasons from other waders by its shape, the contrast of black and white and 'tortoise-shell' in its markings and its *orange* legs. Upperparts dark-brown, mottled black and chestnut; lower back white with second white band curving across upper tail; throat and abdomen white; upper breast broadly black. Bill blackish, robust, slightly tip-tilted. White wing-bar conspicuous in flight. The amount of white on face and head varies considerably, some adults in breeding plumage becoming almost white-headed. Dusky heads and duller colouring easily distinguish young birds when they first arrive.
Voice: A metallic rattle or twittering *kitititit* is heard most commonly. In large mixed flocks of passing waders a ringing *kee-oo* draws attention to Turnstones. A noisy excited version of these notes has been heard from two birds just before they leave for their breeding grounds. It accompanied a swift darting and twisting flight concerned with pair-formation or courtship.
Habitat and range: A holarctic breeder, migrating south. The third most numerous of the arctic waders which regularly reach New Zealand occurring in flocks from Parengarenga to Bluff and even Auckland Islands. Sizeable flocks seem to frequent the main island of the Chathams at all seasons. Tends to avoid smooth sandy beaches and open mudflats, preferring to feed on a shelly or stony foreshore or among rockpools (e.g. Kaikoura). Small flocks of immature non-breeders overwinter mostly in the northern harbours. A marked association of Turnstones with Eastern Golden Plovers has frequently been noticed, the two species together visiting rough ploughland near the sea or even dried out pastures a mile or more inland. An active feeder deftly flicking over stones and tide-wrack with its bill. Stray Turnstones readily join groups of other small waders.

SUB-ANTARCTIC SNIPE   *Coenocorypha aucklandica*
Maori name: Tutukiwi.
Description: 23 cm (9″). Small primitive snipe-like birds—Seebohm's semi-Woodcocks—with long sensitive bill (5 cm), short wings, striped head and richly variegated upper-surface. Legs yellowish-brown. Females rather larger.
Voice: A low hoarse double croak on Big South Cape off Stewart Island (Guthrie-Smith); also a repeated double-whistle, usually given in flight just after dusk (Bell).
   On Snares a repeated whistle as in *C. pusilla* (Fleming).
Habitat and range: These snipe have been aptly described as living fossils, which belong, strictly speaking, to a past geological period. They may be the relic of an ancient stock which at one time had a more northerly or more general

distribution and from which the present-day woodcocks and snipe arose. They have survived because of the long isolation of certain islands and the consequent freedom from ground predators. Four well-marked insular races at (*a*) Auckland Islands (Ewing and Adams Island) (*aucklandica*) paler, only flanks barred, not abdomen; (*b*) Antipodes Island (*meinertzhagenae*) darker above, underparts yellower; (*c*) Snares (*huegeli*) undersurface barred throughout; (*d*) islands off Stewart Island (*iredalei*), rather more rufous, lower abdomen and flanks barred, throat spotted.

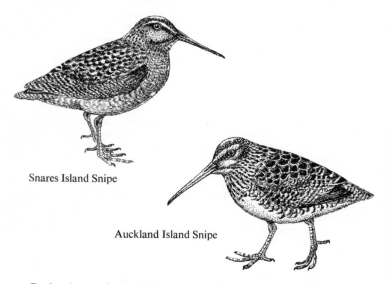

Snares Island Snipe

Auckland Island Snipe

By day they tend to avoid the open, preferring the shelter of bush or scrub. At the Snares they frequent the fringes of the penguin colonies. If disturbed they can fly short distances; but apparently they take wing more readily at night with a swift and woodcock-like flight.

Breeding: Nest often quite a substantial structure, e.g. deep cup of fine grass (Snares); pile of moss, lichen and twigs (Big South Cape). Eggs, October–December. Clutch 2, bluntly ovoid, closely resembling woodcock eggs; markings rather variable, but basically pale brown with dark spots or blotches. Both parents sit. Apparently only one young is reared.

CHATHAM ISLAND SNIPE *Coenocorypha pusilla*   *Pl. 31, p. 136*
Description: 20 cm (8″). Similar to *C. aucklandica* of which it is sometimes treated as a strong subspecies, but distinctly smaller and with lower breast unbarred and abdomen buffy white. Males and females readily distinguishable, the males being smaller in body and bill, and darker in the plumage of the back and more strikingly patterned on the upper-surface. Usually in pairs. Flight,

when suddenly alarmed, fast and fairly strong with a characteristic whirring beat.

Voice: Alarm note a drawn out *cheep* (Bell). A feeding male 'chirruped' softly. The typical call, which is heard more frequently in the evening than in the day-time, begins as 'soft, low, sibilant chirrups' and quickly works up to 'a series of sharp, tuneful, whistles on high B, repeated eight or ten times in about five seconds.' At every whistle the bird's cheeks and throat were seen to vibrate. Two males some distance apart sometimes called at each other and the cries then reach an excited pitch (Fleming). Note of female is pitched lower.

Habitat and range: Formerly surviving only on South-east Island, where it feeds on the rich moist leaf-mould of the forest floor, among rank grasses and on spongy seepages above the rock-fringe. Now introduced with apparent success to Big Mangere Island.

Breeding: Reported to nest among the roots and buttresses of trees or under fallen logs. Clutch 3. Eggs, similar to those of *C. aucklandica*, but slightly smaller. Downy plumage of young is uniformly umber-brown.

JAPANESE SNIPE *Gallinago hardwicki* Pl. 31, p. 136

Description: 33 cm (13″). A typical snipe with long bill (4 cm) and short legs. Upperparts heavily marked brown and black; crown prominently streaked with a buff stripe down the centre; throat and sides of face buffy white; under-parts buffy; flanks barred; chestnut band on tail; bill long and black; legs brown and short. Rises suddenly at feet of observer, with a whirr of wings, usually uttering a harsh note, *kek*. Rapid twisting flight.

Habitat and range: Breeds in Japan, migrating to eastern Australia and Tas-mania where it is not uncommon from late August to March. Seldom reported from New Zealand but has occurred in widely separated districts in both islands. Easily overlooked because of its lurking habits. Feeds by probing the soft mud among short vegetation along the edges of reedy or grassy swamps.

LESSER KNOT *Calidris canutus* Pl. 30, p. 129

Other names: Huahou, Eastern Knot.

Description: 25 cm (10″). A compact short-legged rather nondescript shore-bird, often in very large flocks; and of the arctic waders which migrate to New Zealand, easily the most numerous after the Godwit. Sometimes big flights of 'godwits' over the northern harbours are more than fifty percent Knots.

In winter plumage the upperparts are grey, lightly speckled; eye-stripe whitish; rump barred white and dark brown showing pale in flight; rather indefinite white wing-bar; underparts pale grey or off-white. The moult into red summer plumage begins in February. Head, neck and breast become richly rufous and the black and silver speckling of the mantle more intense. Females are less resplendent than males. By April adults are in full breeding dress. Rather curiously, it is not unusual for flocks of red Knots to remain in New Zealand throughout the winter. Bill (3 cm) robust and straight; legs dull green.

Voice: A throaty *knut knut*. Flocks feeding or flying along the tideline often keep up a subdued not unmusical chatter, with higher-pitched notes *too-it-wit* or *quik-ik* interspersed.

Habitat and range: Breeds in eastern Siberia, migrating south; the bulk of the population of the eastern race (*rogersi*) evidently coming to New Zealand, where very large flocks occur annually in Kaipara, Firth of Thames, Manukau and at Farewell Spit, while smaller numbers visit most suitable harbours and estuaries as far south as Paterson Inlet. Occasionally at the Chathams. Has straggled to Macquarie.

Very much a bird of the tideline, commonly consorting with Godwits; and with them sometimes visiting salt-marshes and coastal pastures to feed where the vegetation is short and the ground wet. Sometimes Knots may be found apart in large unmixed flocks forming a solid grey carpet on sandy flats.

GREAT KNOT   *Calidris tenuirostris*   *Pl. 30, p. 129*

Description: 29 cm (11½″). Like Lesser Knot but larger and does not assume a red nuptial plumage. Upperparts grey, streaked with black; across rump a *narrow white band. Crown striped*, but without clear cut superciliary line. Underparts mainly white, except that foreneck and breast are variably streaked or spotted with brown. In breeding dress the colours of the mantle and scapulars are enriched, heightening the contrast of dark brown, white and chestnut; the underparts are blotched with blackish brown and the breast may become quite black. Bill (4 cm) dusky; legs (3.5 cm) olive-green.

Great Knots observed in New Zealand have been associating with Lesser Knots, among the great and dense flocks of which they are likely to be overlooked.

Habitat and range: Breeds in the mountains of north-eastern Siberia, migrating to winter mainly between India and northern Australia; occasionally overshooting to reach south-eastern Australia and more rarely New Zealand. First recorded Manawatu estuary, three, October 1967; then two, Firth of Thames, February 1970. Others since, one in Manukau in mid-April 1972 being in nuptial plumage.

PECTORAL SANDPIPER   *Calidris melanotos*   *Pl. 30, p. 129*

Description: 22 cm (8½″). Closely resembles the Sharp-tailed Sandpiper and only separable after close and careful scrutiny. Breast densely spotted and streaked, the markings forming a *solid gorget which ends abruptly* and contrasts sharply with the white underparts. In breeding dress does *not* develop crescentic spots on flanks. Superciliary stripe variable. Bill dark, *yellowish at base*; legs usually yellower than in *C. acuminata*. In flight a pale wing-bar shows indistinctly. On the ground has a habit of stretching its neck.

Voice: Rather silent; but call-note, an incisive *kreek* audible at some distance, is very helpful as a means of confirming identification when Sharp-tailed Sandpipers are also present.

Habitat and range: Breeds across arctic America and Siberia west to about Taimyr peninsula, its Siberian breeding range being more extensive than that of the Sharp-tailed Sandpiper. Main migration is to Central and South America; but a few evidently come directly south. Very rarely reported in Australia. Probably regular in very small numbers in New Zealand, where it has been reported from numerous estuaries and coastal lagoons from Kerikeri to Foveaux Strait.

Prefers shallow pools with vegetation to open shore-line. Will feed snipe-like in grassy marshes and can easily escape notice among water plants. In the Firth of Thames and Manukau, where it has frequently been observed on the same pools as parties of Sharp-tailed Sandpipers, it tends to keep near them but apart on the fringe.[1]

SHARP-TAILED SANDPIPER *Calidris acuminata* *Pl. 30, p. 129*
Other name: Siberian Pectoral Sandpiper.
Description: 22 cm (8½″). A brown, richly speckled sandpiper, which never looks really grey. Crown, chestnut streaked black; superciliary stripe whitish and varying in clarity; upperparts dark-brown, striped darker; rump and pointed tail dark brown with white sides; breast mottled grey or buffish with irregular streaks, fading to white on abdomen, but *with no sharp line of demarcation*. Young birds when they arrive in October look tawny and have bright chestnut crowns. In complete eclipse plumage the throat and breast are often quite unspotted. In breeding dress a warm buffy tone suffuses the plumage, the breast becomes more heavily spotted and *crescentic streaks* ('*little boomerangs*') *develop on the flanks*. Bill (2.5 cm) very slightly decurved; legs yellowish-green. Faint wing-bar shows in flight. When these sandpipers are in flocks, it can be seen that they may vary considerably not only in appearance, depending on age and state of moult, but also in size. Their brownness makes them conspicuous when they roost among Wrybills as they often do in Firth of Thames and Manukau.
Voice: Rather silent. A flock, when flushed, may utter some soft *pleeps* or *pips*.
Habitat and range: Breeds in a rather restricted area of north-east Siberia from lower Lena in west to Kolyma delta in east; migrating south mainly to Australia where it is one of the commonest of the arctic waders. A regular migrant to New Zealand, where though not common, it is the most numerous of the smaller sandpipers; occurring in small flocks with some regularity, Firth of Thames, near Napier, Wellington west coast, Lake Ellesmere and near Invercargill. By New Zealand standards a 'big' flock contains more than 30 birds. Will forage on open mudflats with Knots, but prefers shallow brackish lagoons, and may feed effectively hidden among *Salicornia*, *Cotula*, etc. As in Australia, only rarely do any of these sandpipers stay over the winter.

CURLEW SANDPIPER *Calidris ferruginea* *Pl. 30, p. 129*
Description: 22 cm (8½″). A small sandpiper about the same size as a Wrybill but with a *slender distinctly decurved bill*. In flight a narrow white wing-bar and white *upper tail-coverts* show clearly. The Curlew Sandpiper is one of those waders in which there is a striking difference between red summer and pale winter plumage. Curlew Sandpipers seen in New Zealand are usually brownish-grey and white juveniles or adults in eclipse; but some adults when they arrive in September retain traces of rufous nuptial plumage which is quickly lost, though an exceptionally red bird was seen in Manukau late in October 1959. Some adults begin to redden in January and by the end of March are in rich rufous breeding dress. In summer often feeds on the tideline among Knots

---

[1] Our Pectoral Sandpipers do not necessarily come from America. The range of this bird extends into Siberia, actually farther westwards than the rather restricted range of the Sharp-tailed, or Siberian Pectoral Sandpiper, whose breeding range in fact is enclosed within that of the American Pectoral.

where it is difficult to detect.

Voice: A distinct liquid *chirrip*. Small, fast-flying, swerving flocks keep up a musical twittering, *tirri-tirri-tirri*.

Habitat and range: Breeds in arctic Asia. Some annually reach New Zealand from early September onwards and stay till March-April. Occasionally non-breeding juveniles are reported in winter, when they tend to join flocks of Wrybills among which they can easily escape notice. A bird of tidal flats and shallow brackish pools.

The summers of 1969-70 and 1976-77 were marked by irruptions which were most observable in some of the northern inlets. Stead found these sandpipers several times at Lake Ellesmere where they are now being found again, and elsewhere south to Foveaux Strait. A flock of more than 30 birds is exceptional.

DUNLIN *Calidris alpina* *Pl. 32, p. 137*

Other name: Red-backed Sandpiper.

Description: 20 cm (8″). Although the nuptial plumage of Dunlins and Curlew Sandpipers is strikingly different, adults in winter plumage and juveniles at first glance are very alike. The Dunlin, shorter in the neck, bill and legs, has a 'hunched up' stance and the *rump is not white* but *has a dark centre* edged with white. Bill rather thick at base, nearly straight or slightly decurved towards tip. Upperparts scalloped greyish-brown, the colour becoming heightened with the assumption of breeding dress – hence the American name, Red-backed Sandpiper. Underparts, a variable grey wash on the chest with fine streaking; lower *breast* and *belly* whitish, *becoming black for the breeding season*. The local sightings indicate that some black on the belly may still be visible in November and may begin to show in February. In flight white wing-bar and sides of tail show clearly.

Voice: The old English name *Purre* is onomatopeic, based on attempted rendering of the short flight note; also given is a nasal *teerp* or *treer*.

Habitat and range: A holarctic breeder with several valid races. Highly gregarious in winter and one of the commonest shore birds in the Old World. Migratory but wintering mainly in the northern hemisphere, few reaching the tropics and still fewer passing through. A very rare straggler to Australia and New Zealand. Sight records from Manukau (1969) and Kaipara (1974). At Miranda in March 1977 the presence of a Dunlin among Wrybills and Curlew Sandpipers was betrayed by its blackening belly. A Dunlin in New Zealand is likely to belong to the large eastern race *sakhalina*.

BAIRD'S SANDPIPER *Calidris bairdi* *Pl. 32, p. 137*

Description: 19 cm (7½″). Smaller than a Wrybill, marginally larger than a Stint, and somewhat resembling an undersized Pectoral Sandpiper, but with black legs. *Buffy neck and chest are faintly streaked.* Pale margins to feathers on back and wing-coverts create a scaly pattern. Longish wings project beyond the tail; and the standing bird often looks flat and elongated. Rump and tail dark. Bill straight and slender. There is a faint wing stripe.

Because of the lack of any salient feature, extreme care must be taken in identifying this small graceful sandpiper.

Voice: Call note an incisive, high-pitched, trilled *pr-r-r-reet*.

Habitat and range: Breeds in arctic America and north-east Siberia, migrating mainly through the interior. A rare straggler to south-west Pacific; collected Tasmania (1965). Single birds found associating with other small waders Manukau (1970 and 1976) and Firth of Thames (1970-71).

WHITE-RUMPED SANDPIPER *Calidris fuscicollis*   *Pl. 32, p. 137*
Description: 19 cm (7½″). A small slender sandpiper in the same size group as *bairdi*; but greyer, less scaled on the mantle and with a clear *white rump. Grey neck and chest are finely but distinctly streaked.* Flight reveals a thin white wing-bar. Legs dark. Small size and straight bill distinguish *fuscicollis* from Curlew Sandpiper which also has a white rump. As breeding plumage is assumed, back and scapulars become rufous and black.
Voice: The call is a high-pitched *jeet* or *tsick*, reputedly unique and commonly uttered on rising.
Habitat and range: Breeds in arctic America, migrating mainly through the interior. A very rare straggler to New Zealand; two in Manukau (1969) and one at Parengarenga (1971).

RED-NECKED STINT *Calidris ruficollis*   *Pl. 30, p. 129*
Description: 15 cm (6″). The smallest of the arctic waders which visit New Zealand regularly, dwarfed even by Wrybills and Banded Dotterels, with which it habitually associates on the seashore. Adults when they arrive about October may still retain traces of rufous feathering on the neck; but in New Zealand this very small sandpiper is usually a predominantly grey and white bird; the head and sides of neck shaded grey; the back and wings mottled and the underparts white. Bill and *legs black.* Wing-bar just visible in flight. Before leaving for their arctic breeding grounds in April, adults assume nuptial plumage, most noticeable in the reddening of the neck-feathers. The colour spreads upwards till the head seems to be wearing a red balaclava, while the mottling of the back and wings deepens and becomes a richer brown. First year birds retain their grey and white plumage and may stay behind in New Zealand often attached to flocks of wintering Wrybills. A voracious feeder with a sewing-machine action.
Voice: When rising it sometimes utters a weak *chit, tit* or *wik*, repeated two or three times.
Habitat and range: Breeds in north-eastern Siberia. Though said to be the most numerous of the arctic waders which visit Australia, only small numbers annually reach New Zealand. Most frequently recorded from the harbours and estuaries of the north. Possibly a regular visitor to Lake Ellesmere and the Southland lagoons. Two at Enderby Island, January 1963 (B. D. Bell). The biggest flocks seldom exceed 40 birds.

SEMI-PALMATED SANDPIPER *Calidris pusilla*   *Pl. 32, p. 137*
Other name: Sand Peep.
Description: 15 cm (6″). About the same size as a Red-necked Stint but with a *much stouter bill* (2 cm), thick at the base and distinctly tapering. Upperparts greyish even in breeding season. Underparts white, the breast streaked lightly or not at all, and in winter the white of the throat extending above the shoulder

to form a *white half collar*. There is a well marked white superciliary stripe and a thin white wing-bar. The tail and centre of the rump are black, but the sides of the rump are white. Bill and legs black.

Likely to consort with other very small shore birds, stints or peeps.

The tiny webs between the toes are hardly a field character.

Voice: The note on rising is a husky *chrruk* or a hoarse *krip*. A clipped, shriller *chip* indicates alarm.

Habitat and range: The most numerous of the small American shore birds, breeding across the arctic coast from Labrador to Alaska, but apparently not west of Bering Strait; migrating south, commonly in company with Least (*C. minutilla*) and Western (*C. mauri*) Sandpipers.

The evidence that this 'difficult' peep has reached New Zealand is not conclusive, but sightings in Hawkes Bay and Firth of Thames, some supported by photographs, are strongly suggestive.

WESTERN SANDPIPER   *Calidris mauri*   *Pl. 32, p. 137*

Description: 17 cm (6½″). A stint-sized sandpiper with a long tapering black bill (2.5 cm) which in full adults is markedly decurved. Summer and winter plumages are quite distinct, so that birds seen in New Zealand are likely to be in a transitional plumage, which makes certain identification all the more difficult. In full breeding plumage crown, nape, cheeks and upperparts generally are bright rufous and the breast is firmly streaked, the spots becoming V-marks which may extend to the flanks. The tawny or rusty tone of the scapulars may be retained far into winter, when it contrasts with the grey mantle – a useful pointer for identification. In winter plumage also the superciliary stripe which shows only faintly in summer, is much clearer. The head is noticeably pale and the breast is white with a grey wash at the sides. Legs very dark. A very narrow wing-bar just shows in flight.

Voice: The flight call is described as a thin plaintive *kreep* or a squeaky *jeerp*.

Habitat and range: Breeds in extreme north-eastern Siberia and Alaska, migrating mainly down the Pacific coast to Central and South America. A rare vagrant to the south-west Pacific, where it is likely to consort with Red-necked Stints, though it may forage on its own. First recorded in New Zealand at Farewell Spit, October 1964. Further sightings at Rangiputa Bank, November 1970; Firth of Thames, summer of 1970-71; Parengarenga, April 1976.

LEAST SANDPIPER   *Calidris minutilla*   *Pl. 32, p. 137*

Other names: American Stint, Mud Peep.

Description: 15 cm (6″). A diminutive thin-billed sandpiper with *greenish-yellow legs*. In breeding dress feathers of head and back are reddish-brown with black centres which form dark lines down the back; the buffy breast is strongly speckled; a dark line passes through the eye and there is a whitish superciliary stripe. In winter plumage the upper parts are greyish brown and

PLATE 31 Red-necked (Northern) Phalarope (p.141); Red (Grey) Phalarope (p.140); Turnstone (p.129); Oriental Collared Pratincole (p.141); Ruff (p.138); Upland Sandpiper (p.124); Japanese Snipe (p.131); Chatham Island Snipe (p.130).

PLATE 31

RED-NECKED (NORTHERN) PHALAROPES
19 cm

winter

♀

♂

RED (GREY) PHALAROPES
20 cm

summer

winter

summer

TURNSTONES
23 cm

winter

ORIENTAL COLLARED
PRATINCOLES
23 cm

UFF (winter plumage)
cm

UPLAND SANDPIPER
30 cm

JAPANESE SNIPE 33 cm

CHATHAM ISLAND SNIPE 20 cm

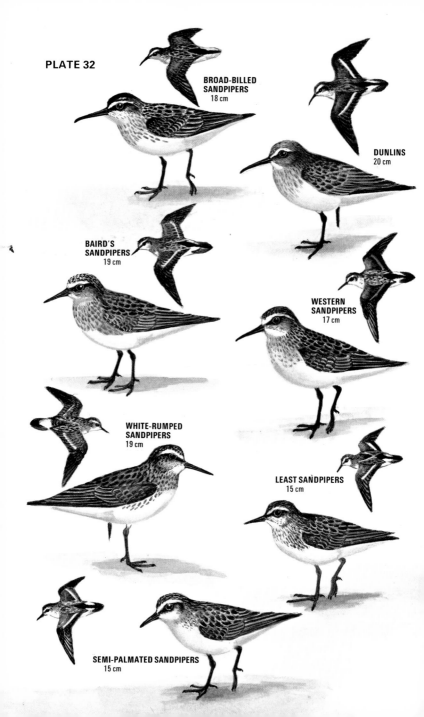

PLATE 32

BROAD-BILLED SANDPIPERS
18 cm

DUNLINS
20 cm

BAIRD'S SANDPIPERS
19 cm

WESTERN SANDPIPERS
17 cm

WHITE-RUMPED SANDPIPERS
19 cm

LEAST SANDPIPERS
15 cm

SEMI-PALMATED SANDPIPERS
15 cm

the breast is ashy-grey with fine dusky streaks. Flight reveals a narrow white wing-bar. Bill black, lighter at base.

Voice: A sharp grating *kreep* and sometimes on rising a longer drawn *quee-ee-eet*.

Habitat and range: Breeds across sub-arctic America from Alaska to Newfoundland; migrating south mainly through America and occasionally straggling east across the Atlantic or west to south-west Pacific.

At least three probable occurrences in New Zealand: Hawkes Bay, November 1952 and November 1953; and one Firth of Thames 1972 whose identification is supported by a colour slide.

LONG-TOED STINT *Calidris subminuta*

Description: 15 cm (6″). *A dark looking stint with greenish legs* and a middle toe about 2.5 cm long. In the field very difficult to distinguish from *minutilla* of which according to some authors it is the Asiatic counterpart, while others treat it as a full species.

Upperparts darkly streaked in such a way that they may resemble tortoiseshell; crown almost black; neck and breast grey; no white in tail, of which outer feathers are brown-grey.

Voice: Described as a shrill piping or rapid high-pitched *chee-che*.

Habitat and range: Breeds across Siberia from Bering Sea to Ural Mountains, migrating south to winter from India to Australia, but rare in southern Australia and not certainly recognised in New Zealand, where it could overlap with *minutilla*.

In Borneo Red-necked and Long-toed Stints tend to occupy distinct habitats, *subminuta* preferring typical 'snipe country', i.e. marshy ground with short grass and inland swamps up to 1000 m.

SANDERLING *Calidris alba*   *Pl. 30, p. 129*

Description: 20 cm (8″). An active, small, plump, short-legged sandpiper, very white about the head, showing *a small dark patch at the bend of the wing* and in flight a prominent white wing-bar. Upperparts pale grey faintly marked; underparts white; dark tail has white sides; in winter plumage the *palest of the sandpipers* resembling a Wrybill; but in April upperparts, head and breast become pale chestnut speckled with black. Bill and legs black. Bill straight and stout. Hind toe entirely absent.

Voice: Flight note a shrill but liquid *twick twick*.

Habitat and range: Breeds mostly in the high arctic; migrating south, small numbers regularly reaching the south-eastern coast of Australia. Recorded from Parengarenga, Bay of Plenty, Waikanae, Farewell Spit, Waimakariri estuary, Lake Ellesmere, Invercargill. Usually single birds reported, but small flocks do occur. Mainly frequents sandy beaches, where it always seems to be in a hurry as it feeds busily close to the tideline.

PLATE 32 Broad-billed Sandpiper (p.138); Dunlin (p.134); Baird's Sandpiper (p.134); Western Sandpiper (p.136); White-rumped Sandpiper (p.135); Least Sandpiper (p.136); Semi-palmated Sandpiper (p.135).

RUFF and REEVE *Philomachus pugnax* *Pl. 31, p. 136*

Description: 29 cm (11½″). Male (Ruff) in breeding dress with ruff and ear tufts spectacularly variable; but in winter plumage resembles the plain and distinctly smaller female (Reeve) (23 cm). Upper-surface brown, the mantle having a scaled appearance from the paler edgings to the feathers; wings darker. Underparts variably buffish or white. In the southern hemisphere, the most reliable features to clinch the identification are the *white oval patches on either side of the dark centre of the tail* revealed in flight, when a narrow white wing-bar also appears. Bill (3.5 cm) robuster in males than females. Legs show a wide range of colours – shades of yellow, green, brown, pink.

Habitat and range: Breeds across northern Eurasia, migrating mainly south-west towards Africa and India; only a straggler in Malaysia and very rare in the Pacific. Australian records are slowly accumulating. One sighting reported in New Zealand, Manukau Harbour (April 1964).

In winter quarters frequents marshes and the muddy shallows of lakes.

BROAD-BILLED SANDPIPER *Limicola falcinellus* *Pl. 32, p. 137*

Description: 18 cm (7″). One of the smallest sandpipers, larger than a Red-necked Stint and smaller than a Wrybill; and with rather snipe-like proportions. Upperparts brown-grey, mottled; feathers of wing-coverts with darker centres and pale margins; *head prominently streaked* with a dark-grey central panel, below which whitish stripes converge on the bill; underparts whitish; chest faintly spotted; tail blackish with white at sides. Bill long (3 cm), robust and black, distinctly *dipping downward near the tip*; legs short, dull green or olive-grey. In flight a narrow pale wing-bar becomes visible.

Voice: Sometimes trills *pürrr*, as it rises. Flight-note also described as a dry *chr-r-r-reet.*

Habitat and range: Breeds in remote arctic regions; migrating south, a few reaching south-eastern Australia. A very scarce visitor, first recorded Firth of Thames, January to March 1960, when one freely associated with other small waders both on the tideline and also at a roost on reclaimed saltmarsh sown with turnips; Karaka, 1/12/63, when one was present among summering Wrybills at a high-tide roost. In its winter quarters from Africa to Australia, this is a notoriously elusive species. In New Zealand the likeliest way of adding to our scanty knowledge of it may be by close examination of flocks of Wrybills in the northern harbours. Two near Miranda, February 1968, and one November 1970; one, Parengarenga, February-March 1970.

STILTS AND AVOCETS: Recurvirostridae

PIED STILT *Himantopus leucocephalus* *Pl. 25, p. 112*
Other names: Stilt, Barker, Poaka, White-headed Stilt, Daddy Longlegs, Torea (Rotorua), Pip (Kaipara).
Description: 38 cm (15″). A black and white wader with very long pink legs (25 cm) which in flight trail far behind the tail. Noisy and gregarious, often breeding in colonies, but isolated pairs may occupy small swamps. Wings, back and hind neck black; head and underparts white. A not uncommon variant has a complete black collar round the lower neck. Most first-year birds have traces of grey on head and lack the black hind neck; but some have almost pure white heads and necks. Bill (6 cm) black, fine and straight.
Voice: A puppy-like yapping *yep yep*. The call of the young is a shriller *kip kip*. Stilts call frequently when migrating by night.
Habitat and range: This is evidently one of the birds which has benefited from European methods of farming in the North and South Islands. In the middle of the nineteenth century it seems to have been relatively rare; but now it is the commonest of the larger waders which breed in New Zealand and it is still seeking new breeding grounds, especially in the north where it hitherto has been a rare and local breeder. After nesting there is a general movement from inland breeding grounds to the coast. Some winter in the South Island; but large numbers move north, though evidence is needed for the crossing of Cook Strait. After midsummer many thousands pour into the great harbours of the north and stay till about July, when the southward migration starts. By the end of August those remaining are the local breeders and immature non-breeders. Most Pied Stilts winter on the coast; but inland some are attracted by the shallows of Lake Rotorua.

Casual visitor to some off-shore islands, e.g. Little Barrier; breeds on Kapiti, Great Barrier, Ruapuke, and has bred on Waiheke. First recorded Stewart Island, 1956, and at Chatham Islands, 1961, when a pair bred.
Breeding: A successful coloniser because of its wide range of breeding habitats among which are the seashore, boulder banks, saline lagoons, swampy paddocks, river beds and lakesides up to more than 750 m. Breeding season, June to February (Auckland). Eggs buff or olive heavily blotched with black and brown spots and streaks; normal clutch four, occasionally five; incubation period 23–7 days; fledging 27–37 days. Incubation shared by both sexes.

BLACK STILT *Himantopus novaezealandiae* *Pl. 25, p. 112*
Maori name: Kaki.
Description: 38 cm (15″). Plumage entirely black with a greenish gloss on upper surface. Bright red eye. Bill (7 cm) black; legs pink. With its longer bill and shorter tarsus it is a bird of different proportions from the Pied Stilt. Both on the ground and in flight, it looks more compact and robust. The immature plumage varies; mainly black, but with smudgy patches showing white, especially on face and throat, thighs and lower abdomen.
Voice: Described as louder and deeper in pitch than that of the Pied Stilt.

139

Habitat and range: Formerly widespread; now rare but persisting in at least four scattered inland colonies in South Canterbury and North Otago. Most, if not all, breeding adults overwinter in the home area after the departure of the Pied Stilts, but some evidence points to a northward dispersal, especially of immature 'smudgies', as small flocks (the largest of 14 birds) have been reported several winters in Kawhia Harbour and odd birds usually reappear in autumn on the Auckland isthmus, including the occasional 'All Black'.

Breeding: Nests both on dry shingle-beds and also on adjacent swamps. Eggs, September to December; similar to those of Pied Stilt, but 'the difference they exhibit is very manifest to the eye, although not easily described' (Buller); normal clutch 4. Both sexes incubate.

RED-NECKED AVOCET *Recurvirostra novaehollandiae* *Pl. 25, p. 112*
Description: 45 cm (18″). White with *chestnut head and neck*; two black lines on mantle; wings brownish-black with broad white band across middle; bill long (9 cm) *upcurved*; legs greenish-blue. In flight legs are stretched out straight behind. Feeds with scythe-like sweep of the bill from side to side.

Habitat and range: An Australian species, but rare in Tasmania and the southeast; apparently tenuously established in New Zealand between 1859 and 1878, perhaps till 1892. Said to have bred in a few localities and reported in small flocks, mainly South Island; only twice North Island, viz. Wellington west coast and Whangarei. The only acceptable twentieth-century records are of one shot at Ellesmere in 1912 and one near Westport 1968-70. Typically a bird of shallow saline lakes and lagoons. Should Australian Avocets again attempt to establish themselves in New Zealand, there would not seem to be a lack of suitable breeding habitats.

PHALAROPES: Phalaropodidae

A small anomalous family (3 species) of sandpiper-like birds, in which *the females are larger and brighter than the males.* Two species are circumpolar, breeding in arctic and sub-arctic latitudes and migrating south to certain definite areas of the equatorial and southern oceans. In winter they are truly pelagic, living on the surface of the open sea and swimming buoyantly, sometimes in very large flocks.

At sea they feed on plankton. Hence they are sometimes known as 'whalebirds' or 'mackerel-birds' to sailors who believe that flocks of phalaropes indicate the presence of crustacea-eating whales and fish. As an adaptation to aquatic life their feet are partially webbed (lobed) and their under-plumage is thick.

RED (GREY) PHALAROPE *Phalaropus fulicarius* *Pl. 31, p. 136*
Description: 20 cm (8″). Females in breeding plumage with rich red underparts, white cheeks and dark crown are unmistakable. Males are paler. Upperparts boldly striated; broad white wing-bar conspicuous in flight. In winter fairly uniform blue-grey above, with white head and underparts, rather like a Sanderling, but with a dark mark through the eye. *Bill relatively heavy and broad, yellow* with dark tip. *Legs yellowish.* Appears a stockier and thicker-

necked bird than the Red-necked Phalarope.

Habitat and range: Breeding range more northerly than that of the other phalaropes. The only known wintering ground in the Pacific is off the west coast of Central and South America to about Lat. 50°S., especially on the off-shore border of the Humboldt current. A rare wanderer to New Zealand. Rather curiously, the three specimens collected here have all been females in breeding dress from the east coast. Waimate South (1883), Lake Ellesmere (1925), Hastings (1934). Continuous gales may drive phalaropes to seek the shelter of coastal lagoons. The fourth record (possibly a male) is of one in reddish plumage at Kaituna, Bay of Plenty, in June 1977.

RED-NECKED (NORTHERN) PHALAROPE *Phalaropus lobatus*

Pl. 31, p. 136

Description: 19 cm (7½″). Similar in habits to Red Phalarope, but perhaps more dainty and graceful. Easily recognisable in breeding plumage by white throat and underparts and *orange patch down sides of neck*. Bill black *slender and needle-like*; *legs blackish*. In winter the darker grey back, conspicuously streaked and the darker wings on which by contrast the white wing-bar is shown up more vividly, are useful field characters. As in the Red Phalarope there is a dark eye-to-ear patch.

Flight rapid and often erratic. Swims jerkily and may 'pirouette' when feeding among surface weeds on shallow water. Appears long-bodied as compared with a Sanderling. Notably approachable and indifferent to man.

Habitat and range: Breeding range less northerly than that of the Red Phalarope. Known wintering grounds in the Pacific are in the seas adjacent to Borneo and to the north of New Guinea; also with Red Phalaropes along Humboldt current.

A rare wanderer to New Zealand recorded from Lake Ellesmere (1929), Wanganui estuary (1935), Washdyke (1961).

PRATINCOLES: Glareolidae

Short decurved bill, forked tail and swallow-like flight in pursuit of insects set the pratincoles or swallow-plovers apart from other waders.

ORIENTAL COLLARED PRATINCOLE *Glareola maldivarum*

Pl. 31, p. 136

Description: 23 cm (9″). Looks unusual either in flight or on the ground. Upperparts olive-brown, darker on head; *rump white*, tail white with dark tip, *deeply forked*; throat buff, enclosed by a black line (less distinct in juveniles), which passes up the side of the neck to join the dark lores; breast rufous buff; abdomen white. Legs black and short; bill short (1.3 cm) and curved with a *scarlet margin to the gape*. Wings long, dark and pointed; *axillaries chestnut*. During the aerial hawking of insects, shape and action suggest a big brown swallow. On the ground has an almost tiptoe stance; walks or runs rapidly.

Voice: A soft plover-like note *towheet towheet* uttered as the bird rises has been

described. Flocks of the typical race *G. pratincola* are noisy in flight making a sharp rippling call *kikki kirrik* with variants; and also a simpler *kik kik kik*.
Habitat and range: Breeds widely in Asia in paddy plains, desert places and the drier areas of marshes; migrating south to Australia, but only occasionally in the south-east. A very rare straggler to New Zealand recorded Westport (1898), a flock of at least five on the beach; Appleby, one, May 1959; Port Adventure, Stewart Island, one, April 1963; L. Wainono, 1977, one hawking over feeding Pied Stilts.

SKUAS: Stercorariidae

Skuas, sometimes called Jaegers, are strong-flying pelagic birds allied to the gulls, with hooked beaks and piratical habits. In New Zealand waters they are most frequently seen pursuing terns and forcing them to drop or disgorge their food. They also attack gulls and other seabirds and will feed on offal.

Of the four species which regularly occur in New Zealand seas one (*lonnbergi*) breeds commonly in the sub-antarctic region; one (*maccormicki*) is a rare transient from the antarctic continent; two (*parasiticus* and *pomarinus*) are summer visitors from the arctic, the one common and the other rare. The adults of these two species are dimorphic, having light and dark phases; the plumage of immature birds shows a bewildering range of variations. A single example of a third arctic species (*longicaudus*) was found stranded at Muriwai.

SOUTHERN SKUA *Catharacta lonnbergi*   *Pl. 33, p. 144*
Other names: Sea-hawk, Hakoakoa.
Description: 63 cm (25″). Mainly dark-brown; superficially resembling a young Black-backed Gull in the brown plumage of its first autumn; but with conspicuous white patches in the wings at the base of the primaries and with some yellow showing in the feathering of the neck. Wings broad and rounded, not so angled and pointed as in the two northern skuas. Bill and feet black. Females are slightly larger than males.
Voice: Noisy at nesting site only, where there is a loud display call *charr-charr-charr*; single or double clucking notes and a thin wheezy call made with the beak open.
Habitat and range: Breeds sparingly in Fiordland; abundantly on Stewart Island and outliers and most sub-antarctic islands, north to the Chathams, south to Macquarie, usually in the vicinity of penguin or petrel colonies. Breeding grounds are deserted June-August, when it ceases to be a shore scavenger and becomes an ocean raider, reaching northern waters of New Zealand, but seldom reported near land except after persistent gales. Verification of flocks in Otago coastal waters in late summer is needed. Little known of its winter habits. Prions may be its main prey. One caught in a hawk trap on Awhitu peninsula.
Breeding: Some adults return to breeding grounds in August; most in September. Eggs dark stone colour with irregular blotches of dark brown, laid late October-early November. Incubation period about 27 days. Normal

clutch 2, but usually only one chick reared. Chicks in down are uniformly cinnamon brown. Three adults often reported in attendance at one nest.

ANTARCTIC SKUA   *Catharacta maccormicki*   *Pl. 33, p. 144*
Description: 53 cm (21″). Similar to Southern Skua but smaller and lighter in colour. *Adults*, but not first winter young birds, *have feathers of neck conspicuously streaked with yellow.*
Voice: A similar range of notes to that recorded for *lonnbergi.*
Habitat and range: The skua of the coast of Antarctica and the pack ice; has been found farther south than any other bird in the world. Occasionally wanders north in autumn and winter to New Zealand waters, but so far only four recorded, all wrecked on the long west coast of the North Island.

These skuas may visit and pass through New Zealand seas more often than is suspected, as they appear every May off the coast of Japan where they constantly attack shearwaters especially *P. tenuirostris* during the northern summer.
Breeding: The nest is commonly a mere scrape near a large breeding colony of penguins, petrels or seals. Eggs slightly paler in ground colour than those of *lonnbergi*; clutch 2. Down of nestlings is pale grey with a faint buffy tinge.

ARCTIC SKUA   *Stercorarius parasiticus*   *Pl. 33, p. 144*
Description: 43 cm (17″) (excluding any projecting tail-feathers). A dimorphic species about the size of a Red-billed Gull. Light phase—upperparts sooty-brown, sides of head and neck yellowish, underparts whitish, white patch in wings at base of primaries. Dark phase—almost entirely dark brown, with a little white usually visible at the base of the primaries, but sometimes difficult to see. Tail wedge-shaped with the central feathers elongated to a point in the adults. These develop about April. (It does not seem to be easy in New Zealand to see adults with these tail feathers fully elongated.) Immature birds in mottled plumage of different shades are very variable. Wings sharply pointed and angled. Before and after a dashing attack on terns, skuas usually fly low. Often hunt in pairs, but gatherings of up to fifty birds have been reported.
Habitat and range: Summer visitor to New Zealand from arctic regions where it is a circumpolar breeder. Easily the most numerous skua off the coasts of the North and South Islands south to Foveaux Strait. Commonly seen near breeding colonies of White-fronted Terns; rarely attacks Caspian Terns. Some immature birds remain over the winter, when they have been seen to harry Red-billed Gulls and to pursue a small passerine. These skuas are seldom on or over land; but occasionally one will settle on a beach near terns or gulls.

POMARINE SKUA   *Stercorarius pomarinus*   *Pl. 33, p. 144*
Description: 48 cm (19″) (excluding projecting tail feathers which, when present, are paddle-shaped and curiously twisted). A dimorphic species similar to Arctic Skua but bigger and more powerful. Easily distinguished if the central tail feathers are developed. Otherwise not easily separable from the Arctic Skua; but size, larger extent of white in the wings, and, *in immature birds, the pale rump*—upper tail-coverts white or black barred white—are useful pointers.
Habitat and range: Breeds mainly within the Arctic Circle. Scarce but probably

regular summer visitor to New Zealand south to Cook Strait, especially Farewell Spit, where they haunt the gull and tern colonies and appear to molest the big flocks of waders. Fairly common off the eastern and south-east coasts of Australia, where they habitually follow ships.

LONG-TAILED SKUA *Stercorarius longicaudus* *Pl. 33, p. 144*
Description: 35 cm (14″), excluding the long flexible central tail feathers which may project up to 22 cm in breeding plumage, which is unlikely to be seen in New Zealand waters. The smallest of the skuas, more streamlined than a Red-billed Gull, and tending to fly high and soar with a floating tern-like action.

Crown brownish-black, clear cut and contrasting with white collar and grey back. Cheeks and neck yellow. Upper surface generally dark ash grey, but flight feathers and tail almost black. Breast and underparts white merging into grey on lower belly. Bill black; legs grey. Young birds resemble young *parasiticus*; and though greyer and slightly smaller, are doubtfully distinguishable at sea.
Habitat and range: A holarctic breeder, migrating to the southern hemisphere. In the Pacific Ocean its main wintering area is off the west coast of South America. Very scarce in south-west Pacific, whence come a few inconclusive sightings and one specimen wrecked at Muriwai (January 1964).

GULLS, TERNS AND NODDIES: Laridae

Three species of gull are among the familiar birds of New Zealand. Two of them are conspicuous at most ports and along the popular beaches. In some districts the three occur together. The least plentiful is the endemic Black-billed Gull, which is primarily a bird of the South Island, where over large areas it replaces the Red-billed. All three species may be found well inland and the two smaller gulls readily follow the plough. Considerable skill is sometimes needed in differentiating between Red-billed and Black-billed Gulls. When they are in first year or subadult plumage, before the colours of bills and legs have become fixed, the surest and safest guide to identification is the shape of the wings, and the pattern of the primaries as seen in flight.

In view of the great variety of climates and habitats in the New Zealand region, it is not surprising that the terns and noddies are strongly represented. Fifteen species are known to occur, of which nine breed; three are scarce but possibly regular migrants from the northern hemisphere; and three are unusual stragglers from Australia or the tropical south-west Pacific.

The Sooty Tern and three small kinds of noddy nest at the sub-tropical Kermadecs. Caspian and White-fronted Terns frequent the coasts of the main

---

PLATE 33 Arctic Skua (p.143); Pomarine Skua (p.143); White-fronted Tern (p.151); Long-tailed Skua (p.144); Antarctic Skua (p.143); Southern Black-backed Gull (p.145); Southern Skua (p.142)

PLATE 33

ARCTIC SKUAS 42 cm

dark phase

light phase

dark phase

light phase

White-fronted Terns

POMARINE SKUAS
48 cm

LONG-TAILED SKUA
(non-breeding plumage)
35 cm

ANTARCTIC SKUAS
53 cm

THERN
K-BACKED
imm.
also
34)

SOUTHERN
SKUAS
63 cm

PLATE 34

SOUTHERN BLACK-BACKED GULLS 60 cm

first

seco

adult

RED-BILLED GULLS 37 cm

imm.

adult

BLACK-BILLED GULLS 37 cm

imm.

adult

GULL-BILLED TERN 43 cm

ARCTIC TERNS 38 cm

breeding

islands. The Fairy Tern seems to be confined for nesting to a single stretch of sandy coast in Northland. The marsh-terns are represented by the Black-fronted Tern, which breeds widely in the South Island east of the Alps. The Antarctic Tern has colonies at all the truly subantarctic island groups and reaches the northern limit of its breeding range at Stewart Island.

Little difficulty will be experienced in identifying most New Zealand terns when they are in breeding dress. But it can be very hard to diagnose adults of the several black-capped species, both resident and migratory, in eclipse, when the black cap is lost or recedes and the colour of the bill is dulled, and young birds in first-year plumage, even when closely observed.

SOUTHERN BLACK-BACKED GULL   *Larus dominicanus*

Pls. 33, 34, pp. 144, 145

Maori name: Karoro, Ngoiro (imm).

Description: 60 cm (24″). A large gull, with head, neck, upper tail-coverts, tail, and all underparts including underwing, white. Back and wings above are black, but tertials and secondaries are broadly tipped with white forming two bands when the wings are closed. The four outer primaries are also white-tipped and the outermost has a second sub-terminal patch of white, sometimes repeated on a smaller scale on the next. Bill yellow, with a splash of red at the angle of the gonys: gape and eyelid orange: iris pale hazel; feet mustard yellow

A typical gull bill

or olive-green according to age or season; female smaller and more slender than the male. This plumage is not attained until the bird's third winter. In first winter plumage the general tone is dark clove-brown all over, varied with buff-edged feathers dorsally, mottled beneath and barred brown and white on rump and tail-coverts above and below. Flight feathers and tail are uniformly brown, bill blackish, eye brown, feet grey. As most of the body feathers are

PLATE 34 Southern Black-backed Gull (p.145); Red-billed Gull (p.146); Black-billed Gull (p.147); Gull-billed Tern (p.148); Arctic Tern (p.153).

basally dull white the plumage rapidly becomes paler with wear. The first moult produces some dark scapulars and more white on the body, and the progress to maturity is accompanied by colour change in bill, iris and feet. The rate of change is not uniform and birds of the same age often appear superficially older or younger.

Voice: A wide range of calls used in varying circumstances has been fully described by Fordham (*Notornis x*, 5, 1963). (See page 224.)

Habitat and range: Although as a species it has a circumpolar distribution in the Southern Hemisphere this gull is sedentary and not pelagic. It frequents estuaries, harbours and open coastline, outlying and off-shore islands, river systems, lakes and alpine tarns. Scavenging and predation enable it to survive in non-marine localities, but its numbers are greatest near supplies of offal and smallest where it depends on shellfish and other sea-food. Rare straggler to the Kermadecs and Norfolk Islands.

Breeding: Colonies are found on coastal sand dunes, rocky islands, grassy seaward slopes, river-beds well inland and even on the mountains up to 1500 m. Isolated pairs may nest on rock stacks. Nests are often substantial, and may have a depression nearly as deep as the short diameter of the egg; eggs, normally three to a clutch, are greenish-bluish or buff in ground colour with purple or brown spots and blotches. Incubation period, 24–25 days. Downy chicks are mainly stone grey broadly spotted blackish on head and back, shading to greyish white on belly. Bill and feet leaden colour.

RED-BILLED GULL *Larus scopulinus* *Pl. 34, p. 145*

Other names: Tarapunga, Mackerel Gull, Jackie (Chathams).

Description: 37 cm (14½″). A small gull related closely to the Silver Gull (*Larus novaehollandiae*) of Australia. New Zealand populations are by no means uniform, the sub-antarctic race having a shorter, stouter bill and slightly darker plumage. The entire plumage of head, neck, underparts and tail is white. The mantle, back and wing-coverts are uniformly pale pearly grey as are the under wing-coverts. The primaries are mainly black but all are white-tipped in fresh plumage having hidden basal patches of white, and the two outermost have broad sub-terminal white bands on both webs. Bill, eyelids and feet are scarlet; the iris silvery white; males are larger and more robust than females. In the first immature plumage the feathers of the mantle have pale buffy tips and a dark band on the wing is formed by brownish patches on the secondaries. There is much less white on the primaries in this plumage. Bills are dark brownish black; eyes brown and feet purplish brown. The nestling down is warm greyish buff mottled with darker spots on the upper surface and paling to white on the abdomen.

Voice: A strident and tremulous scream is the usual alarm note associated with a short sharp cry. Skirling calls and softer notes are part of an elaborate display in the nesting season.

Habitat and range: In the main inhabitants of coasts and off-shore islands, these gulls are also found in small numbers inland on the larger lakes. Densely packed nesting colonies occur on many rock stacks and cliffs, but large colonies are also known from sandbanks and flat areas near the mouths of rivers. A small colony in Hokianga occurs on piles of an old jetty. Although fairly successful as predators on small post-larval fish, these gulls are also scavengers and have a wide range of diet including earth worms, insects and occasionally berries. Rare straggler to the Kermadecs and Norfolk Islands.

Breeding: In the situations already mentioned the nest is usually well formed of grass and other adaptable material. The usual clutch is two eggs, sometimes three, of variable ground colour, but mainly brownish-ochre, with the dark spotting and blotching characteristic of gulls' eggs generally. Incubation period *c.* 21 days. The sub-antarctic forms, already mentioned as distinguishable, have also a distinctive nesting habit, the nests being found in caves and cavities and rarely exposed in the open. Both sexes incubate.

BLACK-BILLED GULL *Larus bulleri*   *Pl. 34, p. 145*
Other name: Buller's Gull.

Description: 37 cm (14½″). Superficially similar to the Red-billed Gull, this species has nevertheless the more delicate structure and characteristic wing pattern of the several Black-headed Gulls of the Northern Hemisphere. It resembles them also in its habitat preference. Entire plumage of the head, neck, underparts and tail is white. Mantle and upper wing-coverts are very pale pearly grey as are the under wing-coverts. *The pattern of black and white on the primaries* is the most conspicuous field character, the *outer primaries being mainly white* for the greater part of their length with a small sub-terminal area and border of black. As in most other gulls, they are white-tipped. Bill black with reddish gape and interior; feet dark reddish black; eyelid dark red; iris white. In immature plumage there are buffy tips to most of the mantle feathers. Sometimes a trace of black in the tail and brown patches sub-terminal in the secondaries. In very young birds the bills are pale pinkish brown and the feet about the same colour; iris brown. However, the first stage of change in bill and feet is in the direction of red which becomes quite bright in the second year and is a field character causing some confusion with the Red-billed Gull, as in fact the immature brownish-black bill of the latter causes it to be sometimes misidentified as a Black-billed Gull. The downy plumage of chicks is pale buff, sometimes almost pinkish, with a light blotching of darker tufts. Belly down is whitish.

Voice: Very similar to that of the Red-billed Gull, but more high-pitched and less powerful.

Habitat and range: This is essentially an inland gull of the larger river systems and lakes of the South Island, although it moves to the coast in winter, when fair numbers drift northwards and cross Cook Strait. Many colonies in association with Red-billed Gulls occur near the mouths of the larger rivers. In the North Island the only known regular breeding colony was at Rotorua; but up to 15 pairs now nest near Gisborne and in the 1970s the breeding range was extended north to the Firth of Thames. Non-breeders are the dominant small gull at Hawkes Bay estuaries in summer. A flock of some hundreds winters on the Miranda Coast of the Firth of Thames; and smaller numbers occur at Bay of Plenty estuaries. A few visit Stewart Island. Recorded as a straggler at the Snares.

Aquatic and terrestrial insects form much of its diet but it also feeds in flocks over farmland and obtains a good deal of marine food from estuaries and shallow coasts. Less inclined than the Red-billed Gull to become parasitic on man.

Breeding: Nesting habits, except its preference for river-beds well inland, are very similar to those recorded for the Red-billed Gull. The eggs are usually somewhat light in colour and have less intensity of spotting and blotching. In the mixed colony at Rotorua, Black-billed Gulls lay two or three weeks later than the Red-billed. Clutch, normally 2. Incubation period, 20–24 days. Chicks are covered with a streaky grey, brown and white down. Both sexes incubate.

GULL-BILLED TERN   *Gelochelidon nilotica*   *Pl. 34, p. 145*
Description: 43 cm (17″). An obvious tern, but distinguished from the typical terns by its *thick black gull-like bill*, less forked tail and longish legs. Upperparts greyish-white; crown and forehead black; underparts white; outer webs of outermost primaries slate-grey; legs black. In winter plumage head is nearly white. Long tarsus (4 cm) gives rather high stance.
Voice: The calls of the typical race have been described as a 'throaty rasping *za-za-sa* or *kayweek*'. Those of the Australian race have been recorded as *kuh-wuk kuh-wuk* repeated several times; and a *che-ah*.
Habitat and range: Mainly a freshwater tern, which commonly feeds over pasture, marsh and still water. An almost cosmopolitan species, represented in Australia by *macrotarsa*, but not common in south-east Australia or Tasmania. It is not inconceivable that the migratory race *affinis* from eastern Asia is reaching New Zealand.

Two were found associating with gulls and waders on the short turf of Invercargill airport in May 1955 and were reported still present two months later. After sightings of single birds at Southland lagoons in 1964 and 1965, there was an upsurge of records in the mid-1970s, e.g. from estuaries on both sides of Cook Strait and most notably from the southern shore of Manukau Harbour, where at least 8 summered in 1975-76 and 6 in 1976-77.

BLACK-FRONTED TERN   *Chlidonias albostriatus*   *Pl. 35, p. 152*
Other names: Tara, Sea Martin, Ploughboy, Inland Tern, Riverbed Tern.
Description: 30 cm (12″). The common inland tern of the South Island; rather dusky and markedly smaller and greyer than the White-fronted Tern with which it sometimes associates at river mouths and on sea beaches. Adults in breeding dress are dapper and colourful. Top of head and nape deep velvety black; broad white stripe below the eye; mantle, upper surface, tail and underparts a delicate blue-grey; *rump white particularly noticeable in flight*; *bill* and *feet bright orange-red*. During the postnuptial moult the black cap is lost and the top of head and nape are a very pale grey. Many adults have assumed their distinctive breeding dress by the end of May.

Young resemble adults in eclipse; but show some brown speckling on the upper surface, have a white throat and paler breast; bill at first dusky, then yellowish with dark tip and legs dull yellow.
Voice: The common call is 'a high-pitched, staccato, whistling note given at intervals' (Stead). Variations of this sharp *ki-kit* include *ki-ki-kit*, *ki-ki-ki-ki-kit* and sometimes a single *kit*. Intruders near the nest are assaulted with a harsh angry *yark*; and an additional call when disturbed is a *curr*, like protest note

of the White fronted Tern.

Habitat and range: Now known to breed only in the South Island east of the main range, on river-beds and lake shores up to the foot of the glaciers, from Marlborough to Southland. Scarce in Westland. Formerly bred in the North Island 'far up the course of the Whangaehu River' near the south-east base of Ruapehu, and may yet be discovered breeding on some river-beds of Hawkes Bay, where some are found every winter at the estuaries.

In autumn there is a general movement from the breeding grounds down to the coast. Some go south to Stewart Island and some hundreds cross Cook Strait to winter on the Wellington coast especially at Waikanae, where biggest flock recently recorded in North Island was *c.* 320 on 18/5/58; and Palliser Bay. On the west stragglers and even small flocks may reach Auckland, the northern-most records coming from Kaipara.

Another regular wintering ground is in the Bay of Plenty from Whakatane to Matata, especially the estuaries of the Rangitaiki and Tarawera, where in 1952 over 120 were present. The provenance of these birds is unknown.

Inland these terns habitually hawk insects over rivers, lakes, swamps, and damp pastures, and even growing crops; and they will follow the plough. In winter commonly feed offshore.

Found only in New Zealand, the Black-fronted Tern is sometimes treated as a strong subspecies of the Whiskered Tern (*C. hybrida*).

Breeding: Breeds in loose colonies on shingly river-beds often in association with Black-billed Gulls, occasionally beside a brackish lagoon at sea level. Nest a scrape in silt or sand among large round stones. Eggs, late September-January; dark stone copiously marked with light and dark brown blotches. Clutch 1–3, typically 2. Incubation period *c.* 21 days. Both sexes incubate.

WHITE-WINGED BLACK TERN *Chlidonias leucopterus*   *Pl. 35, p. 152*

Description: 23 cm (9″). In breeding dress which is strikingly smart and distinctive, head and body black; *tail conspicuously white* and only slightly forked; wings black, white and grey, the fore-edge above ('shoulder') being white and beneath black, thus showing a quite diagnostic pattern; bill small and reddish; legs red. Breeding dress is assumed between January and April; but these terns in full or almost full breeding dress have been observed in New Zealand in every month of the year.

Adults in eclipse are mainly grey and white; but a black band passes from behind eyes over the back of the crown and joins a club-shaped area of black on the nape. First year birds resemble adults in winter, but have upperparts variably mottled with brown. The plumage changes of the White-winged Black Tern are notoriously puzzling.

Voice: Rather a silent tern. One in Manukau was once heard to utter an incisive *keevit* and a sharp *keet*.

Habitat and range: A typical marsh-tern, breeding across the temperate palaearctic from eastern Europe to eastern Asia. Reported to have bred in Africa south of the equator. Birds from eastern Asia migrate south, to winter especially in Borneo and north-eastern Australia; but juveniles are particularly prone to be over-carried and may reach New Zealand where the same bird may frequent a suitable habitat for several months or even years. Reported from

Bay of Islands to Invercargill, mainly at coastal lagoons, estuaries and marshes; sometimes over high wetlands in the Mackenzie country. A few seem to reach New Zealand annually. History was made in the summer of 1973-74 when a pair bred in South Canterbury.

Shallow pools which attract Pied Stilts are likely to suit wandering White-winged Black Terns. They are largely insectivorous and have been seen to walk round on muddy ground, snapping up flies. The flight is swift, agile and buoyant. In cold blustery weather they seem tireless, and for hours on end they will hawk insects over a pool dipping down to the water but not breaking the surface; flying low they work their way upwind till they reach the edge of the pool; then they swing back to the lee shore and begin the circuit over again. To rest they will settle quite fearlessly among Pied Stilts or other species of terns and on the edge of flocks of waders.

CASPIAN TERN *Hydroprogne caspia*   *Pl. 35, p. 152*

Maori name: Taranui.

Description: 51 cm (20″). The largest of the terns with a wing span of 1.4 m. Upperparts pale grey; underparts white. Forehead, cap and nape of adults black in breeding dress; cap greyish, almost white in winter; but many adults have assumed breeding dress by mid-July. Bill (7 cm) massive orange-red, dusky towards top which is yellow; legs black. Juveniles have top of head more or less streaked; upperparts at first spotted with black and brown; bill duller and feet dusky yellowish. Recently hatched chicks in grey down have orange-red bills.

In flight the *wing-tips* are seen to be *black on the underside* and the tail not deeply forked.

A tern of shallow coastal waters, over which it fishes often hovering characteristically with head pointing downwards; seldom seen far out to sea.

Voice: Commonly a harsh grating corvine *kaah* or *karh-kaa*; also a slow gruff *kuk-kuk*; a faster *kak-kak-kak* and a scolding *yakketi-yak*. Several months after fledging young birds will still badger adults with a peevish mewing or high pitched squeaky whistle *queea-queea*.

Habitat and range: Widely but unevenly distributed in tropic and temperate zones. Fairly plentiful around the coasts of the North and South Islands; most numerous in the north, but becoming scarce south of Canterbury and Westland, though breeding regularly near Bluff. Not yet reported from Stewart or Chatham Islands.

Commonly frequents estuaries and penetrates rivers especially in the North Island to inland lakes. Regular at Rotorua where a few pairs breed at *c*. 300 m a.s.l. and winter roosting flock may number 50. In autumn the large shallow harbours of the north receive an influx; and it is quite normal to see groups of 100-200 resting on shellbanks at high tide among waders. There is growing evidence that birds from the south tend to move north for the winter. Banding has shown that there is considerable local movement in the province of Auckland, and one bird banded in Northland has been recovered in the South Island.

Breeding: Mainly a colonial nester on shingle banks, beaches and sand-dunes. A normal colony has 5–20 pairs; but at least two in the north have more than

100 pairs. Sometimes isolated pairs will breed on promontories or rocky islets. Inland nesting occurs at Rotorua, near or in the colony of Red-billed and Black-billed Gulls. Eggs, September-January, light stone or pale blue-green thickly sprinkled with dark brown spots and blotches; clutch 1–3, most frequently 2. Incubation *c.* 21 days; fledging at least four weeks. Inopportune gales with high tides or blown sand cause many casualties among eggs and chicks. Both sexes incubate.

WHITE-FRONTED TERN *Sterna striata*   *Pl. 35, p. 152*
Other names: Sea-swallow, Kahawai Bird, Tara, Blackcap, Grenadier, Swallow-tail, Noddy (Chathams), Tikkitak (Stewart Is.).
Description: 42 cm (16½″). A typical sea-swallow and by far the commonest tern around the New Zealand coast. *Forehead* and *lores white*; crown and nape black; upperparts pearl grey; outer web of first primary brownish black; underparts white; breast sometimes showing a transient pink. Bill black; legs dusky or dull red. Some adults assume breeding dress, as indicated by *narrow white forehead* and long tail-streamers, by midwinter. Adults in eclipse have more white on forehead and a mottled crown; subadults (second year birds) are similar, but above the *high white forehead* are black on the crown. First winter birds have crown and nape streaked with black, white and buff; mantle barred and mottled, a blackish wash on the shoulders of the wings, and a dusky edging to fork of tail. Tail, white in adults, deeply forked, the depth of the fork varying according to the season.
Voice: Call note a high-pitched *siet*, *tsit* or *zitt*, frequently used in flight either by day or night or e.g. when 'working' over a shoal of fish. When molested the protest note is a rasping *kee-eet* or harsh *keark*, or *keh*, *keeahk*, *keeakh*.
Habitat and range: Breeds only in New Zealand (not Three Kings), from Aupori Peninsula south to Chatham and Auckland Islands. In autumn large numbers, especially young birds, migrate to south-eastern Australia, where widespread May-November on coasts of New South Wales, Victoria and Tasmania, a few ranging west to Southern Australia or north to Queensland.

The annual trans-Tasman migrations of this tern give it a certain unique distinction. Ringing has shown that birds from both Lake Ellesmere and the Firth of Thames may cross to Australia. Many, however, remain in New Zealand throughout the winter.

Said to be completely absent from Chatham Islands from about end of March to mid-August.

Rarely reported inland; but has visited Taupo and Rotorua. Feeds mainly in coastal waters, sometimes a few miles out to sea, forming great 'swirls' over shoaling fish with gannets and shearwaters; in autumn especially a few may fish up tidal creeks and rivers.
Breeding: Breeds in colonies among sand-dunes, at estuaries on shingle-banks, rock-stacks and cliffs; many colonies in inshore waters containing hundreds of pairs; others, especially on the outer off-shore islands of the north, only a few, 10–20 pairs. Notoriously capricious; a site successfully used one year may not be used the next; or else a few pairs will return, lay a few eggs in a rather desultory way and then abandon the site for the rest of the season.

In the north these terns start revisiting nesting grounds in August; but the first eggs do not appear until mid-October. Some young are on the wing before Christmas. Casualties are heavy and egg-laying may continue into January, but, more often than not, the young which are hatched from late eggs are abandoned before they can fly. Eggs, almost indescribably variable; clutch commonly 1, sometimes 2. Incubation *c.* 24 days; fledging *c.* 4 weeks. Both sexes incubate.

CRESTED TERN *Sterna bergii* *Pl. 36, p. 153*
Description: 47 cm (18½″). Markedly larger than a White-fronted Tern and with much greyer upperparts. *Forehead white*; crown and nape black with elongated feathers which can be raised to form a crest; underparts snow-white. Bill (6 cm) powerful, *greenish-yellow*; feet dull red or brownish black. Juveniles and adults in eclipse have crown streaked or mottled black and white.
Voice: A throaty dissyllable variously recorded as *kurrik, kyark, kair-rik, kārruk.*
Habitat and range: In the Indian Ocean and south-west Pacific, a common and widespread species, of which the form *cristata* is plentiful on the coasts of Australia and Tasmania, habitually fishing in estuaries and penetrating rivers. A very rare straggler to New Zealand: Raoul Island (April 1910); Spirits Bay, one ashore dead (March 1951); Farewell Spit, one among White-fronted Terns (January 1960); Firth of Thames one (March 1974). In Australian waters often feeds well out to sea, e.g. among shearwaters.

ANTARCTIC TERN *Sterna vittata* *Pl. 36, p. 153*
Description: 40 cm (16″). Rather smaller than a White-fronted Tern. Forehead, crown, nape black; a broad streak of white from gape below eye to nape, upper surface a soft shade of light bluish grey; outer webs of outermost primaries blackish; rump and tail white, only the outer webs of the tail feathers being pale grey; underparts, including throat, greyish white; but undertail-coverts white. Bill vermilion or coral red; legs orange-red. Tail deeply forked, white. In eclipse April to October, forehead and crown are white; bill and feet dusky red. In their first winter young birds closely resemble adults in eclipse, but have pure white underparts.
   Flight undulating. Boldly attacks Southern Skuas, if they pass near the nest.
Voice: Shrill and high-pitched.
Habitat and range: Circumpolar, represented in New Zealand by the subspecies *bethunei*, which breeds in all groups of the sub-antarctic islands from Macquarie to the Snares and Stewart Islands. No evidence of migration in the New Zealand region.
Breeding: Nest a shallow scratching with some protection usually afforded by vegetation on rocks near the sea and on cliffs up to 120 m a.s.l. Eggs, November to January, dark green, olive or olive-brown with spots of black or dark brown and underlying markings of grey. Clutch 1–2.

PLATE 35 Fairy Tern (p.154); Little Tern (p.154); White-winged Black Tern (p.149); Black-fronted Tern (p.148); White-fronted Tern (p.151); Caspian Tern (p.150)

PLATE 35

FAIRY TERN 25 cm

LITTLE TERNS 25 cm

WHITE-WINGED BLACK TERNS 23 cm

imm.

BLACK-FRONTED TERNS 30 cm

imm.

WHITE-FRONTED TERNS 41 cm

imm.

CASPIAN TERNS 51 cm

imm.

PLATE 36

WHITE TERNS 31 cm

WHITE-CAPPED NODDIES 34 cm

COMMON NODDY 39 cm

GREY TERNLETS 28 cm

ANTARCTIC TERNS 40 cm

SOOTY TERNS 45 cm

CRESTED TERN 47 cm

ARCTIC TERN   *Sterna macrura*   *Pl. 34, p. 145*

Description: 38 cm (15″). Distinctly smaller than a White-fronted Tern. The salient features of breeding dress are: black cap, contrasting with white streak below; bill blood-red, without dark tip; legs coral red; tail deeply forked with long streamers projecting a little beyond wing-tips, when perched; throat, breast and abdomen pale grey. It is just possible that northward bound Arctic Terns, showing these characteristics, in April, might pause on the coast.

However, most Arctic Terns in New Zealand seas are likely to be in eclipse, immature (first winter) or subadult plumage with bill and legs blackish; forehead and crown white or streaked black and white; undersurface white, not grey.

In breeding dress Antarctic and Arctic Terns would be almost indistinguishable in the field; but where the two species occur together in the southern oceans, Antarctic Terns are generally in nuptial plumage, whereas Arctic Terns are not and are without their long tail streamers; but subadult non-breeding Antarctic Terns complicate an already difficult problem of field identification. The following guide to distinguishing the two species in the Antarctic has been proposed by M. C. Downes (*Emu* 1952, 307).

Arctic Tern	*Antarctic Tern*
slighter build	bigger body
shorter wings and tail	longer new feathers
dives up and down frequently	dives more decisively
straight flight	undulating flight
black bill and feet	red bill and feet
white or slightly grey underparts	deeper grey underparts
sometimes brown patchy mantle and back of wings	even grey on mantle wings
dark cubital band	no cubital band

The *very short tarsus* of the Arctic Terns is a useful aid to identification, if they are seen perched. The narrow grey band on the inner web next to the shaft of the outermost primaries and the dark grey outer webs of the outside tail feathers are hardly field characters; but are pointers to establishing the identity of a bird in the hand.

Voice: A high whistling note *kee-kee* rising in pitch is said to be characteristic.

Habitat and range: In the course of a year an Arctic Tern enjoys more daylight than any other bird. In the northern autumn these terns set out for Antarctica, migrating mainly by two routes, one down the eastern side of the Atlantic, the other down the eastern side of the Pacific. Those that reach antarctic and sub-antarctic seas south of New Zealand probably do so by the Atlantic route and are swept eastwards by the prevailing westerlies.

They are certainly more numerous in the New Zealand region than the few records suggest.

Probably a regular visitor to our sub-antarctic islands where they have been

PLATE 36 White Tern (p.156); White-capped Noddy (p.156); Grey Ternlet (p.157); Common Noddy (p.155); Antarctic Tern (p.152); Sooty Tern (p.155); Crested Tern (p.152).

reported from Macquarie, Auckland and Campbell Islands. Very rarely recorded from the main islands, mostly west coast of North Island as north-bound migrants, possibly off course, since there is some evidence to show that these terns keep well out to sea on their long journeys to and from Antarctica. **Note:** The dark-billed Eastern Common Tern (*S. hirundo longipennis*) may reach the Tasman Sea at the southern limit of its migration. It has been recorded several times from Lord Howe Island and the south-eastern coast of Australia. Its claim to be on the New Zealand list depended on the fragmentary remains of a single bird found at Karekare on the Auckland west coast on 23/8/1959 till one appeared on Lake Horowhenua in 1977.

FAIRY TERN *Sterna nereis* *Pl. 35, p. 152*
Description: 25 cm (10″). The smallest and rarest of the terns which breed in New Zealand. Very pale grey above, white below, with crown of head and nape black and a black band extending forward from eye, *ending about half a centimetre from bill*; forehead white. Bill yellow, *without dark tip*; legs orange. Though the tails of breeding birds are forked, the outer tail feathers are not markedly elongated. Immature birds have dusky legs and bills and are said to be inseparable in the field from *S. albifrons*.
Voice: Call note a high-pitched rasping *zwit* or *zewit*. If disturbed near nest the protest note is a repeated *tee-tee*, followed by the rasping *zwit*.
Habitat and range: Primarily an Australian species, breeding commonly on the south and west coasts, but not in eastern Australia or Tasmania where it is replaced by *S. albifrons*. Now known as a breeding bird in New Zealand only from Northland, where probably fewer than ten pairs attempt to nest. A hundred years ago it is said to have been more widespread and even to have bred inland on the river-beds of the South Island. This small tern is not a colonial nester, the few pairs being scattered over many miles of open sandhills. It seems that for some months in winter the breeding area is deserted and it is not known where the few New Zealand Fairy Terns go.
Breeding: Fairy Terns reappear at breeding grounds in September and begin to make trial nest scrapes in the sand. Eggs, November to January; clutch usually 2; pale buff blotched and spotted with black, dark grey and brown. Incubation at least 18 days; fledging *c.* 24 days. Both sexes incubate.

LITTLE TERN *Sterna albifrons* *Pl. 35, p. 152*
Description: 25 cm (10″). Separable in the field from *S. nereis* only in breeding plumage by colour of bill, *yellow with black tip*, and pattern of black and white on head, viz. a black narrowing streak from eye *forward to bill*; black crown well forward and white recess below forming *an acute angle* above eye, not rounded as in *S. nereis*. Immature birds, with blackish patch on 'shoulder' of wing, and adults with crown mostly white, bill and legs dusky, appear in spring, especially November, in the northern harbours, in small flocks and stay over the summer, the adults assuming breeding dress between February and April when they disappear; a few presumably immature birds have been seen in winter. The tail which, over most of the summer, is so short as to be stumpy, is well forked by April.
Voice: A sharp *kweek* or a rasping *zweek* which seemed to be a note of alarm

was made by each of seven as they rose from among Wrybills. While hovering an urgent *peep-peep-peep* may be often repeated. A lively pleasant chattering *chi-chi-chi-chi* or an excited chittering may accompany what appears to be pair formation or courtship flights.

Habitat and range: An almost cosmopolitan species, represented in the western Pacific by *S. a. sinensis*, which breeds from China and Japan to eastern Australia and Tasmania. Small terns adjudged to be *sinensis* regularly associate with the big mixed flocks of waders in summer, feeding over the shallows in the large northern harbours, and some scores may gather at high tide roosts. In the South Island small dark-billed, short-tailed terns have recently been reported from the estuaries of Taramakau and Wairau (Blenheim), Lake Ellesmere, Otago Harbour and the Southland lagoons. States of plumage, times of moult and seasonal behaviour of most of these small terns postulate an origin in the northern hemisphere.

SOOTY TERN   *Sterna fuscata*   *Pl. 36, p. 153*
Other name: Wideawake.

Description: 45 cm (18″). Entirely dark brownish black above, except for *white forehead*, and *white recess above the eye* from which a narrowing black stripe runs forward to beak. White below, *including underwing*. Tail deeply forked, the outer tail feathers having the appearance of streamers, though their length and the depth of the fork varies considerably. The outer edge of the longest tail feathers is white. Bill and legs black. Flying low at a distance, this tern looks jet black till the white underparts become visible.

Voice: Not unlike the word *wideawake* spoken in a squeaky voice or with a twang, the accent being on the first and last syllables. A protest note at the nest *go-ak*.

Habitat and range: Ranges over most tropical and sub-tropical seas. Though it breeds abundantly at Lord Howe, Norfolk and Kermadec Islands, it is seldom reported from New Zealand proper. The recorded occurrences form an interesting pattern. Most are from late summer, following northerly gales, but at least six from the tail-end of winter when New Zealand waters are at their coldest. Sooty Terns are sometimes blown inland. The most southerly records are from Cook Strait.

Breeding: The first Wideawakes return to Raoul about mid-August. Most eggs are laid between mid-October and the end of December. Clutch 1. Incubation *c.* 24 days. Some young are on the wing in mid-February. By the end of April the breeding grounds are almost deserted.

COMMON NODDY   *Anous stolidus*   *Pl. 36, p. 153*
Other names: Noddy Tern, Brown Noddy.

Description: 39 cm (15½″). Forehead almost white, top of head pale grey; lores black, sharply contrasting with whitish forehead; plumage otherwise dark brown, with primaries and tail nearly black; underwing and throat greyer. Bill stout (4.5 cm), black; feet brownish-black with yellowish webs. Tail rounded, not forked.

Voice: A harsh corvine *kar-r-rk* or *kwok-kwok*.

Habitat and range: Tropical and sub-tropical waters of the Atlantic and Pacific.

The subspecies *pileatus* ranges throughout the south-west Pacific, its southern-most breeding stations being at Lord Howe and Norfolk Islands. Rather anomalously this noddy has not been reported from the Kermadecs and its claim to be on the New Zealand list is based on two rather unsatisfactory nineteenth-century reports. It is curious that it should be so scarce in New Zealand waters, for in the Atlantic it breeds as far south as Tristan da Cunha, in the same latitude as Auckland.

WHITE-CAPPED NODDY   *Anous minutus*   *Pl. 36, p. 153*
Other names: Lesser Noddy, Black Noddy.
Description: 34 cm (13½"). Forehead and top of head silvery white; plumage otherwise black, but not uniformly; wings very dark; tail brownish-black; lores, band through eye and throat jet black. Bill slender (4 cm), black; feet dark brown.
Habitat and range: Several subspecies have been described from tropical seas. The form *minutus*, which breeds at Norfolk and Kermadec Islands, ranges from New Guinea and Queensland to the Tuamotu Archipelago. From New Zealand proper it is seldom reported. An exhausted bird flew into a tree at South Kaipara Heads during a north-westerly gale (October 1953); another was seen sitting among White-fronted Terns on Farewell Spit and then flying strongly out to sea (January 1961). Others have since occurred in Northland after tropical storms, and one reached Otago in autumn 1977.
Breeding: On Meyer Islet, a nest of forest debris occasionally with some seaweed is built in a tree, karaka, ngaio or pohutukawa. On Macauley Is., in the almost complete absence of woody plants, the nest is placed on rock ledges and in caves. Laying begins in October. Clutch 1. Incubation 35 days; fledging *c.* 51 days. Most young are on the wing by the end of March.

WHITE TERN   *Gygis alba*   *Pl. 36, p. 153*
Other names: White Noddy, Love Tern, or rather confusingly, Fairy Tern.
Description: 31 cm (12½"). The most ethereal of seabirds. Ivory white, with a narrow black ring round the eye and usually dusky shafts to the primaries and tail feathers. Bill (4 cm) rather stout, black, blue at base; feet black or bluish with yellowish webs. Juveniles have a black spot behind the eye, darker shafts to the wing-quills and tail feathers; and the feathers of the mantle are tipped with rusty brown. Against the sunlight the wings and forked tail of these elfin-like terns appear translucent. Flight swift and erratic.
Voice: Of the Atlantic form, Murphy remarks, 'They have a way of fluttering just in front of one's face, not attacking, but merely staring, hovering like over-grown mosquitoes, and wheezing in a way to suggest the buzz of some such noxious insect.'
Habitat and range: Six subspecies have been described from tropical seas. The race *royana* breeds at Norfolk and Kermadec Islands. Though it is the sort of seabird that might be expected in New Zealand coastal waters after a northerly blow, there are only three recorded occurrences; Waipu (1885), Ettrick, Otago (March 1945), Bethells (May 1960).
Breeding: White Terns begin to return to Raoul Island early in September and most have left the island by the end of April. Eggs may be found from mid-

October to the end of January. The single egg is laid usually on a tree preferably at a considerable height. Eggs are described as being more uniformly elliptical than those of most terns and decidedly blunt at both ends.

GREY TERNLET *Procelsterna albivitta* *Pl. 36, p. 153*
Other names: Little Blue Petrel (Norfolk Island), Grey Noddy, Blue Billy (Lord Howe).
Description: 28 cm (11″). A small predominantly grey tern with rather long legs and large feet. Head and underparts greyish white; upperparts and undertail feathers ash-grey; underwing white; a ring around the eye is black in front and white behind. Bill (3 cm) short and weak, black; feet black with yellow webs.
Voice: A noisy scream comes from birds on the wing at the breeding cliffs. Birds sitting on the rocks seem to be more curious than alarmed and keep up a kind of purring note like *cror-r-r-r*.
Habitat and range: Sub-tropical south-west Pacific, breeding at Lord Howe, Norfolk, Kermadec and Friendly Islands, wandering to the coast of the North Island in summer. The great gale of mid-April 1968 swept one down to Banks Peninsula. In the summer of 1969-70 hundreds frequented the Bay of Plenty, and it appeared that substantial numbers bred at Volkner Rocks, off White Is.
Breeding: At the Kermadecs nesting starts in August. The nest is invariably in the shade on a niche in a cliff or under vegetation or boulders. Clutch 1. Fledging *c*. 36 days. Double-brooded. At Phillip and Nepean Islands in the Norfolk Group the eggs are usually placed in niches on inaccessible cliffs.

PIGEONS AND DOVES: Columbidae

The New Zealand Pigeon belongs to one of several subfamilies that feed largely on fruit and berries; subfamily Treroninae (S.E. Asia, Malaya and Africa).

NEW ZEALAND PIGEON *Hemiphaga novaeseelandiae* *Pl. 37, p. 160*
Maori names: Kereru, kuku, kukupa.
Description: 51 cm (20″). Can generally be seen at close quarters on a reasonably cautious approach, when the rich coloration of the back and purplish-crimson bill and feet are prominent; forehead, face, throat and upper breast metallic green with purple reflections; back of head, nape, scapulars and lesser wing-coverts deep purple with blue-grey sheen; a zone of bronze reflections between purple of head and neck, and green of throat and breast; lower back pale green with grey sheen, wing quills and greater coverts green (bronze reflections), with grey to pale grey centres; tail quills above dark brown with metallic green edges at base, below silvery grey, broad dark brown band towards tip; *underparts* from the line of green breast *white*. At some angles the light may produce a mainly grey appearance on the back; the white underparts and pale grey-green lower back distinctive in flight; pale grey at base of primaries also shows in flight. Iris crimson, eyelids purplish crimson; bill tip yellowish; legs and feet dark blood red.

Soft swish of wings, sometimes including wing-clapping, is a distinctive feature; there is also much flapping as the birds move about the branches feeding on foliage and fruits giving an indication of their presence before they are seen.

In juvenal undertail-coverts pale buff.

Voice: A single soft, but occasionally quite penetrating, *ku*; also low scarcely audible variant of the same note or a soft moan. Further variants given at the nest are a growl, faint whistle and a 'double sound of a grunt and whistle' (Guthrie-Smith).

Habitat and range: Throughout in forests at European settlement and, after a period of decrease throughout the early settlement period, now well established and probably increasing in the remaining forest areas and residual forest remnants. From native vegetation now freely transfers feeding activity to exotic trees, e.g. poplar, willow, orchard trees, but these in the main do not supply the fruit in its diet.

Food comprises a large proportion of young leaves, and fruits of trees and shrubs of which some species are available practically throughout the year: although few fruits are available in late winter and spring. Fruits of the following trees or shrubs taken: konini (fuchsia), puriri, mangeao, makomako (wineberry), tawa, taraire, matai, miro, kahikatea, titoki, maire, hinau, porokaiwhiria (pigeonwood), mahoe, supplejack, poroporo, five-finger, karamu, nikau, cabbage-tree and karaka; also the introduced acmena, holly, cherry, rowan and sweetbriar. In addition to the leaves of a wide range of native trees or shrubs (especially kowhai, wineberry, and the common liane, *Parsonsia*), it has been known to eat foliage of various introduced species: willow, poplar, tree lucerne, apple, laburnum. It will freely descend to the ground for clover. Flowers of kowhai and of introduced shrubs (broom, tree lucerne, laburnum) form an important element in its diet.

Restriction on the shooting of Pigeons was found necessary as early as 1864; total protection since 1921 has probably been the most important factor restoring populations.

The Chatham Island Pigeon (subspecies *chathamensis*) has purple head and breast with bronze and green reflections; pale grey lower back (*cf.* grey-green); greenish-grey greater wing-coverts and extensive grey bases to the primaries; bronze-green undertail-coverts. Rapidly decreased on the main island of the group with European settlement, persisting in fair numbers until recently on Pitt Island, but its status on the main island and even on Pitt Island is now evidently precarious; originally occurred also on Mangere Island but absent from other outlying islands.

Breeding: Nest a flimsy structure of twigs and sticks supported on several smaller branches, at 3–9 m from the ground, even lower on off-shore islands; sometimes overhanging a cliff. Breeding November-March (occasionally September); possibly double-brooded as eggs recorded as late as June-July; one egg, white. Incubation period *c.* 30 days. Down yellowish-white, sparse; bare on abdomen and round eye. Fledging 6–7 weeks.

ROCK PIGEON   *Columba livia*   *Pl. 37, p. 160*
Other name: Blue Rock Dove.
Description: 33 cm (13″). From the wild Rock Pigeon have been derived more than 200 breeds of dovecote and racing pigeons, many of which have gone 'wild'. Hence the motley assortment of pigeons which may now be seen in many public parks and squares. In the wild form, the plumage is mainly blue-grey; *rump whitish; two prominent black bars across the wings*; sides of neck glossy green and purple; tail broadly tipped black; *underwing white*; bill leaden; feet pinkish. When the many domestic strains are crossed, the original type tends to emerge.
Voice: *oor-roo-cooo* and variants.
Habitat and range: Introduced in the early days of settlement and now established in many towns, breeding on ledges or in niches on buildings. In some districts, notably Auckland west coast, Hawkes Bay and Banks Peninsula, the Rock Pigeon has gone truly feral and reverted to its traditional habitat, breeding in caves on sea-cliffs and inland cliffs.

SPOTTED DOVE   *Streptopelia chinensis*   *Pl. 37, p. 160*
Other names: Turtle Dove, Laceneck, Spotted-necked Dove.
Description: 30 cm (12″). Upperparts pinkish-brown with darker markings; hindneck and upper back black finely spotted with white; outer tail-feathers black, broadly tipped with white, conspicuous when the tail is fanned; underparts greyish pink, paler on the throat; undertail-coverts whitish. Bill black; legs pink. Has a swift, direct, level flight.
Voice: A cooing call of two, three or four notes varying in rhythm and emphasis, e.g. *croo-croo*; *cuck-croo-cuck*; *cu-cu-croo-crook*. Cooing occurs at all seasons, with apparent peak periods in autumn and spring.
Habitat and range: Introduced from Asia as a cage-bird and now breeding wild in the suburbs of Auckland from Albany—not common on the North Shore—south to Papakura and Karaka. Prefers well-treed gardens and parks. Somewhat elusive; but perches openly on roof-tops and commonly feeds on the ground, especially on lawns and gritty tracks.
Breeding: Has an extended breeding-season. Increased cooing in autumn may indicate pair-formation. A spectacular part of display is a steep upward flight and a downward glide with wings and tail stiffly spread. Nest a flimsy platform of twigs, well concealed in a big, thick tree. Eggs two, white. Probably more than one brood a year.

BARBARY DOVE   *Streptopelia risoria*   *Pl. 37, p. 160*
Description: 28 cm (11″). The general tone of the plumage is a warm creamy buff shading virtually to white on chin, belly and undertail-coverts. The primaries are dull grey and the wing-tips inconspicuously white. At the back of the head is a black, white-edged half-collar. In flight the basal half of the tail is revealed as brownish-black. Juveniles lack the black half-collar and have pale bills.
Voice: Normally a rather pleasant mellow crooning. Also a high-pitched excitement cry *heh-heh-heh*, sounding like a 'jeering laugh'.
Habitat and range: A feral population of this long-domesticated breed has

been known around Whakatane for some years and another became established around Masterton about 1970. Survival is likely to depend on handouts from man.

Barbary Doves are related closely to African (*roseogrisea*) and Eurasian (*decaocto*) Collared Doves.

Breeding: Not so far studied with wild birds in New Zealand.

PARROTS AND PARAKEETS: Psittacidae

KAKAPO   *Strigops habroptilus*   *Pl. 38, p. 161*

Description: 63 cm (25″). Colours mainly *moss-green* (bluish sheen in strong light) *above, greenish-yellow below*; forehead and face below eyes yellowish-brown, faintly streaked paler, and throat yellowish white; tail and wing quills barred brown and dull yellow. More or less distinct yellow eyebrow-stripe divides the brownish face from the green crown. The feathers of the back with dark brown and yellow crossbars inside the green tip, and this results in a somewhat irregular mottled effect where brown and yellow coloration shows under green; the dorsal feathers also have irregular central longitudinal stripes which may be visible as yellow streaks. A similar barred and streaked effect on the yellowish underparts, the longitudinal streaks tending to be especially noticeable on the upper breast. Cere pale brown; bill yellowish white, with a varying area of brown at base of upper mandible and generally brown along the fluting of lower mandible; feet brownish grey. The abundant stiff, brownish bristles round the base of the bill are characteristic; this, together with the brown facial disc and strongly arched bill, give an owl-like appearance (hence the old colonial name of 'Owl-parrot'). Male averages larger than female, generally with distinctly larger bill.

Voice: The most characteristic call is a series of bittern-like booms heard during the breeding season: other calls are hisses, croaks, screams and mewings (Williams).

Habitat and range: Now one of New Zealand's rarest birds, the only populations known with certainty being those discovered by officers of the Wildlife Service, Department of Internal Affairs, from 1958 onwards in various areas in the vicinity of Milford Sound and on Stewart Island. Early explorers' accounts and ornithological writings, however, give a fairly satisfactory picture of its original range: this was apparently almost exclusively the beech forests of the North and South Islands, more especially in mountain districts although in some areas (especially Fiordland) extending down to sea-level. G. R. Williams, in a survey of its pre- and post-European distribution, considers that its range and numbers had been shrinking before the effects of man— European and Polynesian—were felt; still abundant in certain localities of western South Island until *c.* 1900 after which it decreased rapidly. Occurred

---

PLATE 37 Crimson Rosella (p.167); Eastern Rosella (p.166); New Zealand Pigeon (p.157); White Cockatoo (p.167); Rock Pigeon (p.159); Barbary Dove (p.159); Spotted Dove (p.159).

PLATE 37

IMSON SELLA 36 cm

EASTERN ROSELLA 33 cm

NEW ZEALAND PIGEONS 51 cm

WHITE COCKATOO 50 cm

ROCK PIGEON 33 cm

BARBARY DOVE 28 cm

SPOTTED DOVE 30 cm

PLATE 38

YELLOW-CROWNED PARAKEET 25 cm

ORANGE-FRONTED PARAKEET 22 cm

RED-CROWNED PARAKEET 28 cm

ANTIPODES ISLAND PARAKEET 31 cm

KAKA (South Island) 45 cm

KAKA (North Island) 45 cm

KEAS 46 cm

KAKAPO 62 cm

in the North Island at the time of European discovery only in small numbers mainly in the central mountain ranges. On Stewart Island occurs in rata-podocarp forest. The Kakapo's habitat extends above the forest into the subalpine and alpine zone: this proximity of herbaceous and shrubby vegetation may well have been a factor limiting its distribution, as fruits of subalpine shrubs, and leaves and roots of grassland species formed an important food source. In grassland the blades of tussock grasses are chewed and fibrous material is left hanging in loose balls on the plant. The latter become bleached by sun and rain, providing an indicator of the presence of the species in any area; various types of fibrous plant matter, in addition to tussock, may be chewed in this way. Other items of diet recorded include ferns, mosses, fungi, lizards. The Kakapos recently kept in captivity by the Department of Internal Affairs in an attempt to establish a breeding stock have shown a strong liking for sweet substances, obtainable in the wild by chewing nectar-bearing flowers.

Early accounts make special mention of the tracks cleared by the Kakapo through low vegetation, especially on ridges and spurs; shallow depressions may be bowls used for both dusting and booming. As this species is incapable of upward flight, it progresses by walking along these tracks, or clambering up leaning trunks and branches; the wings are large and with these the bird can perform a downward glide of as much as 100 m. It is closely nocturnal, spending the day in natural crevices or excavated burrows.

Three subspecies described (one from North Island, two South Island) are still not satisfactorily defined.

Breeding: Nest in a hollow amongst tree roots, a crevice or excavated burrow, extending back as far as 3 m; the eggs placed on powdered wood with the addition of some feathers. Breeding December-February (records also for May, suggesting sometimes a second brood); eggs 2–4, white. The female is said to be responsible for incubation. Downy young white. The claim (by Richard Henry, caretaker of Resolution Island sanctuary) that all birds bred only in alternate years would, as pointed out by G. R. Williams, be very surprising if true; Henry based this view on the incidence of 'booming' (or 'drumming'), which he maintained was produced only by the males throughout the breeding season, and on his lack of any evidence of nesting when no birds were heard drumming. Sometimes more than one year was missed, and on one occasion the Kakapos drummed in two succeeding years.

KAKA *Nestor meridionalis* Pl. 38, p. 161

Description: 45 cm (18"). Harsh call is often heard before the bird is seen. Large size in comparison with other forest species (except pigeon), and heavy bill, together with dark coloration are characteristic when amongst foliage: predominating colours seen closely are olive browns or dull greens (see description of subspecies below) and reds; *crimson rump and abdomen*; *grey to greyish- or greenish-white crown*; *tawny-orange patch below eye*; *underwing*

PLATE 38 Yellow-crowned Parakeet (p.165); Orange-fronted Parakeet (p.165); Red-crowned Parakeet (p.163); Antipodes Island Parakeet (p.165); Kaka (p.161); Kea (p.162); Kakapo (p.160).

scarlet. In flight the head is prominent owing to size of bill; scarlet underwing (coverts and axillaries) conspicuous in suitable light. Bill of adult male more arched than in female, upper mandible being distinctly longer. Cere brown; bill dark brown to dark steel grey; feet dark grey.

Voice: Common call a harsh *ka-aa*; also ringing, musical whistle *u-wiia* (both calls commonly in flight); a musical subsong to the chicks sometimes delivered at the nest; a call, perhaps also given to the young, *chock, chock, chock* is described by Guthrie-Smith.

Habitat and range: More or less continuous native forest tracts form the present habitat of this species; a decrease even in such areas on mainland is likely, as early accounts suggest that it was present in great numbers. Unlike various native forest species, the Kaka has shown only a very limited tendency to spread into exotic plantations or settled districts, exceptions being individuals attracted to nectar-bearing trees and shrubs—Kakas have under these circumstances been known to appear in city gardens. On sanctuaries (Little Barrier and Kapiti) orchard fruits readily taken. Mainly a fruit and insect eater; tears up decaying wood to obtain insect larvae, especially the grubs of wood-boring beetles. Also eats leaves and obtains nectar from the flowers of rata (*Metrosideros* spp.) and other forest trees or shrubs.

Flight powerful when travelling any distance; small flocks of up to 10, probably family parties, may be seen above the forest. Often heard at night, and is possibly to some extent nocturnal.

The North Island (*septentrionalis*) subspecies is of smaller average size and duller plumage (olive brown above, feathers with darker crescentic tips, and the collar somewhat obscurely mottled with crimson and gold feathers; crown grey to greyish-white): distribution of this subspecies includes native forest areas of the North Island, and larger coastal islands—Hen and Chickens Islands, Great and Little Barrier, Fanal, Mayor, Kapiti. South Island (*meridionalis*) subspecies of more vivid coloration (greenish brown above, the green brighter in male; crimson collar of gold-tipped feathers prominent in male, less distinct in female; crimson underparts exceptionally extend over the whole breast in the male; crown much paler than in *septentrionalis*—greyish- or greenish-white): found throughout the South Island, Stewart Island, and on islands of the latter area.

Breeding: In a large hollow tree, a site being used year after year and probably by successive pairs; entrance generally a hole 3–9 m from the ground; opening often widened in either dead or living wood by the birds; eggs laid on powdered wood. Breeding, October-February; eggs 4–5, white. Incubation period *c*. 21 days. Down of chicks pale grey; bill and facial skin lemon-yellow. Fledging 10 weeks (J. R. Jackson).

KEA   *Nestor notabilis*   *Pl. 38, p. 161*

Description: 46 cm (18½″). *Olive-green above and below*, underparts a little fainter green; *scarlet underwing* (coverts and axillaries); *dull scarlet rump*; *blue outer margins wing quills*; feathers of body plumage and wing-coverts all with dark crescentic tips. Tail quills blue-green with a subterminal black band, and a series of orange-yellow bars on the inner web of each feather. Brown patch below eye. Adult: cere dark brown; bill dark brown; feet dark grey. In young birds cere, eyelids and base lower mandible are yellow, feet yellowish; this colour lost finally at the end of the second year in the female and at end of third year in male (J. R. Jackson). In juvenal plumage crown yellowish.

The Kea has a much slimmer bill than the Kaka; upper mandible hardly arched in female, longer and prominently arched in male.

When Kea is seen in forest, where it may be confused with Kaka, the presence of much green in the plumage is a reliable field marking; both species have scarlet underwing patches.

Voice: Call *keaa* is delivered mainly in flight; has a variety of softer and conversational calls. It lacks the musical whistle of the Kaka but has a similar subsong at the nest (J. R. Jackson).

Habitat and range: Restricted to the South Island mountain area; until *c.* 1870 only in southern districts (S. of Hurunui River), including Fiordland, but has subsequently extended into high country of Nelson and Marlborough. Despite this habitat, the Kea is not limited to the alpine zone; recent field studies by J. R. Jackson have shown that it obtains much of its food (leaves, buds and fruits together with insects) in the forests clothing mountain valleys, and, further, nests in high-level forests or near the forest edge. Ranges widely to the alpine grassland and subalpine scrub for the fruits abundant in autumn; commonly feeds also on the open river flats. Takes nectar when available.

The Kea has received wide publicity as an inveterate sheep-killer: while Keas certainly feed on dead sheep and carrion, they can at most be accused of only the occasional killing of healthy animals. J. R. Jackson, after assessing all the evidence available on the subject, states: 'It is credible that Keas do attack sheep trapped in snow, sick sheep, sheep injured by falls or sheep they mistake as dead. When such a sheep reacted they would take flight, but return when it relaxed. If such occurs, the evidence suggests it must be very rarely.' (*Notornis*, 10, 33–8: 1962.)

Breeding: Nests on the ground in a hole or crevice between rocks, sometimes in a hollow log; twigs, leaves, etc. are used as nesting material, although in a hollow log only powdered wood may be used. Site is commonly at the base of a rocky outcrop breaking through forest canopy. Breeding July-January (peak of laying in October); eggs 2–4, white. Incubation period over 21 days; mainly by female. Down of chicks is pale grey; bill and facial skin a vivid orange-yellow. Fledged in 13–14 weeks (J. R. Jackson).

RED-CROWNED PARAKEET *Cyanoramphus novaezelandiae*   Pl. 38, p. 161

Other names: Kakariki, New Zealand Parakeet.

Description: Males 28 cm (11″), females 25.5 cm (10″). Although male is larger, and difference in size between the sexes is clearly seen in fresh plumage, note that this may be less distinct in the field when tail worn or moulted: the larger head and heavier bill of male is distinctive when pair seen together. Green above, yellowish green below; *crimson forehead and crown*, extending back to a little behind the eye; *crimson stripe forehead to eye*; *crimson patch* (larger in male) *immediately behind the eye*; outer webs of inner portion of wing quills and primary coverts *violet-blue*, visible when wings slightly spread or in flight; a *crimson patch on each side of rump*. Upper mandible pale steel blue, tip black, lower mandible blue-grey, darker at tip; feet greyish brown. The plumage is notably cryptic in effect amongst foliage, the bird being commonly located only by movement or call. Note that size of male of yellow-crowned species is equal to that of red-crowned female: it is not safe to distinguish these species on size alone. Yellow-crowned and Orange-fronted Parakeets lack red patch behind the eye.

Flight is direct and rapid, sometimes with side-slipping through the trees, and trailing tail is generally a useful guide to identification. The broad, graduated tail is spread as the bird swoops up to alight.

Voice: A rapid chatter is commonly given in flight, *ki-ki-ki-ki-ki* (enables the bird to be located *after* it has taken flight). When perching this call may be given as a more relaxed, conversational chattering (often abbreviated); also a shriller one- to three-syllable call when perching, which is commonly rendered as 'pretty dick,' 'do-be-quick,' etc.; and a soft musical *tu-tu-tu-tu*, as well as a variety of conversational notes.

Habitat and range: Both Red-crowned and Yellow-crowned Parakeets were apparently birds of the mainland forest at all altitudes when European settlement began: subsequently after a brief period when they were reported in plague numbers in orchards and on crops, and seemed likely to have a potential as injurious species, both greatly decreased. The Red-crowned Parakeet is now very rare on the mainland, found only in larger forest tracts, especially those of the Huiarau and Raukumara Ranges, and of the Urewera (North Island); and of Nelson, Arthur's Pass and Fiordland National Parks, and Wakatipu and Dunedin district (South Island) (cf. present distribution of Yellow-crowned Parakeet, below). It occurred on nearly all coastal islands, and was widespread (see subspecies) on New Zealand's outlying islands; most of the island populations remain in a flourishing state. Food consists of an extremely wide variety of vegetable matter ranging from fruits and seeds to leaves and buds. Commonly observed where abundant on islands obtaining such food as seeds of biddybid (*Acaena*), centres of ice-plant flowers, on the ground.

Coastal islands on which it occurs include Three Kings, Poor Knights, Hen and Chickens, Little Barrier, Arid, Mokohinau, Mercuries, Aldermen, Kapiti, and Stewart Island with its numerous outliers. The Auckland Islands population cannot be separated from *novaezelandiae* of the mainland. Introduced to Cuvier and Tiri Tiri Islands. Subspecies occupy: (*a*) Kermadec Islands—distinguished by the greater amount of blue on wings and bluish green tail (*cyanurus*); (*b*) Chatham Islands—larger size, emerald green facial area (*chathamensis*); (*c*) Antipodes Island—larger size, plumage distinctly yellower above and below, blue on wings more faint, orange-red (rather than crimson) crown, eye-stripe and rump spots (*hochstetteri*); Macquarie Island—characters as for the Antipodes I. subspecies (*erythrotis*) (extinct). Also extralimital subspecies of the Red-crowned Parakeet on Lord Howe Island (extinct), Norfolk Island and New Caledonia.

Breeding: In hollow tree, eggs on powdered wood; on islands commonly in rock crevices. Breeding October–March; eggs 5–9, white. Laying interval 24–48 hours, incubation starting with second egg; incubation period 18–20 days; performed entirely by female (M. E. FitzGerald) (in captivity). Chicks grey down. Fledging 5–6 weeks; male assists in feeding chicks (food mainly transferred to female, but male feeds chicks if female absent).

YELLOW-CROWNED PARAKEET *Cyanoramphus auriceps* *Pl. 38, p. 161*
Maori name: Kakariki.
Description: Males 25.5 cm (10″), females 23 cm (9″). Differs from preceding species in smaller size (size range of male overlaps female of Red-crowned: note under Red-crowned Parakeet) and *absence of red patch behind eye*; *crimson forehead* and *golden-yellow crown* (to a little behind eye); crimson stripe from forehead to eye; *crimson patch on each side of rump*. *Violet-blue* on wings. Bill and feet as in Red-crowned.
Voice: The same range of calls as in Red-crowned. Calls tend to be higher pitched and weaker, and flight call *ki-ki-ki-ki-ki* is noticeably so.
Habitat and range: As noted under Red-crowned Parakeet, both species were originally widely distributed on the mainland; after a period of decrease there has apparently been a fairly recent expansion of this species which reports suggest is now moderately common in larger forest tracts in both North and South Island (central mountain chain of North, mountains from Nelson to Fiordland in the South Island). Food, as far as known, the same as that of the Red-crowned Parakeet, but observations on islands where it occurs suggest that it is less dependent on ground plants.

Occurs on Three Kings, Hen, Big Chicken, Little Barrier, Kapiti, and Stewart Island and surrounding smaller islands. On Solander and Auckland Islands the mainland subspecies (*auriceps*) occurs. The Chatham Island subspecies (*forbesi*) was originally found on Pitt, Mangere, Little Mangere Islands of this group, but is now represented only by *c.* 100 birds on Little Mangere: larger size, and brighter generally, with more yellowish underparts and emerald green on sides of face.
Breeding: As for Red-crowned; breeding recorded August-April; eggs 5–9, white. Incubation 18–20 days; fledging 5–6 weeks (in captivity).

ORANGE-FRONTED PARAKEET *Cyanoramphus malherbi* *Pl. 38, p. 161*
Description: Males 22 cm (8½″), females 20.5 cm (8″). Like Yellow-crowned parakeet, but smaller with comparatively weak bill; rich green and yellowish-green of the two previous species is lacking, plumage being distinctly less yellowish ('cold pure green,' Buller); *forehead bright orange* and *paler orange stripe forehead to eye*; *pale yellow crown* (to a little behind eye); *orange patch on each side of rump*; no patch behind eye. *Violet-blue* on wings. Bill and feet as in Red-crowned.
Voice: Apparently closely resembling Red- and Yellow-crowned.
Habitat and range: South Island only (records claimed from Hen and Little Barrier Islands unacceptable). It was apparently never common, but records assembled by M. Harrison indicate that it probably occurred in the forest in most districts of the South Island and on Stewart Island; now known only from mid- and north-west Nelson.
Breeding: General breeding habits probably like the above species, but nothing recorded (except in captivity).

ANTIPODES ISLAND PARAKEET *Cyanoramphus unicolor* *Pl. 38, p. 161*
Description: Males 31.5 cm (12½″), females 29 cm (11½″). The two species of parakeet occurring on Antipodes Island may be distinguished without difficulty:

unicolor being the largest of the New Zealand parakeets, and lacking prominent red or yellow markings. Body plumage slightly yellowish green above, strongly yellowish below—the yellow element is approximately as strong as in the Antipodes Red-crowned Parakeet. Wing quills and primary coverts violet-blue as in other species. *Crown* to immediately behind eye and *whole facial area a brilliant emerald green* which shows prominently in the field and may have a bluish sheen. Head and bill massive as compared with Red-crowned, and the pale basal portion (blue-grey or bluish-white) of the bill is prominent in the field; the bill is comparatively broad and blunt. Feet stouter than in Red-crowned, greyish brown.

Voice: Calls much the same as in Red-crowned, although conversational notes seemed softer and deeper (E. G. T.).

Habitat and range: Antipodes Island consists of steep seaward slopes rising to a tableland, the highest point, Mount Galloway, reaching 400 m. In area the island is approximately 62 sq. km. The slopes and plateau are largely clothed in tussock, with extensive areas of prickly-fern (*Polystichum*); a little low scrub includes various species of *Coprosma*. Both parakeets occur throughout on slopes and tableland; considerable portions of the slopes are invaded by penguins in October-May, and the colonies are freely entered by this unique species. Observations on a visit in November 1950 (E. G. T.) suggested that *unicolor* depended to a considerable extent on food derived from the penguin colonies: skins and carcases of dead penguins which had been eaten by skuas were constantly investigated for fat and probably fragments of flesh; older dried skins seemed to be especially attractive to the parakeets; eggs broken by skuas were also examined for remains of yolk and albumen. Observations of *hochstetteri* in November 1950 were all of leaf- and seed-feeding. R. H. Taylor made extensive observations on the feeding habits of the two forms in the course of field work on the island in February 1969, his results indicating that the diet of *hochstetteri* contained a high proportion of seeds, together with flowers, berries and invertebrates; on the other hand *unicolor* was seen feeding mainly on leaves, supplemented with seeds, berries and the remains of dead penguins and other sea birds.

This species flies quite strongly.

Breeding: In holes in ground, or in bases of taller tussocks. Eggs white.

EASTERN ROSELLA *Platycercus eximius*   *Pl. 37, p. 160*

Description: 33 cm (13″). Larger and more gaily coloured than any of the native parakeets. Head, neck and breast red; cheeks and lower throat white; 'shoulders' blue; back black and yellow; *rump pale green*, very noticeable as bird flies away; abdomen yellow and green; under tail-coverts scarlet; tail tipped pale blue.

Often feeds on the ground. Where plentiful, gregarious after the nesting season.

Voice: A crisp, ringing *kwink*, sometimes single, sometimes rapidly reiterated.

Habitat and range: An Australian species, which became naturalised when caged birds escaped into the Waitakeres; now strongly established between Raglan and Houhora; increasing south of Auckland and extending its range eastwards. There appear to be expanding pockets on Coromandel and north of Wellington. Prefers open or lightly timbered country, but will enter denser forest. Disliked by orchardists.

In the South Island a small population surviving in the hills near Dunedin is said to include hybrids between Eastern (*P. eximius*) and Crimson Rosellas (*P. elegans*), which were released from a ship off Otago Heads about 1910. **Breeding:** Not studied in New Zealand, though the bird has clearly been breeding very successfully in the north.

CRIMSON ROSELLA *Platycercus elegans*   *Pl. 37, p. 160*
Description: 36 cm (14″). Bigger than Eastern Rosella. Plumage mainly deep crimson, but upper back heavily mottled with black; *cheeks and throat violet blue*; wings and tail mostly blue or black. Young birds are predominantly green, but some blue and red are usually beginning to show.
Voice: A low-pitched *kweek-kweek-kweek*, the middle note on a lower scale. The alarm call is a shrill metallic screech. Feeding birds chatter softly.
Habitat and range: A robust species from south-eastern Australia, which since 1963 appears to have become established in the wooded hills around Wellington.

WHITE COCKATOO *Kakatoe galerita*   *Pl. 37, p. 160*
Other name: Sulphur-crested Cockatoo.
Description: 50 cm (20″). White with a bright yellow crest; and a yellow tinge on underwing and undertail-coverts. Bill and feet black.

Flies strongly on broad rounded wings. Often feeds on the ground. Gregarious outside the breeding season. Very alert.
Voice: A raucous screech.
Habitat and range: A familiar Australian species, now well established in the North Island in two localities (*a*) the limestone country between the lower Waikato and Raglan; (*b*) the watersheds of the Turakina and Rangitikei. Also a small colony Wainuiomata Valley, Wellington. The hundreds of these cockatoos now wild in New Zealand are said to be sprung from escaped caged-birds, but some may be self-introduced. It is curious that the two main populations are near the west coast, where wind-blown stragglers might make a landfall; and it may be significant that in May 1959 after three days of strong westerlies a White Cockatoo was seen at South Kaipara Heads, so tired that it could fly only downwind.
Breeding: Little recorded in New Zealand. Said to nest in a hole high in a big tree; perhaps also in limestone cliffs; but one of the few nests found in New Zealand was on the top of a pile of hay-bales close under the roof of a barn. Eggs 2–3, glossy white.

CUCKOOS: Cuculidae

The many species of true cuckoos (subfamily Cuculinae) which inhabit the Old World have few diagnostic features in common except that they lay their eggs in the nests of other birds. They have long been a byword for parasitism and general rascality.

Six members of this subfamily are known from New Zealand. The two which are essentially Neo-zelanic, namely the Shining and Long-tailed Cuckoos, are not at all alike in size, shape, colouring or voice. Both have achieved a certain distinction because of the very long oceanic crossings which their migrations entail before and after a breeding season spent in New Zealand.

The flying ability of cuckoos must be deceptively strong, as four other species reach New Zealand, despite its far isolation, as casual strays. Of these, three breed in Australia and Tasmania, two commonly, one rather more sparingly; the fourth breeds in eastern Asia and, like its European near-relative, migrates south towards the end of the northern summer.

ORIENTAL CUCKOO   *Cuculus saturatus*   *Pl. 39, p. 168*
Description: 33 cm (13″). Closely resembles the famous cuckoo (*Cuculus canorus*) of the Old World. Head and back blue-grey; tail slaty-black spotted and tipped with white; wing-surface dark brown spotted white on the inner webs of the outer primaries; throat pale grey; *breast and abdomen closely barred black and white*. Eyelids yellow. Bill blackish above, greenish below; yellow round the gape. Legs and feet yellow. Juveniles are browner. This cuckoo like *C. canorus* has a rufous or 'hepatic' phase.
Voice: 'Four dull booming notes on a monotonous *hoo-hoo-hoo-hoo* not unlike the call of a "Hoopoe" ' or 'a mellow triple hoot, *hoop, hoop-hoop*.' (Smithies) One on Little Barrier uttered a quiet regular *tsoo-tsoo-tsoo* about a dozen times.
Habitat and range: Breeds in eastern Asia and migrates southwards, some reaching south-east Australia. A surprising number have been taken at Lord Howe Island. About ten widely scattered records since 1950. One at Whangaroa perched on posts from which it dived to the ground to take worms.

PALLID CUCKOO   *Cuculus pallidus*   *Pl. 41, p. 176*
Description: 30 cm (12″). Paler and slightly smaller than *C. saturatus*, and *without the abdominal barring*. Upperparts a light uniform brownish-grey with white spotting on the wings and outer tail-feathers and a small white patch on the fore-edge of the wing; underparts light grey, the underwing being grey-brown barred with white. Females differ in being copiously marked with chestnut and buff on the head and back and the spotting on wings and tail is buff rather than white. Eyelids yellow. Glides like a hawk and often mobbed by small birds. Habitually perches on fence-posts.
Voice: 'At times it seems to endeavour to run up a chromatic scale; so it is called the Scale Bird. At other times after three running notes, it repeats one note strongly. So persistent is the call that it is named in places the Brain-fever Bird.' (Leach.) Often calls at night. The female's call is a hoarse single-noted *cheer* or *kheer*.
Habitat and range: The commonest and best-known cuckoo in Australia, where it is a migrant from the north arriving in Tasmania early in the spring.

PLATE 39 Long-tailed Cuckoo (p.170); Shining Cuckoo (p.169); Oriental Cuckoo (p.168); Morepork (p.171); Little Owl (p.173); Australian Barn Owl (p.174); Laughing Owl (p.172).

PLATE 39

imm.

LONG-TAILED CUCKOOS
40 cm

SHINING CUCKOO
16 cm

ORIENTAL CUCKOO
33 cm

MOREPORKS 27 cm

LITTLE OWL
23 cm

AUSTRALIAN BARN OWL 34 cm

LAUGHING OWL
38 cm

PLATE 40

AUSTRALIAN TREE MARTIN 14 cm

FORK-TAILED SW 18 c

SPINE-TAILED SWIFT 20 cm

MASKED WOOD-SWALLOW 19 cm

WELCOME SWALLOW 15 cm

WHITE-BROWE WOOD-SWALLO 19 cm

NEW ZEALAND KINGFISHERS 24 cm

imm.

KOOKABURRA 45 cm

A very rare straggler to New Zealand recorded from Craig Flat (1941), Okarito (1941), Greymouth (1942) and Wairarapa (1977). In Australia honeyeaters are favoured as foster parents, but many other passerines are also victimised.

FAN-TAILED CUCKOO *Cacomantis pyrrhophanus* Pl. 41, p. 176
Description: 25 cm (10″). Head and upperparts dark blue-grey except for a white patch on the fore-edge of the wing below the 'shoulder'; throat light-grey; breast rust-red, abdomen paler; tail dusky with white spots; eyelids yellow; legs and feet yellowish brown. Habitually raises and lowers its tail several times before and after flight.
Voice: A loud plaintive call often heard at night; or a shrill trisyllabic whistle; also a murmuring note, a melancholy *coo-coo* slurred. In Tasmania the first calls are heard in July.
Habitat and range: A common Australian species only partly migratory; some wintering even in Tasmania; but nomadic after the breeding season. Parasitic on a wide variety of small song-birds. Only once so far recorded from New Zealand; Governor's Bay, Canterbury, 1960.

SHINING CUCKOO *Chalcites lucidus* Pl. 39, p. 168
Other names: Pipiwharauroa, Whistler.
Description: 16 cm (6½″). A small cuckoo, much more often heard than seen; about the size of a sparrow. Its true colours can only be appreciated in a good light. Upper surface metallic green with a golden or coppery glint; sides of face and underparts white, finely barred with glossy green, which may look black; lateral tail-feathers barred with white. Females similar but crown and nape more purplish bronze and the abdominal bars more bronzy. Bill black, rather broad. Feet black with yellowish soles. Young birds have prominent stripes on flanks; but barring on throat and breast is obscure.
Voice: 'A series of double notes,' upward slurs, several times repeated, followed by fewer downward slurs, the whole in a musical whistle with ventriloquistic effects (Oliver). The full summer song is represented in Maori as *kui, kui, whiti-whiti ora, tio-o.* The call note, a clear *tsee-ew* or *tsiu,* may be heard from Shining Cuckoos as they pass in the night; and is much used at any time of the day when several of these cuckoos gather in a tall tree and fly in and out, chasing and calling excitedly.
Habitat and range: A summer migrant arriving from mid-August onwards but not widely distributed till October. Parasitic mainly on the Grey Warbler and so found throughout main islands south to Stewart and up to *c.* 1200 m a.s.l. Feeds mainly on insects, especially on the black hairy caterpillars of the Magpie Moth and often killed by cats among the cinerarias. Often also a casualty from flying into windows.

Singing ceases early in February and these cuckoos slip unobtrusively away to their winter quarters which extend over the Solomon Islands and Bismarck

PLATE 40 Spine-tailed Swift (p.175); Australian Tree Martin (p.182); Fork-tailed Swift (p.175); Masked Wood-swallow (p.215); New Zealand Kingfisher (p.175); White-browed Wood-swallow (p.215); Kookaburra (p.177); Welcome Swallow (p.182).

Archipelago. The New Zealand subspecies (*C. l. lucidus*) occurs irregularly on migration on Lord Howe and Norfolk Islands; and as a straggler in eastern Australia. Sometimes reported as wintering, especially in the north of the North Island.

Breeding: Needs intensive study. Courtship feeding occurs. Average number of eggs laid by one female in a season is quite unknown. Eggs greenish or bluish white to olive brown or dark greenish brown. Incubation period *c*. 12 days. The Grey Warbler is the usual foster-parent; but eggs have also been found in nests of Fantail, Tomtit, Silvereye and some of the smaller introduced passerines. In the Chatham Islands victimises the endemic warbler.

LONG-TAILED CUCKOO *Eudynamis taitensis* Pl. 39, p. 168

Maori names: Koekoea, Kawekawea, Kohoperoa.

Description: 40 cm (16″). More often heard than seen; but voice and flight silhouette with very long tail are diagnostic. Upperparts dark brown, barred and spotted rufous, with white spots on head, back and wings; underparts white with dark longitudinal streaks. Females more rufous and slightly smaller. In juveniles the underparts are rufous; throat has broad dark stripes or irregular spots; and the white spots on back and wings are larger and much more conspicuous. Legs greenish-yellow.

Voice: A harsh, piercing, long drawn out screech *zzwheesht*, unlike any other sound in the bush. This call is used at night by these cuckoos on migration and in northern New Zealand is often the only evidence of their landfall in October. Another call is a rapid, ringing, prolonged *zip-zip-zip-zip*; or a loud *rrrp pe-pe-pe-pe-pe*. 'The *rrrp* had a ringing quality and was sometimes uttered alone, without the series of sharp *pe-pe-pe* notes' (A. T. Edgar).

Habitat and range: Arrives mostly in October. Breeds from Little Barrier to Stewart Island, its distribution depending almost entirely on the presence of suitable foster parents, i.e. in the North Island, Whiteheads, which it has followed into the exotic pine forests; and in the South and Stewart Islands, Yellowheads and Brown Creepers. On Kapiti has been watched hunting and catching sunbathing skinks. During February there is a steady, if not very noticeable, movement northward throughout the main islands, and small flocks may be formed, e.g. 10 on 1/2/70 flying north at Otaio Gorge, Canterbury. The winter range covers a vast arc of the Pacific from the Marquesas and Austral Islands in the east, north to the Marshall and Caroline Islands and west to New Guinea. Present at all seasons on Raoul.

Breeding: Comparatively unknown. The three typical fosterers are: Whitehead, Yellowhead and Brown Creeper. Other species known to have been victimised are: Tomtit, Robin, Silvereye, Fantail (once), Greenfinch, Song Thrush; but nesting Tuis are strongly hostile and Bellbirds mass to mob one. Egg, variable, e.g. creamy white blotched all over with purplish brown and grey; or pale flesh prettily spotted with brownish red and vandyke brown.

CHANNEL-BILLED CUCKOO *Scythrops novaehollandiae* Pl. 41, p. 176

Description: 61 cm (24″). The giant of the cuckoos with a massive yellowish bill and a conspicuous patch of bare red skin round the eye. Head, neck and underparts light grey; back and wings brownish-grey with some blackish barring; flanks finely pencilled; tail large and fanlike with a broad black sub-terminal band and a white terminal band narrowest at the tip.

Voice: A loud call often heard as this cuckoo flies high during rainy weather; described by Gould as a 'frightful scream'; but Sharland considers it 'melodious, though certainly strange in its trumpeting quality.'

Habitat and range: Migrates from Indonesia to breed in Australia where 'it recruits the aid of magpies, crows and currawongs to rear its offspring;' rare in the south-east and Tasmania. Known to have straggled to New Zealand only once; Invercargill, 1924.

OWLS: Strigidae

Only one species of owl, the Morepork or Ruru, is at all widespread in New Zealand. It belongs to an Australasian genus, *Ninox*, containing some sixteen species which extend to Japan, India and even Madagascar. Because of their rather long tails, they are sometimes referred to as Southern Hawk-owls. In Australia the counterpart of the Morepork is called the Boobook.

Also placed among the Southern Hawk-owls but in a special genus is the endemic Laughing Owl. For reasons not fully understood, it has declined in the last century to the point of extinction.

Very rarely, it seems, an Australian Barn Owl is wafted across the Tasman Sea. To the north the Polynesian Barn Owl (*lulu*) is quite common in Fiji and, rather suggestively, bones of a Barn Owl have been uncovered at Tom Bowling Bay.

In the seventy years since they were introduced from Europe into Otago, Little Owls have spread into most settled districts of the South Island up to the foothills.

MOREPORK   *Ninox novaeseelandiae*   *Pl. 39, p. 168*
Maori name: Ruru.

Description: 29 cm (11½"). *Brown above* with scattered buff flecks on head and neck, whitish flecks on remainder of upperparts (flecks may form a collar on hindneck, and crown may lack spots or they may take the form of radiating stripes); white forehead and face at base of bill, the bristles black; wing quills spotted white or buff on upper, and prominently barred white or buff on lower surface; tail dark brown with obscure paler brown bars; *feathers of undersurface have brown centres, and prominent white spots or stripes on outer margin, giving a mottled pattern*, the whole undersurface being more or less washed with orange-brown (age differences or local variation in pattern of the Morepork remain to be clarified); brown and white barred undertail coverts; tarsus (feathered) yellowish brown to reddish buff; toes yellow or brownish yellow, dark brown claws; bill varies from dark brown with white ridge on upper mandible to white or yellow with dark brown cutting edges on both mandibles; iris golden yellow.

Distinguished from the Little Owl by the much browner general coloration; also by larger size, comparatively long tail and the more rounded outline of the head.

Voice: Characteristic call a clear and individually variable *more-pork* (also rendered, probably more accurately, as *quor-coo*); a common variation is repetitive and often prolonged *more-pork-pork-pork* ... Also a scream apparently used in hunting, a vibrating *cree-cree* mainly heard in the breeding season (Moon).

Habitat and range: Settled districts throughout New Zealand, as well as in forest; early records show that it was one of the native forest birds which adopted modified and exotic vegetation in the earliest stages of settlement; also in larger exotic plantations.

Commonly seen at dusk when it begins to hawk for insects from a prominent perch, frequently mobbed by small birds in the day-time. Food largely insects, wetas, moths, beetles and also spiders; pellets examined by Cunningham (in the urban area of Masterton) in nearly every month of the year yielded remains of a high proportion of moths, with spiders and beetles of lesser importance, and a few remains of other invertebrates; other food items lizards, small birds, especially House Sparrows, rats and mice (Cunningham recorded bird remains throughout the year). According to Moon flying insects such as moths and huhu beetles are caught with the talons before being transferred to the beak. On outlying islands diet includes smaller petrels; Kiore (*Rattus exulans*); Short-tailed Bat once recorded (Stead). Cunningham found that the time of ejection of pellets was generally mid-afternoon or late afternoon.

Distribution includes nearly all of the off-lying islands including Three Kings south to Stewart, but not Chathams or sub-antarctic islands. Present in the Christchurch urban area until some time in the 1930s but is reported to have begun to decrease at about the time of a marked increase of the Little Owl.

Other subspecies range from Australia, and Norfolk and Lord Howe Islands, to New Guinea.

Breeding: Nests in hollow tree or dense clump of vegetation (especially *Astelia*); sometimes in the open on a platform provided by a fork, or even in a depression on top of an old Sparrow's nest (Stead); once in a nesting-box. Breeding October-November; eggs 2 (occasionally 3), white. Laying at two-day intervals, incubation starting with the first egg; incubation period 30–31 days; by female (Moon). Chicks have first coat of white down when newly-hatched, gradually replaced (beginning at 10 days old) by the second down which is dark smoky brown (Stead). The chicks leave the nest at about 5 weeks old, at which stage much of the second coat of down remains and shreds of the first down form a white 'halo' on the crown and nape; young brooded during day by the female until well fledged, the male remaining hidden nearby. Moon found that the male at first transferred food to the female, but later fed the chicks himself.

LAUGHING OWL   *Sceloglaux albifacies*   *Pl. 39, p. 168*
Maori name: Whekau.
Description: 38 cm (15″). A large owl with *yellowish-brown plumage striped with brown*; white stripes on scapulars (sometimes also feathers edged white rather than yellowish-brown on hindneck and mantle); *face white behind and below eyes, greyish towards the centre*, the feathers with brown shaft-lines; wings and tail brown with brownish-white bars; tarsus (feathered) yellowish to reddish-buff; toes 'fleshy brown' or 'pale-yellow' (Buller), dark brown claws; bill horn-colour, black at base; iris 'dark reddish brown' (Buller).

Apart from size, the Laughing Owl differs from the Morepork in proportions, the tail being comparatively short.

Voice: According to early accounts the call from which this species received its name is heard mainly on dark nights accompanied by rain or drizzle, or before rain: it is 'a loud cry made up of a series of dismal shrieks frequently repeated' (Potts). Buller records 'a peculiar barking noise . . . just like the yelping of a young dog'; a melancholy hooting (or 'cooeying') note; also various whistling, chuckling and mewing notes (Buller's observations were on birds in captivity).

Habitat and range: Apparently, from early accounts and localities of specimens, inhabited mainly the low-rainfall districts of the South Island (Nelson, Canterbury and Otago), but penetrated deeply into the mountains of the central chain; also probably into Fiordland. Stewart Island, specimens obtained *c.* 1880. Buller thought from his observations of captive birds that it fed much on the ground, and notes that the legs are long for an owl; most of the early specimens were obtained from fissures in rocky areas.

It was plentiful during the first 40 years of colonisation, but by 1880 was extremely rare; no fully substantiated record since July 1914 (specimen found at Blue Cliffs, South Canterbury, by Mrs. A. E. Woodhouse), but occasionally claimed, localities including South Canterbury (Hakataramea and adjacent districts), Wanaka and Te Anau.

The Laughing Owl occurred according to Maori tradition in the Urewera, but only two specimens have been collected (both in forest districts) in the North Island (Mt. Egmont, *c.* 1856; Wairarapa, *c.* 1868), the second forming the basis of Buller's description of the North Island subspecies (*S.a. rufifacies*). Sight records from Porirua and Te Karaka.

Food as shown by pellets included beetles, rats and mice (W. W. Smith), and all of these items were eaten in captivity; raw meat and lizards also readily taken.

Breeding: Amongst rocks, nest being lined with dry grass. Breeding, September-October; eggs 2, white. W. W. Smith who observed the breeding habits of several pairs in captivity found that incubation was carried out by the female. Nestling when freshly hatched covered with coarse yellowish-white down (Buller).

LITTLE OWL   *Athene noctua*   *Pl. 39, p. 168*
Local name: German Owl.
Description: 23 cm (9″). Upperparts dark brown liberally flecked with white; underparts whitish broadly streaked with dark brown; tail brown crossed by four whitish bands and tipped white. Flat-topped skull, low forehead and yellow eyes produce a stern frowning look. Distinguishable from Morepork by much smaller size, whitish face, broad band across throat and whitish boldly streaked undersurface; generally greyer. Female slightly bigger than male. Flight dipping.

Less nocturnal than Morepork. May often be seen on the wing by day and will feed on carrion, e.g. a car-killed rabbit, in strong sunlight. Sometimes also seems deliberately to choose a perch where it can bask in the sun. Walks freely on ground.

Voice: Some calls are soft and plaintive; others louder and more strident. The call heard at any season is a clear arresting *kiewick* or terse whistled *whiu* or *kiew*. A slower, more rounded, rather melancholy *pee-oo* or *pāw-ut* is used at dusk in the breeding season.

Habitat and range: Between 1906 and 1910 several shipments from Europe were liberated in Otago whence other districts were stocked. Now established in the South Island east of the main range from Southland (Puysegur Point) to Marlborough and Golden Bay; more recently Westland, where probably increasing. Some were transferred to the North Island, where its status is uncertain, since a number of reported sightings have not been confirmed. Hunts mostly over open country, taking much of its prey on the ground; even digging for earthworms.

Breeding: Nest-site is usually a hole in an old building, tree or bank, e.g. rabbit burrow. Eggs 2–5, near Queenstown, normally 3; white, rounded. Incubation period 28 days; fledging *c.* 26 days.

AUSTRALIAN BARN OWL   *Tyto alba*   *Pl. 39, p. 168*
Other names: White Owl, Screech Owl.
Description: 34 cm (13½″). Upperparts a beautiful soft light greyish brown tinged yellow, finely spotted blackish brown and white; underparts white; facial disc heart-shaped, large and prominent, white with buff margins; tail grey barred with buff. Flight soft, silent and buoyant. 'Lovely are the curves of the white owl sweeping, Wavy in the dusk lit by one large star.' (George Meredith.)
Voice: A menacing, long-drawn *skiirrr*, sometimes uttered during hunting-flight. Young in nest hiss and snore.
Habitat and range: The Barn Owl is the most widely distributed land-bird[1] that exists. Three specimens of the Australian race (*delicatula*) have been found in Westland, at Barrytown (1947), Haast (1955), Runanga (1960). There is no evidence that this useful rodent-eater has bred in New Zealand, but it could become established through wind-drifted strays from Australia.

Bones believed to be of a Barn Owl have been recovered from Tom Bowling Bay. The subspecies *lulu* is common in Fiji.

SWIFTS: Apodidae

Somewhat swallow-like in appearance and behaviour, but with very long narrow scythe-like wings and short tails. Structurally quite distinct, especially the feet, of which the toes are directed forward. Hence swifts do not perch like swallows but, for rest, cling to the sides of trees, rocks or walls. In fine weather swifts generally fly high and fast and so escape notice, but depressions may force them to fly low over open water where insects are abundant.

Two species which breed in north and east Asia commonly migrate to Australia. Only rarely are they reported in New Zealand. A third palaearctic species may have strayed far off course to reach New Zealand. On 4/12/68 a single dark swift, believed to be *Apus apus*, was watched by two eminent ornithologists as it flew around the western tip of Motunau Island, north Canterbury.

[1] The House Sparrow's wide distribution has been brought about by man.

FORK-TAILED SWIFT *Apus pacificus* *Pl. 40, p. 169*
Description: 18 cm (7″). Upperparts brownish black with greenish gloss; *rump white*; *tail strongly forked*; chin and throat whitish; underparts obscurely barred. Wings long and slim with a span of 40 cm. In Australia has been noted hawking insects in company with Tree-martins, which by comparison look diminutive.
Voice: A shrill excited chattering, audible up to 400 m.
Habitat and range: Breeds in eastern Asia, migrating south and sometimes straggling to New Zealand, viz. Taranaki, December 1884; six sightings since 1950, up to 4 birds at a time, usually near the coast or over sea-cliffs.

SPINE-TAILED SWIFT *Chaetura caudacuta* *Pl. 40, p. 169*
Description: 20 cm (8″). At first glance very dark, with swept-back wings. Larger than Fork-tailed Swift; forehead, chin, throat and *undertail-coverts white*, the white passing up the flanks to lower back; chest, abdomen and back brown; crown, wings and tail shiny gun-metal blue; tail short and squarish with feather-shafts protruding as fine spines, probably too small to be seen in a bird flying free. Wing-span 48 cm.
Habitat and range: Breeds in north-eastern Asia, migrating south, regularly to Tasmania but in varying numbers. Has straggled to Macquarie. From time to time considerable invasions occur, the most notable being in 1942–3 when, between November and March, strays were widely reported from Whangarei to Stewart Island and flocks appeared in Westland. On numerous occasions these powerful swifts, in small flocks or as individuals, have been noted circling hilltops or small steep islands, or flying about sea-cliffs and headlands from North Cape to Bluff Hill. The accumulating records suggest that some may reach New Zealand every year.

KINGFISHERS: Alcedinidae

Forest kingfishers (subfamily Daceloninae)—including both the New Zealand Kingfisher and the Kookaburra—are an Old World group, differing from the fishing kingfishers (subfamily Alcedininae) in their broader, more flattened bills and more varied habits; the subfamily includes a number of species which never go near water, and others which live on both aquatic and terrestrial foods.

NEW ZEALAND KINGFISHER *Halcyon sancta* *Pl. 40, p. 169*
Maori name: Kotare.
Description: 24 cm (9½″). Crown, mantle and scapulars *deep sea-green*, tinged with olive; back, rump and wing-coverts *ultramarine with green reflections*; *wing and tail quills cobalt*, brown inner webs; a broad band of black passing back from angle of mouth encircles the neck and below this is a buff or reddish-buff collar; crown edged with ultramarine (often a white or buff spot or band divides this from the black hindneck); a spot of buff or reddish-buff behind nostrils passes back as a faint stripe above the eye; underwing-coverts and axillaries buff; throat white to buffy-white; *breast buffy-white to deep reddish-*

buff (the latter only strongly developed in the male, probably intensified with age); bill black, base of lower mandible pinkish-white; feet brown.

Immature plumage like adult, but feathers of breast and of pale collar are broadly margined with brown; successive plumages retain narrow brown margins, most adults showing some trace.

Voice: A penetrating *kik-kik-kik-kik* is given occasionally throughout the year, but delivered repeatedly in spring and summer. For about a month before nesting begins, chasing and other mating displays are accompanied by a loud *kreel*, generally repeated from six to eight times, or by a scream; the scream is also given as an alarm note, especially when an intruder is near the nest.

Habitat and range: Occupies a remarkably wide range of habitats, and, as these include nearly all types of habitat associated with man, it has probably increased as the result of settlement: it is a bird of the more open portions of the forest, and of open country with scattered trees, lake shores, rivers and streams, and the coast (especially tidal estuaries). Commonly uses power and telephone wires as a perch and man-made excavations, including road cuttings, provide nesting sites.

Food items recorded are: worms, insects and spiders, crabs and other crustaceans, shell-fish, small fish, tadpoles, lizards, mice and occasionally small birds, even ducklings. Prey is captured by a sudden dash from a prominent perch; killed by beating against the perch before swallowing. Stead found that flies and other insects were caught in his garden at flowering shrubs in winter, the Kingfishers either taking the insect off the flower in passing, or diving straight on to the foliage, stopping themselves from penetrating too far by keeping their wings spread. According to Stead's observations, when diving for fish or water insects the Kingfisher may 'flop' into the water with outstretched neck, so that its body is barely submerged; sometimes, however, it dives into the water 'going in with bill, neck and body in a straight line, and wings clapped tight to the sides, after the manner of a Gannet.'

Moon states that a Kingfisher was seen bathing from an overhanging branch; it splashed clumsily into the water several times in succession, each time giving a few wing-beats in the water before flying back to its perch, and finally began to preen.

There are numerous observations of a seasonal change in distribution, although possibly increased numbers, e.g. on coastal estuaries in winter, result from a local dispersal to a new food supply rather than migration; some are always present throughout the year in inland districts.

The New Zealand Kingfisher (sub-specifically *vagans*) is found throughout the country and on most off-lying islands from Kermadecs and Three Kings south to Stewart but not at Chathams or sub-antarctic islands. Very common in northern districts, ranging up to *c*. 750 m in the centre of the North Island; rather scarce over much of the South Island, especially inland. The species ranges from the Loyalty Islands to New Caledonia, Australia, Norfolk Island

---

PLATE 41 White-winged Triller (p.183); Satin Flycatcher (p.190); Broad-billed Roller (p.178); Red Wattle-bird (p.205); Fan-tailed Cuckoo (p.169); Black-faced Cuckoo Shrike (p.183); Pallid Cuckoo (p.168); Channel-billed Cuckoo (p.170).

PLATE 41

WHITE-WINGED TRILLERS 20 cm

♀

♂

SATIN FLYCATCHERS 16 cm

♀

♂

BROAD-BILLED ROLLER 29 cm

RED WATTLE-BIRD 34 cm

AN-TAILED CUCKOO
cm

BLACK-FACED CUCKOO-SHRIKE 33 cm

PALLID CUCKOO 30 cm

CHANNEL-BILLED CUCKOO 61 cm

PLATE 42

PIED FANTAIL
16 cm

BLACK FANTAIL
16 cm

NORTH ISLAND TOMTITS
13 cm

♂

♀

SOUTH ISLAND TOMTIT
13 cm

SNARES ISLAND TOMTIT 13 cm

♀

AUCKLAND ISLAND TOMTITS
13 cm

♂

NORTH ISLAND ROBINS
18 cm

♀

SOUTH ISLAND ROBIN 18 cm

♂

CHATHAM ISLAND ROBIN
15 cm

and Lord Howe Island.

Breeding: A hole is bored in a rotting tree or bank; tunnelling is started by perching opposite the site and flying straight at the selected spot; the birds strike with some force and drive the bill into the wood or earth; finally when the hole is some centimetres deep they sit in it and begin to peck at the material. Tunnel is inclined slightly upwards, length 10–23 cm; the nest-chamber 15–20 cm in diameter. The same tunnel may be occupied year after year. Eggs placed on earth or wood without nesting material. Breeding October-January; eggs 4–5, white. Incubation period *c*. 18 days (Moon). Chicks naked when hatched, but soon sprout spiny pin-feathers and these break out to reveal the juvenal plumage; food remains and excrement are allowed to accumulate in the nesting tunnel. Moon found that the chicks were fed (by both parents) at intervals of 10–30 minutes; chicks have a characteristic rasping note and call frequently. Fledging *c*. 24 days.

KOOKABURRA   *Dacelo gigas*   Pl. 40, p. 169

Other name: Laughing Jackass.

Description: 45 cm (18″). A giant kingfisher, not highly coloured, which escapes notice by sitting still on top of a pole or stump. Head, neck and underparts buffy-white; crown streaked brown; dark stripe through eye; back and wings brown; *pale blue spots* on shoulder and *white patch* at base of wing quills, conspicuous in flight which is laboured and undulating; tail brown, barred with black and tipped white. Bill long and heavy, black above and white below.

Voice: A loud raucous laugh, most often heard at dawn and sunset. When one bird starts laughing, others in the vicinity will join in.

Habitat and range: Several small shipments from Australia were liberated between 1866 and 1880. The only district in which a small, but apparently fairly stable, population survives is along the western shore of the Hauraki Gulf among the creeks and islands between Cape Rodney and Whangaparaoa Peninsula. Wanderers sometimes reach Little Barrier, Auckland, Kaipara and Whangarei. Elsewhere Kookaburras have been reported in places and circumstances which strongly suggest that they were wind-blown strays from Australia.

Breeding: Nest in a hole in a tree or bank. Eggs 2—4, white, rounded. Little known about breeding in New Zealand. Apparently only one or two young are reared.

PLATE 42 Pied Fantail (p.185); Black Fantail (p.185); North Island Tomtit (p.186); South Island Tomtit (p.186); Auckland Island Tomtit (p.186); Snares Island Tomtit (p.186); North Island Robin (p.187); South Island Robin (p.187); Chatham Island Robin (p.189).

ROLLERS: Coraciidae

Rollers, so named from their spectacular aerial acrobatics, are found throughout the temperate and tropical countries of the Old World. One successful eastern species (*Eurystomus orientalis*) has numerous subspecies, one of which (*pacificus*) is a common summer migrant to eastern Australia from the tropics and an occasional visitor to New Zealand.

BROAD-BILLED ROLLER *Eurystomus pacificus* *Pl. 41, p. 176*
  Other names: Australian Roller, Dollar-bird.
  Description: 29 cm (11½"). Head and neck dark brown; throat dark blue; upperparts brownish green; underparts pale green; wings blue and green with a *greenish white or silvery blue patch on the primaries*, conspicuous in flight; tail bluish green with black tip. Bill and feet red. Juveniles are less brightly coloured with greenish throat and dusky bill.
  Flight strong and buoyant with slow, steady wing-beats. Attention may be drawn to a Dollar-bird by its peculiar aerial antics as it hawks insects near trees or over open country.
  Voice: A harsh grating chuckle or rough *treek treek* commonly uttered during swallow-like flight towards dusk, when these birds become more active.
  Habitat and range: Dollar-birds arrive in south-eastern Australia from the tropics from late September onwards; and after breeding, leave between February and April. Though very rare in Tasmania, they have been recorded in New Zealand about 16 times since 1881, 5 since 1950, mostly from districts near the west coast as far south as Ross, but also from Great Barrier and as far east as Havelock North and Tikitiki, and as far south as Fortrose (1967). Some of the occurrences have been in spring, especially November, but most have been in late summer, when young birds on northward passage from south-eastern Australia may be drifted across the Tasman by adverse winds.

NEW ZEALAND WRENS: Acanthisittidae

An endemic family, of doubtful relationships as affinity has been suggested both with the Old World pittas and South American antpipits.

RIFLEMAN *Acanthisitta chloris* *Pl. 43, p. 184*
  Other names: Titipounamu, Thumbie (Nelson).
  Description: 8 cm (3"). A forest species generally located by very high-pitched 'zipt' notes given by pairs or family groups passing through the trees. Sexes differ: *male* clear bright yellowish-green above, white (tinged buff) below; wing with *yellow bar and behind this a white spot*; yellow rump and flanks; faint dark eye-stripe and above this *distinct white eyebrow-stripe*; tail black tipped with buff: slightly upturned black bill; *female* striped dark and light

178

brown above but otherwise like the male. In summer and autumn family parties include immatures, both sexes striped as in the female. The wholly white underparts provide the best distinguishing feature at a distance in the upper foliage. Distinctly smaller than the Grey Warbler and other small forest species but appears much smaller because of comparatively short tail. A distinctive feature is vigorous flicking movement of the wings when standing on a branch, not seen in any other bush bird.

Voice: Irregular sharp, high-pitched *zipt-zipt-zipt-zipt*; sometimes a single *zipt* but often rapid bursts. When bursts heard two or more birds probably often call together. Fledged young *tsit-tsit* (Soper).

Habitat and range: Now found throughout North Island (except northern third from a line approximately through Te Aroha), South Island and Stewart Island in all bush areas; also Great Barrier and Little Barrier Islands. Also readily occupies modified habitats with some native forest remnants. Feeds freely in exotic trees near native forest, and has been recorded in larger exotic plantations although it is not one of the abundant species in the latter (has been recorded in hedgerows in Taranaki, and gorse near Wellington). Its range now includes a high proportion of higher altitude beech forest on the mountain chains of both main islands but it was probably originally widely distributed in lowland mixed forest. Habits are to a large extent those of a tree-creeper, searching crevices in bark, and amongst epiphytic mosses and lichens, on trunks and branches of larger trees; also explores all portions of the tree as far as the twigs, both in the second storey and canopy. Only rarely feeds on the forest floor. May be seen arching neck to extract food items with the comparatively large bill, and hanging under a twig. Believed to feed mainly on insects but also takes spiders.

The subspecies described for the North (*granti*) and South Island (*chloris*) are doubtfully distinct, the yellow rump being greenish in *granti*. In Fiordland and mountain districts of Otago and Nelson specimens with brighter yellow rump and flanks have been obtained and distinguished subspecifically (*citrina*), but further field work and taxonomic study are needed.

Breeding: Nest ground-level to 18 m (usually 3–6 m), generally in a hollow limb or crevice in bark; clay banks of old bush roads are often favoured; constructed of abundant material, loosely woven with lining of feathers, entrance at the side. Has nested in settled habitats in the neighbourhood of native vegetation, sites including stone walls, hollow posts and beneath a corrugated iron roof. R. S. Gray, in Dunedin, found that nest boxes were used readily. Double-brooded; breeding recorded August-January; eggs 2–4, white. Both parents incubate and feed chicks, which are fed mainly by male after departure from nest. Incubation period 20–21 days, fledging *c.* 24 days. According to M. F. Soper, the young of the first brood sometimes assist in feeding second, and Soper's observations show that this species is frequently polygamous.

BUSH WREN   *Xenicus longipes*   *Pl. 43, p. 184*
Other names: Matuhi, Tom Thumb Bird (Stewart Is.).
Description: 9.5 cm (3¾″). In comparison with Rifleman of generally stouter build. Dark brown head and face; dark green back and wings; *above eye prominent*

white stripe; prominent *yellow patch surrounded by dark brown* at angle of wing; underparts *grey on breast and abdomen, yellowish-green sides and under tail*. Female duller. Slightly upturned bill. The Bush Wren shares with the next species, the Rock Wren, the habit of bobbing the whole body, a vigorous action repeated frequently on alighting.

Voice: Common call note a 'subdued trill' (Buller); Guthrie-Smith records a 'faint rasping sound' and a loud cheep for the Stewart Island Bush Wren.

Habitat and range: In remote forests, and of extremely limited range in North Island (in recent years observed only at Waikaremoana) and rare in the South Island. Formerly widespread (apparently not in northern North Island), although never as abundant as the Rifleman.

Little known of its habits, but it is apparently less creeper-like than the Rifleman; feeds less on trunks and more amongst foliage, and according to Buller only rarely on the ground. Entirely insectivorous as far as known.

North Island (*stokesi*) and South Island (*longipes*) subspecies distinguished only by minor differences—mainly yellower sides in *stokesi*—have been described; a third and more distinctive subspecies on Stewart Island and its neighbouring islets (*variabilis*) has generally browner plumage and less distinct eyebrow-stripe.

Breeding: Nesting habits probably as in Rifleman, although little information on record. On the mainland it probably nests above ground level; on the outlying islets of Stewart Island the nest is commonly in an old petrel burrow, or other hollow in the ground, and sometimes in a prostrate log or clump of fern. Eggs, December (South Island); November-December (Stewart Island area), 2–3, white. Incubation by both parents, and young fed by both (Stewart Island Bush Wren).

ROCK WREN *Xenicus gilviventris*   Pl. 43, p. 184

Description: 9.5 cm (3¾"). Habitat is distinctive, mainly open screes, moraines and fell-fields of mountains above the bushline; also enters the zone of sub-alpine scrub. In colour general shade browner than the preceding species, dull green above and grey-brown below, with a yellow wash on the sides; *creamy white stripe above eye*; *narrow pale yellow stripe* with *black surrounding patch* at the angle of the wing. The sexes differ slightly, the back being brown faintly washed with green in the female. The comparatively large feet and long hind toe form an additional distinguishing feature. Bobs the body vigorously on alighting; also a 'bowing movement' (Soper).

Voice: Common call consists of three notes, the first being accentuated; also a thin pipe. Calls penetrating and may carry for some distance.

Habitat and range: Only in South Island, where it extends from Nelson to Fiordland. Found in Fiordland at lower altitudes in subalpine scrub; a sub-species described from Fiordland (*rineyi*), with brighter green upper surface and brighter yellow on the sides, is still of doubtful status.

Feeds actively on the ground amongst alpine vegetation, and in scattered shrubs or dense subalpine scrub; the latter also furnishes shelter and is probably often inhabited in bad weather. Can fly fairly strongly, but normally flies only 5–6 yards between rocks when feeding. Feeds on fruits of alpine plants as well as insects, spiders, etc.

Breeding: In rock crevices in comparable sites to those of the two arboreal wrens; nest bulky, with entrance at side, and lined with feathers; eggs, September–November, 2–3, white. Both parents feed the young; food observed at Homer Tunnel was grasshoppers, moths, beetles, caterpillars and grubs (Soper).

A fourth species of wren, the Stephen Island Wren (*Xenicus lyalli*) discovered in 1894, became extinct almost as soon as discovered, the population on the island at that time being destroyed by a cat. In colour this species was mottled brown above, and yellowish below; the bill was stouter than in the mainland wrens. Although weak flight is suggested by the short, rounded wings and soft plumage, there is no clear evidence of flightlessness. The only observations were those of the lighthouse keeper on the island, Lyall, who saw them but twice, on both occasions in the evening. They ran like a mouse and 'did not fly at all' (Rothschild).

LARKS: Alaudidae

SKYLARK *Alauda arvensis*   *Pl. 43, p. 184*
Description: 18 cm (7″). Upperparts brown heavily streaked with dark brown, especially on the crown, with a whitish eye-stripe and a crest which can be raised at will; underparts buffish white with breast boldly streaked; outer tail feathers pure white, conspicuous as bird arises; when also greyish-white edging along rear of wings is revealed. Bill short; hind-toe furnished with a very long claw. Has a crouching walk. Flight strong and slightly undulating with alternate spells of wing beats and 'shooting' with closed wings. Often takes dust baths on country roads.
Voice: Note a liquid *chirrup*. Song a torrent of trills and runs, fast, variable and sustained—sometimes for as long as 5 minutes—delivered as it soars steeply or while poised at a considerable height, head to wind, or as it drops earthwards. Sometimes sings on the ground. Song may be heard in all months, but at a minimum mid-February to mid-April.
Habitat and range: Imported by the hundreds and widely released from 1864 onwards, they quickly became established in all types of open country up to 1600 m. Introduced to Chatham Islands; self-introduced to Auckland Islands and Kermadecs. Some flocking in autumn and local movement, but no evidence as yet in New Zealand of regular migration. In Auckland in spring loose flocks are still present in country where local birds are paired and males singing strongly on territory.
Breeding: Nest a neat grass-lined cup in a hollow of the ground, e.g. hoof-print, well concealed by grass. Eggs, October-January, 3–7, greyish white thickly speckled brown, frequently with a darker zone. Incubation period *c*. 11 days; fledging up to 20 days. Two or three broods.

SWALLOWS AND MARTINS: Hirundinidae

WELCOME SWALLOW   *Hirundo neoxena*   *Pl. 40, p. 169*
 Description: 15 cm (6″). Forehead, throat and chest rufous; head and back
 blue-black; wings and tail dark brown; abdomen and underwing greyish white;
 tail forked, outer feathers elongated, inner feathers having a subterminal row
 of white spots. Flight swift, darting and graceful.
 Voice: A twittering *twsit, twsit, twsit.*
 Habitat and range: The Welcome Swallow, now usually treated as a race of the
 widely distributed Pacific Swallow (*H. tahitica*) is common in Australia, but
 prior to 1958 was known only as a rare vagrant to New Zealand, reported
 Northland (1920), Auckland Islands (1943), Stewart Island (1953), Farewell
 Spit (1955). In 1958 at least three pairs are known to have nested near Rangaunu
 Bay, and others perhaps near Kawakawa. The increase has been spectacular.
 Common throughout lowlands of North Island up to Volcanic Plateau;
 breeding as high as Taupo and visiting Tongariro National Park. In South
 Island, reported all provinces; breeding at Lake Ellesmere since 1961 and now
 generally, except in the south where it is a common autumn and winter visitor.
 This dynamic species has now colonised some offshore islands and was
 reported at the Chathams in August 1975; and four were flitting above roosting
 waders at The Old Neck, Stewart Island, in May 1977.
 Breeding: Nest a mud cup, strengthened with grass and lined with feathers.
 Most nests so far found in New Zealand have been in man-made sites, e.g.
 under concrete and wooden bridges, concrete culverts, a ramshackle jetty,
 a neglected launch swinging at anchor. A few pairs are using coastal caves
 or rocky overhangs. Long breeding season, 2 or 3 broods being raised. Eggs
 August-February, 3–5, white, variably freckled with brown, sometimes with a
 denser zone towards the upper end. Incubation period *c.* 15 days; fledging
 17–22 days. For some time after flying young return to nest to roost.

AUSTRALIAN TREE MARTIN   *Hylochelidon nigricans*   *Pl. 40, p. 169*
 Other name: Tree Swallow.
 Description: 14 cm (5½″). Upperparts steely black *except rump which is dull
 white*; forehead rust-red; throat and chest grey; rest of underparts dull white.
 Tail slightly forked. Viewed from below brown undertail-coverts contrast with
 white of the remainder of the underparts. Smaller than Welcome Swallow from
 which it is readily distinguishable by white rump, small amount of red on head,
 and tail not deeply forked.
 Habitat and range: Widespread in Australia and a common summer visitor to
 Tasmania, forming large flocks before departure. From time to time vagrants
 and even small flocks reach New Zealand; rarely in spring, more often in
 autumn when wind-drifted migrants, probably from Tasmania, have occurred,
 especially in the far south and in the province of Nelson or near Farewell Spit.
 Elsewhere widely reported, but rather anomalously, not from Auckland or
 Northland. Reported as wintering Blenheim (1878) and Featherston (1946).

A typical swallow in its feeding habits, hovering and dipping over rivers and lakes or hawking insects around trees.

Breeding: A pair is said to have nested successfully in a mill at Oamaru in 1893. In Australia normally nests in holes in trees, but sometimes uses ventilators and suitable cavities in buildings.

CUCKOO-SHRIKES: Campephagidae

BLACK-FACED CUCKOO-SHRIKE *Coracina novaehollandiae* *Pl. 41, p. 176*
Description: 33 cm (13"). Mainly a uniform bluish dove-grey; but forehead, face, throat and primaries black; abdomen and *tip of tail white*, conspicuous in flight. Instead of a black face, young birds have a dark line through the eye, and whitish underparts. Flight strong and undulating. Easily approachable.
Voice: A curious soft churring or croaky purr.
Habitat and range: This is a highly successful species, of which there are nineteen accepted races extending over India, south-eastern China and Australasia. Common in Australia and Tasmania where it is a partial migrant. Recorded in New Zealand about a dozen times from Invercargill to Kaipara, mostly near the west coast. It appears that most of those which have reached New Zealand have been young birds, wind-drifted across the Tasman on their first northward migration. One at Pouto, near North Kaipara Heads, was present from June to September. Habitually chooses a conspicuous perch from which to swoop cuckoo-like upon its prey. Will feed on the ground on insects and worms. Also eats fruit, such as mulberries and boxthorn berries.

WHITE-WINGED TRILLER *Lalage sueurii* *Pl. 41, p. 176*
Description: 20 cm (8"). Male, crown, nape, back and tail black; rump grey; top of wing black with prominent thick white bar on 'shoulder'; underparts white. Female, brown above with a buffy eye-stripe; underparts pale grey.
This species is unique among the Trillers in that most males have distinct breeding and non-breeding plumages; i.e. when nesting is over, they moult into a plumage which somewhat resembles that of the female. From July onwards they begin to moult into breeding plumage.
Voice: Autumn song, distinct and 'rather liquid, descending and with a similar pattern to the first part of a Chaffinch's song', was heard at dawn and dusk from a male at Macandrew Bay.
Habitat and range: A regular migrant in south-eastern Australia, moving south in August-September and heading north in February; frequenting lightly timbered areas including parks and gardens.
A male, an off-course wind-drifted migrant, was observed between February and June 1969 in a suburban setting on the Otago Peninsula.

BULBULS: Pycnonotidae

Bulbuls are a large tropical family of Africa and Southern Asia. Some species are popular cage-birds and have become established as wild birds outside their normal range. Thus the Red-whiskered Bulbul (*Pycnonotus jocosus*) is now common in the suburbs of Sydney N.S.W.; and the Red-vented Bulbul (*P. cafer*) thrives in Fiji.

In 1952 it was suspected that a species of bulbul was present in Auckland; but their identity as Red-vented Bulbuls was not established till 1954 when pairs were proved to have bred or to be breeding in at least three suburbs. The Department of Agriculture decided that they were undesirable aliens and a determined and apparently successful attempt was made to exterminate them. None has been reported since 1955.

RED-VENTED BULBUL   *Pycnonotus cafer*

Description: 20 cm (8″). About the same size as a Starling, but slimmer and with a longer tail. Head and throat glossy black; breast dusky; back sooty brown with wavy grey lines. Rump white, noticeable in flight; tail black with white tip. Abdomen grey, undertail-coverts red. Bill and feet black. Sexes alike. An important field character is the triangular crest, 'like a Roman helmet'.

Voice: Described as 'cheerful and attractive' though it has 'only one or two call notes and no song' (Whistler). The most common call-note heard in Auckland was a low, scratchy, double croak *cark-cark*, but single notes of more musical quality were sometimes uttered.

Habitat and range: The species has a wide range in India and south-eastern Asia with numerous races. Apparently about 1952 some (of the subspecies *bengalensis*) escaped or were released from a ship in the Auckland harbour and adapted themselves to a new climate and environment. None seems to have survived the order for their suppression.

FLYCATCHERS: Muscicapidae

In this large Old World family (distribution: Europe, Africa, Asia together with many Pacific Islands) the bill is typically broad at the base surrounded by abundant bristles. A habit almost universal in the family (except in the whistlers) is to capture insects in the air with short flights from a prominent perch; flight when hawking erratic. The characteristics mentioned so far apply to the fantails

---

PLATE 43 Rifleman (p.178); Bush Wren (p.179); Rock Wren (p.180); New Zealand Pipit (p.199); Skylark (p.181).

184

PLATE 43

RIFLEMAN
8 cm
♀

RIFLEMAN
8 cm
♂

BUSH WRENS
9 cm
♀

♂

ROCK
WRENS
9 cm
♂

♀

NEW ZEALAND
PIPIT 19 cm

SKYLARK 18 cm

BROWN CREEPER 13 cm

WHITEHEA[D] 15 cm

♀

PLATE 44

YELLOWHEAD 15 cm

♂

GREY WARBLER 11 cm

FERNBIRD 18 cm

SILVEREYE 12 cm

CHATHAM ISLAND WARBLER 12 cm

(Pacific, Australia, New Zealand) which constitute a subfamily—Rhipidurinae. In the genus *Petroica* (Pacific, Australia and New Zealand) facial bristles are sparse, and the legs comparatively long (especially long in the New Zealand Robin): birds of this genus obtain insects by searching in foliage and on branches, or on the ground—almost never by hawking. The family includes also the subfamilies Monarchinae (paradise flycatchers and allies of Africa, Asia and Australia) and Pachycephalinae (the whistlers of Australia and the Pacific).

FANTAIL   *Rhipidura fuliginosa*   *Pl. 42, p. 177*
Maori name: Piwakawaka.
Description: 16 cm (6½″) (tail 8 cm beyond coverts). Readily identified by characteristic proportions—rounded head and long tail—and frequently spread tail; tail closed in flight except when manoeuvring. Birds of normal colour pattern ('Pied Fantail') make up most of the population in North Island, but the 'Black Fantail' (i.e. dark phase) accounts for perhaps a quarter of the population of the South Island subspecies; dark phase absent in Chatham Island subspecies. Pied Fantail dark olive brown above, darker on the head, with rich yellowish buff underparts; white throat, and band of sooty black across the upper breast; white eyebrow stripe and faint buffy-white wing-bar; the two central tail feathers are dark, and the remaining feathers have white inner webs, producing vertical stripes on the spread tail; bill black and feet dark brown. In the Black Fantail plumage is sooty black above, chocolate brown below: a small white patch may be present behind the eye.

Lively movements include sidling and posturing with tail fully spread, but tail sometimes folded when it frequently hangs down.
Voice: Common note a penetrating *cheet*; also repetitive chattering derived from the same note. Call notes sometimes merge into a not unmusical song, which may be well sustained.
Habitat and range: Common in forest of all types, but just as familiar in town and country gardens, parks, hedgerows, shelter belts and exotic plantations; it evidently adopted man-made environments and modified native vegetation at an early stage of settlement, and has extended its range into all settled districts providing trees and shrubs. Present on most of the nearer islands, including Three Kings, Poor Knights, Hen and Chickens, Great and Little Barrier, Mayor, Kapiti, Stewart Island and outliers, but not on distant outlying islands except the Chatham Islands.

The North Island (*placabilis*), South Island (*fuliginosa*) and Chatham Island (*penitus*) subspecies are distinguished by the amount of white on the tail feathers (except for two dark central feathers): approximately half of each feather white in North Island subspecies, two-thirds of feather in South Island subspecies and three-quarters in Chatham Island subspecies. In the North Island form undersurface of spread tail greyish-white, in South Island and Chatham forms almost pure white; breast is somewhat darker in South Island and Chatham

---

PLATE 44 Brown Creeper (p.192); Whitehead (p.193); Yellowhead (p.194); Grey Warbler (p.195); Silvereye (p.205); Chatham Island Warbler (p.197); Fernbird (p.190).

Island than in North Island form.

Breeding: Nest a compact, often tailed, cup on a slender branch or fork 2–6 m from the ground, constructed of fibres, moss, bark, horsehair, etc., and finished off with an outer coating of spider's web. Three, four or even five broods August-January; eggs 3–4, cream, spotted grey and brown, most abundantly at the larger end where a ring of denser spots may be present. Both parents build first nest, incubate, and feed the nestlings; only female builds subsequent nests and incubates while male feeds the fledglings (female takes some part in feeding young of final clutch) (A. Blackburn). Incubation period 15 days, fledging 15 days in North Island Fantails.

TOMTIT *Petroica macrocephala*   *Pl. 42, p. 177*
  Other names: Miromiro, Pied Tit (North Island), Ngirungiru (South Island), Wheedler, Butcher-bird (Taranaki).
  Description: 13 cm (5″). Large-headed and short-tailed. Sexes differ: *Male*– prominent pattern of black and white: head and upperparts jet black, the black throat forming a clear-cut line above the breast; a small white forehead spot and *prominent white L-shaped wing-bar*; three outer tail feathers on each side white with black tips forming *conspicuous white patch on each side of tail* when spread, or partly spread; bill black; feet brown, orange-yellow soles. *Female— above greyish-brown*; brownish-white forehead spot is somewhat indistinct; wing-bar small and faint as compared with that of the male, and washed with buff; *tail-patches white*. *Immature male* resembles adult female, except that the head and throat are dark grey.

  Comes readily—especially the male—to examine an intruder, and aggressive behaviour, including raising of frontal feathers, wing drooping or fluttering and darting flights accompanied by bill snapping, is characteristic.
  Voice: Call note of male a penetrating *swee*; faint *seet* in female. Male song a high-pitched trill that has been vocalised as, *Willoughby willoughby* (Buller); *ti oly oly ho* and *yodi yodi yodi* (Fleming). According to Fleming the female occasionally, when excited, utters a whispered warble similar to the male's song.
  Habitat and range: Forest, forest remnants, mature exotic plantations, even mainly exotic cover near native forest, are inhabited by this species: original range—reduced greatly by forest clearing—is thus to some extent being recovered, and this is one of several forest species at present showing a tendency to expand under settled conditions. According to Fleming is 'sedentary, undertaking few small-scale and no large-scale seasonal movements' and in most areas pairs evidently remain together, in the general area of their nesting territory, all through the year. Insectivorous, much of its food being obtained from trunks and branches, and some from the forest floor; Fleming describes the typical 'darting from a watching perch to pick up insects on the bark.'

  The North Island Tomtit (*P. m. toitoi*) (slightly smaller than South Island and Chatham Island subspecies, male with pure white underparts, female greyish white underparts) is distributed throughout the North Island (rare in Northland where it is restricted to larger forest areas); also Hen and Chickens, Little and Great Barrier and Kapiti Islands. The South Island Tomtit (*P. m. macrocephala*) (size larger; breast and abdomen yellow, colour being of varying intensity ranging in the male from lemon-yellow, with deep orange on the upper breast, to individuals that 'appear white-breasted in the field'; underparts of female faintly washed with yellow) is found throughout the South Island, on Stewart Island and outliers, and on Solander Island. The Chatham Island Tomtit (*P. m. chathamensis*) (like the South Island Tomtit, differing mainly in the browner upperparts of the female, and the greater length of tarsus) is now restricted to the larger forest remnants on the main island of the group; also Pitt Island, Mangere, Little Mangere and South East Island.

The two remaining Tomtits of the New Zealand region exhibit notable departures from the description given above for the species, although they may be regarded as strong subspecies of *P. macrocephala*. The Auckland Island Tomtit (*P. m. marrineri*) is, like the South Island and Chatham Island forms, yellow-breasted; however, the female is superficially similar in plumage pattern to the male, and thus strikingly different from females of other subspecies; the upperparts of the female are dull black instead of glossy black; the fledgling plumages also differ in more nearly resembling the adult condition. Fleming, who pointed out these characters in *marrineri*, states that a tendency towards 'maleness' can be observed in the plumage of many females of the Chatham Island Tomtit, *P. m. chathamensis*.

The Snares Island Tomtit (*P. m. dannefaerdi*) is entirely glossy black except for wing and tail which are brownish black; female plumage with slightly less gloss. According to Fleming, field observations in 1944 (R. A. Falla) and in 1947 (R. A. Falla, C. A. Fleming, E. F. Stead) showed that the song and habits agree with those of the New Zealand Tomtits; 'the song is a typical Tomtit warble, which could be matched within the range of variation in other races of *macrocephala*.' The total population is of the order of some hundreds of breeding pairs; mainly in the *Olearia lyallii* scrub that clothes much of the main island; nests well hidden in hollow logs or holes in trees, generally close to the ground, also among rocks in tussock areas.

Breeding: Nests from ground level to 9 m; usually 2–4.5 m (except Snares Island Tomtit which nests near ground level). Site is generally sheltered from above in a hollow in a trunk, a rock crevice or under vegetation, but occasionally in an unsheltered position in a fork. Material moss, scraps of bark, cobwebs, with lining of feathers; built by female rarely assisted by male. Female fed by male throughout nesting period. Highly territorial; male selects nest site. Breeding August-February; double-brooded; eggs 3–5, cream, with delicate yellowish- and purplish-brown spots, usually forming a denser zone at large end. Incubation by female. Incubation period of North Island Tomtit *c*. 17 days, fledging 17–18 days (Wilkinson); incubation of South Island Tomtit, 15 days (Jensen), 16 days (Potts). Both parents feed young.

ROBIN *Petroica australis*   *Pl. 42, p. 177*
Maori name: Toutouwai.
Description: 18 cm (7"). Dark slaty grey upper surface, together with long legs and upright stance are characteristic. Differs from Tomtit in absence of tail pattern, faint wing-bar and much reduced sexual dimorphism. *Male*—head, upperparts, sides and throat dark grey, meeting the pale underparts in a definite line; wings and tail brownish black; white forehead spot; on inner webs of the mid-wing feathers is a white spot which is not generally visible, but faint buff

spots on the outer webs of the same feathers form a weak wing-bar; bill black; feet brown. *Female*—slightly browner and paler, with a reduced pale breast and abdomen, and with throat and sides not sharply marked off from the pale underparts.

Tameness and tendency silently to inspect the intruder are characteristic, and it has a pattern of aggressive behaviour essentially similar to that described above for the Tomtit; a habit often noted is spreading of white frontal spot especially to warn off a straying Robin in the territory, but also in display to a human intruder.

Voice: Call note is a short chirp. The song is varied and sustained, according to Wilkinson's observations on Kapiti, delivered frequently for half an hour at a stretch, and broken only by very short pauses. 'Beginning with slow, almost plaintive notes, the song soon gains in volume, until it is ringing through the bush with almost startling vehemence. The variety of notes is astonishing . . . When near the end of its song, the pauses become more frequent and of longer duration, until it ceases altogether.'

Habitat and range: The present discontinuous distribution of the Robin is difficult to explain: although 'chiefly confined to native forest in districts at least moderately remote from areas with high human populations' (Fleming), it readily enters second-growth scrub (e.g. on Kapiti Island and Stewart Island); is one of the forest species now increasing in the exotic plantations of the Volcanic Plateau. Originally it was probably distributed universally in forest or scrub. Like the Tomtit is insectivorous, but a much higher proportion of the food is taken on the ground; it does not make darting flights like those of the Tomtit to pick up food, and unlike the Tomtit spends much time hopping over the forest floor. Food includes worms (not regularly taken by the Tomtit) and a variety of invertebrates. The habit of 'caching' surplus food has been several times observed. Fleming describes the Robin as 'a bird of the lower stratum of the forest.'

Like the Tomtit is sedentary and probably territorial throughout the year.

The North Island Robin (*P. a. longipes*) (throat mottled white; feathers of crown and back with white shaft streaks; breast, abdomen and undertail-coverts ivory white) is distributed discontinuously in forested areas of the central North Island from Mamaku (near Rotorua) to the East Cape district, and south to East Taranaki; east of Otaki (Tararua Range); also Little Barrier and Kapiti Islands. The South Island Robin (*P. a. australis*) (largest subspecies in average dimensions, and with proportionately shorter wing and longer tail; breast washed with lemon-yellow in male, this colour being of varying intensity; female whitish below; brownish dorsal plumage) is found on D'Urville, Chetwode and Pickersgill Islands (Marlborough Sounds region); scattered throughout Marlborough and Nelson in habitats ranging from manuka scrub to deep forest tracts; west of the Alps in Westland; and in scattered localities in Otago and Southland (comparatively abundant in the Manapouri–Te Anau area). The Stewart Island Robin (*P. a. rakiura*) (similar to *australis*, but slightly darker above; breast ivory white like that of North Island Robin) is found in the Stewart Island area on the main island and on Green, Jacques Lees, Tamaitemioka and Pokowaitai, on which two last the population is unusually dense (Blackburn).

Breeding: Nest in similar situations to those chosen by Tomtit, but usually favours lower level. Nest rather bulky, of twigs, fibres, moss, etc., bound together with spider web, and lined with treefern scales or soft grasses, etc.; built by female. Breeding September-February, double-brooded; eggs 2–3, cream with purplish-brown spots, denser at the larger end. Incubation by female; male's feeding of female persists throughout the period of mating, nest-building, incubation and fledging of the young. Incubation period of North Island Robin *c*. 17 days, fledging 19 days (Parkin); incubation of South Island Robin, 20 days, fledging 21 days (Richdale).

CHATHAM ISLAND ROBIN *Petroica traversi* Pl. 42, p. 177

Description: 15 cm (6″). Entirely brownish black; bill black; legs brownish black.

Habits as in Robin of mainland, including the characteristic erect posture (probably a character 'related to the long tarsus shared by both species' Fleming).

Voice: Recent extensive investigations on Little Mangere Island by the Wildlife Service included a study of the vocalizations of the species and comparison with those of *P. australis*. Common call consists of a single syllable; also a call of descending notes, heard most commonly in summer and autumn. The song is clear and sustained, although less complex than that of *P. australis*; song period lasts from the beginning of the breeding season to early summer.

Habitat and range: Fleming states—'It is inferred that the species at one time ranged throughout the Chatham Islands, but it had become extinct on the main Chatham Island before 1871.' By 1937, when an estimate for the total population of 20–35 pairs was given by Fleming, the remaining population of the Chatham Island Robin was restricted to the coastal forests and the ledges of scrubby vegetation on the cliffs of Little Mangere Island (approximately 6 hectares). The recent field studies by the Wildlife Service suggest that Fleming's figures were probably an overestimate; however, the vegetation on the species' last refuge was also evidently in a state of deterioration and the population was by 1972, when the current investigations began, only about 17—this had become reduced to 7 in June, 1976. Five birds, including the only two females, were transferred to nearby Mangere Island in September, 1976, and immediately started nesting.

Breeding: The Wildlife Service field studies have included extensive work on breeding, territoriality, etc. The pairs are maintained throughout the year, full territorial song beginning in late autumn and ending in December or early January. Laying mid-October to early December; nest building is by the female. Nest lightly constructed of plant fibres, lined with feathers. Clutch 2, colour of eggs as *P. australis*.

SATIN FLYCATCHER *Myiagra cyanoleuca* *Pl. 41, p. 176*
  Description: 16 cm (6½″). Slightly longer than a Fantail and noticeably larger in the body. Males and females are very different. *Male*–back, wings and tail glossy, blackish green; throat black; lower breast and abdomen white. *Female*–crown and nape dull blue black; rest of upperparts brown with faint bluish wash; *throat and breast rust red or tinted orange-red*, brightest on lower part of the throat; underparts dull white, sharply defined from the red of the lower breast. The tail of both sexes has narrow very pale brown, almost whitish, outer edges. Bill broad and short with typical flycatcher hairs round the base. Feathers at rear of crown slightly raised, but not forming a crest. Maintains a constant tremulous movement of the tail.
  The female of the duller and slightly smaller Leaden Flycatcher (*M. rubecula*), a summer visitor to eastern Australia which might straggle to New Zealand, is very similar; but the red on throat and breast is less vivid and the lines of demarcation between the red and adjacent areas are less clearly defined.
  Voice: A cheerful, loud piping whistle, *chee-ee, chee-ee*; and also a short rasping note.
  Habitat and range: A fairly common summer migrant to the eastern states of Australia, reaching Tasmania in some numbers. Has been noted on board ships during its crossing of Bass Strait. Moves north in autumn to North Queensland and apparently to New Guinea and adjacent islands.
  Only once recorded in New Zealand, a very active female near Gisborne, June 1963.

WARBLERS: Sylviidae

A large family of four rather diverse subfamilies, typical members small and with thin bill; bristles at base of bill well developed or absent. With few exceptions have a musical—often powerful—song; movements active as they search for food in foliage and crannies of twigs and branches. Insectivorous.
  Subfamily Sylviinae (Europe, Africa, Asia, Indonesia, Australia and the Pacific) contains approximately three-quarters of the total species including *Bowdleria* of New Zealand. The Regulinae (goldcrests, known as kinglets in North America) are Eurasian and North American; Polioptilinae (gnatcatchers) restricted to the New World (United States to Brazil); Malurinae (East Indies to the S. W. Pacific, Australia and New Zealand) contains the blue wrens (*Malurus*) and their near allies of Australia and New Guinea, and some 20 aberrant genera, among which are *Gerygone* (East Indies, South-west Pacific, Australia and New Zealand), *Finschia* (New Zealand) and *Mohoua* (New Zealand).

FERNBIRD *Bowdleria punctata* *Pl. 44, p. 185*
  Other names: Matata, Tataki Thrush (Foveaux St).
  Description: 18 cm (7″). Warm brown above, streaked dark brown; white

below, with dark brown spots on throat and breast; flanks brown with dark brown streaks. Forehead and anterior portion of crown chestnut. *Tail feathers have a spine-like appearance* owing to the disconnected barbs of the webs and dark brown shafts; webs often much frayed.

Characteristically reluctant to take flight and will remain hidden even though movement of foliage is visible when moving through swamp vegetation, etc. Flight is for short distances (exceptionally, 50 metres). In flight the tail trails hanging down.

Voice: Mechanical double call consisting of a low and a sharp metallic note, also a single soft *click*. Rarely a warbled song of about six rather metallic notes (B. D. Bell). Pairs travelling through scrub may keep in touch, one calling *plik* and the other *choot*. A male observed on Codfish Island gave a song consisting of 'an upward cadence of two very musical notes, with a timbre akin to that of the Bellbird' (Blackburn).

Habitat and range: Reduction of swamp- and fern-lands through agricultural development has greatly reduced the range of the Fernbird, which on the mainland inhabited drier swamps and adjacent scrub, bracken and the low rushes and stunted scrub clothing saltmarsh, gumland, *pakihi* and other poorer lands, up to 1000 m. It is nevertheless widespread, although local. The early stages of settlement may have locally increased its range as bracken or low scrub regenerated on cleared forest lands, but most of these areas were subsequently developed, and became grassland. Now mainly in swamps, and the remaining undeveloped poorer lands (including the considerable *pakihi* areas of north-western and western South Island).

Pending a full study, both North and South Island Fernbirds are treated as *punctata* (size of spots on under surface, used as a character to distinguish *vealeae* of North Island from *punctata* of South Island, is variable); this form occurs on Great Barrier and on two of the Alderman Islands (on the latter lives in *Poa anceps* on steep slopes and low scrub); also formerly on Great Island, Three Kings group. The Stewart Island (*stewartiana*) subspecies (Stewart Island and outliers except Codfish Island) is unsatisfactorily defined, but is apparently dimorphic (either spotted on both throat and breast as in *punctata*, or with throat devoid of spots, or very faintly spotted: the latter type was described by E. F. Stead as a new subspecies, *insularis*). The Codfish Island (*wilsoni*) subspecies is distinguished from *punctata* by the heavy pattern of large spots on throat and breast, and darker upper surface (feathers black with only narrow brown edges). (*Note.*—Stewart and Codfish Island forms occur both on the coast in low vegetation—swamp, grass and low scrub—and in the scrub and adjacent grasslands of the higher slopes; also swamps and bogs on the main island.) The Snares Island (*caudata*) subspecies is a more uniform brown above, with obscure dark streaking, and with a strong wash of brown below; tail quills broader than in other subspecies, the barbs weakly connected; feet comparatively robust (this form obtains cover from tussock, but unlike other subspecies is also seen constantly in the open: it feeds in penguin colonies, and on the open floor of *Olearia lyallii* forest). The Chatham Island (*rufescens*) subspecies is believed to have become extinct in *c.* 1900: dark chestnut brown above, back streaked with dark brown; undersurface lacking spots, or a few obscure spots on throat and upper breast (occurred on Chatham, Pitt and Mangere Islands:

practically nothing recorded of its habits, but apparently like the mainland form kept to denser vegetation).

Breeding: Nest deep in sedges, rushes, shrubs or other low vegetation, from a few centimetres to *c.* 1 m above the ground (according to Guthrie-Smith when in swamps usually over water or damper portions); a deep cup of neatly woven dry rushes, grasses, etc., with lining of feathers which frequently conceal or partly conceal the eggs. Nest built by both adults. Breeding September–February. Eggs 2–3, white or pinkish heavily flecked brown and purplish-brown, usually a denser zone (or broad band) at large end. Incubation period 12½ days; fledging 12–13 days (Soper). Both adults feed young with crane-flies, moths, grubs and caterpillars (Guthrie-Smith, Buddle).

B. p. caudata of the Snares nests in dense ground vegetation (fern, grasses)—occasionally in a hollow log—nest resembling that of the mainland subspecies; according to Stead's observations both adults incubate; during Stead's visit in late November–early December a pair accompanied by newly-fledged young were seen building a second nest, i.e. double-brooded.

BROWN CREEPER　　*Finschia novaeseelandiae*　　　　*Pl. 44, p. 185*

Maori name: Pipipi.

Description: 13 cm (5¼″). Reddish-brown forehead, crown, lower back, rump and tail, this colour strongest on rump and tail but merging gradually with ashy grey on upper back; a zone of ashy grey, shaded with brown on nape and upper back and this passes forward without interruption to face which is pure ashy grey; wings dark brown, quills with buff edges; underparts including throat pale cinnamon brown; *narrow pale throat meets ashy grey of cheeks in a sharp line situated well below the eye*; a faint pale buff stripe behind the eye; dark brown spots at one-third from tip of each tail quill, except centre pair, form a band when tail is spread; bill and feet pale brown.

In flocks, pairs or family parties (see below); seldom silent, maintains contact with constant flocking call.

Voice: Call has some resemblance to call note of Yellowhead (*q.v.*) but with experience readily distinguished; it consists of a rapid succession of somewhat harsh notes *chi-chi-dee-dee-dee-dee-dee-dee*. Notes are rapidly repeated; may be partial or a *chi* or *dee* given singly (the single *chi* can be a prolonged note). Flocking calls may be broken with fragments of song. The song consists of from five to six highly musical notes, of which the third is emphasised, viz. *chi-roh-rée-roh-ree* (or final *ree-ree*).

Habitat and range: South Island, and Stewart Island and its outliers; in forest throughout, but much more widely distributed than commonly believed and present in a surprising range of smaller native forest remnants; where remnants are adjacent to gardens, etc., containing old-established exotic vegetation it will enter this freely (e.g. on Banks Peninsula occurs in vegetation consisting mainly of oaks and other well-grown exotic trees); in second-growth forest and scrub;

PLATE 45 Bellbird (p.202); Stitchbird (p.200); Tui (p. 204); Song Thrush (p.197); Blackbird (p.198).

PLATE 45

BELLBIRDS
20 cm

♀

♂

STITCHBIRDS
19 cm

♂

♀

TUIS 31 cm

♂

♀

imm.

SONG THRUSH
23 cm

BLACKBIRDS
25 cm

♂

♀

imm.

PLATE 46

REDPOLLS
12 cm

♀

♂

GOLDFINCH
12.5 cm

♀

♂

GREEN-
FINCHES
15 cm

♀

♂

CHAFFINCHES
15 cm

♀

♂

YELLOWHAMMER
16 cm

♀

CIRL
BUNTINGS
16 cm

♂

HOUSE
SPARROWS
14.5 cm

♀

♂

HEDGE SPARROW
14.5 cm

also reported established in pine plantations at Golden Downs, Nelson. Reaches the timber line in the mountains, but not normally found in sub-alpine scrub.

Flocks or pairs move characteristically through the trees when feeding among branches and in canopy, a vigorous inspection being made of bark crevices, leaf bases, etc.; frequently clings upside down to a twig or allows itself to swing down as the foliage gives under its weight. Food apparently consists of insects only.

Large flocks are sometimes formed: a flock of *c.* 50 was noted on 24th February in the Craigieburn Range, Canterbury (E. G. T.).

Breeding: Nest an open cup 1.5 to 9 m from the ground, generally in canopy or in bush lawyer and other vines; sometimes in a fork. Material dry grasses, fibres, small twigs, moss, bound together with spiders' web, and lined feathers. Strongly territorial; pairs feed together in territories (observed 23/10/1961; probably shortly before nesting) (E. G. T.). Breeding October-January; probably double-brooded. Eggs 3–4, of extremely variable colour and pattern (pink or pinkish-white with scattered reddish-brown blotches, white with dense brown blotching, white with scattered brown and purplish spots, etc.). Incubation *c.* 17 days. Only female incubates and is fed on nest by male (Soper).

WHITEHEAD *Mohoua albicilla*   *Pl. 44, p. 185*
Maori name: Popokatea.
Description: 15 cm (6″). Upper-surface, wings and tail pale brown; this colour also extends on to the sides and flanks; rump and base of tail quills tinged to a varying degree with reddish-brown; *head and underparts white*, slightly tinged with brown; head almost pure white in adult male, shaded brown on nape and crown in female and immature; bill black, feet bluish-black.

Generally in flocks or family parties, located in the forest by flocking call.
Voice: Calls varied, the commonest consisting of a rapid series of chirping notes which may be compared with opening portion of song of Chaffinch; frequently heard is a hard single *zit* (R. B. S. found that on Little Barrier Island this could be mistaken for the typical note of the Stitchbird). Song composed of clear canary-like notes, which are commonly interspersed with harsher notes (Reischek described a song of this type consisting 'first, of three notes, like *viu, viu, viu*, then four, like *zir, zir, zir, zir*'). In spring it adds a five-note chime like a Bellbird's (R.A.F.).
Habitat and range: North Island; Great and Little Barrier, Arid and Kapiti Islands: now found on the mainland only south of a line approximately through Te Aroha and Pirongia. Found in the larger remaining forest areas up to *c.* 1300 m (and adjacent second-growth forest), but may be close to settlement, e.g. east of Wellington; abundant on Little Barrier and Kapiti Islands. On the Volcanic Plateau one of the species established in exotic pine forests.

Main food is insects, searched for vigorously in canopy, on tree trunks, logs,

PLATE 46 Redpoll (p.209); Goldfinch (p.208); Chaffinch (p.210); Greenfinch (p.207); Yellowhammer (p.210); Cirl Bunting (p.211); House Sparrow (p.212); Hedge Sparrow (p.198).

and 'even, on occasion, the forest floor' (Wilkinson), whose observations on Kapiti show that it also eats fruits (mahoe, matipo, toro, horoeka, hangehange, kaikomako and kotukutuku); like the Brown Creeper and Yellowhead often hangs downwards on a branch or twig.

Breeding: Cup-shaped nest of twigs, rootlets, grass, bark, bound together with spiders' web; lined with fragments of bark and sometimes a few feathers; common site is canopy of shrub or low tree 1–3 m above the ground, but may be at 9 m or more; commonly in a fork; sometimes 'hung from light twigs or branches like that of the Silvereye' (Buddle); in mainland forest (Urewera) a common site according to R. St. Paul is leaf of treefern 30–60 cm from trunk. Breeding October-February; probably double-brooded. Eggs 2–4, variable (white or pinkish-white with reddish-brown blotches; white with reddish-brown and purplish spots; densely blotched red, almost obscuring the ground colour; white with only faint indication of spots, etc.). Wilkinson, on Kapiti Island, found that the nest took about four days to build, after which there might be a delay of several days before the first egg was laid; incubation *c.* 17 days, by both parents; fledging 16–17 days (Wilkinson). Young fed by both adults: at a nest on Little Barrier Island (November 1947) the female returned with food approximately every 7 minutes, the male every 30 minutes; food included caterpillars, grubs, moths, beetles, a blow-fly, spiders (Buddle, E. G. T.).

'Quartets' combining to incubate and feed young were noted by Guthrie-Smith in his investigation of the breeding habits of this species on Little Barrier Island and in Hawkes Bay; he was doubtful whether two pairs were involved, or a male and three females, but as according to Soper's recent observations the male Yellowhead (see below) is commonly polygamous it seems likely that the latter explanation is the correct one. Guthrie-Smith found four adults present at most of the nests examined, but at some there was only a single pair.

YELLOWHEAD *Mohoua ochrocephala*   *Pl. 44, p.185*

Other names: Mohua, Bush Canary.

Description: 15 cm (6″). Back olive-brown, tinged with yellow: rump and tail brownish-yellow; wing quills brown, yellowish-brown on outer edge; *head and underparts bright canary-yellow*; lower abdomen greyish white; undertail-coverts yellow; nape shaded olive-brown in female and immature; bill and feet black. Tip of tail quills nearly always much abraded, shaft projecting (see below).

Identification of the call note is even more important than for Brown Creeper and Whitehead as the Yellowhead feeds mainly in the tops of the trees; in pairs, family parties or small flocks.

Voice: A louder and more mechanical call than the Brown Creeper's, consisting of 6–8 notes rapidly repeated; a high-pitched ratchety buzzing (notes have a vibrating quality that has been compared with a pneumatic drill); the call is much varied, e.g. Soper found that during incubation the male's call increases in volume as soon as the female leaves the nest; according to Soper a characteristic call note, *lukaart, lukaart*, is given by the female for the few days prior to hatching and after hatching. Song a variable number of musical, canary-like notes; sometimes ends in a guttural *curr*. When the notes are much drawn out they have a strong resemblance to certain notes of the Bellbird.

Habitat and range: South Island, Stewart Island (doubtful). In the large areas of native forest, i.e. Marlborough, Nelson, Westland, and western Otago and Southland (also some smaller areas of forest near Dunedin); formerly Banks Peninsula but last recorded *c*. 1900.

Soper states that although it feeds mostly in the tops of the trees, it has 'a fondness for rooting through the accumulations of rubbish that fall down and collect in the forks . . . they grip the bark with one foot . . . dig their tail, which is supplied with spines, into the trunk, and scratch vigorously with the other foot sending down a shower of debris.' In the search for insects, it thoroughly investigates leaves, twigs, branches and higher portions of the trunk. The tail feathers rapidly become abraded, presumably through use in feeding on branches and trunks, and it is quite normal for the spines formed by the projecting shafts to be about 1 cm long (similar abrasion appears in the White-head but is much less marked). Actions are vigorous, hanging head downwards from a twig, or swinging on tops of smaller branches to examine foliage. So far as known entirely insectivorous.

Breeding: Differs from the Brown Creeper and Whitehead in that it is apparently always hole-nesting: according to field studies by Soper, the site may be 2.5–18 m above the ground, but usually over 9 m. All the nests he examined were in cavities in dead or dying trees; nest cup-shaped, composed of moss, rootlets and spiders' webs, lined with fine grass (Soper suggests that hole-nesting has been comparatively recently acquired, as the construction of the nest conforms to that used in the open by the related Brown Creeper and Whitehead). Breeding November–December; eggs 3–4, pinkish-white evenly blotched with reddish-brown. Incubation by female, at least 21 days (Soper). Soper found that for the first five or six days after hatching the chicks were fed by regurgitation; later they received 'insects, grubs and caterpillars of all kinds' (fed by both adults); the chicks left the nest on their eighteenth day. He records courtship feeding early in the season, and, according to his observations at one nest, the nest site is chosen by the male.

Soper has shown that polygamy is of regular occurrence in this species. He was able to observe the breeding cycle closely at five nests and found that three birds (a male and two females) were associated at two of the nests, the females being of different ages and thus distinguishable by the degree of shading on the nape. The number of eggs in these nests was three or four, the same number as in nests with one female; both females shared the work of incubation.

GREY WARBLER *Gerygone igata* Pl. 44, p. 185

Maori name: Riroriro.

Description: 11 cm (4¼″). Greenish-grey above; pale grey throat and breast; white abdomen and undertail-coverts; a yellow tinge varying in intensity on sides and flanks, but this may be absent (not present in juvenal); on anterior margin, at bend of wing, a narrow white streak may be visible; *short, rounded tail*; conspicuous *white patch on either side of dark brown tail seen in flight* (the tail quills have a subterminal or terminal white spot except the centre pair); bill black; feet blackish brown.

Commonly seen fluttering on perimeter of foliage or emerging for a short flight to the next feeding point; usually in pairs. Song, heard throughout the year, is the most familiar feature.

Voice: Song a sweet trill, may be varied by reduction of the number of notes, or suppression of the latter part; also delivered in a somewhat rambling fashion (this, however, may be juvenile song or a local variation). A shorter song consisting of three comparatively weak, unmusical notes is commonly repeated at intervals when feeding; these notes sometimes given as a preliminary to the trill. (*Note.*—Local variations are commonly distinguished, but further study is required.) In calm weather the warble has remarkable carrying power.

Observations in Dunedin by Marples showed that while the Grey Warbler sings at all times of the year, a marked diminution occurs in the winter months during which there are usually a few weeks when it is not recorded. He found that the main peak of singing activity came in September or October, but it fell to a low level in December, reaching another peak in February or March.

Habitat and range: A familiar bird of all settled districts, having like the Fantail adopted modified native forest and exotic trees and shrubs. It entered the man-made habitats resulting from settlement rapidly, and Buller could refer to it in 1873 as 'the familiar frequenter of our gardens and hedgerows.' Now occurs in exotic vegetation, e.g. willows, pine shelter belts, gorse hedges, gardens, remote from forest or forest remnants; also in pine and other exotic plantations, in remnant or second-growth native forest and scrub up to *c.* 1400 m., and in larger native forests. In forest it is evenly distributed, but appears to be more abundant in modified and second-growth forest than in unmodified forest.

Insects and spiders provide main food; searches leaves, twigs, bark and characteristically flutters at foliage to feed; has been seen hovering to catch a spider in front of web (H. C. Abraham); 'hawks' small moths on the wing (Moon).

North, South, Stewart Island and nearer outlying islands, including the Solander Islands. Study of possible subspecies is required: several have been described but present information does not justify their recognition.

Breeding: Suspended nest is pear-shaped and has a side entrance near the top, frequently hooded; composed of grasses, moss, sometimes small twigs, spiders' webs, thistledown and even wool, lined with feathers. Nest situated 1.5–7.5 m from the ground. (Of 23 nests examined by Moon most were hanging from the canopy of the outermost branches; the point of suspension was 'firmly woven around a branch, with the lower part secured at one or more sides to prevent it from swinging'.) Built by female, male assisting with gathering of material; a nest observed by P. C. Bull was built in 7 days. Breeding August–January; double-brooded. (*Note.*—August–September broods escape parasitism by the Shining Cuckoo, *q.v.*: the latter is then arriving in New Zealand from winter quarters, lays in November–December.) Eggs 3–6, pinkish white evenly covered with small reddish-brown or purplish spots, a dense zone or band at larger end (sometimes almost unspotted except at large end). Incubation period 17–19 days, fledging 17–19 days (J. M. Cunningham). Both adults feed young at intervals of 3–6 minutes, foraging within a short distance of the nest (Moon). Chicks fed for three weeks after departure. Chicks have a most distinctive, high-pitched call *cheef* in addition to the begging call at this stage.

CHATHAM ISLAND WARBLER *Gerygone albofrontata* *Pl. 44, p. 185*
Local name: Woodpecker.
Description: 12 cm (4¾″). Olive-brown above; upper tail-coverts and base of tail pale reddish-brown; forehead, line above eye and whole of underparts white; only obscure whitish spots on outer tail quills; sides and flanks tinged yellow; bill and feet dark brown. The Chatham Island Warbler has a much larger bill than the Grey Warbler.
Voice: 'Three rather weak notes repeated several times with a break in between' (B. D. Bell).
Habitat and range: Originally in forest throughout, but now of very local distribution. Fleming in 1937 gained the impression that it was 'not nearly so abundant in the changed conditions in settled country as is its New Zealand representative [the Grey Warbler].' Since 1937 it has become more restricted in distribution on the main island, being found only in bush remnants of the southern half (B. D. Bell). Also in bush remnants on Pitt Island; present on South East Island (abundant) and Little Mangere Island.
  According to Fleming its general habits and movements resemble those of the Grey Warbler, as do its feeding habits, differences apparent to the observer being 'merely correlated with the Chatham bird's larger size.'
Breeding: Nest very like Grey Warbler's: materials recorded are roots, fibres, moss, leaves, cobwebs, with lining of feathers. Two nests recorded by Fleming on the main island were 6–9 m from the ground, one in a tangle of vine and the other hanging from a lofty limb in the open; a nest on South East Island was about 2 m up in a tangle of *Muehlenbeckia*. Breeding recorded November–January, but this is probably the second brood (parasitised by the Shining Cuckoo). Eggs 4, pinkish white with reddish-brown spots, a dense zone at the large end. The behaviour of the adults when feeding young in the nest closely resembles the behaviour of the Grey Warbler; family parties of three or four young with their parents are normal (November–January).

THRUSHES: Turdidae

The true thrushes are a very big almost cosmopolitan family, missing only from much of Polynesia and New Zealand; though one variable species, the Island Thrush (*Turdus poliocephalus*) is widely distributed in the south-west Pacific and came as close to New Zealand as Norfolk Island. Song Thrushes and Blackbirds were first introduced from England in 1862; since when they have proved such successful colonisers that they are now among the most numerous birds in the country.

SONG THRUSH *Turdus philomelos* *Pl. 45, p. 192*
Description: 23 cm (9″). Above warm olive-brown, with paler underparts, boldly spotted breast and reddish buff under wing. Bill brownish; legs pinkish brown. Young have mantle speckled buff. By midsummer upperparts of many adults are grey-brown with bleaching.
Voice: Song, April-January, a 'fine careless rapture', bold, varied, musical, the

clear-cut phrases often repeated with brief pauses, usually delivered from a conspicuous perch. Alarm note a loud *chuk* or *tchik* rapidly repeated; flight note a thin *seep* or soft *sip*.

Occasionally a mimic; has been heard to incorporate notes of Pied Stilt and Red-billed Gull in its song.

Habitat and range: Throughout New Zealand in all types of country including dense bush up to *c.* 1300 m. Now present on most off-shore and outlying islands north to Kermadecs and south to Campbell. Feeds mostly on the ground using regular 'anvils' for smashing snails; but also takes some berries and small fruit.

Breeding: Nest, seldom high, often conspicuous, smoothly lined with mud or wood-pulp, a mixture of rotten wood and saliva, where no mud is available, e.g. Rangitoto. Eggs, June–January, 3–6 clear greenish blue with black spots. Incubation period 13–14 days; fledging 13–14 days.

BLACKBIRD   *Turdus merula*   *Pl. 45, P. 192*
Description: 25 cm (10″). Male a robust all-black bird with clear orange-yellow bill; female dark brown with grey chin and brown bill; juvenile more rufous-brown with some speckling (hence popular fallacy of hybrids between Blackbird and Song Thrush). Partial albinos are not uncommon, but seem to be much more numerous in some years than others.
Voice: Song clear, fluent, tuneful, mellower and more fluty than that of the Song Thrush. Song period, July-January, considerably shorter than that of Song Thrush. In late summer and early autumn Blackbirds may sing quietly a soft inward warble while remaining hidden in the heart of a thick leafy shrub. Alarm notes an anxious *tchook*, an angry screech and a persistent *tchink*, *tchink* which becomes particularly resonant when vermin, cat or owl, is being mobbed.
Habitat and range: Throughout New Zealand up to *c.* 1400 m. Rather a more thrustful coloniser than the Song Thrush of off-shore and outlying islands from Kermadecs to Campbell. Wild and shy in insular habitats. Feeds mainly on ground, but much more partial to fruit than the Song Thrush.
Breeding: Nest generally low and ill-concealed, strengthened but not lined with mud; frequently now in out-buildings. Eggs, 2–5, July–December, bluish-green freckled with red-brown, but showing considerable variation. Incubation period 13–14 days; fledging 12–15 days.

ACCENTORS: Prunellidae

A small palaearctic genus of rather colourless sparrow-like birds but with fine pointed bills, probably related to the thrushes and warblers. None native to New Zealand. One species, first introduced in 1868, has shown itself a most successful coloniser.

HEDGE SPARROW   *Prunella modularis*   *Pl. 46, p. 193*
Local names: Dunnock, Hedgie.
Description: 14.5 cm (5¾″). Upperparts brown streaked black; throat and chest

slate-grey, underparts paler with heavily streaked flanks. Inconspicuous rather than skulking. Perhaps most evident in autumn when song restarts, males are challenging and pairs are formed. Seldom seen to fly far. Feeds on ground, moving with a slow shuffling gait, often with a flicking of the wings.

Voice: Call-note a sharp insistent *tseep*. Song, a hurried warble faster and stronger than that of a Grey Warbler (*weeso, sissy-weeso, sissy-weeso, sissy-wee* W. Garstang).

Habitat and range: At home in all kinds of cover from sea-level to 1600 m; saltmarsh, mangroves, gumlands, gardens, shrubberies, sand-dune lupins, wind-flattened taupata, gorse hedges, pine plantations, mountain scrub. Has spread to most off-shore islands and into the sub-antarctic as far as Campbell Island.

Breeding: Nest usually low down in thick cover. Eggs, August–January, 3–5, clear deep blue. Incubation period *c.* 12 days. Fledging 11–15 days.

PIPITS AND WAGTAILS: Motacillidae

The pipits and wagtails are largely insectivorous birds, characterised by slender form and comparatively long tail. The wagtails are with one exception restricted to the Old World, being absent from New Zealand and occurring only accidentally in Australia; pipits nearly cosmopolitan, although absent from most Pacific islands.

NEW ZEALAND PIPIT *Anthus novaeseelandiae* *Pl. 43, p. 184*
Other names: Pihoihoi, Sandlark (Chathams).
Description: 19 cm (7½″). Brown above (feathers with darker centres) and white below with dark-brown streaked upper breast; *fairly prominent white eyebrow-stripe* and *white outer tail feathers*. The Skylark, with which it is commonly confused, lives in pasture land where the Pipit is generally absent, but ranges of the two species overlap in rough open country, etc. The main field differences between Skylark and Pipit are the more slender form (including comparatively long tail) of the latter, and the raised head feathers forming a short crest in the Skylark; colour of Skylark generally more strongly buff; both have white outer tail feathers. Skylark's aerial song is unmistakable (Pipit sings briefly from a prominent perch, only occasionally on the wing: see under 'Voice' below). Both Pipit and Skylark walk and run, rarely hop. Note also the distinctive habit in the Pipit of spasmodically moving tail up and down either when walking or standing.

The juvenal plumage characterised by crescentic warm buff dorsal feathers, and zone of dark streaks on upper breast more distinct than in adults.
Voice: Common call a high-pitched *scree* or a rasping drawn out *zwee*; in spring male repeatedly calls from a prominent perch *pi-pit* and sometimes gives the musical trilling song, *tsew-tsēr weet-tsrrr*, or more briefly *tzu-weet*; song may be delivered from a prominent perch or in flight as the bird descends in short glides, wings and tail elevated; the song flight commonly ends in a quick run on alighting.

Habitat and range: The most obvious habitat restriction under modern conditions is the avoidance by the Pipit of pure pasture land as mentioned above, but elsewhere on rougher farmland, roadsides and in open country generally it is found throughout and fairly common. Under conditions of early settlement it probably greatly increased in range as forest was cleared, although it was perhaps limited in abundance by introduced predators; before European settlement probably restricted to lowland and alpine tussock grasslands, river-beds and the coastal zone. In mountain districts widely distributed on the open rocky tops. Almost entirely insectivorous, insects occasionally captured on the wing; some seeds also taken.

A member of a wide-ranging species (from East Europe to Australia and New Zealand) including *A. n. richardi*, Richard's Pipit. On most coastal islands surrounding New Zealand, and Chatham, Antipodes, Auckland and Campbell Islands (straggling to Kermadec and Snares Islands). The populations of our sub-antarctic islands differ subspecifically. Of several forms described, *aucklandicus* (Auckland Is.), *steindachneri* (Antipodes), *chathamensis* (Chathams) are acceptable.

Breeding: Nest a deep cup—the lining of dry grass generally substantial—well concealed at the base of a tussock, or amongst grasses, low bracken and similar vegetation, which may enclose nest in a tunnel. Two- to three-brooded. Breeding August-March; eggs 3–4 (heavily blotched brown or purplish-brown, and grey). Incubation period *c.* 14 days; fledging 14–16 days; young fed by both parents. When visiting the nest, adults alight at some distance off, but usually fly directly off the nest after feeding chicks.

HONEYEATERS: Meliphagidae

A family restricted—but for the doubtfully assigned South African genus *Promerops*—to Indonesia, Australia and New Zealand and the South-west Pacific (also Hawaii); in Australia, the main centre of distribution, there are numerous common and conspicuous species. Tongue brush-tipped.

STITCHBIRD *Notiomystis cincta*　　　　　　　　Pl. 45, p. 192
Maori name: Hihi.
Description: *Male*—19 cm (7½″). *Velvety black head, throat, upper breast and mantle*, with a *tuft of white feathers on each side of head behind eye* (white tufts can be erected when disturbed); *a band of golden-yellow* passes from the 'shoulders' and lesser wing-coverts across the breast; *white wing-bar*; back olive-brown; wings and tail brown with olive-brown outer webs; underparts pale greyish brown, with irregular streaks of dark brown mainly towards sides. *Female*—18 cm (7″). *Olive-brown above*; a faint white spot on each side of head corresponds to ear tuft of male; *pale brown below*, darkest on throat and upper

---

PLATE 47 Starling (p.212); Myna (p.213); Rook (p.214); Black-backed Magpie (p.216); White-backed Magpie (p.216).

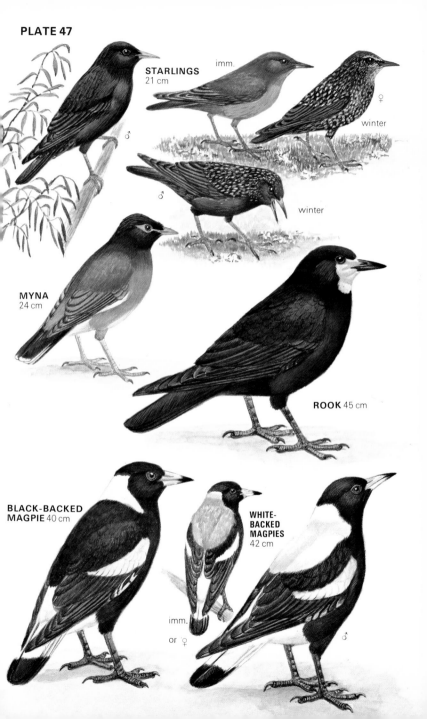

PLATE 47

STARLINGS
21 cm

imm.

♀
winter

♂
winter

MYNA
24 cm

ROOK 45 cm

BLACK-BACKED
MAGPIE 40 cm

WHITE-
BACKED
MAGPIES
42 cm

imm.

or ♀

♂

PLATE 48

SADDLEBACKS
25 cm

North
Island

South Isl
immature
Jackbird

South Islan

NEW
ZEALAND
THRUSH
North
Island
26 cm

NEW ZEALA
THRUSH So
Island 26 cm

KOKAKO
North Island
38 cm

KOKAKO
South
Islan
38

HUIAS

♂
45 cm

♀
48 cm

breast, obscurely marked with dark brown streaks; a faint yellow wash on lesser wing-coverts; *white wing-bar*. Bill brownish-black; feet pale brown (both sexes). Plumage of immature male similar to that of female; female and immature might be mistaken for female Bellbird but can be distinguished by less slender build, comparatively short tail and white wing-bar.

Tail is commonly tilted.

Voice: The common call *tzit* (from this the bird's name is derived as, in Buller's words, 'it has a fanciful resemblance to the word 'stitch' ') is given by both sexes. Female also has a repeated *pek, pek, pek, pek* (like alarm note of Bellbird); feeding call of young is a continuous, high-pitched *sit, sit, sit*. Sibson also recorded a softer call *tseet*, in addition to the common *tzit*; and also on one occasion heard 'a two-note call like part of the exuberant bubble-song of the Bellbird.' The male has a vigorous song: Sibson's description states that 'it began with the typical *tzit*, and went to *tsiu, tsiu, tsiu*; it ended quite abruptly and was not repeated.' Also a soft warbling by the male (recorded both in spring and in mid-December, i.e. towards the end of the nesting season).

Habitat and range: Originally the North Island, and Great and Little Barrier and Kapiti Islands, but has been extinct on the mainland since about 1885. It is doubtful whether it was originally evenly distributed on the North Island mainland; however, Buller described it as 'comparatively common in the southern parts of the North Island' in 1872. It was apparently rare north of a line approximately through northern Taranaki and the Bay of Plenty; according to Maori tradition, was plentiful in the Upper Wanganui, Rotorua and Urewera districts. A last remnant of the species exists on Little Barrier Island, where it appears to be thriving.

It inhabits forest of varying types at all altitudes on Little Barrier, although not frequently seen in the second-growth manuka of former clearings; like the Bellbird and Tui it is strongly attracted to nectar-bearing trees and shrubs, and a marked attraction to the coast when flax (*Phormium*) was in flower was noted by Parkin. Food includes insects and fruits (Buller states that A. Reischek found 'some minute seeds as well as insect-remains' in stomachs of specimens); however, observations on Little Barrier Island, especially (see below) feeding of the young in the nest (Guthrie-Smith, Sibson), suggest that it is more dependent than the other New Zealand honeyeaters on nectar. On Little Barrier it has been recorded feeding on the nectar of (amongst others) puriri, pohutukawa, kohekohe, *Alseuosmia* and flax.

Breeding: In holes in trunks and branches, 3–18 m from the ground; nest substantially built of sticks and rootlets, lined with treefern scales and a few feathers (Guthrie-Smith). Breeding November–December; eggs 3–5, white. Guthrie-Smith's observations on Little Barrier showed that both parents feed the young; he believed that nectar alone was given to the chicks (he notes that the parents often wiped the bill on a branch as if sticky, and that insect or other food was not at any time seen in the parent's bill). At two nests found more recently (Sibson, Parkin) the same observations were made; however, at the nest discovered in early January, 1948, Sibson found that only the female came in with food. The nest observed by Parkin contained small young on 21st December, 1955, and the young left the nest on 3rd January, 1956: fledging thus occupies not less than two weeks.

BELLBIRD   *Anthornis melanura*   *Pl. 45, p. 192*
Other names: Korimako, Makomako, Mockie.
Description: *Male* 20 cm (8″). *Soft olive-green*, yellowish green on sides and abdomen; gloss of iridescent purple on forehead, crown, face and chin (this is of variable extent); *tuft of yellow feathers on each side* situated near angle of closed wings; *undertail-coverts pale yellow*; wing and tail quills brownish black. *Female*—19 cm (7½″). *Plumage is much more drab than the male*; olive-brown above, yellowish-brown with tinge of olive below; purple on head much reduced; the tuft on the sides and the undertail-coverts yellowish-white; *a narrow white stripe from gape passes below eye*. In both sexes: bill black; feet blue-grey, claws brown. Iris cherry-red (male); brown (female).

Located by song throughout the year; movements vigorous and lively, and silhouette distinctive, with slender proportions, distinctly arched bill and slender tail with shallow fork.
Voice: Song a sequence of liquid notes, of which the more powerful at a distance sound remarkably bell-like. Songs consist of phrases which, as recorded by numerous observers, vary from district to district (see Marples's observations below). Female sings in comparatively short phrases, and song weaker.

Marples recorded the songs heard in the Town Belt of Dunedin over 3½ years (1941–4); he noted a different periodicity for three different and easily recognisable songs. The song he designated as No. 1, a distinct phrase of seven notes, was heard constantly at all times of the year, but there was a peak of this type of song in May and a period of minimum song in October (in 1941 there was a late peak in August). Song No. 2 consisted of two notes followed by a *zizz*, followed by the two notes again, and finally a phrase of six notes, the third being a high one heavily accented—at times groups of male Bellbirds were seen sitting a few feet apart, all singing this song with great energy: periodicity of No. 2 song was similar to No. 1, the peak falling in June or July; however, it was not heard at all during four or five spring and summer months. No. 3 consisted of a series of descending notes, usually four but sometimes three or five, in which the last note was slurred or accented; periodicity of this song was identical with that of No. 2 but nothing comparable with the group singing of No. 2 was noted. Marples's observations included records of four other songs, well marked and easy to recognise, but only heard for short periods; it was suggested that these records were of strange birds passing through the area.

Alarm call a series of rapidly repeated harsh notes *pek*, *pek*, *pek*, *pek* or *yeng*, *yeng*, *yeng*, *yeng*.
Habitat and range: Found in forest, forest remnants and second-growth forest throughout New Zealand (except around and north of Auckland: see below); also in exotic vegetation, orchards, gardens, etc., in some districts, but mainly in the neighbourhood of forest remnants. It may, however, be in the process of expanding into settled districts. Established in the large exotic plantations.

In winter, like the Tui, reaches nectar-bearing trees and shrubs at some distance from its breeding areas.

Up to *c.* 1860 it was abundant but a marked decline, which it is suggested may have been due to disease, subsequently affected populations throughout New Zealand. It decreased in numbers until *c.* 1910 but after this recovered in nearly all districts (Stead states that in Canterbury numbers were maintained until *c.* 1900, recovering after about 10 years of low ebb in *c.* 1910). In North Auckland and about Auckland became locally extinct: has been noted in recent years at two isolated points (Whangarei Heads, Warkworth), suggesting that recolonisation may be occurring in these areas. There was no decrease of the populations of the Three Kings, Poor Knights, Hen and Chickens, Little Barrier, Kapiti and certain inner islands.

Food the same as that of the Tui—insects, fruits and nectar. More information on the proportions of the three types of food in the diet of these two species is required, but the Bellbird's feeding habits suggest that it takes a higher proportion of insects: it appears to spend much time at all seasons searching for insects in crevices in bark, and on twigs and branches; and sometimes on the ground.

Common sources of nectar in forest are: puriri, rata, pohutukawa, kowhai, rewarewa, native fuchsia, kohekohe; also flax (*Phormium*), and numerous exotics including tree lucerne, gums, wattles, *Banksia* and various garden shrubs. Honeydew (produced by mealybugs) is a major food in much southern beech (*Nothofagus*) forest (the sooty mould which grows on the trees in association with the mealybug gives a characteristic appearance to forests where honeydew is available). Artificial foods (sweetened water, honey, etc.) freely taken.

Fruits include those of a number of native trees and shrubs (including *Coprosma* spp., native fuchsia, cabbage tree and mistletoe), and of berry-bearing exotic trees and shrubs of all kinds; may also take grapes, and figs, apples and peaches if close to orchards.

Mainland (*melanura*) subspecies (mainland and most nearer islands) is also found on the Auckland Islands; the Three Kings (*obscura*) subspecies is a little larger and plumage less yellow, with patches on sides and undertail-coverts creamy-white instead of yellow; Chatham Island (*melanocephala*) subspecies larger, head deep purple and reduced patch on the sides (extinct since 1906). **Breeding:** Usually in fork at 1–12 m from the ground; generally in dense cover but sometimes conspicuous from the ground; sometimes in an open cavity in a trunk; rarely almost at ground level. Nest has a somewhat loosely-constructed base of dry twigs and fibres, and a deep well-lined cup (lining fine grass, sometimes wholly feathers). Breeding September–January; double-brooded; eggs 3–4, pinkish (pale pinkish-white to rich pink) with reddish brown spots and blotches, densest at large end. Incubation by female; may be fed on nest by her mate. Incubation period 14 days; fledging 14 days. Young are fed by both adults, feeding continues for about 10 days after departure from the nest. Stead found that the young were fed entirely on insects; Buddle, at a nest observed on the Poor Knights, noted that for three days after hatching the chicks were given nectar alone; insects were then added to their diet in increasing numbers.

TUI *Prosthemadera novaeseelandiae* *Pl. 45, p. 192*

Other name: Parson Bird.

Description: Male 31 cm (12½″), female 29 cm (11½″). Iridescent metallic green with bluish-purple reflections (varies according to light and appears black at a distance); the back and scapulars dark brown with bronze reflections, and the abdomen and sides reddish brown; undertail-coverts metallic green; *double white throat-tuft* composed of curled feathers; a lacy white collar on back and sides of neck (formed by white-shafted filamentous feathers which curl forwards on the side of the neck); *white wing-bar*. Bill and feet blackish brown.

Female has smaller throat-tufts, and paler reddish brown abdomen.

Immature plumage slaty black, except wing and tail quills which have metallic green outer webs; a crescentic mark or extensive patch of greyish white on the throat; dusky white wing-bar. Buller states that a well-grown fledgling taken from the nest and kept in captivity began to sprout throat-tufts within a month; at the end of another six weeks it was changing into the full adult plumage, and metallic coloration appeared first in irregular tracts on the breast and sides of the body.

Movements are vigorous like those of the Bellbird, and flight is often noisy especially when darting through the trees at a high speed; performs aerobatics, often plunging down with closed wings from some height.

Voice: Closely resembles that of the Bellbird, and like the Bellbird varies song from district to district. However, it has a much greater tendency than the Bellbird to intersperse harsher sounds among the notes (variously described as croaks, coughs, clicks, grunts, rattles, wheezes and chuckles). Richer notes are more fluid and resonant than any notes of the Bellbird.

Also has notes evidently of high frequency and beyond the range of human hearing, for the bird is seen singing energetically although only faint squeaky sounds are to be heard.

A high-pitched plaintive cry *ke-e-e-e* is apparently an alarm note. Also sometimes uttered is a high-pitched jackdaw-like *tchack*.

Habitat and range: Although like the Bellbird often seen obtaining nectar in settled districts, the Tui has so far remained a forest bird to a greater extent. However, it appears that more and more it is adopting settled habitats, and (especially in Auckland) will under suitable conditions nest in suburban and even urban areas; nest sites may be in pines and other exotic trees and shrubs. Appears only as an occasional visitor in the larger exotic plantations. Found in most of the larger forest tracts, up to *c.* 1000 m and even in comparatively small remnants; also second-growth forest, and manuka scrub if this contains some forest remnants. Does not favour southern beech (*Nothofagus*) forests e.g. almost absent on the eastern side of the divide at Arthur's Pass but abundant on the western side.

Food insects, fruits and nectar: fruits probably bulk larger in the diet than for the Bellbird. The following have been recorded (probably many others): for fruits, mahoe, *Coprosma*, supplejack, maire, makomako, karaka, totara, kiekie; for nectar, puriri, rata, pohutukawa, kowhai, rewarewa, native fuchsia, flax (*Phormium*). In settled districts tree lucerne, wattles, gums and a number of others provide nectar, while fruits are obtained from various ornamental trees and shrubs; Tuis commonly feed on nectar from garden flowers at the homestead of Little Barrier Island sanctuary, such flowers as freesias and lachenaleas being visited eagerly. May be fed artificially.

The typical subspecies (*novaeseelandiae*) is distributed over the mainland of New Zealand, Stewart Island, many of the off-lying islands (including formerly the Three Kings), and the Kermadecs and Aucklands; Chatham Island (*chathamensis*) subspecies larger, with longer throat-plumes and breast of deeper blue (main island, and Pitt and South East Islands).

Breeding: Generally in a fork in the outer branches or canopy, 3–15 m above the ground; base a bulky structure of sticks and twigs up to 25 cm in diameter, and the cup is lined with treefern scales, grasses or other finer material, or with moss; sometimes a few feathers. Breeding November–January (occasionally September and October); probably often double-brooded. Eggs 2–4, white or pale pink, with reddish-brown specks or blotches mainly at the larger end. Incubation by female; throughout incubation male sings from a nearby tree. Incubation period 14 days; fledging *c.* 21 days. Moon noted that the female alone fed the chicks for the first four days, the male subsequently assisting. He found that the movements of the adults were so rapid that it was only with the aid of a slow-motion movie camera and electronic flash exposures that the food could be identified—insect food and possibly nectar during the first 4–5 days and later a number of berries and larger insects (insects identified included moths and stick insects).

RED WATTLE-BIRD   *Anthochaera carunculata*   *Pl. 41, p. 176*
Description: 34 cm (13½″). Brownish-grey strongly streaked with white above; pale grey with brown and white streaks below; tail and wing quills with white tips; *a yellow patch in middle of abdomen*; *small red fleshy wattle* hangs behind the eye; bill black, feet brownish-grey.
Voice: 'Raucous notes' (Serventy and Whittell); in addition to these loud, harsh notes, has double whistling alarm call.
Habitat and range: Twice recorded as a straggler: Matakana, North Auckland (*c.* 1865) and Rahotu, Taranaki (1882). In Australia distributed from southern Queensland to Victoria (not Tasmania), and westward to the south-west of Western Australia; a partial migrant. Feeds on insects, nectar, and fruits (sometimes including orchard fruits); common at nectar-bearing trees and shrubs, including those of towns and cities.

SILVEREYES: Zosteropidae

A family of about 85 species found in Africa, southern Asia from Arabia eastwards, China and Japan, Indonesia, Australia (a recent colonist to New Zealand) and many Pacific Islands.

SILVEREYE   *Zosterops lateralis*   *Pl. 44, p. 185*
Other names: Tauhou; Waxeye, White-eye, Blightbird, Blightie.
Description: 12 cm (4¾″). Head, upper surface of wings, rump and upper tail-coverts bright yellowish-green; wing and tail quills brown with yellowish-

green on outer webs; upper back and scapulars grey tinged with yellowish-green; underparts pale greyish-white (throat and undertail-coverts—or undertail-coverts alone—may be tinged yellow, and the whole of the under-surface may be darkened to a distinct grey); sides and flanks chestnut brown; underwing-coverts white; *eye-ring white*, with a line of black in front and below. Bill brown, paler at base; feet pale brown.

Female can be distinguished by less intense (pale cinnamon brown) colour of sides and flanks. Eye-ring absent in immature.

Active and noisy in flocks, which are conspicuous in autumn and winter. It is the species most commonly fed artificially (fat, fruit, sugar, honey, syrup, jam, bread), and as it is readily trapped and banded has been the subject of a number of studies of life history, social behaviour, etc. Dispersal or migration is as yet largely unknown.

Voice: Flocking call especially in flight a chirping *cli-cli-cli* . . . and a further common flocking note is a rather plaintive *cree*. Fleming describes the nest-alarm call as a grating or nasal *swang* (rare except in the breeding season but liable to occur if a Kingfisher, Morepork or cat is near); when birds are actually flushed from the nest this is modified as *swang di-di-di-di-di*. Special calls (modification of the *cree*) when incubating, feeding young, etc., and as a threat call. There are also according to Kikkawa a number of imitative call notes.

Song of male in breeding season was divided by Fleming into: (*a*) *warbling song*—apparently during earliest stages of establishment of territory—of slender volume but varied, including trills, warbles and slurs; (*b*) *challenge song*—normally begins after mating and before building—made up of a rapid succession of high-pitched call notes with rare trills interposed, has less range in tone and pitch than the warbling song but louder; (*c*) *whisper song* (by both sexes), consisting of whispered trills punctuated by a normal call note: inaudible outside a range of a few yards. Challenge song somewhat similar to the song of the Hedge Sparrow, but less powerful.

The chick after leaving nest has a characteristic begging call *ee-chéeta*.

Habitat and range: Common generally up to *c.* 1000 m, has reached Kermadec, Chatham, Snares, Auckland, Campbell and Macquarie Islands, though curiously scarce as a breeding bird on many northern off-shore islands. In all types of settled habitat with tree-cover; also in native forest (although here numbers are relatively few) and subalpine scrub.

Distribution eastern and south-eastern Australia and Tasmania (a partial migrant). In June 1856 (i.e. the early settlement phase) large flocks appeared on the Wellington coast at Waikanae; arrived in Canterbury in July of the same year (Potts). Some other dates of appearance are Nelson, 1856; Otago, 1860; Wanganui, 1863; Auckland, 1865; Bay of Islands, 1867. It thus seems probable that spread throughout New Zealand began with the invasion of 1856, and that any further invasions have been subsequent to the dispersal of the 1856 stock throughout New Zealand. Earlier than 1856 there had evidently been scattered records in Otago and Southland (earliest was 1832, Milford Sound).

Food mainly insects and fruits, but eagerly takes nectar (Kikkawa records that when Bellbirds were drinking syrup at a feeding station they rarely allowed Silvereyes to feed; nectar-feeding from flowers in many localities may thus be limited by the two honeyeaters). In forest, fruits of a number of trees and shrubs are taken, and in subalpine scrub fruits of *Coprosma, Hymenanthera*, etc. Many introduced plants provide fruits and nectar.

Kikkawa in a study of behaviour noted various displays associated with aggressive behaviour, including the commonly observed 'wing fluttering' and, in addition, 'head-up' posture, 'beak clattering' and pecking. Chasing occurred among breeding birds as a means of defending territory.

Breeding: Nest, a cup woven strongly of fine grasses, fibres, fragments of moss, etc., and spiders' webs and attached to twigs or foliage hammock-wise at the rim; generally in outermost foliage at a height of 1–9 m; other sites recorded include bracken fern and a clump of bamboo (nest between two slender stems 2 m above ground). Kikkawa found that mated birds remain together in the winter flocks; flock disintegration is brought about as pairs leave the flock to establish individual territory, and the first-year birds form pairs while in the winter flock. Strongly territorial; eggs, August–February, two, and sometimes three, broods in a season. Eggs 3–4, pale blue. Incubation by both parents; incubation period 10–11 days, beginning with the second egg; fledging 9–12 days. Both adults feed the chicks. Moon found that the food as recorded on a series of flashlight photographs included grubs, caterpillars, fruits and occasionally adult insects and spiders. The first flocks—probably resulting from fusion of family parties and young of early broods—were noted by Fleming in mid-February (at Auckland).

FINCHES AND BUNTINGS: Fringillidae

A huge family of seed-eating birds with short strong bills. Males are usually more brightly plumaged than females; and juveniles resemble adult females. None is native to New Zealand but six species were successfully introduced from 1862 onwards and five of these are now among the commonest passerines in the North and South Islands. In winter these birds form flocks, which sometimes contain thousands of individuals of several species, frequenting untidy arable wastelands, paddocks where hay is fed out, and especially saltings and rough land along the coast. Because finches have plump bodies and comparatively short wings their flight is undulating.

GREENFINCH *Chloris chloris*   *Pl. 46, p. 193*
Local name: Green Linnet.
Description: 15 cm (6″). A plump stockily built finch with a short distinctly forked tail and a pale heavy bill. Male, olive-green with yellower rump and with bright yellow patches on the fore-edge of the wings and at the sides of the black-tipped tail. Female and juvenile much duller, the green having a brownish wash.
Voice: The distinctive spring and summer call is a harsh drawn out *dzwee*. A pleasant twittering song with slower variants *chichichichichit-teu-teu-teu-teu* may be delivered from a conspicuous perch or during an ecstatic, darting, bat-like flight. Young in family parties call persistently.

Habitat and range: Widely but unevenly distributed and locally abundant up to *c.* 600 m. Self-introduced to Chatham Islands, and a straggler to many sub-antarctic islands: but not a persistent coloniser of off-shore islands. Apparently partial to exotic pines. Forms large flocks in autumn. Winter roosts often with House Sparrows in thick hedges and shrubberies.

Breeding: Nest in a bush or tree usually below 6 m. Eggs, September–January, 4–6, dirty white with reddish spots or streaks, rather variable. Incubation period 13–14 days; fledging 13–16 days. Usually double-brooded.

GOLDFINCH *Carduelis carduelis*   *Pl. 46, p. 193*
Local name: Goldie.

Description: 12.5 cm (5″). The gayest of the finches. Sexes alike. Head a striking pattern of red (crimson mask), white and black; back brown; rump whitish; wings black with broad band of bright yellow and white terminal spots on the quills; tail black with white tips, forked; underparts white, washed with brown on the flanks. Juvenile streaked and comparatively sober-hued.

Sociable. Larger flocks or family parties (charms) fly with a light lilting motion. Commonly seen feeding on thistleheads.

Song chart for eight introduced European birds near Auckland

Continuous line—most adult males in full song
Dashes—some adult males in full song; others tuning up or fading
Dots—incomplete song by a few males or tentative song by young birds

NOTE. Auckland, at latitude 37°S, has a milder climate than most of New Zealand. Accordingly adjustments to the song chart must be made for latitude and altitude

Voice: Call, a shrill clear *pee-yu*. Song a distinctive, fast, liquid, tinkling *tswitt-witt-witt*, which in spring can be elaborated into a vibrant canary-like song.

Habitat and range: Abundant over large areas of the North and South Islands, becoming scarce above *c.* 1000 m and apparently uncommon in Westland. Self-introduced to Kermadecs and strays to sub-antarctic islands south to Campbell; but breeds only sparingly away from main islands. Big winter flocks often frequent coastal saltings especially in the north, e.g. *c.* 2000 feeding on *Salicornia australis* in the Firth of Thames. Many birds remain together in flocks feeding on close-mown turf well into the spring, when local breeding birds already have nests and eggs.

Breeding: The nest, one of the most beautiful, is usually among green leaves, 1.5 to 3.5 m from the ground. Eggs 4–7, bluish white with spots and streaks of reddish brown. Incubation period 12–13 days; fledging 13—14 days. Normally double-brooded. Some young are on the wing by the end of October.

REDPOLL   *Carduelis flammea*   *Pl. 46, p. 193*

Description: 12 cm (4¾″). The smallest of the introduced finches; streaked grey-brown; but close observation reveals *crimson forehead, black chin*, and buff or whitish double wing-bar. Male in summer has pink flush on breast. A sprightly acrobat as it feeds on the swaying heads of rushes or catkins of birch and alder. The distinctive flight-call (q.v.) is often the first indication that these superficially drab finches are present. Flight commonly rather high, 20–60 m; airy and confident.

Voice: Flight call a metallic twitter *chich-ich-ich-ich*. Alarm a plaintive *tsooeet*. Song a short rippling trill, often preceded by flight-call, and delivered either in flight or from a perch.

Habitat and range: Now at home in New Zealand in a remarkable variety of habitats. Rather rare in the north, but a few breed near the sea on the sun-baked gumlands of Parengarenga and there is a long thin zone where breeding occurs among the sand-dunes and broken scrub country of the Auckland west coast. Redpolls become more plentiful on the Volcanic Plateau and breed commonly above the bush-line in the ranges especially, e.g. Egmont, and in the south of the North Island. In the South Island they are abundant from sea-level to 1600 m. Self-introduced to most sub-antarctic islands, they are now perhaps the commonest passerine on Campbell Island and are established on Macquarie. After the breeding season mixed flocks of finches in the lowlands may contain large numbers of Redpolls. In winter coastal wasteland is a favourite feeding ground.

Breeding: Nest, small and compact, in scrub, seldom above 3.5 m. Eggs, September–January, 4–6, bluish-green, glossless, spotted and streaked light-brown, sometimes unmarked. Incubation period 10–12 days; fledging 11–14 days. Sometimes double-brooded. Redpolls are sometimes almost colonial nesters, forming local pockets, e.g. where a patch of rough country remains among tamed green farmland.

Note: From a critical examination of many Redpolls trapped at Lincoln College, D. Stenhouse has concluded that Redpolls in New Zealand are descended from two subspecies, Lesser (*cabaret*) and Mealy (*flammea*). Some individuals with white rather than buff wing-bars are too large and too pale to be considered typical *cabaret*, but more closely resemble *flammea*. It may be significant that in the winter before the first introduction of Redpolls to New Zealand, great numbers of Mealies appeared in Britain and many are likely to have been caught in the bird-catchers' nets.

According to Stenhouse (*a*) the bulk of the population is composed of *cabaret* type individuals; (*b*) perhaps 10–15 per cent of the population are of *flammea* type; (*c*) the two types are inter-breeding.

In the North Island, Redpolls showing strong 'mealy' characters have been noted in the Firth of Thames and on Great Mercury Island.

CHAFFINCH   *Fringilla coelebs*   *Pl. 46, p. 193*
Description: 15 cm (6″). Males are strikingly handsome; *crown and nape slate-blue*; forehead black; mantle chestnut; rump greenish; sides of heads and *underparts pinkish-brown*; wings blackish with conspicuous *white patch on the 'shoulder'*, and lower, a white wing-bar; tail blackish with *white outer tail feathers*. Females and juveniles lack the bright colours and look greyish-green or yellowish-brown. In flight the white in wings and tail shows clearly.
Voice: Ordinary call-note a metallic *pink* or *chwink*; also in summer from males, a loud but rather plaintive *cheet*; flight-note a soft *tsip*. Song, a loud bustling rattle leading up to a terminal flourish—*chip chip chip tell tell tell cherry-erry-erry tissi cheweeo* (W. Garstang). At the start and end of the singing season, July to January, the terminal flourish is missing or incomplete. Broken snatches of song can be heard in autumn.
Habitat and range: The commonest finch in New Zealand, though sometimes obvious only to the ear, evenly distributed wherever there are trees or shrubs from sea-level to 1400 m and penetrating the bush as no other finch has done. It can, e.g. be the dominant singer in the beech forest of the North Island above 1000 m. A vigorous coloniser of off-shore and sub-antarctic islands, breeding as far south as Campbell Island. Winter behaviour in New Zealand needs studying. Small flocks of brightly plumaged males have been noted near the coast in winter; and also in high country in spring before they take up nesting territories; also larger loose flocks of females and juveniles.
Breeding: Nest, 'a beautiful piece of workmanship,' firmly placed in a crutch or fork, usually below 6 m. Eggs, 4–6, September–January, generally greenish-blue with spots and streaks of dark purplish-brown. Incubation period 11–13 days; fledging 13–14 days.

YELLOWHAMMER   *Emberiza citrinella*   *Pl. 46, p. 193*
Description: 16 cm (6½″). Adult males with bright *yellow head and underparts* are unmistakable; but extent and depth of yellow varies; upperparts chestnut streaked black; across chest a streaky cinnamon band not always easily seen; rump chestnut; *white on outer tail feathers* conspicuous in flight. Female duller with much less yellow and head decidedly dusky; closely resembling female Cirl Bunting except in *chestnut* rump. Juveniles and young females still duskier, only faintly yellow below.
Voice: Call notes a ringing *tink* or *chip*; a single *twick* used in flight and a more liquid *twitup* or *twitic*, characteristic of winter flocks. Song popularly worded

as 'Little bit of bread and no cheese' (*tintintintintink-sweee* or *chitty-chitty-chitty . . . swee*) the 'cheese' (*swee*) omitted at start and end of singing season, August–February, and emphasised in full song; usually delivered from conspicuous perch. In early spring some males still in flocks start singing. Song continues well into February after other introduced songsters have fallen silent. A soft tuneful warbling has been heard in May from birds in flocks at Kaipara, Rotorua and Lake Forsyth.

Habitat and range: Widely distributed in all types of open country, sometimes ranging to alpine tussock at 1600 m, often feeding on exposed sea beaches and occasionally breeding on saltings, and along the ditchbanks of marshes. In autumn and winter flocks visit gardens, parks and playing fields and stragglers cross considerable distances of open sea to off-shore islands, e.g. Little Barrier, Mokohinau. Southward, has established itself as a breeder at Chatham Island, and stragglers have been reported from the remoter sub-antarctic islands. Northward it is known from Lord Howe Island and has been found breeding at Raoul in the Kermadecs.

Breeding: Nest usually close to the ground in scrub, fern, gorse, bramble; commonly on rough roadside banks and in hedge-bottoms. Eggs, October–February, 3–5, whitish or pinkish cream, pencilled with fine hair-lines of dark brown and few spots (hence local English names of Scribbling Lark and Snakebird). Incubation period 12–14 days; fledging 12–13 days. Usually double-brooded.

CIRL BUNTING *Emberiza cirlus* Pl. 46, p. 193

Description: 16 cm (6½″). Resembles Yellowhammer, but adult males at once distinguishable by *black throat*, bold black eye-stripe, with yellow stripes above and below, *dark crown* and *greyish-green*—not cinnamon—band across chest; sides of breast and back rich chestnut, underparts below chest-band yellow; flanks streaked; *rump olive-brown*, not chestnut. Female and young only reliably separable from Yellowhammer by *olive-brown rump*. Cirl Buntings look compact; Yellowhammers longer.

Voice: Call note a thin *zit*, *sip* or *zib-zib*, sometimes run together in flight to form a sibilant *sissi-sissi-sip*. Song a monotonous metallic rattle or sharp high-pitched trill *tirrrr*, recalling a Yellowhammer's song without the 'cheese', but readily distinguishable with practice. Singing season in New Zealand not recorded, probably August to February, possibly longer. Males near Oamaru often sing from telegraph-poles and wires.

Habitat and range: Rather rare, except perhaps in a few favoured localities, e.g. limestone country near Oamaru. The population may fluctuate. Recently reported from the southern portion of the North Island, and widely in the South Island east of the Alps from Nelson to Otago. Nomadic in winter, frequenting farmlands and coastal wasteland; and sometimes perhaps crossing Cook Strait.

Breeding: Nest usually within a metre of the ground in thick cover (more precise details for New Zealand lacking). Eggs 3–5, greenish or bluish with almost black streaks and hairlines, generally more boldly marked than eggs of Yellowhammer. Incubation period 11–13 days; fledging 11–13 days. Usually double-brooded.

SPARROWS AND WEAVERS: Ploceidae

HOUSE SPARROW *Passer domesticus*   Pl. 46, p. 193
Description: 14.5 cm (5¾″). Females and juveniles are dull brown above, with dark streaks on mantles and 'shoulders', and dingy white below. Adult males easily separable by dark grey crown, chestnut nape, black throat, whitish cheeks and short white wing-bar.

Partial albinos, particularly with the white in wings or tail, are not uncommon.

Gregarious, garrulous and quarrelsome.
Voice: Has a variety of penetrating calls, but not a note of real music; though chirping by several males together may develop into a 'fairly regular song of 8–10 notes with some approach to rhythm.'
Habitat and range: The survivors of several shipments were liberated in the 1860s. Their descendants are now widely distributed and not always in association with man. Sparrows are said to have introduced themselves to the Chatham Islands about 1880 and have straggled to other sub-antarctic islands. In the north they have followed settlement of the off-shore islands. In northern districts where little grain is grown large flocks visit saltings and even mangroves in winter.
Breeding: Commonly nests in buildings; but colonies of untidy nests may be seen near the top of tall trees, e.g. 25–metre gums; and a few birds nest in remote sea-caves. Eggs 5–7, variable on a whitish ground. Incubation period, c. 13 days; fledging 15 days. During the lengthy breeding season, five or even more broods may be reared (Kirk).

STARLINGS: Sturnidae

Though there are no native members of this family, the European Starling, first liberated in 1862, is now one of the most familiar birds in New Zealand; and the Indian Myna, which was widely introduced in the 1870s, is firmly established over much of the North Island.

Starlings are stocky birds with short tails, long pointed bills, an upright stance and a jaunty walk. They are noisy, perky and self-confident. They feed mostly on open ground, sometimes in trees. The sexes are alike.

STARLING *Sturnus vulgaris*   Pl. 47, p. 200
Description: 21 cm (8½″). Blackish with a green and purple gloss; wings short and pointed; tail short; bill robust, pointed, yellow in nesting season – some males acquire yellow bills as early as May – otherwise dusky. Winter plumage

speckled with white, especially on the underparts; females appearing more richly spangled than males. Juveniles drably brown with whitish throat.

Voice: A drawn-out descending whistle, *cheeoo*, is characteristic. Song a 'lively rambling melody of throaty warbling, chirruping, clicking and gurgling notes interspersed with musical whistles and pervaded by a peculiar creaky quality.' Many Starlings are clever mimics with a wide range of imitations, but choosing especially to reproduce the calls of the California Quail and Pukeko. A Starling has been seen attempting to imitate both voice and actions of a Fantail on a wire.

Habitat and range: Abundant everywhere except in dense bush and above *c.* 1200 m. In large numbers on Kermadec and Norfolk Islands. Has colonised even the remote sub-antarctic islands, e.g. Campbell and Macquarie. In winter large flocks converge at dusk on favoured roosts, several of which are on islands, even as far off-shore as Motuharakeke (Cavallis) and Kapiti. Near the coast, Starlings often feed on the foreshore and have been dubbed in jest 'pseudo-waders.'

Feeding flocks will rise in a cloud to mob a passing Harrier, Bush Hawk or even a Black Shag.

Breeding: Nests in a hole commonly about buildings but also in trees, clay banks—often in disused Kingfisher tunnel—and sea cliffs. Eggs 4–7, very pale blue with a faint gloss. Incubation period *c.* 13 days; fledging period *c.* 21 days. Usually single-brooded. Family parties of Starlings descend upon the paddocks when the first hay is cut.

MYNA *Acridotheres tristis* *Pl. 47, p. 200*

Description: 24 cm (9½″). Rather bigger than a Starling; but a showy bird in flight when *white patches* in broad rounded wings and *white tip to black fanned tail* are very conspicuous. Head and neck black, glossed green; body *mainly vinous brown*, paler underneath; abdomen and undertail-coverts white. Bill, bare skin on face and legs *yellow*. Male and female alike.

Voice: A rowdy medley of notes, raucous, gurgling, chattering, even bell-like, in rapid sequence. Adults with young utter a harsh *skwark*, and the call of flying young is a noisy, persistent *chi-chi-chi*.

Habitat and range: Released widely in the South Island from which it is said to have disappeared before 1890; but two seen near Nelson, 1956. Common in the North Island, north of Wanganui and southern Hawkes Bay; increasing on Volcanic Plateau where it first became established in middle 1940s, ascending above 600 m a.s.l. at Mamaku and Kaingaroa and above 900 m on Desert Road, 1966; still spreading northwards and reached Bay of Islands, 1960, and Doubtless Bay, 1965. Now in many parts a characteristic bird of the roadside. Large flocks occur about dumps and rubbish-tips; smaller parties often feed on the seashore. Often perches on sheep and cattle. Local night roosts in winter may be found by following flight lines. Biggest roost so far described (Ardmore) contained nearly 1000 birds. In districts where they are grown, Phoenix Palms are favourite dormitories.

Breeding: Rather a late nester. Nest usually in a building; sometimes in a hole in a tree or bank. Eggs 3–6, pale blue, rounder than those of a Starling. First broods fly in late December; some young are still in the nest in mid-March.

CROWS: Corvidae

This almost cosmopolitan family is now represented in New Zealand only by the introduced English Rook. An extinct crow (*Palaeocorax moriorum*) once widespread, is known from sub-fossil bones. Between October 1945 and January 1949 there were several sightings on the outer islands of the Hauraki Gulf of a large corvine bird which may have been an Australian Raven (*Corvus coronoides*).

ROOK *Corvus frugilegus*   *Pl. 47, p. 200*

   Description: 45 cm (18″). Almost entirely black with purplish gloss; but *face bare and whitish*. Bill greyish-black. Thighs of rooks on the ground look shaggy. Walks sedately with occasional hops. Flight strong and direct. Very sociable. Juveniles have the face feathered—an important point to note in the identification of stray 'crows.'

   Voice: Usual note is *caw* or *kaah*; but a variety of other notes is used especially at rookeries and roosts. A rookery in spring is pleasantly noisy.

   Habitat and range: Rooks were liberated in Nelson, Auckland and Christchurch, between 1862 and 1873 but only the Christchurch liberation was successful. Rooks are now well established in two North Island districts (Hawkes Bay and Southern Wairarapa) and in three South Island ones (Christchurch, Banks Peninsula and Peel Forest). Most of the rookeries are located in districts of yellow-grey earth where the growing of crops is an important aspect of farm management. In 1956 the main centres of population were near Hastings and near Christchurch, but subsequently the latter population was much reduced by systematic poisoning. Communal winter roosts may contain some thousands of Rooks. Perhaps as a result of persecution Rooks have dispersed and established colonies in areas where they were unknown twenty years ago. The most southerly rookery is near Sutton, Otago, and the most northerly in the Firth of Thames. Some vagrancy, especially by young birds, is to be expected. A Rook has reached the Chatham Islands.

   Breeding: Carrying of nesting material has been observed in August. Nests mainly in tall eucalypts and exotic pines, especially *P. radiata*, occasionally in Lombardy Poplars and Norfolk Island Pines. Eggs September–October, 2–5, pale bluish-green fairly evenly marked with blotches of dark and light brown. Incubation period 16–18 days; fledging *c*. 30 days.

WOOD-SWALLOWS: Artamidae

The so-called Wood-swallows or Swallow-shrikes form a distinct and peculiar family belonging primarily to the Australo-Papuan region, but extending westwards to India and eastwards to Fiji. Although there are six species in Australia, and one, the Dusky Wood-swallow (*Artamus cyanopterus*), is common in Tasmania, both as a resident and a migrant, the genus was unknown in New

Zealand till the summer of 1971-72 when examples of two sociable and nomadic species were discovered in Central Otago.

Wood-swallows are not closely related to the true Swallows (Hirundinidae). Their affinities may lie rather with the Cracticidae. It is likely that they received their popular name because after the Swallows they are the most accomplished fliers among the passerines, soaring and gliding with superb ease and grace as they hunt insects or play in a thermal. Some species have slightly forked tails.

MASKED WOOD-SWALLOW *Artamus personatus* Pl. 40, p. 169

Description: 19 cm (7½″). Sexes different. Male has a black facial mask bordered with white; upperparts light grey: underparts paler silvery-grey, shading to almost white undertail-coverts; tail slightly forked, white-tipped. Bill blue-grey, tipped black; legs black. Female duskier, with the same pattern blurred. In first flying plumage, young are speckled with white on the back and faintly barred on the belly and flanks.

Largely insectivorous, but will descend to earth, and a family party in New Zealand visited a bird table to take bread, honey water, meat and household scraps.

Habitat and range: Australia generally, but not in Tasmania and of irregular occurrence in the south-east. A pair together with four male White-browed Wood-swallows appeared at Naseby Forest (Otago), a plantation of exotic pines, in the summer of 1971-72. They survived the winter and reared two young in the late summer of 1972-73, but were not seen again after the 1973 winter.

Breeding: In parts of Australia mixed colonies of Masked and White-browed Wood-swallows are normal. Both species build flimsy nests. Normal clutch 2, sometimes 3. Incubation *c.* 16 days; fledging *c.* 15 days. In New Zealand only known breeding was in 1972-73, probably at Naseby Forest.

WHITE-BROWED WOOD-SWALLOW *Artamus superciliosus* Pl. 40, p. 169

Description: 19 cm (7½″). Sexes different. *Male*—head and neck black with prominent white eyebrow; upperparts—back dark grey; rump, wings and tail bluish-grey; tail slightly forked, outer feathers tipped with white; underparts a rich chestnut; underwing and undertail whitish. Bill blue-grey with black tip; legs black. *Female*—duller; head and upperparts grey-blue; lores black; eyebrow less obvious; underparts greyish chestnut.

Habitat and range: Common in eastern Australia, excluding Tasmania, where it is known only as an accidental visitor. Of six Wood-swallows which appeared in Central Otago in the summer of 1971-72, four were males of this species. Having survived almost two winters, they were last seen in late winter 1973.

The birds became quite tame, visiting a bird table or the lawn only a little way from a house, where they would feed on honey water, bread, tomato, banana and, in fact, almost anything offered.

AUSTRALIAN BELL-MAGPIES: Cracticidae

White-backed Magpies ('white crows that sing') were imported from Australia and liberated widely in New Zealand in the third quarter of the nineteenth century. They have proved successful and aggressive colonists. Evidently at the same time some Black-backed Magpies were introduced. Though their increase has been slower, there are pockets of country in which they are now strongly entrenched. The two species may sometimes interbreed. Grassland farming, with its attendant shelter-belts of pines and gums, suits these magpies. In some districts both species occur side by side.

BLACK-BACKED MAGPIE *Gymnorhina tibicen* Pl. 47, p. 200

Description: 40 cm (16"). Head, *back* and underparts black; hindneck and lower back white; shoulders of wings and base of tail white. Female similar to male, but with hindneck mottled grey.

Voice: 'To describe the note of this bird is beyond the power of my pen' (Gould). 'Wonderfully modulated whistle unequalled among European birds' (Alfred Russel Wallace).

Habitat and range: Formerly known in New Zealand only from North Canterbury, whence it has spread into Marlborough. First recognised in the North Island near Hastings in 1946, and now known to be widely distributed in Hawkes Bay and some districts to the south. Stragglers have appeared as far north as Manukau and Kaipara.

Breeding: Badly in need of study in New Zealand.

WHITE-BACKED MAGPIE *Gymnorhina hypoleuca* Pl. 47, p. 200

Description: 42 cm (17"). Common and conspicuous over large areas. About the size and shape of a Rook. Male similar to Black-backed Magpie but with *hindneck and back strikingly white*. The back of the female is grey. Adult males, females and young of the two species appear to be readily distinguishable, if the colour of the nape and back can be seen.

Voice: A 'glorious carol' of flute-like notes, similar to that of *tibicen*; at its best soon after daybreak or in the evenings when the birds are going to roost. *Quardle oodle ardle wardle doodle* (Denis Glover).

Habitat and range: Widely but unevenly distributed in the North and South Islands, ranging up to 1000 m in the Tongariro National Park and on the eastern side of the Southern Alps; still spreading, e.g. on Volcanic Plateau as more sheep-country is broken in; missing from the extreme north and south of both islands and from the western side of the Southern Alps. Occasionally reported as a wanderer to off-shore islands, e.g. Kapiti, Little Barrier. Readily becomes a suburban dweller, frequenting parks, playing fields and airports.

Breeding: Nesting may start as early as June. The nest is usually in a tall tree; but hedges of gorse and hawthorn are mentioned as sites in Canterbury. Eggs 2–5, very variable on a bluish-green ground.

216

NEW ZEALAND WATTLE-BIRDS: Callaeidae

Various relationships have been suggested for this endemic family; it is included by Mayr and Amadon (*Am. Museum Novitates No. 1496*: 1951) in the group of Australian and Papuan families comprising the Cracticidae (Bell Magpies), Grallinidae (Magpie-larks, White-winged Chough, Apostle-bird), Ptilonorhynchidae (Bower-birds) and Paradisaeidae (Birds of Paradise): probably closest to Grallinidae. Mayr and Amadon regard these families as the descendants of a very early crow-like stock.

SADDLEBACK   *Philesturnus carunculatus*   *Pl. 48, p. 201*

Maori name: Tieke.

Description: 25 cm (10″). Glossy black; wing quills dark brown with glossy black outer webs; *bright chestnut saddle*, composed of back, scapulars, wing-coverts, rump and uppertail-coverts; undertail-coverts chestnut; *wattles orange*; bill and feet black.

Immature: see under subspecies.

Voice: Buller's description of the Saddleback as a 'clamorous' bird is apt. The common call is a loud, penetrating *cheep – te-te-te-te* ('chatter song'), delivered by both sexes (as many as 30 short notes may follow the long, steady-toned introductory note). Males also sing a 'loud rhythmical song' consisting of two high pitched *zeet* notes, followed by from three to seven similar repeated phrases, the latter varying greatly from song to song (young males acquire the phrase types by imitation of their territorial neighbours and do not inherit them from their fathers). Softer notes – some low pitched and musical, others harsh – are constantly interchanged between two birds of a pair; duetting, in which the female sings the chatter song, and the male the loud song with its dialectal component, is common. An anxiety note, an irregularly repeated, high pitched *zit*, is commonly given when the observer approaches the pair, but is very difficult to locate. (Information on 'Voice' kindly provided by P. F. Jenkins.)

Habitat and range: Originally in forests of North Island, South Island, Stewart Island and outliers, and Little Barrier Island, Great Barrier Island, Cuvier Island, Kapiti Island and Stephen Island. It had greatly decreased in most areas by 1880 (Buller in 1873 described it as more abundant in the South than in the North Island, but it was still well established to the south of the lower Waikato; by 1888 it was 'extremely scarce in the North Island'). Richard Henry's observations in Fiordland show that the Saddleback, Kokako and New Zealand Thrush remained in thriving populations until the 1890s, but a decline was observed at about this time quite suddenly; Henry attributed the decline to stoats which arrived in the area in the 1890s. However, the decrease of the three species mentioned as pointed out by G. R. Williams had begun throughout much of New Zealand before stoats and other mustelids could have had any effect. (Present range under subspecies.)

Its progress through the trees typically consists of short flights, and rapid hops from branch to branch; flight is vigorous but the bird is incapable of maintaining a level course for more than a few metres. Pairs remain together all through the year, and are seen moving through the forest examining crevices for insects, often tearing away loose bark with the powerful beak. Feeds in twigs and foliage of second-storey trees or shrubs but does not commonly enter the high canopy. Commonly feeds on the forest floor (on Hen Island observed almost hidden in the litter). Roosts in holes in trees, or dense vegetation (E. G. T.).

Food, insects and other invertebrates and fruits; occasionally nectar. A wide variety of fruits is probably taken: on Hen Island pate (*Schefflera digitata*) and whauwhaupaku (*Pseudopanax arboreus*), and on Cuvier kawakawa (*Macropiper excelsum*) and houpara (*Pseudopanax lessonii*), are important berry sources.

The North Island (*rufusater*) subspecies has a narrow yellowish-buff line along the front of the 'saddle'. The two subspecies differ in the pattern of the immature plumage: in the North Island subspecies the immature is like the adult (plumage brownish-black, with dull chestnut 'saddle'); in the South Island subspecies (*carunculatus*) the immature plumage is markedly dissimilar (described as a separate species and known in early literature as the 'Jack-bird') (uniform olive-brown, a little paler below, with reddish-brown upper and undertail-coverts). Wattles of immature comparatively small in both subspecies; the young may pair off before the end of their first year ('engagement period'), and Stead recorded a 'Jack-bird' in transitional plumage paired with a fully adult male; breeding probably does not start until the end of the second year (P. F. Jenkins).

The North Island subspecies was known to survive for certain only on Hen Island when the 1964 series of experimental introductions to suitable islands was made by the Wildlife Service. It now breeds – in addition to Hen Island – on two of the Chickens group (Lady Alice, Whatupuke), Cuvier and Red Mercury, and present (possibly breeding) on Fanal Island. The South Island subspecies had survived on three of the South Cape islands (to south-west of Stewart Island)– fears for its continued survival were aroused by the evidence in 1964 of an irruption on all three islands of the ship rat (*Rattus rattus*); steps were taken to save the subspecies when the Wildlife Service successfully transferred birds from the threatened stock, of which none now survive, to smaller islands in the general area.

There are unconfirmed comparatively recent reports from both North Island (East Cape district) and South Island (Marlborough Sounds and north-west Nelson); no recent reports from Stewart Island.

Breeding: Nest in a hollow tree or in dense cover of epiphytes, etc., mainly close to the ground on South Cape islands (Guthrie-Smith) but *c.* 2 m or more above ground on Hen Island. Guthrie-Smith found a nest in a flax kit which was hanging inside a mutton-birder's hut. Nest loosely and crudely constructed of twigs, with lining of finer material (fibres, grasses, bark, treefern scales). Breeding October–January; eggs 2 (occasionally 3), pale grey or white, with reddish-brown and pale purple spots or blotches. Observations by Guthrie-Smith on the South Cape group showed that the female incubates, and afterwards broods the chicks; incubation period *c.* 21 days, begins with the second egg; food is gathered mainly by the male but on his return to the nest female takes part of the food to distribute among the chicks. The male also feeds the female off the nest when incubation and brooding are in progress. Double broods recorded on Cuvier Island (P. F. Jenkins). The young probably accompany their parents for some months – a number of family groups were still together on Hen Island in May, although some families had broken up as immatures not attached to adults were observed (E. G. T.).

HUIA *Heteralocha acutirostris*   *Pl. 48, p. 201*
Description: Male 45 cm (18″) (bill stout, arched); female 48 cm (19″) (bill slender, scimitar-shaped). Plumage glossy black, with bluish iridescence; rounded orange wattle; tail tipped for 2.5–3.0 cm with white. Bill ivory-white, greyish at base; feet bluish-grey, pale brown claws.
Immature duller black plumage, and white tips of tail feathers tinged with reddish-buff; wattles small and pale-coloured; bill of immature female only slightly curved (Buller).
Voice: 'A soft and clear whistle'; also a loud whistling note of higher pitch, and various chuckling and whining notes (Buller).
Habitat and range: Presumed extinct. Restricted to the North Island, and in European times apparently confined to parts of the Rimutaka, Tararua, Ruahine and Kaimanawa Ranges and adjacent forests at least as far as the Turakina River to the west. It survived longest in the rough mountainous portions of its range, but has probably been extinct since *c.* 1907. Collectors obtained skins in such numbers that its fate would probably have been sealed whether affected by other factors or not.
Buller's fairly lengthy account indicates that it was almost invariably met with in pairs (once a solitary male bird was recorded, and sometimes parties of 'four or more'). It flew only when necessary to traverse an opening in the forest, or cross from one tree to another. It normally moved rapidly along the ground or from tree to tree 'by a series of bounds or jumps.'
Food both insects and fruits. Buller records wetas and other orthopterous insects, grubs, caterpillars and spiders. Wood-boring larvae, especially the huhu—the large, succulent grub of the longicorn beetle *Prionoplus recticularis* — were obtained from rotting wood. Buller states that a pair in captivity immediately attacked a log of decayed wood, the male breaking off softer material and the female probing holes in harder portions, to obtain the grubs; when a grub was extracted, the bird would place one foot firmly upon it in order to tear off the hard parts, and then, throwing the grub upwards to secure it lengthwise in the bill, would swallow it whole.
Breeding: In a hollow tree or in a mass of dense vegetation; nest a substantial structure of sticks and twigs, with finer material lining the cup. Potts recorded the finding of a nest containing one chick on 18 November; it was taken from the nest and reared on huhu. A further nest reported to Potts containing three young was also found in November. Supposed egg in New Zealand's National Museum pale brownish-grey, with brown and dull purple spots and blotches.

KOKAKO *Callaeas cinerea*   *Pl. 48, p. 201*
Other names: Wattled Crow, Organ-bird, Gill-bird, Bluegill (N.I.).
Description: 38 cm (15″). *Dark bluish-grey*, shaded olive-brown on wing-coverts,

lower back, rump, uppertail-coverts, lower abdomen and undertail-coverts; wing and tail quills blackish-brown with a slaty wash; a broad band of velvety black passes back from base of bill to the eye and encircles eye as a narrow ring. Wattles blue or orange according to subspecies (q.v.). Bill and feet black.

In immature plumage the brown shading extends on to the upper back; wattles smaller and paler than in adult.

In silhouette the long legs are distinctive, and this and the large size (distinctly larger than Tui) are aids to identification; almost invariably located by voice. **Voice:** A variety of notes, in addition to the rich musical song, have been identified in the course of recent observations by H. R. McKenzie and others in the Hunua area, south of Auckland. Maning has summarised the calls as: (*a*) an alarm or curiosity note *took-took-took-took* (audible only at very close quarters); (*b*) a low mewing note, also of small range, apparently used by the pairs in keeping touch; (*c*) a double call (short bell-like note followed by a sharp *kik*); (*d*) abbreviated versions of these calls.

Song and calls are given most often in the morning and evening.

Habitat and range: Although originally throughout forests of North, South and Stewart Islands, it seems probable from Buller's account that the Kokako was of somewhat uneven distribution before it could have been affected by European settlement. However, it was locally common in many districts. By 1880 it had greatly decreased (like the Saddleback and New Zealand Thrush). (Present range under subspecies.)

Its characteristic mode of progression is to hop vigorously up trunk and limbs; it then glides to the next tree, perhaps losing a good deal of height, the process being repeated. It rarely makes a sustained flight, but is likely to be seen gliding between trees, or making longer glides of up to 70 metres across a gully. Pairs keep together all through the year.

Buller mentions that the foot is used, parrot-fashion, when feeding.

Food mainly vegetable, insects may be included but not conclusively recorded in recent observations. Much of its time is spent on the outer branches where leaves, flowers and fruits are obtained (fruits of bush lawyer, pigeonwood, supplejack, native fuchsia and *Coprosma* recorded); has also been seen examining moss on larger branches (for insects?) (J. W. St. Paul).

North Island Kokako (subspecies *wilsoni*) has *ultramarine-blue wattles*; well-developed olive-brown shading on wing-coverts, etc.; there is a narrow zone of pale grey round margin of the black facial area shading off into the blue-grey plumage. In the South Island Kokako (subspecies *cinerea*) the *wattles* are *rich orange*, blue at the base; olive-brown shading on wing-coverts, etc., reduced; no pale edge to the black facial area; tail quills dark bluish-grey like the body plumage, with only tips (4–5 cm) blackish-brown.

The North Island Kokako is apparently still quite widely distributed: it has been recorded recently from North Auckland (Mangamuka, Pakotai, Tutamoe and possibly other localities); Great Barrier Island; Waitakere and Hunua Ranges, near Auckland; near Ngaruawahia; near Raglan; Mt. Pirongia, south of Kawhia; some parts of the King Country; North and South Taranaki; the Coromandel Range south to about Te Aroha; parts of the Volcanic Plateau; and the Bay of Plenty side of the Urewera forest area.

The South Island Kokako is likely to survive only in a few isolated areas:

the only recent records are from the head of Lake Monowai, 7 with Yellow-heads, February 1946 (W. Axbey); the Wilkin Valley, North-west Otago in 1958 (A. Chapman); the Maitai Valley 1961; and Picton. Last reported on Stewart Island in the 1940s (Martin).

Breeding: A somewhat massively-constructed nest in a fork or tangle of branches 2.5–9.0 m above the ground; composed of a platform of small branches and twigs up to 60 cm long, and above this, finer material and fragments of rotting wood; cup consists of moss and finally treefern scales or other fine lining. Breeding November–March; probably single brooded. Eggs 3 (occasionally 2); pale brownish-grey, with brown and purplish-brown spots and blotches. Little was recorded of breeding habits until the discovery of a nest in the Hunua Ranges in December 1950; subsequently observations have been made at two further nests by H. R. McKenzie (December 1952) and R. and J. W. St. Paul (January 1962). Observations by McKenzie and a number of others showed that incubation was performed by the female, but the male helped to feed the chicks; food consisted mainly of fruits e.g. supplejack, pigeonwood and *Coprosma australis*, together with macerated foliage (the quantity of the latter was increased as the chicks grew older). Fledging 27–28 days. R. St. Paul in January 1962 found that the male helped to build the nest, and his observations showed that the incubation period was *c*. 25 days. The nestling has a little dark brown down on the crown, back and legs; mouth inside purplish red, bluish towards gape.

NEW ZEALAND THRUSHES: Turnagridae

An endemic family of doubtful position: its relationships are possibly with the southern crow-like birds including the Callaeidae. Some authorities consider *Turnagra* the New Zealand representative of the Catbirds and Bowerbirds (Ptilonorhynchidae) and compare it especially with the Stagemaker Bowerbird *Scenopoeetes*.

NEW ZEALAND THRUSH   *Turnagra capensis*   *Pl. 48, p. 201*
Maori name: Piopio.
Description: 26 cm (10½″). North Island Thrush (subspecies *tanagra*) has *white throat*; olive-grey breast and abdomen, darkest on breast (the abdomen and undertail-coverts with a wash of yellow); olive-brown sides. The South Island Thrush (subspecies *capensis*) is *broadly streaked with brown and white below*; the striped plumage on the throat and sides of the neck tinged reddish-brown; yellow wash on abdomen and undertail-coverts; feathers of forehead, crown and face tipped rust red; feathers of wing-coverts tipped irregularly with rust red. (In immatures of the North Island Thrush the feathers of forehead, crown, face, upper breast and wing-coverts are tipped with rust red, and breast is brown; in the South Island Thrush the amount of the red coloration on the head, throat, sides of neck and wing-coverts much increased.)

In both subspecies, upper parts olive-brown; *uppertail-coverts and tail quills except centre pair rust red*; centre tail quills olive-brown; bill and feet dark brown.

Voice: Buller states that the common call (whence the Maori name Piopio is derived) is a 'short, sharp, whistling cry, quickly repeated.' The song according to Buller is remarkably varied and sustained: it consists of 'five distinct bars, each of which is repeated six or seven times in succession'; the bird often stops abruptly to introduce a variety of other notes, including a rattle and a loud rasping cry; there is also a short flute-note. When singing, spreads the tail and slightly droops wings (Potts).

Potts states that both the male and female use a low purring *chur-r-r* as a threat to intruders at the nest.

Habitat and range: Probably extinct. The early settlers found the South Island Thrush a common bird of the forests, particularly in the west, yet, like the Wattle-birds, it was reported to be fast disappearing by 1880; Buller attributed the decrease to the ravages of cats and dogs, 'to which this species, from its ground-feeding habits, falls an easy prey.' In Fiordland, and a few other remote areas, it remained well established, like the Saddleback (q.v.) and Kokako, until the 1890s, when a further significant reduction seems to have been contemporaneous with the spread of mustelids, particularly the stoat, and possibly also the Ship Rat *Rattus rattus*. There have been no fully authenticated reports of the South Island Thrush for more than half a century and such very few recent reports as have been made do not give much hope for its continued existence. The North Island Thrush has never been common in European times and the few records available indicate that its distribution in those times was confined to the more remote and rugged forested areas of the southern portion of the island. The last authentic record of this subspecies is of two birds in the eastern Ureweras in 1908, one of which is preserved in the Auckland Museum. There have been a number of unconfirmed reports in recent times, particularly from the Ureweras, but its continued survival seems at present unlikely.

All early accounts give prominence to its tameness – thus Buller quotes James Hector to the effect that it was very abundant during Hector's exploration of the West Coast in 1862-3; Hector '. . . on one occasion counted no less than forty in the immediate vicinity of his camp. They were very tame, sometimes hopping up to the very door of his tent to pick up crumbs.'

Its flight is evidently direct and powerful: Buller describes the flight as 'short and rapid', and adds: 'It haunts the undergrowth of the forest, darting from tree to tree, and occasionally descending to the ground, but rarely performing any long passage on the wing.'

Food apparently extremely varied: insects and other invertebrates, and vegetable matter, including fruits, seeds and foliage. Henry saw it eating fruits of native fuchsia. It evidently obtains much of its food from the forest floor, and Buller's account includes mention of one seen 'grubbing with its bill among dry leaves and other forest debris.' Buller found that in captivity the North Island Thrush was markedly omnivorous (grain, raw meat, earthworms, insects fruits, green vegetable matter).

Breeding: (In South Island Thrush) nest compactly built of twigs and moss, lined with grasses, treefern scales or other fine material, from 1.2–3.5 m from the ground, usually 2 m (Potts); all eggs recorded found in December (Potts considered that it probably bred twice in the season); eggs 2, white or pinkish-white, with scattered black or brown spots, and sometimes with additional purplish blotches at the larger end. Nothing is recorded of the breeding of the North Island Thrush.

Calls of Black-backed Gulls

(After Fordham, *Notornis* 10: 208-214.)

1. Calls related to Courtship and Nesting:
   (a) A non-contagious cry *gorah gorah* mainly from breeding adults, but occasionally throughout the year.
   (b) A very contagious long call heard especially in breeding colonies which are continually swept by it. Sounds like *uh, uh, eeah-ha-ha-ha-ha-ha-ha*. Also described as a musical *kaloo-kaloo-kloo-kloo*, the last syllable being repeated several times.
   (c) Mew call – a non-contagious wailing, drawn out *waaaaah*, usually given by a bird walking slowly to its mate, and never on water. Used in courtship, nest-relief and to call chicks to food or shelter.
   (d) Choking-sounds like *wo-wo-wo-wo-wo*, and is concerned mainly with nest-building; but sometimes with aggression. It may occur on land or sea; and may be contagious.
   (e) A non-contagious soft fluty cry *kle-oo-kleoo* heard when females are begging food from their mates or as a prelude to mating.
   (f) A non-contagious call given by the male only during mating – a rapidly repeated *cor-cor-cor* which may become a harsh *car-car-car*.

2. Calls of Alarm, Anxiety and Aggression:
   (a) The anxiety call *ha-ha-haha*, *kok-kok-kok* or *ha-ha haro* is mostly given by breeding birds in flight. It begins as a slightly contagious chatter.
   (b) It may be followed by a contagious, loud, staccato *kwe-ah kwe-ah*.
   (c) A muffled moan is uttered by some birds when a roosting flock is disturbed.
   (d) The 'charge' call is a sudden piercing screem *oo-waaaaah* made in flight and directed at a possible predator from above. Likely to be heard only near the nest during the breeding season.

ADDENDA   OCTOBER 1980

The following have been admitted to the official New Zealand list.

MAGELLANIC PENGUIN *Spheniscus magellanicus*
  One ashore at Hawke Bay, March 1972.
JUAN FERNANDEZ PETREL *Pterodroma externa*
  One found inland, Waikato, October 1971.
RED-KNEED DOTTEREL *Erythrogonys cinctus*
  One at Manawatu estuary, March 1976.
WHISKERED TERN *Chlidonias hybrida*
  At least two probably more, visited L. Horowhenua and the Waikato estuary
  between 1977 and 1980. They were easily distinguishable from endemic
  Black-fronted Terns.

The following changes in scientific names have been accepted or are recommended.

p.22. LITTLE BLUE PENGUIN; the name of the middle region form is *variabilis*,
  not *septentrionalis*.
p.23. ROCKHOPPER PENGUIN; for *crestatus* read *chrysocome*.
p.24. SNARES CRESTED PENGUIN; for *atratus* read *robustus*.
p.47. LESSER FAIRY PRION; for *fallai* read *subantarctica*.
p.153. ARCTIC TERN; for *macrura* read *paradisaea*.
p.157. GREY TERNLET; for *albivitta* read *cerulea*.

Recent information of interest concerning some of the rarer birds already
mentioned in the *New Guide*.

ROCKHOPPER PENGUIN (p.23, Habitat), after 'represented . . . ' the text should
  read 'in the South Atlantic and Indian Oceans by the sub-species *moseleyi* which
  has straggled to the Chatham Islands'.
AUSTRALIAN LITTLE GREBE (p.28) appears to be breeding and establishing
  itself on small lakes with cover, especially in South Island where there is no
  competition from the N.Z. Dabchick.
BLACK-BROWED MOLLYMAWK (p.32). Those which breed on Bollons Island
  in the Antipodes are now known to be of the typical circumpolar form, and differ
  from *impavida* of Campbell Island.
GIANT PETREL (p.36). *giganteus* and *halli* are now generally held to be distinct
  species; but, for the ocean-going bird-watcher, their separation is fraught with
  difficulties.
ANTARCTIC PETREL (p.39). In 1978 there was an unprecedented irruption and
  many were wrecked, mainly along the west coast.
SOFT-PLUMAGED PETREL (p.42). Breeding at Antipodes Island has been
  confirmed and the colonists appear to be prospering.
GOULD'S PETREL (p.43). The origin of the puzzling *leucoptera* petrels which are
  stranded on the west coast is believed to be islands in the region of New
  Caledonia.
BLACK-WINGED PETREL (p.45). This enterprising colonist now breeds on
  Portland Island, Hawke Bay, and is prospecting the headlands of the Far Norh.
LEACH'S FORK-TAILED STORM PETREL (p.54). In 1978 the second and third
  specimens for New Zealand were found storm-wrecked near Matamata (April)
  and Dargaville (August).

225

226 ADDENDA

SOUTH GEORGIAN DIVING PETREL (p.57) has been found breeding at Codfish Island (off Stewart Island).

WHITE-TAILED TROPIC BIRD (p.59). In 1979 three were wrecked on the west coast between Taranaki and Dargaville.

AUSTRALIAN PELICAN (p.61). A minor invasion, summer '77-78, seems to have petered out.

PLUMED EGRET (p.73). One spent part of the 1979 winter with Cattle Egrets in the lower Waikato.

CATTLE EGRET (p.75). The annual winter expectation now exceeds 600. Adults evidently continue to return to Australia to breed, though flocks with some birds in rich colour are now summering in New Zealand.

ROYAL SPOONBILL (p.78). A new breeding colony of at least three pairs has been found — a hopeful advance.

AUSTRALIAN WOOD DUCK (p.89). One was shot, mid-April 1980, in Marlborough.

AUSTRALIAN COOT (p.101). Hamilton lake now has a lusty population in a suburban setting.

SPUR-WINGED PLOVER (p.111). Although there are gaps, some have settled near Parengarenga. They have now gone northwards about as far as they can go.

AUCKLAND ISLANDS BANDED DOTTEREL (p.113-4). In 1978 this was described as a new sub-species and named *exilis*. During April 1980 no fewer than 155 were counted by R.J. Pierce.

MONGOLIAN DOTTEREL (p.118). One in brilliant breeding dress was seen on Farewell Spit, May 1980.

GREENSHANK (p.125). One reached Chatham Island, summer '77-78.

COMMON SANDPIPER (p.128). Sightings at Ruakaka and Karioitahi (near Waiuku), summer '79-80, bring the New Zealand total up to eight.

DUNLIN (p.134). One in striking nuptial plumage spent the winter of 1979 in Manukau Harbour.

GREY TERNLET (p.157). Summer '78-79, some hundreds were presumed to have bred at Poor Knights.

SPINE-TAILED SWIFT (p.175). A flock of 60+ at Tautuka Lodge, Otago, February 1979, far exceeds any other reported in New Zealand.

KOOKABURRA (p.177). Two sightings, January 1980, Raglan and Hastings, after a westerly storm, may support the theory of natural arrival from Australia.

CHATHAM ISLAND ROBIN (p.189). Young have been raised on Big Mangere and the future of the species, though not assured, is more hopeful.

HEDGE SPARROW (p.198). In northern New Zealand there appears to have been a marked decline.

NEW ZEALAND PIPIT (p.199). Now quite scarce over much of northern New Zealand, except perhaps on the west coast.

STITCHBIRD (p.200). On Little Barrier the population is in good heart, perhaps because feral cats have been virtually exterminated. In April 1980 30 birds were transferred to Hen Island.

ROOK (p.214). Southwards, rookeries have sprung up in the lower Clutha.

WHITE-BACKED MAGPIE (p.216) has extended its range south to Invercargill.

SADDLEBACK (p.217). Experimental transfers of both sub-species to selected 'vermin-free' offshore islands have succeeded beyond all expectations.

GLOSSARY
ACKNOWLEDGEMENTS
BIBLIOGRAPHY
INDEX

GLOSSARY

alar bar a bar or band, usually white or whitish, in the wing, concealed in some species when the wing is folded, but revealed in flight.

axillaries the feathers in the 'armpit'.

caruncle fleshy or wartlike growths on the facial skin of some shags near the nostrils.

cere fleshy covering of the upper bill in some orders of birds, e.g. hawks, parrots, pigeons.

cline a gradual change, within a population from one end of its range to the other, of such characters as size, markings and colour of plumage, possibly exemplified in New Zealand by Little Shag and Variable Oystercatcher.

congeners members of the same family or genus.

cryptic aiding concealment or camouflage.

cubital band a band of usually dark feathering in the wing between wrist (carpal joint) and elbow, noticeable particularly in some species of terns when immature.

dertrum the hooked or curved tip of the upper mandible as, e.g., in some plovers and pigeons.

dimorphism the existence in a species of two colour-phases irrespective of age or sex, e.g. Arctic Skua with dark-breasted and light-breasted forms; Stewart Island Shag with pied and bronze forms. *But* sexual dimorphism implies a difference in shape, size or colour, attributable to sex as, e.g., in Huia, Stitchbird and many species of ducks and game birds.

distensible capable of stretching.

dorsal of or on the back.

facial disc a conspicuous feature of some species of owl.

filamentous like fine hairlike silky threads.

filo-plumes silky threadlike plumes without vanes.

frontal plate horny shield on the forehead, taking the place of feathers as, e.g., in coots.

frontal shield *v.* frontal plate.

gape either the open mouth revealing the throat or the area where upper and lower mandibles meet.

gonys the ridge, beginning with a projection, and formed by the fusion of the two rami (side-bones) of the lower mandible; very evident in gulls and terns.

gorget throat- or chest-band.

gular sac or pouch elastic skin of throat that can be filled with food or air.

hepatic liver-coloured, i.e. dark brownish-red.

holarctic including the whole of the arctic; circumpolar in the far north, embracing both palearctic and nearctic.

horn (colour) dirty yellowish and with the apparent texture of cows' horn.

juvenile (juvenal, American) immature, especially of birds in their first year; but neither term seems to have been precisely defined. In any case, immaturity and juvenility are a matter of degree according to the type of bird under discussion. At seven years a Silvereye or Fantail would be very old, but an Albatross would just qualify as a young adult.

228

lobe-footed having the toes separately fringed by lobes, e.g. Coot, as distinct from having the toes connected by webs.

malar pertaining to the cheek.

maxilla the upper mandible or upper jaw.

median streak or stripe a strip of contrasting colour running from bill and over the top of the crown, as, e.g., in Whimbrel.

melanism darkness of plumage resulting from abnormal development of black pigment (melanin); exemplified with puzzling frequency in several widely different genera of birds in New Zealand.

morphology the branch of biology dealing with the form and structure of plants and animals.

mustelid generic term embracing polecats, ferrets, stoats and weasels, all feral in New Zealand but none native.

nearctic belonging to the arctic zone of North America and Greenland.

nuchal collar a band on the nape or upper neck.

nuchal plumes plumes springing from the nape.

orbital ring coloured band encircling the eye.

pakihi open, rather barren land, sometimes boggy, sometimes dry.

palaearctic belonging to the arctic zone of the Old World, i.e. North Atlantic to Bering Sea.

palmate having three toes connected by webs.

papilla coloured warty spots like small caruncles (q.v.) on the facial skin of some Pink-footed Shags.

pectoral band band of spots, streaks or colour across chest, cf. gorget.

pelagic belonging to the open ocean.

plumule small downy feather.

pyriform pear-shaped.

ratites flightless birds with unkeeled raftlike breastbones, e.g. moa, kiwi, emu, ostrich, rhea, cassowary.

scalation appearance of overlapping scales, sometimes present in the arrangement and markings of feathers.

semi-palmate having three toes connected by much reduced webs.

shield horny forehead as in coot.

subspecies geographical race or simply race; i.e. a local or geographically isolated population, the members of which can be separated morphologically from the typical species or other local subdivisions of that species.

    strong subspecies a population so long isolated from the typical species and 'going its own way' that it has marked characteristics of appearance and/or behaviour, and may be isolated genetically.

    weak subspecies a local population which is doubtfully separable from the typical species, although it shows small, but constant, differences in size, shape, colour or behaviour.

wattles colourful fleshy excrescences on either side of the gape in Saddleback, Kokako, Huia (Callaeidae).

Pictorial Glossary

OUTER VANES OR WEBS

INNER VANES OR WEBS

SHAFT (RACHIS)

QUILL (CALAMUS)

SEMI-PALMATED
Foot of Sandpiper

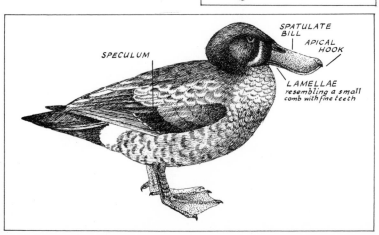

SPATULATE BILL

APICAL HOOK

SPECULUM

LAMELLAE
resembling a small
comb with fine teeth

ACKNOWLEDGEMENTS

Special thanks for encouragement, helpful criticism and precise information on some doubtful points are gladly given to Mrs M. L. Barlow, A. Blackburn, B. D. Bell, D. H. Brathwaite, T. A. Caithness, P. Child, Miss M. M. Davis, A. T. Edgar, D. G. Fenwick, M. E. Fitzgerald, Sir Charles Fleming, Dr J. A. D. Flack, B. D. Heather, M. J. Imber, J. R. Jackson, J. G. F. Jenkins, Dr. P. F. Jenkins, J. Kikkawa, H. R. McKenzie, D. G. Medway, D. V. Merton, K. H. Miers, G. J. H. Moon, C. J. R. Robertson, H. L. Secker, Dr M. F. Soper, P. A. S. Stein, R. H. D. Stidolph, C. R. Veitch, Dr G. R. Williams, Dr M. J. Williams, Mrs A. E. Woodhouse.

We also acknowledge our debt to the many who have added so much in general conversation over the years to our store of knowledge. Some have been mentioned in the text where attribution is definite.

We are also deeply indebted to F. C. Kinsky, R. J. Scarlett and Mrs S. M. Reed who have greatly assisted our artist by the loan of valuable specimens from the National, Canterbury and Auckland Museums respectively.

I am grateful to Mrs B. M. Shimmin, Mrs L. E. Walker, Miss Susan Millar for long hours of painstaking typing, and more recently to Mrs Margaret Forde for her discerning judgment in the preparation of the text; and finally to W. E. Forde whose gentle firmness and inspired attention to detail have held me steadily to my task and lightened my labours.

R. B. S

BIBLIOGRAPHY

The literature listed in two bibliographies has been frequently and profitably consulted to check, from list (*a*), the discovery, history and changing fortunes of New Zealand birds; from list (*b*), their migrations, range, distribution and affinities in other lands.

(*a*)

1882 POTTS, T. H., *Out in the Open*. Lyttelton Times Co.
1882 BULLER, W. L., *Manual of the Birds of New Zealand*. Colonial Museum and Geological Survey Dept., Wellington.
1888 BULLER, W. L., *History of the Birds of New Zealand*. 2nd edition. The author, London.
1905 BULLER, W. L., *Supplement*. The author, London.
1914 GUTHRIE-SMITH, H., *Mutton Birds and Other Birds*. Whitcombe & Tombs, Christchurch.
1925 GUTHRIE-SMITH, H., *Bird Life on Island and Shore*. Wm. Blackwood & Sons, Edinburgh and London.
1927 GUTHRIE-SMITH, H., *Birds of the Water, Wood and Waste*, 2nd edition. Whitcombe & Tombs, Christchurch.
1936 GUTHRIE-SMITH, H., *Sorrows and Joys of a New Zealand Naturalist*. A. H. & A. W. Reed, Wellington.
1925 MONCRIEFF, PERRINE, *New Zealand Birds and How to Identify Them*. Whitcombe & Tombs, Christchurch.
1926 THOMSON, G. M., *Introduced Birds and Fishes in New Zealand*. Government Printer, Wellington.
1930 OLIVER, W. R. B., *New Zealand Birds*, 1st edition. Fine Arts (N.Z.). Wellington.
1932 STEAD, E. F., *Life Histories of New Zealand Birds*. Search, London.
1937 FALLA, R. A., *B.A.N.Z.A.R.E. Reports* (*B*). Published by the Committee, Adelaide.
1939 FLEMING, C. A., 'Birds of the Chatham Islands', *Emu*, vol. 38.
1947 TURBOTT, E. G., *New Zealand Bird Life*. A. H. & A. W. Reed, Wellington.
1951 BUDDLE, G. A., *Bird Secrets*. A. H. & A. W. Reed, Wellington.
1952 WILKINSON, A. S. and A., *Kapiti Bird Sanctuary*. Stidolph, Masterton.
1953 FLEMING, C. A. *et al*., *Check List of New Zealand Birds*. A. H. & A. W. Reed, Wellington.
1955 OLIVER, W. R. B., *New Zealand Birds*, 2nd edition. A. H. & A. W. Reed, Wellington.
1957 MOON, G. J. H., *Focus on New Zealand Birds*. A. H. & A. W. Reed, Wellington.
1959 WILSON, R. A., *Bird Islands of New Zealand*. Whitcombe & Tombs, Christchurch.

1967   MOON, G. J. H., *Refocus on New Zealand Birds*. A. H. & A. W. Reed, Wellington.
1967   TURBOTT, E. G., *Buller's Birds of New Zealand*. Whitcombe & Tombs, Christchurch.
1970   KINSKY, F. C. *et al.*, *Annotated Checklist of the Birds of New Zealand*. A. H. & A. W. Reed, Wellington.
1971   STIDOLPH, R. H. D., *The Birds Around Us*. Hedley's Bookshop, Masterton.
1972   McKENZIE, H. R., *In Search of Birds in New Zealand*. A. H. & A. W. Reed, Wellington.
1974   HARPER, P. C. and KINSKY, F. C., *New Zealand Albatrosses and Petrels*. Biological Society, Victoria University of Wellington.
1976   SOPER, M. F., *New Zealand Birds*, 2nd edition. Whitcoulls Limited, Christchurch.
1939-50   *New Zealand Bird Notes*, I-III.
1950-77   *Notornis*, 4–24.

(*b*)

ALEXANDER, W. B. (1955), *Birds of the Ocean*. Putnam, New York and London.
ALI SALIM and RIPLEY, S. D. (1968–74), *Handbook of the Birds of India and Pakistan*. Oxford University Press, Bombay.
AUSTIN, O. L. and KURODA, N. (1953), *The Birds of Japan; their status and distribution*. Museum of Comparative Zoology, Harvard University.
CONDON, H. T. and McGILL, A. R. (1960), *Field Guide to the Waders*. Bird Observers' Club, Melbourne.
CONDON, H. T. (1975), *Checklist of the Birds of Australia, Part I – Non-Passerines*. Royal Australasian Ornithologists' Union.
DELACOUR, J. and SCOTT, PETER (1954–9), *The Waterfowl of the World*. Country Life, London.
Emu, The Quarterly Magazine of the R.A.O.U.
GLENISTER, A. G. (1951), *Birds of the Malay Peninsula*. Oxford University Press, London.
GODFREY, W. E. (1966), *The Birds of Canada*. National Museum of Canada, Ottawa.
HENRY, G. M. (1955), *A Guide to the Birds of Ceylon*. Oxford University Press, London.
HINDWOOD, K. A. (1940), *Birds of Lord Howe Island*.
HINDWOOD, K. A. and McGILL, A. R. (1958), *The Birds of Sydney*. Royal Zoological Society of New South Wales.
LEACH, J. A. (1958), *An Australian Bird Book*, new edition. Whitcombe & Tombs, Melbourne.
MACDONALD, J. D. (1973), *Birds of Australia*. A. H. & A. W. Reed, Sydney.
MATHEWS, G. M. (1928), *Birds of Norfolk and Lord Howe Islands and the Australian South Polar Quadrant*. Witherby, London.
MAYR, E. (1941), *List of New Guinea Birds*. American Museum of Natural History, New York.

MAYR, E. (1945), *Birds of the Southwest Pacific*. Macmillan, New York.

MAYR, E. and DELACOUR, J. (1946), *Birds of the Philippines*. Macmillan, New York.

MURPHY, R. C. (1936), *Oceanic Birds of South America*. American Museum of Natural History, New York.

RAND, A. L. and GILLIARD, E. T. (1967), *Handbook of New Guinea Birds*. Weidenfeld & Nicholson, London.

SERVENTY, D. L. and WHITTELL, H. M. (1948), *Birds of Western Australia*. Paterson Brokensha Pty. Ltd., Perth, W.A.

SERVENTY, D. L., SERVENTY, V. and WARHAM, J. (1971), *Handbook of Australian Seabirds*. A. H. & A. W. Reed, Sydney.

SHARLAND, M. (1958), *Tasmanian Birds*, 3rd edition. Angus & Robertson, Sydney.

SMYTHIES, B. E. (1953), *The Birds of Burma*. Oliver & Boyd, Edinburgh.

SMYTHIES, B. E. (1960), *The Birds of Borneo*. Oliver & Boyd, Edinburgh.

VAURIE, C. (1965), *Birds of the Palearctic Fauna*. Witherby, London.

WHISTLER, H. (1949), *Popular Handbook of Indian Birds*. Oliver & Boyd, Edinburgh.

WITHERBY, H. F. *et al.* (1938–41), *Handbook of British Birds*. Witherby, London.

INDEX

Numerals in **bold type** refer to illustrations.

SOUTH ISLAND

Scale of Kilometres

0   40   80   120   160

N

COOK STRAIT

Farewell Spit
Golden Bay
D'Urville I.
Stephen I.
Pelorus Sd.
Queen Charlotte Sound

Nelson
Blenheim
Cape Campbell

Wairau R.
L. Grassmere
L. Roto-iti
L. Rotoroa
Clarence R.

Kaikoura

Buller R.

Lewis Pass

Westport

Grey R.
L. Sumner
L. Brunner
Waiau R.
Hurunui R.
Cheviot
Motunau I.

Greymouth
Hokitika
L. Kaniere
Arthur's Pass
Waipara R.
Ashley R.

Waimakariri R.
CHRISTCHURCH
Banks Pen
L. Ellesmere

L. Ianthe

Rakaia R.

Okarito
L. Mapourika
Franz Josef Glacier